THE
BREAKING
POINT

THE
BREAKING
POINT

Profit from the Coming Money Cataclysm

JAMES DALE DAVIDSON

Humanix Books
www.humanixbooks.com

Humanix Books

The Breaking Point
Copyright © 2017 by Humanix Books
All rights reserved

Humanix Books, P.O. Box 20989, West Palm Beach, FL 33416, USA
www.humanixbooks.com | info@humanixbooks.com

Library of Congress Cataloging-in-Publication Data is available from the Library
of Congress.

Interior Design: Scribe Inc.

Humanix Books is a division of Humanix Publishing, LLC. Its trademark,
consisting of the words "Humanix" is registered in the Patent and Trademark
Office and in other countries.

Disclaimer: The information presented in this book is meant to be used for
general resource purposes only; it is not intended as specific financial advice
for any individual and should not substitute financial advice from a finance
professional.

ISBN: 978-1-63006-060-2 (Hardcover)
ISBN: 978-1-63006-061-9 (E-book)

Printed in the United States of America
10 9 8 7 6 5 4 3 2 1

To my indispensable Sabine,
who proves again, as e.e. cummings wrote, that
"unless you love someone, nothing else makes sense"

Contents

Foreword

By Bill Bonner

Something went wrong on the way to tomorrow. From the turn of the century in 1900 through the end of Cold War in 1989 to the next turn of the century in 2000, almost every view of the future looked as though it had been photoshopped. Imperfections were few.

In 1900, a survey was done. "What do you see coming?" asked the pollsters.

All those questions forecast better times ahead. Machines were just making their debut, but already people saw their potential. You can see some of that optimism on display in the Paris metro today. In the Montparnasse station is an illustration from the 1800s of what the artist imagined for the next century. It is a fantastic vision of flying vehicles, elevated sidewalks, and incredible mechanical devices.

But when asked what lay ahead, the most remarkable opinion, at least from our point of view, was that government would decline. Almost everyone thought so. Why would that happen? We wouldn't need so much government, they said. People will all be rich. Wealthy people may engage in fraud and finagling, but they don't wait in dark allies to bop people over the head and steal their wallets. And they don't need government pensions or government health care either.

Nor do they attack their neighbors. Norman Angell wrote a best-selling book, *The Great Illusion*, in which he explained why. Wealth is no longer based on land, he argued. Instead, it depends on factories, finance, commerce, and delicate relationships between suppliers, manufacturers, and consumers. As capitalism makes people better off, he said, they won't want to do anything to interfere with it. If you disrupt them, you only make yourself poorer, he pointed out.

One of his most important readers was Viscount Escher of England's War Committee. He told listeners that "new economic factors clearly prove the inanity of aggressive wars."

Capitalism flourishes in times of peace, sound money, respect for property rights, and free trade. One of the most important components of the wealth of the late nineteenth century was international commerce. It was clear that everyone benefitted from "globalized" trade. Who would want to upset that apple cart?

"War must soon be a thing of the past," said Escher.

But in August 1914, the cart fell over anyway. The Great War began five years after Angell's book hit the best-seller lists. On the first day of the Battle of the Somme alone—one hundred years ago—there were more than 70,000 casualties. And when Americans arrived in 1917, the average soldier arriving at the front lines had a life expectancy of only twenty-one days. By the time of the Armistice on the eleventh day of the eleventh month at 11 a.m. of 1918, the war had killed 17 million people, wounded another 20 million, and knocked off the major ruling families of Europe—the Hohenzollerns, the Hapsburgs, and the Romanoffs (the Bourbons and Bonapartes were already gone from France).

Hic hoc. Stuff happens.

James Dale Davidson's new book, *The Breaking Point*, is an attempt to explain why stuff happens the way it does. Using his theory of "megapolitics," he also takes some guesses about what happens next.

After WWI came a thirty-year spell of trouble. In keeping with the metaphor of the Machine Age, the disintegration of prewar institutions broke the tie rods that connected civilized economies to their governments. Reparations imposed on Germany caused hyperinflation in Germany, while America enjoyed a "Roaring '20s" as Europeans paid their debts—in gold—to US lenders. But that joyride came to an end in '29 . . . and then the feds flooded the carburetor with disastrously maladroit efforts to get the motor started again, including the Smoot-Hawley Act, which restricted cross-border trade. The "isms"—fascism, communism, syndicalism, socialism, anarchism—offered solutions. Then finally, the brittle rubber of communism (aided by modern democratic capitalism) met the mean streets of fascism, in another huge bout of government-led violence—WWII.

By the end of this period, the West had had enough. Europe settled down with bourgeois governments of various social-democrat forms. America went back to business, with order books filled and its factories still intact. The "isms" held firm in the Soviet Union and moved to the Orient, with further wear and tear on the machinery of warfare in Korea—and later Vietnam.

Finally in 1979, Deng Tsaoping announced that while the ruling Communist Party would stay in control of China, the country would abandon its Marxist–Leninist–Maoist creed. China joined the world economy with its own version of state-guided capitalism. Then, ten years later, the Soviet Union gave up even more completely—rejecting both the Communist Party and communism itself.

This was the event hailed in a silly essay by Francis Fukuyama, "The End of History?" The battle was finally won, he suggested. It is the "endpoint of mankind's ideological evolution and the universalization of western liberal democracy as the final form of human government," he wrote. With the Cold War over, modern democratic capitalism would be perfected. And now US companies could hustle their products to 1.5 billion more consumers.

But the most obvious and immediate benefit America was to get a "peace dividend," as billions of dollars could now be liberated from the defense budget and put to better use elsewhere.

Things were looking up. As China and the Soviet Union went, so went the rest of the world—with everyone trying to learn the latest buzz words from globalized business schools, setting up factories to make things for people who really couldn't afford them, gambling on Third World debt, trading stocks of companies that used to belong to the government, and aiming to get their sons and daughters into Harvard so they would be first in line for a job at Goldman Sachs.

But wait. Things got even better when, in the late '90s, it looked like the Information Age had freed us from the constraints of the Machine Age. Two things held back growth rates, or so it was said at the time: ignorance and resources. You needed educated scientists and trained engineers to design and build a railroad. You also needed material inputs—iron ore, copper tin, and most important, energy.

Education took time and money. And Harvard could only handle a few thousand people. Most people—especially those in Africa, Asia, and Oklahoma—had no easy access to the information they needed to get ahead.

The Internet changed that. You want to build a nuclear reactor? Google it! You want to know how Say's Law works? Or Boyle's Law? Or the Law of Unintended Consequences? It's all there. With enough imagination, you can almost see an Okie in a trailer in Muskogee, studying metallurgy online. Then you can almost imagine him driving up to Koch Industries in Wichita with a plan for a new way to process tungsten. And if you drink enough and squint, you can almost bring into focus a whole world of people, studying, comparing, inventing, innovating—which leads, at the speed of an electron going home to a hard drive, to a whole, fabulous world of hyperprogress.

MIT has only 11,319 students. But with the Internet, millions of people all over the world now have access to more or less the same information. And there are even free universities that package learning, making it easy to study and follow along. Now there can be an almost unlimited number of scientists and engineers ready to put on their thinking caps to make a better world. Surely, we will see an explosion of new patents, new ideas, and new inventions.

As for resources, the lid had been taken off that pot too. In the new Information Age, you don't need so much steel or so much energy. A few electrons are all it takes to become a billionaire. After all, how much rolled steel did Bill Gates make? How much dirt did Larry Ellison move?

The capital that really matters is intellectual capital, not physical resources. Or so they said. If you used your brain, you could actually reduce the need for energy and resources. Energy use declined in the developed economies as people used it more efficiently. So did the need for hard metals and heavy industries. The new economy was light, fast-moving, and infinitely enriching. There were no known limits on how fast this new economy could grow!

Those were the gassy ideas in the air in the late '90s. They drove up the prices of "dot-com" companies to dizzy levels. And then, of course, the Nasdaq crashed.

And then, one by one, the illusions, scams and conceits of the late twentieth century—like pieces of bleak puzzle—came together:

No "peace dividend"—the military and its crony suppliers actually increased their budgets.

No "end of history"—that was all too obvious on September 11, 2001.

No hypergrowth, no great moderation, no great prosperity—all that came to an end September 15, 2008, when Lehman Brothers declared bankruptcy.

And as far as producing real, measurable wealth—the Internet, too, was a dud.

And then, as the new century matured into a sullen teenager, the ground was littered with scales fallen from the eyes of millions of parents. The entire twenty-first century—from 2000 to 2016—was a failure. People hadn't gotten richer at all. Instead, they had gotten poorer. Depending on how you measured it, the typical white man had lost as much as 40 percent of his real earnings since the century began.

People rubbed their eyes and looked harder; the picture came into sharper and more ghastly focus. The promise of material progress and political freedom had begun to break down many years before. In America, growth rates fell in every decade since the '70s. Real wage growth slowed too—and even reversed. The government was more powerful, more intrusive, and more overbearing than ever and now able to borrow at the lowest rates in history. But so twisted had the financial system become that the least productive sector—the government—was the only one with easy access to capital.

There were signs of a deeper breakdown too. Soldiers returning from the Mideast were killing themselves in record numbers. The fellow in the trailer in Muskogee was likely to be a minimum-wage meth addict watching porn on the Internet rather than studying metallurgy. Debt had reached a record high—at 335 percent of GDP. Real peace seemed as remote as real prosperity.

And then, the Republican Party chose Donald Trump—the most unlikely standard bearer for a major political party in US history.

How these things came to be, and where they lead, is the subject of *The Breaking Point*.

The delight of the book is that it approaches these issues in an original and interesting way. Picketty (the rich get richer), Gordon (the important innovations are already behind us), and Tainter (it's too complicated) all have theories about why the twenty-first century is such a disappointment. James Dale Davidson connects the dots, but more dots—and more unexpected dots—than perhaps anyone.

Chapter One

Will the United States Go the Way of the Soviet Union?

Maybe the hardest thing in writing is simply to tell the truth about things as we see them.

—John Steinbeck

The thesis of this book is that the United States is no longer a dynamic, free market economy but a stagnant, rigged economy all but certain to collapse. The American political economy has been perverted by decades of antimarket plunder into a consortium of crony capitalist rackets, propped up by trillions in "fictitious capital"—credit conjured out of thin air. The semblance of prosperity sporadically enjoyed in recent decades was simulated by spending from an empty pocket, funded by history's greatest debt bubble. Simple math shows that the United States is headed for economic disaster. In the decade after 2007, nominal economic growth in the United States averaged 2.92 percent. Over that period, $60 trillion in public and private debt was added, bringing the total to about $200 trillion, or about 300 percent of GDP. If the average interest rate is 2 percent, then the 300 percent debt-to-GDP ratio means that in order to cover interest, the economy would need to grow at a nominal rate of 6 percent. In fact, average nominal GDP growth in the decade since 2007 now involves an annual shortfall of half a trillion dollars below the growth margin required to cover interest. An economy that depends for growth on ever-increasing amounts of

1

debt that cannot even be serviced at the lowest interest rates in 5,000 years must inevitably reach the Breaking Point.

The Breaking Point is where the "long run" meets the present. It is the point where the car runs out of road—where systems that no longer pay their way exhaust their credit and go broke. The Breaking Point is a nonlinear departure on the road to nowhere. It occurs when collateral collapses, burying the public's faith in fiat money and the institutions that create and regulate it.

The day will come when the debt can no longer be kited. Ever-diminishing returns from operating a system built for rapid growth at stall speed imply that the Breaking Point will come soon. Overly large and overly costly institutions will break down. Commerce will seize up. Malinvestments will be exposed and repriced on a gargantuan scale. Wealth will evaporate. Complex systems will be superseded by simpler, cheaper ways of doing things. And the discontents implied by change on that unexpected scale, manifested by the unexpected popularity of Donald Trump and Bernie Sanders, will mount to full-throated fury.

Of course, the jeopardy I explore here may seem unlikely to those inclined to believe official pronouncements. Donald Trump told you that it was "all lies." But Donald also said that he could "make America great again." Those two propositions may be too far apart to straddle the normal span of credibility. Any way you look at it, you are at a disadvantage in trying to deconstruct the fabric of lies that shrouds your view of the future. Judging from past experience, forecasts of discontinuities are seldom credible in advance.

Starting in the mid-1980s, the late Lord William Rees-Mogg and I risked our dignity (of which he had considerably more than I) on the "crazy" forecast that the Soviet Union was on the threshold of collapse.

Unhappily, there is less dignity at stake with this analysis. Lord Rees-Mogg died of throat cancer in 2012, so he cannot be held to account for my errant hunches, deductions, and grumblings about the looming "terminal crisis" that will bring the US imperium to the Breaking Point.

Megapolitics Revisited

How were Rees-Mogg and I able to foresee the collapse of the Soviet Union when the experts in academia and the CIA missed it? Very simple. While they were focusing on the present through the lens of conventional thinking, we looked ahead and saw an unsustainable situation. The main factor informing our confidence in the brazen prediction that the Soviet Union would collapse was a theory of "megapolitics." Megapolitics is an analysis of the boundary forces that set the rules for life's games. Resorting to analyzing megapolitics represents a departure from the normal practice of projecting the future through a simple-minded linear projection of trends.

Most attempts at forward vision rely almost solely on extrapolation of trends. To see what I mean, try googling "World population in 2100." *Science News* offers this factoid "World population likely to surpass 11 billion in 2100." Will it? I consider that projection most unlikely, notwithstanding the fact that it is endorsed by the United Nations, the American Statistical Association, and hordes of "population experts." You can better understand their approach courtesy of the website OurWorldInData.org. A post on "World Population Growth" makes clear that the only factors incorporated in the forecast of the growth of world population to 11 billion in 2100 are the data incorporated in existing trend lines: "The rate of growth corresponds to the slope of the line tracing the total world population over time."

Lord Rees-Mogg was fond of saying, "Trees don't grow to the heavens." No one with a basic grasp of reality expects a tree that has grown fifty feet high to continue growing until it stretches fifty miles into the sky. We formulated "megapolitics" as a framework for understanding some of the basic factors that counteract and reverse apparently well-established trends. To help specify those factors, we turned to a lost 211-year-old treasure trove of investment secrets: *An Inquiry into the Permanent Causes of the Decline and Fall of Powerful and Wealthy Nations* by William Playfair. Ironically, Playfair was the genius who invented the trend line, the pie chart, the bar graph, and the other familiar formats for the representation of statistical information. But Playfair did not stop there. He was a technological visionary and assistant to James Watt, inventor of the steam engine. Playfair understood that technology changes power relations and thereby changes societies. Playfair wrote:

> The invention of gunpowder . . . changed the art of war, not only in its manner, but in its effect . . . While human force was the power by which men were annoyed, in cases of hostility, bodily strength laid the foundation for the greatness of individual men, as well as of whole nations. So long as this was the case, it was impossible for any nation to cultivate the arts of peace, (as at the present time.) without becoming much inferior in physical force to nations that preferred hunting and made war their study; or to such as preferred exercising the body, as rude nations do, to gratifying the appetites as practised in wealthy ones. To be wealthy and powerful was then impossible . . .
>
> Those discoveries, then, by altering the physical powers of men, by changing their relations and their connections, as well as by opening new fields for commerce, and new channels for carrying it on, form a very distinct epoch in the history of wealth and power.[1]

The theory of megapolitics, as developed here, is an attempt to identify and decipher the boundary forces that inform life's games. Roughly speaking, there are three such games you must understand:

soared to a record $118.32 billion, as reported by Robert Wiedemer in *The Aftershock Investor Report.*[7]

Don't believe official statistics that portray an accelerating rebound. They are a current version of what economist Peter Boettke dubbed "the malpractice of economic measurement" in *Why Perestroika Failed*, his study of Soviet economic collapse.[8]

Today, the personalities are different, and the alphabet is Latin rather than Cyrillic, but the dedication to fabricating a fake prosperity is the same. In spite of the fact that the total number of US business closures exceeded the total number of businesses being created during every year of Barack Obama's presidency, you are told that the economy is recovering. There is supposed to be a robust recovery in real GDP under way. Don't believe it. Forget the headline GDP reports. You are far better advised to gauge the strength of the economy, or lack thereof, on the basis of reported nominal GDP growth. That series is not distorted by the government's phony deflator calculations. On a nominal basis, GDP has flat-lined since 2010. Or worse.

Consider that nominal GDP over the past three business cycles shows a strong secular trend toward slowing. During the recovery from the Savings and Loan Crisis (S&L Crisis) in the 1990s, nominal GDP grew at a 5.6 percent annual rate. After the dot-com bubble burst, nominal GDP grew at 5.3 percent during the recovery into the subprime bubble after 2001. After that bubble collapsed into the Great Recession of 2008–9, nominal GDP grew at a rate of 4 percent during the first three years of "recovery after the bottom." Since Q2 of 2012, nominal GDP growth has been steadily decelerating. In looking at Q3 of 2015, we saw a sad 2.9 percent GDP growth over the prior year, further proving that the US economy was continuing to stall.

Of course, the rate of nominal growth is crucial to determining how heavily the deflationary burden of debt weighs on the economy. Servicing $62.1 trillion in credit market debt outstanding—an amount equal to about 350 percent of reported

GDP—obviously grows more difficult the further the rate of nominal GDP growth sinks below the carry cost of debt.

Bureaucrats in the TsSU, the Central Statistical Agency of the Soviet Union, issued glowing economic reports portraying what was evidently fake prosperity right up until the Soviet state collapsed. They were reporting a comfortable 3 percent national income growth, higher than the reported average US real GDP growth of 2.37 percent since 2009. Meanwhile, however, dissident statistician G. I. Khanin, who disclosed that official statistics overstated the growth of Soviet national income from 1928 through 1985 by thirteenfold, saw a sharp compound decline in the Soviet economy beginning in the late '80s. History has shown who was right.

Remember, as well, that fabricated growth and "make believe well-being" reported by Soviet statisticians seem to have hoaxed Western experts, as well as the mainstream news media. As late as May 1988, The RAND Corporation was reporting that "the Soviet Union [had] transformed itself from an undeveloped economy into a modern industrial state with a GNP second only to that of the United States."[9]

More amazing, as late as 1989, Nobel Prize–winning economist Paul Samuelson declared in the thirteenth edition of his textbook that "the Soviet economy is proof that, contrary to what many skeptics had earlier believed, a socialist command economy can function and even thrive."[10] Shows how little they knew.

It also hints at the common ground that corporatist, welfare state capitalism shared with the "state capitalist" (Lenin's term) system known popularly as Communism. Both systems were varieties of crony capitalism in different guises. Both involved the hoarding of antimarket privileges created at the expense of the general public. Both were all about rewarding the insiders, a.k.a. the *nomenklatura*. This similarity was veiled by the very different political theater in Washington and Moscow. But appearances aside, both systems shared common roots in what Sir John Hicks called "the modern phase of fixed industrial capitalism."[11] The more monopolistic and brittle of the two—the Soviet "state capitalist"/"Communist" system—collapsed first.

Remember that by his own account, Lenin aspired to a utopia "organized on the lines of a state capitalist monopoly." He declared his ambition "to organize the whole national economy on the lines of the postal service" and said "that the technicians, foreman, bookkeepers, as well as all officials, shall receive salaries no higher than 'a workman's wage,' all under the control and leadership of the armed proletariat—this is our immediate aim."[12]

Boettke well described the Soviet system: "Throughout its history the defining characteristic of the mature model of Soviet-style socialism was political and economic monopoly. The vast system of interlocked monopolies, and the nomenklatura system, worked to provide perquisites to those in positions of power and controlled access to these positions. The Soviet system created a loyal caste of bureaucrats who benefited directly from maintaining the system."[13] But while Western economists were celebrating the imaginary economic success of the Soviet Union, promises of future abundance rang hollow to the Russian masses. They saw that the Soviet economy was imploding.

By the final days of the Soviet Union, in the words of economic historian Mark Harrison, "the scale of the downturn in the Soviet economy had already substantially exceeded that of Western market economies in the slump of 1929–1932, but with the difference that there was no prospect of recovery."[14] Today, the bureaucrats who report on US economic performance are just as enthusiastic about their fake statistics as were their Soviet counterparts.

The danger of economic lies and exaggerations, as illustrated by the Soviet collapse, is that they "blanked out the true picture."[15] A realistic understanding of the challenges you face is a prerequisite for getting the better of the bureaucrats. You will be hard-pressed to make the necessary adjustments to prosper in a rapidly changing world if you are complacently swaddled in official lies.

"Things Fall Apart"

The age of big government is over, not just in the Soviet Union, but throughout the globe. The nation-state endures as a not-so-colorful, well-surveyed abstraction, but it has lost its vitality and is now a dysfunctional legacy institution trading on past glories. In the years since the collapse of the subprime bubble almost brought down the world financial system, it has been kept on life support with trillions of dollars created out of thin air by central banks and more trillions spent from an empty treasury by bankrupt central states.

Popularly known as "kicking the can down the road," this game of "extend and pretend" has not resolved the fundamental structural problems. To the contrary, it has made them worse. The phony remedies to past crises only increase the amplitude of the terminal crisis to come that will eventually bring the tottering system to the Breaking Point.

From Pastels to Earth Tones

In this sense, it is appropriate that the latest edition of the *National Geographic* map of the world depicts nations in somber earth tones rather than the bright pastels I remember from the maps of my mid-twentieth-century childhood. Somalia appears as a flat stretch of ochre, bordering the Indian Ocean. Syria along the Mediterranean is the same color. Iraq and Yemen are represented to scale, more or less, in burnt umber; Argentina is a purplish gray, while Pakistan is brown; and Libya, Afghanistan, and Nigeria appear in an unlovely shade of green that I believe interior designers call "olive drab." The colors offer no clue to distinguish failed and failing states from apparently more stable jurisdictions at the core that share similar tones and hues elsewhere on the map. But that doesn't change the reality that the collapse of the nation-state that began on the periphery is working its way toward the center.

A group like ISIS (the Islamic State of Iraq and the Levant, or "Daesh," after its Arabic abbreviation *[al-Dawla al-Islamiya al-Iraq al-Sham])* is both a catalyst and consequence of the breakdown of nation-states, as the poet foresaw almost a century ago:

> Things fall apart; the centre cannot hold;
> Mere anarchy is loosed upon the world,
> The blood-dimmed tide is loosed, and everywhere
> The ceremony of innocence is drowned;
> The best lack all conviction, while the worst
> Are full of passionate intensity.[16]

William Butler Yeats was referring not to ISIS carrying out its pitiless atrocities under "shadows of the indignant desert birds" but to his intuition of "a rough beast . . . slouch[ing] towards Bethlehem to be born," which resonates with the headlines.

In February of 2015, Politifact.com presented reports indicating that ISIS and its supporters post as many as 200,000 social media messages online daily. Their hyperactive use of the Internet for propaganda pays off with astonishing success in recruitment from around the world. The BBC reports that as many as sixty British teenaged girls have flown to the Mideast to join ISIS as jihadi brides.

You are a witness to the spasms of a world system sputtering toward collapse. During major transitions in civilization, it is common that institutions of power that no longer suit the underlying circumstances of their time become dysfunctional. Equally, the leaders of a failing system tend to compound the challenges it faces by cleaving to outdated techniques for asserting power that tend to backfire and aggravate the vulnerability of the system. Just as the late medieval church could not turn back the assault on feudalism launched with gunpowder weapons by threats of excommunication, so air strikes and the "big battalions" will not stem the tide of devolution that is eroding big government everywhere.

This is evident in the fact that the US response to the unraveling of nation-states in the Middle East and Central Asia has been to launch a sequence of ill-conceived military interventions, including attempts at regime changes in Afghanistan, Iraq, Libya, and Syria. The United States also sought to shore up the government of Yemen. These costly wars have been a disaster. The United States quite literally spawned the Islamic State. As detailed in an August 2015 article in *The Times of Israel*, ISIS is led by more than one hundred of Saddam Hussein's former officers, including ex-generals who have created structure and discipline among the jihadist group, developing what some call a "proto-state." US intervention in Iraq clearly let the Islamic State genie out of the bottle.

Rather than stabilizing fraught situations, US interventions only seemed to accelerate the process of collapse, opening the way for the Islamic State to seize control of portions of Iraq, Syria, and Libya, while a resurgent Taliban made gains in Afghanistan, dominating territory on the outskirts of Kabul. And in Yemen, the US-backed government fell to Houthi rebels. Trillions of dollars and many thousands of lives later, chaos reigns supreme.

We live in an obsolete system, though of course obsolete systems can endure long after their "use by" dates. The global financial crisis of 2008 highlighted the dysfunction of systemic leadership carried over from the "Modern Age"—the common nickname for the recent period of history from the end of the fifteenth century through the late twentieth—when the returns to violence were high and rising.

The Start of the Modern Age

The start of the modern era was announced "with a bang" in 1494, when Charles VIII, king of France, invaded Italy with new high-compression bronze siege cannons. (Although usually given second billing, the effectiveness of French artillery was enhanced by the handiwork of brothers Jean and Gaspard Bureau, who supplanted the large rocks previously fired by cannons, with iron cannon balls cast to fit snuggly in the barrel of the cannons.)

The first impact of the high-compression siege cannon firing iron cannon balls was felt at the Tuscan fortress of Fivizzano, which "was quickly reduced to gravel and its garrison ruthlessly slaughtered."[17] But the signal demonstration of the effectiveness of the new weapons was the destruction of the Neapolitan fortress of Monte San Giovanni, whose eleventh-century walls fell after eight hours of bombardment, having previously withstood a siege of seven years.[18] This dramatically highlighted the dominance of "the big battalions." Military historian Max Boot put it this way:

> The cost of both a state-of-the-art fortress and the forces needed to besiege it properly was steep. When Charles VIII's successor, King Louis XII of France, asked what would be necessary carry-out his planned invasion of Milan in 1499, one of his advisers replied bluntly, "money, more money, and again more money." The petty lords of Europe did not have enough money. To compete in the gunpowder age required the resources of a super-Lord, a king, ruling over a large kingdom providing substantial revenues. Thus the dictates of the battlefield—or the siege site—gave a powerful impetus to the development of sovereign states.

The End of the Modern Age

That impetus continued to play out for five centuries before petering out in the last quarter of the twentieth century. Lord Rees-Mogg and I took the view that the Modern Age ended with the death of the Soviet Union in 1991. That epic collapse showed that the "big battalions" now mattered less than they had over the previous five centuries.

But just as every eleventh-century tower did not collapse when Charles VIII opened fire on Monte San Giovanni, so many of the obsolete institutions of the Modern Age still stand. Everywhere on the globe, economies are cluttered with a legacy of dysfunction from the dying nation-state.

Not the least of these legacy issues is the heritage of a debt supercycle dating to 1945, when British hegemony came to an end and the systemic leadership of the United States was inaugurated. The thoroughgoing financialization of the economy by big banks has had far-reaching effects. As former US assistant secretary of the treasury Paul Craig Roberts put it, big banks "are converting the entirety of the economic surplus to paying interest on debt."[19]

The legacy of metastasizing debt is only a part of the overhang from the modern era of nation-states that is destined to be unwound. It is also part of the institutional legacy of fiat money issued through a banking system regulated by central banks. The full story is not yet told, but as the *Telegraph* of London put it, "How might the present explosion in debt end? The only thing that can be said with certainty is 'badly.'"[20]

The Unfree Economy Costs You $125,000 per Year

A related legacy of the obsolete nation-state system is an unfree economy lumbered with innumerable crony capitalist distortions. As a result, many sectors are characterized by declining marginal returns—another way of saying that accelerating inefficiency plagues the economy.

Recent research concludes that the proliferation of regulation has deleterious effects on economic activity. An estimated growth rate reduction of about 2 percent per annum implies a massive compound loss of annual income due to crony capitalism. A 2013 study published in the *Journal of Economic Growth* concludes that increased regulation since 1949 had cost the economy $37 billion in lost annual GDP as of 2011, implying that the average American (man, woman, or child) would have an additional $125,000 to spend per year, if not for the fluorescence of crony capitalist rip-offs.[21]

It would come as a surprise to most victims of this grand larceny to learn that they have been robbed of more than they ever had. In this respect, a faltering education system that leaves many incapable of understanding counterfactuals may temporarily help shore up stability. But ignorance is rarely bliss.

A Legacy of Debt and Dysfunction

To the extent that regulation has dampened growth, the greatest cost of this compound slowdown has undoubtedly been visited on those at the bottom of the income ladder. Evidence of how far the bottom 50 percent of America's wealth distribution has fallen comes from Credit Suisse in its 2014 *Global Wealth Databook*. As interpreted by Mike Krieger, the data show that the bottom half of America's wealth distribution ranks dead last among forty major economies, with 1.3 percent of national wealth. Russia, at 1.9 percent, was the only other major economy of those forty that came close.[22]

But the comparison is even more dismal than Krieger lets on. When the comparison is extended to the sixth decile, the United States ties with Russia at dead last for the smallest percentage of wealth owned by the bottom 60 percent of the population. In both countries, the bottom 60 percent owns only 3.4 percent of the total holdings of wealth according to Credit Suisse. The United States ranks below other countries with famously unequal holdings of wealth; Indonesia (5.6 percent), Brazil (5.8 percent), and Mexico (8.8 percent) all rank considerably above the United States in percentage terms. In other words, a clear majority of Americans are riding the down escalator. Not only is the annual wage of 80 percent of the workforce not growing, but it is in fact collapsing to the lowest levels since the Lehman crisis.

This has troubling implications for your future. For one thing, it says that the majority of Americans appear to be unable to compete economically and create wealth in the twenty-first century. The same Credit Suisse wealth assessment that showed the bottom 60 percent of Americans trailing the world in their share of total wealth, however, also showed that the United States led the world in the number of millionaires and in total wealth creation. According to Credit Suisse, average wealth in the United States in 2014 was 19 percent above the 2006 precrisis peak and 50 percent above the 2008 postcrisis low. Since 2008, $31.5 trillion has been added to US household wealth, which is equivalent to almost two years' GDP.

If you are one of the 14.2 million Americans who are millionaires, not to mention the 62,800 Americans whose net worth exceeds $50 million, the political arithmetic implied by Obama's impoverishment of the middle class gives cause for alarm. While the greatest reason for the wealth and income shortfall for the middle class may well be the accumulation since the middle of the last century of crony capitalist rip-offs, the fact that so many people now seem to find it impossible to compete and recover lost wealth in the face of rigged markets is bad news. It implies that they may well tire of losing a game they apparently can't win.

While one could easily overestimate the influence that voters exert over the direction of policy in Washington, it could also be a mistake to discount their role altogether. There is a high likelihood that disgruntled voters will fail to distinguish between the ill-gotten gains of corporatist crony capitalists who use the political process to pick your pocket and the laudable success of entrepreneurs who create wealth in the free market. If market forces amplify income dispersion in the years to come, there will be a greater risk of this confusion intensifying.

As I explore in the coming chapters, the continued necessity of work does not necessarily imply superior incomes for "the masses." Characteristic technologies of the Information Age do not presage a surge in demand for persons of modest skill. Because the marginal costs of digital goods are vanishingly small, capacity constraints on their sale and distribution are immaterial. This means that one competitor, in principle, could fill orders from millions of customers with few or no employees. This amplifies the "winner-take-all" character of the economy, rewarding the most talented "1 percent" while leaving those in the lower deciles of talent scrambling for jobs as baristas.

The "Education Promise" Broken

At the same time, the more distributed character of the information economy undermines the value of credentials, which were so essential to securing employment in government and private bureaucracies during the heyday of big-business capitalism. The fact that you can no longer dependably secure a superior income by attaining a credential that is essentially irrelevant to your productive capacity compounds the decline in returns to education. Persons of average skills and intellect will be less likely to get ahead through schooling unless it genuinely enhances their capabilities.

One of the implied promises of the bankrupt nation-state is that an individual who gets a good education will be able to get a well-paying job. The Department of Education is still in business and paying its bills, but the "education promise" is already slipping away. The growing realization that about a third of all student loans are likely to go unpaid suggests that the returns to education have already fallen so far that, in many cases, it may no longer make sense to pay the inflated costs of a college degree. Under President Obama, the American dream of upward mobility has become a nightmare with the wealth of all but the top 20 percent sinking like a rock.

Secular Stagnation

The fact that the bottom 60 percent lack the means to spend, while the crony capitalists who enjoy the lion's share of the gains from freebooting have a high propensity to save, leads to an "excess supply of savings" so troubling to Keynesians. Hence the consumers who might otherwise spend eagerly lack the cash flow to fuel a sustainable domestic spending boom. This helps illuminate the twenty-first-century growth slowdown, or "secular stagnation," and its impact on the viability of the system.

Another factor that contributes to the epic deceleration of growth has been the slowdown in the growth of energy inputs as the Energy Return on Energy Invested (EROEI) has plunged over the past several decades. Analysis of the impact of declining EROEI is complicated by the seemingly paradoxical collapse in oil prices, which fell by more than 50 percent after June 2014. As detailed in coming chapters, however, I see this systemic price reversal as another warning signal of a system on the verge of collapse.

Equally, the dramatic slowdown in per capita energy consumption in the United States belies the official data proclaiming strong GDP growth. US annual total energy per capita consumption in British Thermal Units (BTUs) has not recovered but rather fallen since 2008. This is not a matter of energy efficiency but of economic decline.

It is quite a mess. But not to worry. It is not forever, I swear.

Anachronistic Mental Baggage

Still another heritage of centuries of embedded statism is mental baggage—the mental paradigm, or "metageography," that pervades our understanding, imagination, and knowledge as a society. As Peter J. Taylor put it, "A metageography is the collective geographical imagination of a society, the spatial framework through which people order their knowledge of the world. It provides the geographical structures that constitute unexamined discourses pervading all social interpretation."[23] The colorful mosaic map by which the globe is divided into nation-states is only one aspect of embedded statism inherited from the past. It is embedded in the analysis of social, economic, and political patterns and processes within states.

In this sense, the "social sciences" are an anachronism. This is easier to say than it is to grasp. But stay tuned. Sweeping change has many disorienting consequences, most of which lie outside the reach of our wishes. Just as the death of nation-states implies "the breaching of territorial boundaries," so it also implies "a breaching of disciplinary boundaries" and new ways of understanding a changing world.[24]

Like Merlin's enchanted sword, Excalibur, locked deep in the rock, with its conflicting injunctions engraved on opposite sides of the blade—"Take me up" and "Cast me away"— the Breaking Point is destined to cut both ways. We find ourselves at a moment of history pregnant with both promise and anxiety. There is the possibility of a new, freer world taking shape, in keeping with the original promise of America. I confess to writing as an unabashed fan of the Jeffersonian perspective on liberty that informed the early history of the United States. Alas, I suspect that Jefferson would be appalled at the gigantic, all-powerful nation-state that has taken root in the soil he tilled.

The message of this book, however, is one of resilience and hope. It says that you can take control of your life—even in a period of dramatic change. Of course, if you do not face the future with resilience and hope, the prospect of sweeping change could also appear to be a message of doom and gloom.

Because the United States has been the hegemonic power, economic collapse in the United States would mean a transition to a new world system, a result not seen with the collapse of the Soviet Union. Consequently, much of what we take for granted may be up for grabs during and after the Breaking Point. Lord Rees-Mogg and I brushed over this somewhat incendiary point in predicting the collapse of the Soviet Union. Yet in retrospect, the fall of the USSR was only the first tremor in a global earthquake that is also destined to bring the status quo of big government corporatism to an end.

"The Most Extraordinary Scandal of Our Times"

Taking a long view, I also analyze current circumstances in terms of the Secular Cycle—a centuries-long pattern of the growth and collapse of states and empires. The Secular Cycle in turn seems to be a function of the quasi-bicentennial cycle of bad weather.

Coming chapters detail my view that "global warming" is a corporatist scam that has put hundreds of millions of dollars in former vice president Al Gore's pockets. What Dr. Richard Lindzen, professor emeritus of atmospheric sciences at MIT, describes as "global warming hysteria" has led to costly policies that are unable to replace fossil fuels. In the meantime, such policies enrich crony capitalists at the expense of the public, increasing costs across the board and restricting the world's poorest population's access to energy.

Notwithstanding the noisy pretense that the theory of anthropogenic global warming is based on "settled science," it is little more than hucksterism backed by billions of dollars' worth of propaganda spawned at public expense. Not even the temperature data purporting to show rapid warming, as published by NASA and other official agencies, are reliable. The fraudulent data are compounded in computer models forecasting disaster. These computerized alarms are better understood as neo-Scholastic syllogisms akin to medieval "natural philosophy" rather than science.

What the *Telegraph* of London has called "the most extraordinary scandal of our times" extends to phony reports of sea level rise. Coming chapters debunk alarms over rising temperatures and sea levels, exposing the "eco-fascist" project to cartelize world energy. This thought exercise brings together ideas and evidence from many different realms. Along the way, we discuss the transformation of the economy from an open, dynamic free-market capitalist system to a closed, sclerotic system where the rules are rigged against you—unless you happen to be a corporatist insider. The power of law has elevated the privileged antimarket sector at your expense. Big crooks hire lobbyists in thousand-dollar suits to steal your prosperity. This involves issues of inequality, the eclipse of the rule of law, and the prospect of a latter-day version of Adam Smith's "declining state."

Given the unstable and unsustainable nature of our modern global financial, monetary, and economic system, a coming collapse is more likely than most experts suspect. Taken together, the factors informing the terminal crisis of US hegemony amount to a gigantic game of musical chairs. My hope is that this book will help you gain the necessary perspective so you can find a perch when the music stops.

Notes

1   Playfair, William, *An Inquiry into the Permanent Causes of the Decline and Fall of Powerful and Wealthy Nations* (London: W. Marchant, 1805), 4–5.

2   Braudel, Fernand, *The Wheels of Commerce* (New York: Harper & Row, 1982), 229–30.

3   Hayek, F. A., *New Studies in Philosophy, Politics, Economics*

and the History of Ideas (London: Routledge & Kegan Paul, 1978), 197.

4   http://www.bloomberg.com/news/articles/2015-11-02/here-s-how-much-qe-helped-wall-street-steamroll-main-street.

5   https://mises.org/library/our-current-illusion-prosperity.

6   http://www.pewtrusts.org/en/research-and-analysis/issue-briefs/2016/03/household-expenditures-and-income.

7   Wiedemer, Robert, "The Untold Damage of Buyback Billions," *Aftershock Investor Report*, March 5, 2015.

8   Boettke, Peter J., *Why Perestroika Failed: The Politics and Economics of Socialist Transformation* (London: Routledge, 1993), 21.

9   Gur, Ofer, "Soviet Economic Growth: 1928–1985," Rand/UCLA Center for Study of Soviet International Behavior (May 1988).

10   Samuelson, Paul, and William D. Nordhaus, *Economics*, 13th ed. (New York: McGraw-Hill, 1989), 837.

11   See Lane, Frederic C., *Profits from Power* (Albany: State University of New York Press, 1979), 7.

12   Lenin, V. I., "The State and Revolution," *The Collected Works of V. I. Lenin*, trans. Stepan Apresyan and Jim Riodan (Moscow: Progress Publishers, 1964), 25. Available at http://www.marx2mao.com.

13   Boettke, *Why Perestroika Failed*, 5.

14   Harrison, Mark, "Soviet Economic Growth since 1928: The Alternative Statistics of V. I. Khanin," *Europe-Asia Studies* 45, no. 1 (1993): 158.

15   Ibid.

16   Yeats, William Butler, *Michael Robartes and the Dancer* (Churchtown, Dundrum, Ireland: Chuala Press, 1920).

17   Role, Raymond E., "Le Mura Lucca's Fortified Enceonte," *Fort* 25 (1997): 90.

18   Bailey, Jonathan B. A., *Field Artillery and Firepower* (Annapolis: Naval Institute Press, 2004), 147. Note that Bailey reports that San Giovanni fell within three hours, rather than eight hours as usually reported.

19   Long, Gordon T., "Paul Craig Roberts: The Cancer of Financial Repression (And Why You

Can't Do Anything about It)," *Zero Hedge*, February 22, 2015.

20 Warner, Jeremy, "Only Mass Default Will End the World's Addiction to Debt," *Telegraph*, March 3, 2015.

21 Dawson, John W., and John J. Seater, "Federal Regulation and Aggregate Growth," *Journal of Economic Growth,* January 2013.

22 Krieger, Mike, "American Middle Class 'Wealth' Worse than Every Nation but Russia & Indonesia," *Zero Hedge*, November 7, 2014.

23 Taylor, P. J., "A Metageographical Argument on Modernities and Social Science," *GaWC Research Bulletin* 29 (September 4, 2000).

24 Ibid.

Chapter Two

The Megapolitics of a Changing World

*The idea of the future being different from the present is so
repugnant to our conventional modes of thought and behavior that
we, most of us, offer a great resistance to acting on it in practice.*
—Lord Keynes

A crucial but seldom-asked question for you as an investor
and thinking citizen is, what determines the direction of social change? The central conceit of democracy is that this is
determined largely by human choice as evidenced by shows of
hands. Obviously, human desires play some role in determining the direction in which history moves, but probably much
less than we tend to think.

The State of Nature

Even a cursory review shows that one of the rarest of all
historic curiosities is a government actually controlled by its
customers. A more detailed analysis confirms that even governments ostensibly chosen through popular franchise are
anything but popular, hence the Gallup report that popular
approval of the US Congress dipped to an all-time low of
9 percent in 2013. Among other things, the extraordinary
unpopularity of the Congress, and indeed the government
itself, reflects the eclipse of the "one-size-fits-all" mass society. In the diverse American economy of the twenty-first

century, there is literally little consensus in favor of the legacy policies of government. A Gallup poll from March 2015 showed that Americans named "dissatisfaction with government" as the most important problem facing the country.[1]

Having said that, these poll results are more curiosities than determinants of future developments. In my view, the ultimate determinants of human action are the megapolitical factors that inform the current state of nature. The direction of change can be more easily deduced by recognizing these informing factors than by assessing public opinion surveys, much less peering into crystal balls.

Deciphering the "Laws of Nature"

Hence this thought exercise begins with a question that Lord Rees Mogg and I sought to answer. What exactly are "the laws of nature"? Not an easy question. You can't read them in a statute book. They are not inscribed on stone tablets for your inspection. To understand the laws of nature, you have to think for yourself. Are "the laws of nature" or "the law of the jungle" fixed for all time? Or do they fluctuate with circumstances?

Think about it.

The physical strength of individuals does not change markedly from generation to generation. Still, you probably wouldn't like the chances of a middle-aged American in hand-to-hand combat with a battle-tested hero of the ancient world, like Achilles. It requires a bit of imagination to bring Achilles to life from the pages of Homer's *Iliad*, but bear with me. Can you imagine yourself prevailing in such a situation?

I can.

Give you an automatic .40-caliber Glock pistol, and I would bet on you to win a confrontation with Achilles.

As this fanciful example illustrates, the laws of nature that govern the physical force of individuals, or the coalitions groups they are able to form, are not fixed, but fluctuate with various boundary forces such as technology.

Technological innovations in weaponry have obvious mega-political implications for altering the costs and rewards of projecting power. And when you examine them closely, so do other aspects of technology, such as the characteristics that dictate the scale at which enterprises can be most profitably organized. And don't overlook the fact that there are other boundary forces such as climate, microbes, and topography that factor in determining the costs and rewards of violence.

Putting Nature in the Background?

It would be a rank misrepresentation to contend that there is a popular consensus to minimize the role of nature among the various boundary factors that inform the "laws of nature." That said, while nature has not been explicitly discounted, there is ample evidence that we have tended, as a civilization, to push nature to the background as a kind of static setting against which we play out our destinies. If anything other than our decisions in the economic and political realms determines our fate, we suppose it to be technology, hence the prevailing conceit that climate change is determined by human action rather than natural fluctuations.

The "Longue Durée"

In 1958, historian Fernand Braudel wrote an important plea for taking the "the long view" in attempting to understand history. I agree with his view, which has important implications for the current intellectual hysteria over supposed global warming and other climate woes. Well before anyone had invented the concept of anthropogenic global warming, Gustaf Utterstrom observed in "Climatic Fluctuations and Population Problems in Early Modern History" that adverse climate change brought cooler weather to Europe beginning in the fourteenth century, with devastating effects including the Black Death. More generally, Utterstrom chided economists for overlooking the importance of climatic fluctuation in history, including major events in Sweden over the last few thousand years—such as a change in land elevation due to the melting of inland ice—that radically altered how humans live.[2]

Global Warming in Historic Context

At a time when the current American imperium is fiscally exhausted and exhibiting declining returns across a wide range of activities, an abrupt turn toward a colder climate could be a trigger of dramatic change, as it frequently has been in the past.

One of the more pernicious consequences of Al Gore's trumped-up fuss about global warming is its shrouding of all questions of climate in a deep fog of political correctness. (As I detail in later chapters, much of the climate record trumpeted to support claims that the world is getting warmer is simply bogus.) Yet thanks to Gore and his accomplices, rational discourse on questions of climate has been stifled. If you are among the few whose "climate-brain" has not been lobotomized by overexposure to Al Gore's terror of good weather, it may not be too late for you to prepare for an unexpected and potentially dramatic climate change in coming decades that could help precipitate an economic collapse—if the system lasts that long.

Perhaps it would be more bracing to think in terms of a "rapid decline in complexity" as part of a transition to a new and freer world, instead of thinking of it as "collapse." Take your pick. But to avoid an overdose of repugnance at the thought "of the future being different from the present," it may be crucial to stretch your perspective beyond our conventional modes of thought.

For a better perspective on the real risk that climate change poses to economies, you need to forget almost everything you may think you know about the history of climate and its impact on civilization. Unless you studied geology, or you share my gamey taste in reading, you are liable to have internalized something like Al Gore's cartoon view of climate—that it was stable and benign until humans happened along and began to change it.

Wrong.

Climate is dynamic, always changing, and almost entirely outside of human control. Even during the Holocene period over the last twelve thousand years, when the climate has been extraordinarily favorable to human habitation, there have been long centuries when it took a turn for the worse and our ancestors faced a heightened challenge to survive. Looking back, most of these periods of climate lapses, or protracted colder periods, are known variously as the "Dark Centuries," "Greek Dark Ages," "Bronze Age Collapse," or simply "Dark Ages."

Over the longer term, the Earth's climate has been anything but benign. For most of the past 100,000 years, the areas of the northern hemisphere that were the most economically advanced through the twentieth century—including Great Britain and the most industrialized areas of North America—were buried beneath miles of ice. Where Chicago, Detroit, Glasgow, and Stockholm now stand, glaciers more than a mile deep buried everything in sight.

The Megapolitics of Feudalism

In *The Great Reckoning*, *Blood in the Streets*, and *The Sovereign Individual*, Lord Rees Mogg and I cited many examples of how changes in megapolitical conditions in the past, some of them seemingly trivial like the invention of the leather stirrup, had far-reaching consequences in shifting the "laws of nature," thus reorganizing societies. The stirrup came into use in Europe during the Dark Ages in the late sixth or early seventh century. By giving the lateral support to a warrior on horseback, it created a revolutionary new mode of battle: mounted combat. This helped cement the power of the landed aristocracy in feudalism. Roughly speaking, feudalism was a system in which wealthier persons within the hierarchy of poor agricultural societies exercised disproportionate military and economic power.

Personal Rather than Territorial Power

In contrast to the modern system in which the state exercises sovereignty over a distinct territory, the medieval system of rule was one of overlordship, in which a variety of lord-vassal relationships overlapped in the same territories. Professor John G. Ruggie, a political scientist at Harvard, explains that the medieval system of rule was essentially a form of anarchy. In his 1983 article, "Continuity and Transformation in the World Polity: Toward a Neorealist Synthesis," Ruggie described the confusion and chaos in medieval rule that led to overlapping and incomplete rights of government and private authority.

Seen from the modern viewpoint, the feudal system of anarchy is hard to imagine. If the scale of governance plunges, as I suspect it may after the Breaking Point, the intricacies of that time may once again be matters of urgent concern.

For the time being, however, it may be enough to recall that serfs were vassals of the knight. The knight was the vassal of the baron. The baron, in turn, was the vassal of the viscount, as he was the vassal of the earl. The duke lorded over the earl. But the duke was the vassal of the prince. The king, in turn, was superior to the prince, while sometimes, and in some places, the king himself was the vassal of the Pope or the Holy Roman Emperor.

None of the feudal lords, not even the king, was necessarily expected to even reside in his territories, nor were they necessarily contiguous, as national territories have tended to be. Note, for example, that after the Norman Conquest, English monarchs usually did not even reside in England. King William the Conqueror himself spent 75 percent of his time after 1072 living in Normandy.

And it was only after Henry Bolingbroke returned from France to seize the throne in 1399, becoming King Henry IV, that England had a monarch who spoke English as his mother tongue. Henry put an end to the Norman line when he had Richard II murdered in 1400. It was a different world. And probably never quite as bound by tradition as people at the time preferred to believe.

The order of precedence among the European aristocracy, the descendants of feudal warlords, probably continued to puzzle hostesses at upper-class dinner parties at least through World War I. But the raw logic of that deference was established centuries earlier before the ancestors of any titled gentleman made it a regular habit to bathe. Under the medieval system of fragmented power, any local warlord who could seize or erect a castle could operate from an almost impregnable redoubt. In most cases, the agricultural production in the area surrounding the castle would have been sufficient to support a contingent of warhorses and a few armed knights—more than enough to cow the neighboring peasantry into subservience.

The Gunpowder Revolution

As always, this system was destined to change as the state of nature evolved. Power was implicitly democratized when gunpowder weapons gave peasants without expensive horses, or the leisure to practice the military arts, the capacity to defeat mounted shock cavalry of the local warlords. Although feudalism did not collapse when the first shots rang out, gunpowder weapons undermined its megapolitical foundations, at least under the conditions of jurisdictional competition that prevailed in late medieval Europe. "The discovery of gunpowder," as Adam Smith's contemporary William Playfair observed, was "wonderfully adapted for doing away the illusions of knight-errantry, that had such a powerful effect in making war be preferred to commerce."[3]

Big Government Doomed

The argument of this book is that contemporary, big government is a similar anachronism, doomed in much the same way, as was feudalism after the invention of gunpowder weapons. My suspicion is that the speed at which history unfolds has accelerated and that the status quo will falter much faster than feudalism did. Furthermore, the underlying foundations of big government have undergone a seismic shift.

Whereas the returns to scale in organizing violence increased during the past five centuries while government grew, the new megapolitical realities reduce the returns to organizing violence at a large scale. This is why ragtag terrorists and homicidal maniacs operating on their own or in small groups can crowd into the headlines of every broadsheet newspaper in the world. The increasing vulnerability of nation-states to attack by even small bands of fanatics suggests that the coming Breaking Point will happen far faster than the centuries it took to build up the modern nation-state system.

It was indeed a protracted process.

When examined, you can see that the Gunpowder Revolution was not a simple matter of rolling out Howitzers and AK-47s immediately gunpowder was discovered. The Gunpowder Revolution unfolded over centuries as metallurgy improved, making possible higher compression cannons and small guns that would propel heavier shot with greater force. The assembly of greater concentrations of power in mass armies, "the big battalions" as Napoleon described them, went hand-in-hand with the growth of the nation-state, financed by taxing enterprises organized at an ever-larger scale.

Centralization of Power

Whereas power was privatized and disbursed under feudalism, the megapolitical logic of gunpowder weapons pointed toward the consolidation and centralization of power in territorial states. There were great advantages to scale in equipping armies with gunpowder weapons.

While feudalism was a system in which wealthier persons within the hierarchy of poor agricultural societies exercised disproportionate military power, gunpowder weapons empowered poor people within rich societies. (By implication, other things being equal, declining returns to scale in warfare now imply an eclipse in the power of the poor.) As suggested by William Playfair, gunpowder weapons spurred the development of commerce because only wealthy political entities could afford the costs of outfitting ever-larger military forces as the Gunpowder Revolution unfolded.

Put simply, it was so costly to outfit a military force that it became prohibitive for lords, dukes, earls, and other proprietors in the medieval ruling class to remain militarily viable. Hence gunpowder became a propulsive force driving the consolidation of territorial states. As firearms became more effective, the scale of battle rose, and ever-larger armies were required to achieve military effectiveness. Giovanni Arrighi noted, "From about 1550 to about 1640, the number of soldiers mobilized by the great powers of Europe more than doubled, while from 1530 to 1630 the cost of putting each of the soldiers in the field increased on average by a factor of 5."[4]

The coevolution of larger political entities and more effective gunpowder weapons progressed through a number of stages in which different political-economic entities achieved predominance or hegemony.

The Eclipse of Mass Society . . .

It may seem a bit "crazy" to suggest that the megapolitical shifts that made Communism obsolete could also make US-style big government and big business capitalism obsolete. But think about it.

In our analysis of the underlying megapolitics of the Information Age, Lord Rees Mogg and I saw that the microchip had decisively changed the character of the state of nature, reducing scale economies and thus altering the costs and rewards of projecting power. Microprocessing meant the eclipse of what Sir John Hicks, the Nobel Prize–winning economist, identified as the modern phase of fixed industrial capitalism in his 1969 book, *A Theory of Economic History*. As Hicks advised, we looked for clear reasons of why one state of society should give way to another.

We saw that the industrial economy, based primarily upon the manipulation of raw materials at a large scale, was destined to give way to an information economy, based increasingly upon the digital manipulation of data at a micro scale. This necessitated a very different organizational structure than that embodied in the Soviet economy, and indeed, in Western industrial democracy.

One-Size-Fits-All Mass Production

The technological characteristics of enterprise compose an important megapolitical variable. The era of one-size-fits-all mass production found its most extreme expression in the Soviet Union, as we have seen, but it was only a matter of degree. Stalin borrowed his industrial production model from Henry Ford in Detroit. Big business capitalism and the Communist "worker's paradise" in the Soviet Union had the same megapolitical foundation. Economies of scale in mass production were so great that products, like automobiles or tractors, were built in enterprises employing thousands or even one hundred thousand or more people.

During the agricultural era, the fixed supply of land implied declining returns to scale in the absence of new technology. Hence real incomes per capita grew very slowly or not at all. From the year AD 1000, most economic growth was absorbed by a fourfold growth of population. Only after the Industrial Revolution, beginning in England in the final quarter of the eighteenth century, did per capita real income and life expectancy surge.

After long centuries in which power was organized in hegemonies of ever-greater scale organized by nation-states, megapolitical conditions now point to the devolution of power to a smaller scale. During the Industrial Age, especially during the most recent phase of US hegemony, you needed a big government to protect the large, vulnerable capital installations where mass production was geared to mass consumption in a one-size-fits-all mold. Remember Henry Ford's Model T, which you could choose in any color—so long as it was black.

Big Government and Big Business Capitalism

The heavy fixed investment required to build an industrial facility of mass production made the enterprise a sitting duck, vulnerable to shakedowns both by the government and by labor unions. You could not easily pick up and move a factory to another jurisdiction with lower taxes or more amenable labor laws once the installation was built. Big business capitalism went hand-in-hand with big government.

Consider Ford Motor Company's River Rouge Complex. The largest integrated factory in the world, it took 11 years to construct, measuring 1.5 miles wide by 1 mile long, with 93 buildings encompassing nearly 16,000,000 square feet of factory space. It had its own docks and, Ford Motor Company bragged, steel furnaces, coke ovens, rolling mills, glass furnaces and plate-glass rollers. Buildings included a tire-making plant, stamping plant, engine casting plant, frame and assembly plant, transmission plant, radiator plant, tool and die plant, and, at one time, even a paper mill. A massive power plant produced enough electricity to light a city the size of nearby Detroit, and a soybean conversion plant turned soybeans into plastic auto parts. The Rouge had its own railroad with one hundred miles of track and sixteen locomotives.

Mass Production: An Alternative to Free Market Capitalism?

It is scarcely an exaggeration to say that Henry Ford's River Rouge Complex made Stalin and Hitler drool. Economic historian Stefan Link reports that, at the behest of the Supreme Economic Council of the Soviet Union, a commission headed by Stepan Dybets set up shop at Ford Motor Company in the summer of 1929.[5] At Stalin's request, the Soviets later contracted with Ford to build a version of the River Rouge Complex at Gorky, to build tractors and automobiles for the Soviet

Union. Hitler sent Ferdinand Porsche as his emissary to Detroit to borrow Ford's River Rouge program of mass production to make an affordable, mass-produced "people's car," or Volkswagen. Link emphasizes that totalitarian leaders considered Ford's system of mass production an alternative to free market capitalism—what the Communists and the Nazis both called "decadent Anglo-Saxon capitalism." Ford's mass production was an illiberal panacea for their projects of state-led economic growth.

During the 1930s, more than 100,000 workers were employed at River Rouge. Needless to say, the staggering sunk cost of the investment in the River Rouge Complex—billions in today's dollars—meant not only that the plant could not easily be moved to a more competitive location, protecting property rights at a lower cost in taxation, but also that its owners could ill afford for it to sit idle. The Ford family could make money when the River Rouge Complex was cranking out a new car every forty-nine seconds. But they could not make money when the output of the factory was forcibly stopped by a labor union strike. Therefore, they had a strong incentive to avoid or settle any strike that threatened to close the facility, even if that meant agreeing to pay wages that were higher than would have been justified in a free market by the skills of the workers.

"Marx in Detroit"

There is a reason that American factory workers became history's best-paid unskilled labor in the middle of the last century. The unprecedented scale of enterprise, involving vast amounts of fixed investment, gave them an unparalleled leverage to sabotage the profits of their employers. In essence, they used organized force to seize some of their employers' property right to their facilities, extracting higher wages by denying the employers the option to hire anyone else at a market-clearing wage. The employers acceded to the shakedowns by granting wages for unskilled work that were six to seven times higher in real terms than those paid by today's largest US employer, Wal-Mart.

With this in mind, it is perhaps not as surprising as it might at first seem that Marxist philosopher Mario Tronti placed the true epicenter of worldwide class struggle in the United States during the era of big-business, mass-production capitalism. In his 1968 essay "Marx in Detroit," Tronti nods approvingly at labor union shakedowns in the United States, pointing out that if the success of class struggle is measured by how much has been gained, that its most advanced model is that of workers in the mass production industries of mid-century United States. Tronti exulted in the fact that in 1946 there were 4,985 strikes involving 4,600,000 workers out of work—16.5 percent of the entire employed workforce.[6]

Perhaps the signal triumph of the mid-twentieth-century class struggle was the "Treaty of Detroit," between General Motors and the United Auto Workers union, concluded in 1948. As Harold Meyerson details in his article "The Forty-Year Slump," GM agreed to grant its workers a sizable raise, a yearly cost-of-living adjustment matching the rate of inflation, and an "annual improvement factor" raising pay in tandem with the United States' productivity, for a two-year no-strike pledge from the union.[7]

That was at the outset of the Baby Boom in the middle of the previous century. Today, there is no prospect that 16.5 percent of the entire employed workforce could go on strike, as only 11.3 percent are union members. More to the point, a treaty in Detroit, now a "Disneyland of rest and ruin," would lead nowhere. Decentralization of the technology of production gives decidedly less leverage to union shakedowns. Megapolitical conditions have changed.

Notes

1   Newport, Frank, "Congressional Approval Sinks to Record   Low: Current Approval at 9%," *Gallup*, November 12,

2013, http://www.gallup.com/poll/165809/congressional-approval-sinks-record-low.aspx.

2   Utterstrom, Gustaf, "Climatic Fluctuations and Population Problems in Early Modern History," *The Scandinavian Economic History Review* 3, no. 1 (1955).

3   Playfair, William, *An Inquiry into the Permanent Causes of the Decline and Fall of Powerful and Wealthy Nations* (London: W. Marchant, 1805), 73.

4   Arrighi, *The Long Twentieth Century*, new ed. (New York: Verso, 2010), 43.

5   See Link, Stefan, "Transnational Fordism, Ford Motor Company, Nazi Germany, and the Soviet Union in the Interwar Years," http://www.academia.edu/1591016/Introduction_to_Transnational_Fordism._Ford_Motor_Company_Nazi_Germany_and_the_Soviet_Union_in_the_Interwar_Years_.

6   See https://webspace.utexas.edu/hcleaver/www/TrontiWorkersCapital.html.

7   Meyerson, Harold, "The Forty-Year Slump," *The American Prospect*, http://prospect.org/article/40-year-slump.

Chapter Three

The Political Economy of Plunder

People of the same trade seldom meet together, even for merriment and diversion, but the conversation ends in a conspiracy against the public, or in some contrivance to raise prices.
— Adam Smith, *The Wealth of Nations*

As you will have guessed if you have read this far, I am by no means a partisan of income redistribution or the tired political agendas of the "proletariat." Yet being somewhat mindful and alert to civic discourse, I could not help noticing that recent years have brought a revival of interest in the theories of Karl Marx. *The New Yorker* staff writer John Cassidy even hailed Marx as "the next big thinker" in his 1997 piece, "The Return of Karl Marx."[1] Why?

This requires some explanation.

I attribute the revival of interest in Marx mostly to bad branding. Capitalism needs the services of Kim Kardashian's PR agent—but that isn't happening any time soon. Notwithstanding having been around for a couple centuries longer than Kim Kardashian, capitalism has not generated the white heat glare of favorable attention that has been lavished on her well-oiled celebrity ass. (Google reports 1,230,000 entries on that topic; partly, this may be because it is a bit easier to recognize than capitalism.) After all those years on reality TV, people know Kim Kardashian when they see her. Not so with capitalism.

In fact, capitalism suffers from recurring unpopularity mostly due to mistaken identity. As the world economy has stagnated and real income growth stalled in recent decades, many people misattribute the decline in their living standards to capitalism, rather than to corrupt and dysfunctional political systems that deform any semblance of "capitalism" wherever they find it. Deformed, or "crony," capitalism is the universal expression of the political economy of plunder.

I see three different types of corrupt political systems in action fleecing people today:

1. **The Total Kleptocracy**, in which the political oligarchs essentially steal the whole wealth of society. This is seemingly the case in the African nation of Angola, ruled by the Popular Movement for the Liberation of Angola (PMLA), headed since 1979 by Jose Eduardo Dos Santos (whose current net worth is $3.7 billion, according to *Forbes*). Dos Santos came to power with backing from the Soviet Union at the vanguard of a Marxist revolution. The PMLA claimed to be a Marxist-Leninist party until 1991 when the Soviet Union collapsed, taking with it a handy source of cash for the ruling oligarchs. Now, a quarter of a century later, the aging revolutionaries have moved beyond Afro-Stalinism to embrace capitalism. Peter Lewis, a professor of African Studies at Johns Hopkins University's School for Advanced International Studies, explains that Dos Santos and his inner circle have numerous business interests with murky sources of funds and corporate governance. As reported by David Smith in a 2012 *Guardian* article, Elias Isaac of the Open Society Initiative of Southern Africa put it more colorfully, saying that the president had created a system of "blood sucking" in which he was the "main vein," and therefore, he could not be let go. In other words, they steal the money.[2] Isabel Dos Santos, Dos Santos's oldest daughter, has emerged as Africa's richest woman and first female billionaire (worth

$3 billion, according to *Forbes*). For more gaudy details of how a small cadre of Marxist revolutionaries turned "capitalists" stole outsized fortunes in an African country with a poor population and the highest infant mortality rate in the world—one in six Angolan children dies by age five—see *Magnificent and Beggar Land: Angola since the Civil War* by Oxford professor Ricardo Soares de Oliveira. The author reveals surprisingly frank admissions by PMLA officials about how they made money from a new industrial park, filled with obsolete factories—even before it began to operate.[3]

2. **The Quasi-Kleptocracy**, as exemplified by Brazil, in which politicians steal money to enrich themselves, but corruption is more complicated. Part of it, perhaps a big part, is done on the political plunder model. Politicians auction off, or rather rent, government power to the highest bidders to generate campaign finance to keep themselves and their cronies in power. Brazil's corruption is something of a hybrid between Kleptocracy, where political oligarchs use the powers of government to steal as much as possible for their own enrichment, and a Pimpocracy, as exemplified by the United States. You may have heard about the billions of dollars stolen from Brazilian oil giant Petrobras and allegedly funneled into the pockets of top Brazilian politicians, including the speakers of both the Brazilian Senate and Chamber of Deputies. Brazilian politicians, of course, have been hoping to confine this corruption scandal to the footnotes. But an astonishing number of Brazilians seem unwilling to sit still for it. On Sunday, March 15, 2015, an estimated 1.2 million Brazilians took to the streets of São Paulo in a demonstration demanding the impeachment of President Dilma Rousseff (who was duly impeached a year later). Perhaps for our benefit

as outside observers, they obligingly marched behind banners that demanded in English: "Thieves! Bring back our money!" Fat chance. Remember, it was Brazilian president Getulio Vargas who proclaimed the boldest and most succinct statement of corporatist crony capitalism ever uttered: "For my friends anything—for my enemies, the law."[4]

3. **The Pimpocracy**, in which politicians essentially force taxpayers to give up assets or freedoms to the benefit of special interest groups or others. While Brazil provides a striking example of a Pimpocracy in action, Brazilians are amateurs compared to what goes apparently unnoticed in the United States. As I was mulling over the proper technical term to describe the American style of political plunder, I recalled a shrewd observation attributed to Donald J. Boudreaux, then chairman of the economics department of George Mason University, in 2009. As reported in *Washington's Blog*, Boudreaux opined that politicians are not prostitutes but pimps, using other people's property for their own gain.[5] Pimps provide their clients with access to prostitutes' assets, while politicians' clients receive access to taxpayers' assets. The pimps don't actually render the services personally, nor do politicians, and they both pocket the majority of the profits.

Professor Boudreaux's preamble to Pimpocracy provides a useful introduction to a startling study that has been languishing in the footnotes of American life.

The Sunlight Foundation—a nonpartisan watchdog group that tracks lobbyist spending and influence in both parties—reported on research it undertook between 2007 and 2012, tracking 200 of America's most politically active corporations. After examining 14 million records—including data on campaign contributions, lobbying expenditures, and federal budget allocations and spending—they found that, on average, the United States' most politically active corporations received $760 from the government for every dollar spent on influencing politics, for a total of $4.4 trillion (two-thirds of the $6.5 trillion that the federal treasury received from individual taxpayers). As the figure was rounded up slightly, that translates to a 75,900 percent rate of return. Compare that to the 0.25 percent Grandmother gets on her CDs.

Recall our discussion from chapter 1 on the finding, from the *Journal of Economic Growth*, that the proliferation of US government regulation since 1949 has cost every man, woman, and child in the United States about $125,000 of annual income.

A lot of money.

And a lot more than money. Think about it. Unless you're already among the top of the fabled 1 percent, an extra $125,000 of annual income—much less the combined $250,000 if you're married—would mean a different life experience, especially for the 80 percent of Americans whose net worth has declined by 40 percent since 2007. If your income expanded by such a large increment, you would have no need to study the footnotes to protect yourself from being totally ruined by politicians.

A 75,900 Percent Rate of Return at Your Expense

Meanwhile, in a different, but equally revealing exercise, the Sunlight Foundation undertook an extensive research project to quantify the rate of return on money invested in lobbying and spending to buy political favors. This brings parasitism into clearer focus.

According to the Sunlight Foundation's analysis, between 2007 and 2012, 200 of America's most politically active firms dished out a combined total of $5.8 billion to buy laws and spending in their favor. What did they get back? Some $4.4 trillion, or two-thirds of the $6.5 trillion that individual taxpayers paid into the Treasury during that period. Note that those were tax receipts they caged, not outlays, as the government spent trillions from an empty pocket.

On average, for every dollar spent to buy political influence, the special interests got back about $760 from the government. As the figure was rounded up slightly, that translates to a 75,900 percent rate of return. Compare that to the 0.25 percent Grandmother gets on her CDs.

Airlines Seek to Reduce Competition

The 75,900 percent rate of return is only an average calculated from the results actually achieved by the 200 most politically active corporations. Twenty-nine of them received one thousand times, or more, what they invested in politics from the federal government—a 100,000 percent return or more. If Grandmother only had the option of buying an annuity indexed to the payoffs from political plunder, she could be flying first class to Dubai on Emirates for her holiday rather than watching reruns of *I Love Lucy*.

But of course, it can't work that way. The stupendous rates of return pocketed by big investors in politics are leveraged to closing markets and denying Grandmother the choice of flying Emirates—even if she could afford it. In March 2015, John Gapper reported in the *Financial Times* that US airlines were attempting to curtail competition from upstart, nonunionized Gulf Airlines, sounding similar to those airlines that provided mediocre service in the past and complained about energetic rivals. That is just exactly what it is. As one who has flown on Emirates on occasion, I can report that the service and amenities are incomparably superior to anything you could encounter on American Airlines, Delta, or United. At the risk of sounding like a wine snob, the wine list on Emirates rivals what you would find in a Michelin starred restaurant. This strikes me as a particular measure of quality because I was once an investor in a beverage company that sold wine to United Airlines.

From that vantage, I can confirm the impression you are liable to have informed as a consumer. They buy only the cheapest possible plonk for their passengers. Emirates wines would cost a magnitude more than United's. Equally important, the seats on Emirates are extralarge and recline into comfy lie-flat beds. You literally have a choice of thousands of in-flight movies and entertainment options. Grandmother could probably watch her reruns of *I Love Lucy* on-board. And you might note that the grandmothers on board are all passengers. None of the Emirates flight attendants is older than thirty. Many could be mistaken for supermodels. And if watching them makes you all sweaty, there are showers in first class.

Electric Utilities Seek to Ban Rooftop Solar

The effort by US carriers to ban competition from the superlative Gulf Airlines is only one of dozens of similar antimarket efforts being conducted in the shadows every day. Indeed, where the crony capitalists are concerned, sunlight is the enemy.

Consider the campaign being orchestrated by electric utility monopolies. As detailed by investigative reporter Joby Warrick in a March 2015 *Washington Post* article, utilities are working to end a "home-solar insurgency."[6] Warrick reports that regulated electric monopolies are lobbying public utility commissions to impose monthly surcharges on customers who install solar panels. Such surcharges have been approved in Arizona and Wisconsin and are pending in New Mexico.

What can you make of these pick-pocketing maneuvers? Of one thing you can be certain: if US carriers don't want to compete against Emirates, that is probably the most authoritative recommendation you could have to book on Emirates if you are going anywhere they fly. Equally, if regulated electric monopolies want to penalize you for installing solar panels, that's probably a strong hint that it would make sense to do so.

The conclusions from the *Journal of Economic Growth* show the devastating cumulative effect of regulations, most of which were never more than footnotes at the time they were promulgated. If you remember the 1960s and '70s, I am sure that you have no recollection of Walter Cronkite or his contemporary, David Brinkley, leading the nightly news broadcast on CBS or NBC with details about how you and other Americans were being ripped off by hundreds or even thousands of new regulations. With few exceptions, the details would've been mind-numbing. Indeed, that was part of the magic that enabled those who conspired against the public to get away with it. As the huge street demonstrations in Brazil attest, rip-offs that are too easily understood tend to infuriate their victims. Unless you assume that Americans are more complacent and easily fleeced than the Brazilians, you would expect to see millions of demonstrators on the streets of big American cities if Obama and his minions let the gag get as far out into the open as it has in Brazil.

You could shout, "Thieves! Bring back our money!" But good luck with that. There is practically no way of stopping the political plunder from getting worse as it is an inherent feature of the governing system, not an incidental distortion. It is a feature so large and essential to the corrupt corporatist system that it is paradoxically more or less invisible.

How could that be?

Think of DNA that informs biology: it is of paramount importance, but you can only see its consequences, not the DNA itself. Look at a dog. Its DNA is invisible. Yet because of the DNA, you can see it is a dog and not a porcupine.

Fiat Money as the Ultimate in Political Plunder

Equally, funny money is a crucial part of the DNA of the predatory modern state. Money is also the lifeblood of the economy. When the politicians can bring money under their absolute control, they will predictably use it to concentrate wealth in the hands of a small sliver of the population. This is certainly what happened in the United States. The introduction of pure fiat money by Richard Nixon was perhaps the single most telling step toward the impoverishment of the middle class in the history of the United States. Obama's policy of pushing wealth inequality to an extreme since 2009 was only the culmination of the political pillage set in motion by Richard Nixon when he repudiated the last link of the dollar to gold in 1971.

In this sense, it is no coincidence that between 1930 and 1970 it was only the bottom 90 percent who saw their incomes rise, as NPR's "Planet Money" report on February 11, 2015, so convincingly documented. Nixon's move to fiat money halted the gains by the bottom 90 percent in the early 1970s and reignited the concentration of income gains among the top 1 percent of earners, reaching an extreme under Obama.

Of course, Obama would prefer that you forget that he initially sought the White House as the candidate of big banks. As reported by CNN, referencing Federal Election Commission figures, Goldman Sachs executives and PACs associated with Goldman Sachs were the largest corporate contributors to Obama's 2008 campaign for the White House.

In a related development, the Sunlight Foundation reported that President Obama has received more money from Bank of America than any other candidate dating back to 1991. The banks got their money's worth. Obama continued the Bush policy of bailing out the big banks, both explicitly and implicitly. By supporting quantitative easing (QE), he sent trillions of dollars into bank coffers. As of January 2015, 72 percent of money created through QE was sitting idle as excess reserves of private banks. They got this essentially free money, with which they are minting profits, as the Federal Reserve pays them 0.25 percent interest on the excess reserves.

Frederick Soddy, Nobel Prize winner (in chemistry), was a bitter opponent of the modern banking system that gives banks the privilege of creating money. He wrote in *The Role of Money*:

> The Banker as Ruler—from that invention dates the modern era of the banker as ruler. The whole world after that was his for the taking. By the work of pure scientist the laws of conservation of matter and energy were established, and the new ways of life created which depended upon the contemptuous denial of primitive and puerile aspirations as perpetual motion and the ability ever really to get something for nothing. The whole marvelous civilization that has sprung from that physical basis has been handed over, lock, stock, and barrel, to those who could not give and have not given the world as much as a bun without first robbing somebody else of it . . . The skilled creators of wealth [in industry and agriculture] are now become hewers of wood and drawers of water to the creators of debt, who have been doing in secret what they have condemned in public as unsound and immoral finance and have always refused to allow Governments and nations to do openly and above aboard. This without exaggeration is the most gargantuan farce that history has ever staged.[7]

I do not embrace every facet of Soddy's embittered indictment of modern banking. Still, he has a point.

Quantitative easing was evidently designed to enrich the few at the expense of the many. In the first instance, it was a financial death sentence for Grandmother, slashing the annual interest paid on her savings to 0.25 percent. To see this more clearly, assume that Grandmother had $400,000 in savings. Today, her annual interest income is just $1,000. Compare this to the 4 percent (or $16,000) a year she could have earned in bank CDs a year before the 2008 crisis unleashed financial repression.

And it is no better for Grandfather. In 2011, the *Wall Street Journal* profiled Forrest Yeager, a ninety-one-year-old resident of Fort Charlotte, Florida. With remaining savings of only $45,000, Yeager must supplement his monthly Social Security income of $1,500 and his small pension by digging deeper into his principal. According to the *Journal*, Yeager reported that he found himself "betting on dying before his money runs out."[8] For Yeager and others like him, QE really was a death sentence.

While money was pulled out of the pockets of millions of savers, elite bankers were handed trillions that they proceeded to use to drive up stock prices and scoop up foreclosed homes that they turned around and rented to dispossessed homeowners, and they made risk-free money by idling their excess reserves at the Fed. Obviously, it is the big borrowers and speculators who are the big beneficiaries of the Fed's monetary policies.

Of course, I do not pretend for a moment that Richard Nixon, much less Barack Obama, was smart enough to fully understand the extent to which fiat money would concentrate wealth in the hands of a few. Far from it. But one needn't suppose that successful politicians set out with the conscious intention of pauperizing their constituents to see they are cunning enough to recognize where their own best interests lie.

Strangely enough, where politicians depend on majority vote, they are probably more, rather than less, likely to concentrate wealth in the hands of a few, whom they reward with crony capitalist favors at the expense of the many.

Why?

Think about it. Would-be demagogues need needy constituents. (If the consequence of proliferating regulations and reducing the efficiency of the free market is to impoverish the majority, so much the better.) That makes the majority a ready audience for the schemes and nostrums of the politicians. If the average American enjoyed an additional $125,000 year,

Barack Obama could not even draw a crowd as a community organizer. He would not have seen inside the White House, except as a tourist.

Equally, highly concentrated income complements political imperatives in another way. In addition to ensuring that many constituents are needy, it enables politicians to concentrate the cost of income redistribution on a relatively small sliver of the population. Hence fiat money fulfills multiple political purposes. In addition to impoverishing voters, thus making them politically receptive, and enhancing the appearance that the recipients of redistributed income get "something for nothing," it rewards bankers—among the largest and most frequent political contributors.

I did my graduate research at Oxford on the thesis that the structure of decision making in the modern democratic state broadly determines how politics evolves. The result to be expected is ever-greater expansion of the antimarket sector. In my view, the only thing that could stop this is complete economic collapse.

Political Plunder Returns 2,600 Times Greater than Productive Investments

Meanwhile, the process feeds on itself. Do you wonder why? Analysis of the financial results of public companies, reported by David Benoit in a March 2015 column for *Money Beat*, shows that capital investment in the material expansion of the economy seemed recently to yield an average return of 29.2 percent.[9] Compare that with the return of 75,900 percent (much less 100,000 percent) from investments in politics. If the normal assumptions of economists are correct, there will be less capital investment in things like property, plants, and equipment, for an average return of 29.2 percent, and more investment in lobbying and fundraisers for politicians, with the return of 75,900 percent. Indeed, the returns on political plunder could plunge by three magnitudes and still be attractive as compared to productive investment. If plunder only earned a return of 75 percent, it would still attract profit-maximizing businesses to hire lobbyists and subscribe $500-a-plate dinners to fund politicians.

Look at it from a distance, and the results go far toward explaining the artificial economies-to-scale that account for the growing predominance of established firms over start-ups. The legacy firms basically bribe politicians to rig the system in their favor. Hence my view that the immiseration of the middle class is caused more by the political economy of plunder and expansion of the antimarket than by capitalist production, per se, as postulated by Marx.

Marx is not "the next big thinker." That thinking still needs to be done.

Notes

1   Cassidy, John, "The Return of Karl Marx," *The New Yorker*, October 20 and 27, 1997, 248.

2   Smith, David, "Angola's Jose Eduardo Dos Santos: Africa's Least-Known Autocrat," *The Guardian*, August 30, 2012, http://www.theguardian.com/world/2012/aug/30/angola-jose-eduardo-dos-santos.

3   Oliveira, Ricardo Soares de, *Magnificent and Beggar Land: Angola since the Civil War* (London: Hurst, 2015), 65.

4   http://news.bbc.co.uk/2/hi/business/4468042.stm.

5   http://georgewashington2.blogspot.com/2009/10/politicans-are-not-prostitutes-they-are.html.

6   Warrick, Joby, "Utilities Wage Campaign against Rooftop Solar," *Washington Post*, March 7, 2015.

7   Soddy, Frederick, *The Role of Money: What It Should Be, Contrasted with What It Has Become* (London: Routledge, 1934), 51.

8   http://www.wsj.com/articles/SB10001424052748703410604576216830941163492.

9   Benoit, David, "Capex or Capital Returns: The Data behind the Debate on Activism," *Money Beat*, March 11, 2015.

Chapter Four

Would Marx Be a Socialist Today?

*Just as Darwin discovered the law of development of organic
nature, so Marx discovered the law of development of human
history . . . that therefore the production of the immediate material
means, and consequently the degree of economic development
attained by a given people or during a given epoch, form the
foundation upon which the state institutions, the legal conceptions,
art, and even the ideas on religion, of the people concerned have
been evolved, and in the light of which they must, therefore, be
explained, instead of vice versa, as had hitherto been the case.*
—Friedrich Engels's eulogy for Karl Marx,
Highgate Cemetery, London, March 17, 1883

Notwithstanding the abject failure of socialist systems in
practice, as well as the striking failure of the working class to
express its "revolutionary potential" as ardently predicted by
Marx, Marx is back in vogue. Remember the conclusion of the
Communist Manifesto, the second best-selling book of all time,
where Marx and Engels proclaimed, "What the bourgeoisie
therefore produces, above all, are its own grave-diggers. Its
fall and the victory of the proletariat are equally inevitable."[1]

Here you see the confusion between prescription and description that muddled Marx's thought. Marx was much better at historic analysis than as the architect of a better world.

Call it a contradiction, if you will, but this becomes ironic
because Marx's deeper and more interesting insights now point
to a completely opposite conclusion to his prescriptions that
continue to resonate with the so-called proletariat. He offered

a valid framework for understanding the dynamics of social change (i.e., "creative destruction") in *The Poverty of Philosophy*, describing how people will change their mode of production when they acquire new productive forces, leading to a change in how they earn a living and in their social relations.

Take that seriously, combine it with new productive forces then unknown to Marx, and you get an entirely new set of revolutionary possibilities remote from those of which Marx himself was a partisan.

"Steamboats, Viaducts, and Railroads"

As I explore in the balance of this chapter, the new technology of the information economy has far-reaching implications for changing the way people earn their living and, indeed, changing all their social relations. I try to think about the shifting technological underpinnings of the economy in the same spirit expressed in William Wordsworth's "Steamboats, Viaducts, and Railroads," in which he embraced the changes of his time, hoping to gain "that prophetic sense of future change, that point of vision" that illuminates "motions and means."[2] I have no qualms about rummaging in the dusty attic of intellectual history to scavenge whatever insights I can, even from poets, hence my somewhat mischievous willingness to deconstruct Marx's nineteenth-century insights to illuminate the coming transition crisis.

In particular, what we can discern about the development of productive forces in today's society does not confirm that socialism is in any sense a necessary result of current or foreseeable developments. That the working class will foment a revolution against capitalism may be a central tenet of Marxism, but given the indisputable revolution in technology over the past thirteen decades, I see contemporary productive forces pointing to a much different conclusion than Marx imagined.

Now that communism and industrialism are dead, I can no longer blame Marx for the fact that he is known to us mainly as an apostle of industrialism's discontents. As you know, his work was invoked to rationalize some of the greatest abuses of state power during the twentieth century; Lenin, Stalin, Mao Tse Tung, and the murderous Pol Pot all claimed to have been inspired by Marx. I find it ironic that Marx's identification with the underachieving and unskilled continues to resonate with erstwhile followers, particularly academics, while his deeper and more interesting insights are resolutely ignored.

The Antiquated Labor Theory of Value

Like Adam Smith and David Ricardo, Karl Marx embraced the labor theory of value, which is actually an "energy theory of value." During the long centuries when almost all economic activity was powered by human somatic energy, it was more apt to postulate that economic value was indeed created by the hard labor of workers whose muscle power animated commerce and production.

This was all to change, however, as the Industrial Revolution led to the widespread adoption of exogenous hydrocarbon energy to power the economy. A recent, authoritative estimate by Tim Morgan (author, *The End of Growth*) concludes that 99 percent of contemporary economic activity is powered by exogenous energy, while less than 1 percent represents human, somatic energy conversion.[3]

Far from making the somatic energy contribution of the working class more crucial to the functioning of society, a great expansion of the use of exogenous energy, along with increased automation, has made labor less important. If the last century and a third since Marx died has proven anything, it is that the value created by unskilled work pales in comparison to that created by the entrepreneurial imagination.

More to the point, the advent of the information economy has arguably antiquated "the foundation upon which the state institutions, the legal conceptions, the art, and even the religious ideas of the people" have been informed. As you will realize, that quote is lifted directly from Engels's eulogy for Marx, quoted at the top of this chapter. Engels proclaimed, "Just as Darwin discovered the law of evolution and organic nature, so Marx discovered the law of evolution in human nature." Clearly, by giving priority to Marx's insights related to the evolution of society, Engels implied that they were among Marx's more interesting and important contributions. I agree.

Forget the invocations of class struggle, based upon the fossilized notions of the labor theory of value, as well as Marx's observations and projections of megapolitical conditions (though he didn't call them that), particularly scale economies in the production process as they appeared in the middle of the nineteenth century. A lot has changed since then.

If Marx's deeper insights mean anything, it is that the whole nature of the economy, government, law, religious ideas, and yes, concepts of economic justice, are destined to evolve as the megapolitical foundation of production and the organization of violence change.

What Marx Missed

Marx could not have added, because it was outside of nineteenth-century technological imagination, that the 3-D printer gives you individual sovereignty, minimal government, and true free market capitalism.

This is what I believe you will see for yourself in the years to come after the terminal crisis of US hegemony. Given that we're at the threshold of a redefinition of social relations, based on a change in how things are produced, it is an open question whether a reincarnated Marx would see his invocation of socialist revolution as an anachronism today, as I do.

I am not pretending to evaluate priorities among Marx's inner thoughts. It may well be that he was more committed to socialism than to the "law of development of human history." Be that as it may, my point is that the integration of digital information into the production process introduces new factors that should have pointed even Marx toward a realization that the channels of history would open in new directions unforeseen in the nineteenth century.

The Information Age implies a radical devolution of power. It will expose diseconomies of scale embodied in anachronistic forms of bureaucratic, big-business capitalism. And it will even more emphatically undermine the returns to complexity embodied in the overgrown nation-state. It is beyond the scope of this analysis to detail a full litany of the implications of this revolution in human affairs. But broadly and simply, as epitomized by 3-D printing (additive manufacturing), information technology implies that economic and political power will devolve back to the individual. Market forces will replace politics and crony capitalism in determining the distribution of income.

One-size-fits-all mass production in sprawling industrial complexes like River Rouge has already begun to give way to customized production individualized to suit you. The production process will devolve further to a micro scale, even to a personal level. Your work will not be commoditized; it will be whatever you want it to be. You will invent it. Any dissatisfaction it entails will be tempered by the fact that you cannot strike against yourself and a 3-D printer.

Indeed, it is very likely that your worldview will be informed by customized information feeds tailored explicitly to meet, and reinforce, your tastes and requirements. The world you live in will literally be "your world" to a degree that was never conceivable in the past.

When Lord Rees Mogg and I wrote *The Sovereign Individual* on the eve of the millennium, we anticipated that the coming Information Age would mean that "predatory violence will be organized more and more outside of central control. Efforts to contain violence will also evolve in ways that depend more upon efficiency than magnitude of power."[4]

The evolution of 3-D printing provides a compelling illustration that there is an inexorable technological imperative undermining the nation-state in the twilight of American hegemony.

3-D Printing and a Smaller Container of Capitalism

My expectation of a more profound devolution—that which could be distinguished from the systemic chaos that typically accompanies the destruction of old institutions when capitalism outgrows its container in a shift of hegemony—arises from optimism that microtechnology will provide for the emergence of a revolutionary new regime of free market capitalism within a smaller city-state container. Some of this optimism is informed by my appreciation for the productive megapolitical potential of 3-D printing.

The megapolitical implications of 3-D printing were demonstrated in the early spring of 2013 at a shooting range outside of Austin, Texas. While the duly elected members of the US Senate were busily debating stauncher restrictions on gun control, a University of Texas law student went to the shooting range where he loaded an AK-47 with a thirty-shot magazine. And blasted away.

The law student was not content to rest his freedom to bear arms on the Constitution. Instead, he showed that the freedom to bear arms is supported by the "metaconstitution," informed by the megapolitical reality of 3-D printing. You see, while Congress was deliberating legislation to ban high-capacity magazines, the law student had created his own thirty-shot magazine on a 3-D printer. Much to the dismay of Congress, it was also shown that functioning guns could be created using a 3-D printer. Many people tend to think of 3-D printing as a kind of irrelevant novelty, a process for making cheap plastic toys—it is anything but.

3-D printing can be used to create metal parts through a process known as direct metal laser sintering (DMLS). Items can be created that involve intricate geometries and fine detail. Yes, you could make a plastic gun. But you could also build one from a variety of materials including stainless steel, cobalt chrome, bronze, titanium, aluminum, and nickel alloy. A crucial advantage of 3-D products is that they can be customized to the individual needs of specific consumers, transcending the constraints of mass production. This idea is exemplified by Invisalign, a company that uses computer images to customize invisible braces, tailoring them to fit the mouths of individual consumers.

A group of ecologists is now in the design phase for building an automobile, the Urbee 2, using 3-D printing. On one hand, in my opinion, it is one of the ugliest vehicles ever conceived. On the other hand, it promises to get hundreds of miles to the gallon, and it provides an emphatic example of the potential for high-value microproduction using 3-D printing.

Another surprising application of 3-D printing is the creation of replacement body parts. A liver created through 3-D printing techniques has functioned for forty days in a laboratory, matching the performance of a real liver.

3-D Printing Still in Its Infancy

Bear in mind as you consider these illustrations that 3-D printing is still in its infancy. It remains a painstakingly slow process, as products are built up layer by layer. Continuous liquid interface production (CLIP) promises to increase the speed of 3-D printing by tenfold. In a March 2015 *NBC News* article, Joseph DeSimone, a chemistry professor at the University of North Carolina and founder of Carbon3D, explained that CLIP can quickly produce parts with amazing properties within tens of minutes, as compared to hours.[5] It is reasonable to suppose that 3-D printing will become more efficient over time, so more of its potential will be realized.

As ever-greater amounts of digital information are incorporated into the production process, 3-D printing will seem to be the postmodern equivalent of Aladdin's lamp. In the not-too-distant future, you will be able to make anything you please with a 3-D printer—from guns to toys and from automobiles to replacement body parts. To say this is revolutionary is an understatement.

Among other things, it will greatly increase the competition between jurisdictions for mobile capital. Almost any economic activity will be capable of being conducted any place on the planet where individuals can enjoy safety and security from violence. Among other advantages, 3-D printing permits even high-value production to happen in relatively small spaces. You no longer need facilities on the scale of River Rouge to produce an automobile. A barn or perhaps a large garage could suffice.

Because it will no longer be necessary to operate at a large scale, there will be less "hostage to fortune." It will no longer require you to live or work in jurisdictions that impose high costs in order to earn a high income. This means that competition will force governments to downsize voluntarily or collapse. More likely than not, big, complex, and costly nation-states will be replaced by a rich variety of more modest and manageable experiments in governance at a smaller scale.

The Moat Makes a Comeback?

This also implies that the moat will make a comeback. As the costs of projecting force rise, among the areas that will most readily provide the promise of protection from systemic chaos are islands and other regions with easily defensible topography.

Another feature of information technology that minimizes the leverage of violence is that, unlike the industrial facilities that made Hitler and Stalin drool, the tools of the information economy have little hostage value in and of themselves. While you might be able to recover trace amounts of precious metals from salvaging the gold, palladium, silver, and platinum from circuit boards of computers, the attractions of doing so are limited, as evidenced by the fact that 150 million computers will end up in landfills, according to a 1996 *Wall Street Journal* piece by D. P. Hamilton and Dean Takahashi.[6] A 3-D printer could be Aladdin's lamp to someone who knew what to do with it. But to an illiterate thug, it would be only a relatively cheap piece of electronic trash. The lower the leverage for violence, the smaller jurisdictions will tend to be.

Just as mass production gave rise to big government, I believe that microproduction will give rise to "microsovereignties," small states on the scale of cities and provinces rather than continental economies. Remember, there were 300 city-states in Italy alone in 1250. Their time will come again.

My friend Peter Thiel and some other high-tech tycoons have jumped the gun on this twenty-first-century development by laying plans to create a work space for incubating high-tech companies beyond the laws of the United States. Their project, Blueseed, will be an artificial island hosting a startup community for entrepreneurs. It will be launched on a cruise ship anchored in international waters, twelve nautical miles from the coast of San Francisco. This location will allow start-up entrepreneurs from anywhere on the globe to launch or grow companies near Silicon Valley, without the need for US work visas. The ship will be converted into a coworking and coliving space, with high-speed Internet access and daily transportation to the mainland via ferryboat. To date, over 1,500 entrepreneurs from 500 startups in more than 70 countries have expressed interest in living on Blueseed. Think of how much more attractive this option will be when San Francisco becomes a city-state.

After five centuries during which the scale of governance, the scale of warfare, and the organization of business dramatically rose, pushing the development of capitalism into ever-larger "containers," times have changed. That long historical trend has been short-circuited by the invention of microprocessing and the advent of the information economy, as reflected in the paradigm example of 3-D printing. Bear in mind, however, that 3-D printing is only one manifestation of a revolutionary process that is replacing much of the material supply chain with digital information.

Nanotechnologies, Hard AI, and Artificial Life

Other crucial manifestations of the greater incorporation of digital information in the production process include advanced robotics, artificial intelligence (AI), and distributed manufacturing. On the far horizons of dramatic consequences are nanotechnologies and artificial life. It would be difficult from this distance to properly define a limit to the sweeping implications of nanomachines. Eric Dresler, in his pioneering study of nanotechnology, *Engines of Creation*, wrote, "The hand that rocks the AI cradle may rule the world."[7] He could well be right, but an adequate treatment of the consequences and risks of nanotechnology employing self-replicating molecular engines would call for a book in itself. For example, Ray Kurzweil, inventor, futurist, and CEO of KurzweilAI, foresees a future synthetic neocortex engineered with nanobots to amplify brainpower:

> 20 years from now, we'll have nanobots—another exponential trend is the shrinking of technology—that go into our brain through the capillaries and basically connect our synthetic neocortex and the cloud, providing an extension of our neocortex. Now today, you have a computer in your phone, but if you need 10,000 computers for a few seconds to do a complex search, you can access that for a second or two in the cloud. In the 2030s you'll be able to connect to that directly from your brain. I'm walking along, there's Chris Anderson, he's coming my way, I'd better think of something clever to say. I've got three seconds—my

300 million modules in my neocortex won't cut it—I need a billion more. I'll be able to access that in the cloud. Our thinking then will be a hybrid of biological and non-biological thinking.[8]

Moore's Law Becomes a Misdemeanor

Here I interrupt the majestic trajectory of Kurzweil's thought with an observation about diminishing returns as they involve the escalation of computational power. Moore's Law, named for Intel cofounder, Gordon Moore, states that the number of transistors in an affordable dense integrated circuit will double approximately every two years.

Note that Moore's Law, like the concept of EROEI, incorporates affordability as important dimension for understanding. The exponential growth of computational power, up about a millionfold since Moore formulated his law almost half a century ago, would not have been so exciting if the cost of acquiring this computational ability had multiplied by even one thousand.

That would have prohibited developments like the iPhone, the iPad, and the wide dispersal of computational power. My son Arthur would be spending more time reading books and less time playing Minecraft. Recently, the doubling period has stretched out to about 2.5 years. In other words, this implies that the progress in the world over the next decade attributable to extra computing power will be just half of what it otherwise would have been.

Among many implications, Ray Kurzweil's projections in *The Age of Spiritual Machines* that the operation of Moore's law will result in "computers achieving the memory capacity and computing speed of the human brain around the year 2020"[9] now look to be postponed, along with the singularity—the moment when the rising intelligence of computers leads to a merger of man and machine—Kurzweil had that sketched for 2045. But if computational compounding is halved and then halved again in each of the next three decades, we may just have to do a little more thinking for ourselves.

Kurzweil is a man of formidable intelligence with a record of success in technology development—he foresees hard AI within twenty years. Even if the date proves to be postponed, this is equivalent, as Peter Thiel suggests, to a credible forecast that aliens from space will land on earth within the foreseeable future. If you knew that flotillas of flying saucers were soon to hover overhead, looking for a good place to park, what would you think?

Would you be worried that space aliens could do your job more cost-effectively than you? Would you be concerned that they might eat your children? Or would you wish to join the welcome party and host a celebration in their honor?

The implications of, and reactions to, the advent of hard AI covers a similar range of possibilities—almost the whole inventory of science fiction plots from the past half-century could come to life. Rather than trying to rehearse them here, suffice it to say that the implications would be far-reaching and disruptive.

Likewise, the possibility of artificial life, whether it emerged from the evolution of molecular-level assemblers or through the programming into machines—the downloading of human consciousness—as imagined by Kurzweil, could have astonishingly far-reaching implications. These would include the probable emergence of artificial organisms that could do our physical work and collaborate in problem solving.

If these artificial organisms were considered robots, they would displace the need for much human work. If they achieved quasi-human status, they might become varieties of slaves. At the very least, this would suggest the emergence of a hard caste system, in which a range of creatures reminiscent of the bar scene in *Star Wars* jostled for legal status. The puzzles and quandaries this would entail seem certain to perplex the future.

Death Transcended?

The ambition among researchers to decipher the most intimate secrets of biology includes a desire to greatly decelerate or even transcend death. The aforementioned Kurzweil not only forecasts that hard AI will be with us within twenty years, but he boldly believes that the exponential progress of information technology will make heretofore unimaginable miracles possible. As reported by Caroline Daniel in an April 2015 *Financial Times* article, Kurzweil declares that humans will overcome almost all diseases and aging over the next twenty or twenty-five years.[10]

This is a notion about which I am optimistic. The revolution in molecular medicine is based not only on the expansion of computational power, as emphasized by Kurzweil, but also on the 400,000-fold improvement in the power of microscopes in the centuries since Robert Hooke first discovered the cell. Hooke, under commission to King Charles II, discovered the cell with a compound microscope with fifty times the resolution of the human eye. Today, the new STEHM microscope allows researchers to see with a resolution of twenty million times human sight. Science now has the ability to see material as small as a single atom—a million times smaller than a human hair. The deepest secrets of life, literally hidden by invisibility since the dawn of time, are now open for inspection.

Indeed, I am devoting considerable time and effort to help develop therapies that counteract aging, known as "replicative senescence," by extending the length of telomeres—and thus expanding the range of regenerative medicine. Some animals, such as lobsters, whose cells are amply supplied with telomerase—the enzyme that preserves the length of telomeres across cell divisions—do not die of old age. A lobster could live to be hundreds of years old if it could elude the lobster pot, large fish, octopi, and cannibalistic encounters with other lobsters.

Unfortunately, in humans, the telomerase enzyme is usually found in profusion only in the telomeres of chromosomes in germ cells and some cancer cells. Although there are complications, the biology of telomere extension suggests that it could be a potent mechanism of extending human health span.

Google has created its own venture to combat aging, Calico, to which Kurzweil is an advisor. Whether it is Calico, my telomere project, Telometrix, or something entirely different, it would seem to be only a matter of time until the exponential progress of information technology leads to effective regenerative therapies to supersede our inherited biology and counter aging.

For the sake of this thought experiment, imagine that the highly disruptive innovation of "transcending death" only has the effect of doubling the human health span. Think of people enjoying the equivalent of an additional three quarters of a century of vigorous living in what would be a health state equivalent to being in their forties but protracted for decades. Biotechnological breakthroughs that merely permitted greater numbers to reach a decrepit old age would have very different megapolitical implications than innovations that counteract the aging process itself, reprogramming the body to reverse senescence.

Dr. Al Sears shrewdly observes that a significant extension of the health span would open the way for expansion of human capital. You would invest more in developing yourself if you could anticipate many more useful decades of life. Today, people tend to "grow up" in their early twenties, after which they more or less attempt to make the best of the person they have become at that point.

Learn Chinese? Why not? Become an elite athlete? Build a physique like Dwayne "The Rock" Johnson? With enhanced insights into health and fitness, you could become a fair semblance of a superhero with an extra few decades of vigorous life to work on it. Think of the possibilities. Even if you were not an athlete at twenty-one, you could become one at eighty-one, when the scientific basis for reprogramming your body to grow younger is better understood.

Creative Destruction through Survival

You cannot consider the implications of a potentially disruptive innovation like the conquest of aging without recalling that the current corporatist system feasts on the diseases of aging. The pharmaceutical industry, along with the whole sick care establishment, has trillions at stake in the continuation of the current system.

You know what they say; "Life follows art." With that in mind, you might find a better template for grasping the impact of a biotechnological breakthrough to overcome aging by watching *The Fiendish Plot of Fu Manchu*, the last film completed by the late comic Peter Sellers. In this flick, the wicked Fu Manchu is 168 years old, courtesy of his *elixir vitae*, a secret antiaging potion known only to Fu.

If there is another major life extension breakthrough, I would not be surprised if it turned out to be of the Fu Manchu variety: a secret elixir available only to drug dealers and major players in the white slave trade (or maybe some more respectable billionaires), rather than a common tonic administered through systems of socialized medicine. The last thing Social Security could afford would be general progress in life extension. Another century of life would bury the whole gag. Therefore, I would not be surprised if governments sought to suppress therapies that counter senescence.

Needless to say, pay-as-you-go old age benefits like Social Security could hardly survive the transcendence of death. The prospect of extended lifespans through biotechnological innovation is only one of many factors hinting that saving is destined to make a comeback as the principal expedient for addressing life's contingencies.

Retiring Retirement

In all probability, any appreciable progress toward transcending death would rapidly retire the idea of retirement. It would simultaneously open new categories of problems heretofore unknown in society. Removal of death as a universal social laxative would leave the channels of advancement for young people clogged. (That is only one sense in which the transcendence of death would curtail incentives to procreate.)

Another logical consequence of dramatic extension of human health span would be an increase in the physical risk-aversion of the rich. Statistics on "life expectancy" are easier to come by than for "life span." Even so, from what we know, it appears that a twenty-year-old man on the eve of the Civil War in the mid-nineteenth century could have expected to live another 40.1 years. Now imagine the prospect of trebling that life span at a higher level of health. The expected result would be a greater reluctance to undertake the hazards of battle, as persons with revamped biological processes would have four times more to lose than did soldiers with far shorter life spans in the past.

Extended Life Span, Time Preference, and Capital Formation

A framework for understanding time horizons in the economy is the concept of time preference. Time preference refers to the relative valuation placed on a good at an earlier date compared to valuation of that good in the future. An individual with high time preference is one that has a strong preference for immediate gratification and a lesser inclination to invest and defer consumption to the future.

Think of Aesop's tale of "The Grasshopper and the Ant." The grasshopper had high time preference. The ant evidenced low time preference through its inclination to save.

Investopedia gives this capsule background on the concept of time preference: "This theory was initially constructed in 1871 by Carl Menger, an Austrian economist. This theory also stipulates that the consumer's rate of time preference, and therefore the interest required, will probably rise as the consumer's savings increase. This means that the consumer is likely to restrict his or her savings to a level at which the rate of time preference equals the rate of interest paid on savings."[11]

An obvious effect of extending the human life span would be to lower time preference, stimulating more future-regarding behavior (more savings and investment). Other things being equal, this implies more capital formation, higher productivity, and higher living standards all around.

The Austrian economists, who are the connoisseurs of time preference analysis, argue that higher levels of investment lead to what Murray Rothbard described as the "free ride" from the actions of others. They associate civilization with falling time preferences and decivilization with high time preference for immediate gratification over future consumption.

The basics of life dictate that as long as you live, you must consume. To this extent, at least, everyone has high time preferences at mealtime. As Robert F. Mulligan points out in his paper "Property Rights and Time Preference," however, the general level of time preference in an economy has far-reaching implications.[12] Mulligan says that only once people began placing value on, and recognizing, property rights, could they utilize more productive roundabout methods of production. He also says that artificially imposing higher time preference "creates incentives for collectively undesirable behavior." In this sense, if humans, like lobsters, did not die of old age, this would increase the payoff for avoiding conflict and lengthening the structure of production.

Production and Plunder

Professor Hans-Hermann Hoppe, the distinguished Austrian economist, is more emphatic in describing government efforts to artificially raise time preference as decivilizing forces. He was not referring explicitly to the Fed's QE and zero interest rate policies (ZIRP), but the logic he spelled out clearly puts those policies in perspective as "de-civilizing."

In "Time Preference, Government and the Process of De-Civilization: From Monarchy to Democracy," Hoppe points out that government political takings, to which I frequently refer to as "plunder," affect time preference in a systematically different, and more profound, way than crime.[13] He explains that such plunder interferes with private property rights, reducing people's supply of present goods, thus raising their effective time preference rate. People will then associate a permanently higher risk with future production and adjust their expectations downward in regards to the rate of return on future investments. This means that "their expected rate of return on productive, future-oriented action is reduced all around, and accordingly all actual and potential victims become more present-oriented."

Furthermore, if these government property rights violations grow extensive enough, humanity will cease building an ever-growing stock of capital and durable consumer goods. They will become increasingly shortsighted, and their distant goals may not only cease but be reversed toward decivilization. Hoppe states that "formerly provident providers will be turned into drunks and daydreamers, adults into children, civilized men into barbarians and producers into criminals."

Time Preference and Comparative Advantage

The idea that shifts in time preference civilize or decivilize societies is closely correlated with the process by which comparative advantage enshrines or destabilizes property rights, thus shifting time preference in a predictable manner.

Robert Mulligan explains that individuals with comparative disadvantage in production are motivated to use violence against those who have a comparative advantage in creating wealth. He goes on to point out that "in an environment where property rights are insecure, . . . individuals will have short time horizons and high time preference."

Thus the extension of human life span—promised by the incorporation of digital information into the production process—implies a civilizing counterbalance to its impact in increasing the "comparative advantage in violence" of unskilled persons, as well as the impact of systemic chaos in raising time preference. If even a few jurisdictions are capable of efficiently protecting their inhabitants from violence, the result could be an unprecedented flourishing of civilization.

Obviously, there are other pregnant issues associated with the transcendence of death. There is the question of how access to the biotechnologies involved would be priced and shared. If access were less than universal, there would be security issues, larger than those at present, about how those rich enough to afford these life-augmenting therapies could physically protect themselves from others who could not afford them. People would no longer be dying so frequently from what we now know as "natural causes." But they would presumably still be vulnerable to accident, infection, murder, and other external injury. It is reasonable to foresee that unlike the case during the industrial epoch—when low-skilled persons employed the leverage of violence to make hostages of industrial facilities—in the Information Age it is more likely that entrepreneurs will be targeted as potential hostages.

Thus the advent of the Information Age poses the prospect of another epidemiological transition in human history. The major cause of death in hunting and gathering societies was external injuries. That may be the case again. The advent of agriculture brought infectious diseases. The Industrial Age saw cardiovascular disease emerge as the major killer. If the chronic diseases of aging and replicative senescence were conquered, the remaining candidates as the major causes of death would be external injuries, infectious disease, and perhaps the cumulative effect of radiation exposures. Such a sweeping change would leave you a lot to think about.

The Changing Nature of Work and the Eclipse of Economic Equality

Industrial production standardized products, as well as work. Assembly lines were designed so that whether they were manned by geniuses or unskilled persons of modest ability production quality would be the same. Consequently, the factory system gave rise to narrow income dispersion, or historically low levels of income inequality. Because most people had similar marginal productivity, their incomes were similar.

By contrast, the characteristics of information technology are very different. They encourage income dispersion. For one thing, unlike products of mass production, such as automobiles or refrigerators, the marginal costs of many digital goods are vanishingly small. This means that unlike industrial products, the capacity constraints on digital goods are immaterial. As Erik Brynjolfsson and Andrew McAfee put it in *The Second Machine Age*, "A single producer with a website can, in principle, fill the demand from millions or even billions of customers."[14]

The fact that a great amount of value can be created with few employees and without production being rooted in any particular locale has far-reaching megapolitical implications.

For one thing, it emphatically gives the lie to the Labor Theory of Value. We can now easily see that value is created by the entrepreneurial imagination and not necessarily by sweat and toil. The hordes of industrial workers with whom Marx identified are literally superfluous to many high-value operations.

The fact that many information products can be delivered digitally also reduces the leverage of violence in redistributing their rewards. For example, disgruntled truck drivers or dockworkers cannot blockade the loading docks to the World Wide Web. Short of shutting down the Internet altogether, bullying can play little part in determining the compensation derived from sale of digital products.

Even among computer programmers, however, a probable increase in income inequality in the Information Age can be illustrated. Think of comparing two programmers: one may create an algorithm that is essential in robotics and worth millions, while another, who has worked with the same equipment, hasn't come up with anything nearly as valuable. Over the past fifteen years, the income gap between top programmers and the great majority of run-of-the-mill programmers has widened further than your typical union organizers could bring themselves to admit. In *The Second Machine Age*, authors Erik Brynjolfsson and Andrew McAfee report amazing statistics compiled by the *New York Times* showing that three-quarters of software developers in the "app economy" made less than thirty thousand dollars, while only 4 percent of them made over a million dollars. Achieving a relative advantage in digital commerce will lead to domination.[15]

The digital economy works against economic equality. Not only does it mean that the top performers can earn incomes that are many times higher than those of most people, but it also undermines the egalitarian conceit in other ways. For example, today, due to individualization in information technology, it is obvious that programmers who write codes for products rely on their own skills—others cannot claim credit or take responsibility for success as easily as they may have been able to in the past. This also suggests why labor unions play little or no role in the leading companies in the digital economy, apart from a few "old economy" shuttle bus drivers who ferry high-tech Apple, Microsoft, and Facebook workers around San Francisco and its environs.

Another implication of the growing integration of digital information into the production process is that—short of hard AI or artificial life—a great many old areas of employment will be subject to dramatic change. An outline of what to expect was provided in a 2013 Oxford Martin School report, "The Future of Employment: How Susceptible Are Jobs to Computerization?" by Karl Frey and Michael Osborne of Oxford University. They estimate that 47 percent of US jobs are vulnerable to being substituted by computer capital within the next twenty years.[16]

Of course, these projections are subject to the discount that they imply something that is remote from the facts—productivity growth should have been skyrocketing in recent years. But it has not. As you know, productivity is measured in output per hour of human labor. If robots had taken over any considerable fraction of production, by definition this would have caused a surge in productivity that is not in evidence.

That is not to say that robots and AI will not take a bigger role in automating jobs. But the projection is not as convincing as it could be if productivity were already surging. And this, indeed, may be a metamessage confirming that the government has been telling prodigious lies in reporting employment growth in recent years. Obviously, the employees who are no more than statistical figments of the Bureau of Labor Statistics "birth/death" model do not actually contribute to output. Fake jobs may please the stock market and give politicians something to crow about, but they have the drawback of skewing productivity measurement. The millions of fake hires counted in the government's official employment counts disguise productivity growth.

Of course, it is also possible, as Gillian Tett suggests in her August 2015 piece for the *Financial Times*, "The Fed's Productivity Predicament," that there may be a "technological time lag."[17] She notes that in the 1970s and 1980s, a similar swing occurred in which there was another slump after an earlier boom. Exactly. I doubt it is a coincidence that these productivity stalls followed sharp increases in the price of oil. It surged from $3.00 per barrel in 1973 to almost $12.00 per barrel in 1974; then it trebled again early in this century.

If the revolution in employment proves to be even half as far-reaching as Frey and Osborne imagine, however, it presages sweeping change in the way that people earn their livings, and indeed, as Marx suggested, a change in "all production and social relations." But not the type of change that most former Marxists would embrace.

Superficially, people whose thinking is indelibly imprinted with an industrial mind-set—and therefore presuppose a government powerful enough to interrupt, regulate, suppress, and redistribute any outcome informed by markets—are likely to leap to the wrong conclusion. Many will suppose that the falling economic value of unskilled labor requires another costly escalation in social complexity: redistribution on a global scale to ensure a minimum income for everyone.

Consider this from Google's Blaise Agüera y Arcas:

> As machine intelligence, robotics, and technological leverage in general increasingly decouple productivity from labor, we will continue to see unemployment rise even in otherwise healthy economies. The end state is one in which most forms of human labor are simply not required. In 30 years, if not sooner, we will be facing this unprecedented situation—and whether it's heaven or hell depends on whether we're able to let go of capitalism, economic Darwinism and the Calvinist ethics that implicitly underlie these systems. Without a change, of course, we will see mass unemployment drive a radical acceleration of the already dramatic imbalance between the very wealthy few and everyone else, leading to ugly conditions in the cities and ultimately violent uprising.
>
> On the other hand, if we are able to set aside our Calvinism, we will realize that given the technological efficiencies we have achieved, everyone can live well, with or without a job. Capitalism, entrepreneurship and other systems of differential wealth creation could still function on top of this horizontal base; but everyone must be fed and housed decently, have access to free health care and education, and be able to live a good life. I assume the nation-state will still be a relevant legal and economic construct in 30 years (though I'm not sure, as corporations or possibly other structures will complicate the picture); my guess is that we will see both paths taken in different parts of

the world, leading to misery and war in some, where either the benefits of accelerating technology are slow to penetrate or Darwinian economics are left unchecked.[18]

With all due respect to Blaise Agüera y Arcas, who is an accomplished software engineer, I see the expectation that a middle class standard of living will be handed to everyone, as a birthright, as an anachronism. More broadly, egalitarianism, or the demand for equality of economic results, has not been a universal feature of human societies and may not be predominant in the future. A quick review suggests why.

Egalitarianism in the "Garden of Eden"

Redistribution of the hunt was a common feature of primitive, hunter-gatherer bands. Our most distant human ancestors devoted much of their effort to hunting large game animals. Sharing of the hunt must have conveyed substantial survival value by helping ensure the members of the small group against starvation. Given that they had to hunt on foot, armed only with wooden weapons, killing megafauna like woolly mammoths was a dangerous and challenging task. It required cooperation among the hunters in an intimate group that typically numbered about fifty, including women and children.

A woolly mammoth could provide up to eight tons of meat, a more than ample amount for the whole group. Even with an extraordinarily large hunter-gatherer band of 100 individuals, a single mammoth could have provided more than 150 pounds of meat for each person.

In the face of a huge carcass of rotting meat, sharing was the only strategy that made sense. While our primitive ancestors dug ice cellars to preserve meat when climatic conditions permitted during ice ages, more frequently than not, they lacked the capacity to preserve meat for later consumption. In that circumstance, refusal to share provisions harvested in the hunt would only have encouraged overhunting. If each related

corporatist rip-offs and political plunder, especially the perverse effects of fiat money.)

Further to that, before the Industrial Revolution there was no encompassing entity with the power to capture and redistribute much wealth or income. Prior to the advent of the nation-state, wealthy agricultural magnates had their own private armies to protect them against overreaching attempts at taxation.

3. Wherever millenarian fanatics could seize a castle or town, they could always depend upon the support of a segment of the very poor—those that stood to receive some of the money and material goods that these prophets plundered from the church and wealthy merchants.

4. Torture, along with "cruel and unusual punishment," characterized preindustrial governance and warfare in which substate actors played a leading role. In modern industrial warfare between massed armies, torture of captives and grisly executions of dissenters would have amounted to pointless cruelty. Any given soldier, like a worker mobilized for mass production, could be more or less easily replaced by the "next man up." Industrial armies, whether composed of conscripts or hirelings of the nation-state, were not principals of conflict. With few exceptions, they did not choose to initiate combat. And any excruciating torture or execution of soldiers of the nation-state, however grim, would be unlikely to discourage the deployment of new battalions. The soldiers of national armies do not fight for their own private amusement.

By contrast, substate combatants, whether today's "terrorists" or the knights and sociopathic messiahs of the Middle Ages, are indeed principals. They were not deployed to fight; they fought on their own.

Torture becomes more rational when the parties in conflict are principals. It can intimidate and discourage potential combatants, hence the torture of "terrorists" by the CIA and the homicidal antics of ISIS who torture their opponents in a setting where local nation-states are collapsing. The fragile condition of the Iraqi Army, as evidenced by the fact that whole battalions have shed their uniforms and run away, testifies to the effectiveness of fear among individual soldiers that their capture will lead to torture and beheading.

5. Much the same logic applies to efforts by ISIS and other substate actors to collect ransoms on captives. This would not have puzzled the Magna Carta barons for whom the payment of hefty ransoms was a normal hazard of warfare. For example, the feudal baron of Little Dunmow, Essex and chief banneret of the City of London, Lord Robert Fitzwalter, of the Magna Carta fame, was taken prisoner while fighting for King John in Normandy and forced to pay a heavy ransom to King Phillip II of France.

6. Unless the meandering of technology brings a dramatic and unexpected enhancement of the value of infantry in combat, it is more likely that the devaluation of "work"—implied by the integration of digital information into the production process—will lead to a decline in population, rather than the mass provision of a middle-class lifestyle as a birthright. In any event, there will be a transition crisis as the nation-state falls shorter and shorter of paying its way.

7. Information technology entails very different megapolitical implications than did the industrial technology of the twentieth century. The tendency of information technology to concentrate income among a small fraction of individuals competing in a given market is obviously at odds with the equal allocation of votes among noninstitutionalized adults in the democratic nation-state. This points to another obvious sense in which technology is antiquating legacy institutions.

The result to be expected is that democratic capitalism, as embodied in representative and parliamentary government, is likely to be supplanted by something new, perhaps something more akin to the original limited franchise of the early days of the United States in which only property owners could vote. As the longtime leader of Singapore, the late Lee Kuan Yew, shrewdly observed, "I do not believe that one-man, one-vote . . . is the final position."[21]

In short, the law of development of human history seems to have veered off sharply from the trajectory that Marx projected a century and a third ago.

Notes

1 https://www.marxists.org/archive/marx/works/1883/death/burial.htm.

2 Wordsworth, William, "Steamboats, Viaducts, and Railways," in *The Complete Poetical Works of William Wordsworth*, ed. John Morely (London: Macmillan, 1888).

3 Morgan, Tim, *Life after Growth* (Hampshire: Harriman House, 2013), 12.

4 Davidson, James, and Lord William Rees-Mogg, *The Sovereign Individual*, 18.

5 http://www.nbcnews.com/tech/innovation/new-improved-3-d-printer-makes-objects-faster-clip-n324651.

6 Hamilton, D. P., and Dean Tajahashi, "Scientists Are Battling Barriers in Microchip Advances," *Wall Street Journal*, December 6, 1996, A1.

7 Drexler, K. Eric, *Engines of Creation* (Garden City, NY: Anchor/Doubleday, 1986), 76.

8 http://ideas.ted.com/26-ideas-from-the-future/.

9 Kurzweil, Ray, *The Age of Spiritual Machines*, 3.

10 Daniel, Caroline, "We're Going to Overcome Aging," *Financial Times*, April 12, 2015.

11 http://www.investopedia.com/terms/t/time-preference-theory-of-interest.asp#ixzz3Xsq4GdoS.

12 Mulligan, Robert F., "Property Rights and Time Preference," http://paws.wcu/mulligan/www/propertyrights.htm.

13 Hoppe, Hans Hermann, "Time Preference, Government, and

the Process of De-Civilization," *Journal des Economistes et des Etudes Humaines* 5, no. 2/3 (1994), 350.

14 Brynjolfsson, Erik, and Andrew McAfee, *The Second Machine Age* (New York: W. W. Norton, 2014), 154.

15 Ibid., 151.

16 See http://www.futuretech.ox .ac.uk/news-release-oxford -martin-school-study-shows -nearly-half-us-jobs-could -be-risk-computerisation, September 18, 2013—14:3.

17 Tett, Gillian, "The Fed's Productivity Predicament," *Financial Times,* August 21, 2015.

18 Agüera y Arcas, Blaise, "The Future Is Coming: Six Ways It Will Change Everything," http://ideas.ted.com/author/ blaise-aguera-y-arcas/.

19 See Ovid, *Metamorphoses,* trans. Allen Mandelbaum (New York: Houghton Mifflin Harcourt, 1993).

20 Cohn, Norman, *The Pursuit of the Millennium: Revolutionary Millenarians and Mystical Anarchist of the Middle Ages* (Oxford: Oxford University Press, 1970).

21 http://www.ft.com/intl/cms/ s/0/7328512e-bc10-11e4 -b6ec-00144feab7de.html #axzz3VprEkdda.

Chapter Five

Squandering the Spoils of a "Good War"

In the past 11 years in particular we have seen lies, fraud, bogus statistics and Mickey Mouse bookkeeping. For good measure the powers behind government have thrown in the gutting of America's industrial base by outsourcing and offshoring. As an extra temporary measure the Fed has bailed out the financial sectors in the US and Europe and continues to bail out the US Treasury . . . America is slowly discovering that the land of the free and home of the brave has become a corporatist fascist nightmare.
—Bob Chapman, "Economy Debased by Lies, Fraud, and Bogus Statistics," *The International Forecaster*, August 6, 2011

The $800,000,000,000.00 Lie

In 1950, the US government tried to faithfully report increases in the cost of living. But that changed decades ago. Politicians of both parties realized that you and other citizens don't have the time to verify the regular Consumer Price Index (CPI) reports. So they concluded that they could get away with grossly understating the downward trend in household income. They have done such a thorough job of disguising the falling purchasing power of the dollar that current outlays for Social Security, allegedly adjusted for inflation, are just half what they would be if consumer inflation were honestly measured.

Yes, politicians lie.

As part of their ongoing budget negotiations, both Obama and congressional Republicans have embraced proposals incorporating even bigger lies in calculating inflation adjustments for Social Security, with the explicit objective of trimming billions and trillions more from that program's future costs.

Lies. Lies. Lies.

You may not realize that inflation in 2013 was running at an annual rate of 9.6 percent if measured as it was during the Carter administration. But when you look back over six decades you can easily see that the dollar has lost far more of its value than the official statistics suggest. You know that for a family to live a middle-class lifestyle today it would need three or four times $30,591.30—the supposedly inflation-adjusted average income from 1950.

In fact, among the crazy quilt of current federal poverty income levels, the 250 percent ceiling to qualify for "Silver Plan" subsidies count an income of $60,625—198 percent of the supposedly inflation adjusted median income from 1950—as impoverished for a family of four. A joke.[1]

Perhaps one of the reasons politicians were not too devious to honestly report economic statistics in 1950 is that the news then was good. The first three quarters of 1950 were all among the top five quarters for GDP expansion (annualized) during the whole history of the United States. Q1 growth for 1950 was the top ever recorded in the United States at 17.2 percent (annualized)—growth the Chinese would envy today. It slowed to a mere 12.7 percent in Q2 of 1950 before surging again to 16.6 percent in Q3. The United States was at the top of the world then.

Not incidentally, since fathers were economically relevant in 1950, they were present in the lives of their children. When I was a toddler in 1950 Washington, DC, 90 percent of American children lived in families with both parents present. It is a measure of the nation's decline that in some sections of DC today, those proportions are reversed, as detailed by the *Washington Times* in Luke Rosiak's December 2012 article

"Fathers Disappear from Households across America."[2] Rosiak reported that in Southeast Washington, one in ten children live with both parents, while 84 percent live with only their mothers.

The comparison with 1950 is even starker when you consider that widows led almost a third of the female-headed households in 1950. Notwithstanding the almost incessant wars fought by the United States in recent decades, widows headed only 14 percent of female households in 2011.

America at the Summit of the World

America in 1950 was an industrial colossus. As Winston Churchill said of postwar America, "America at this moment stands at the summit of the world."[3]

According to the International Organization of Motor Vehicle Manufacturers, the United States in 1950 produced 80 percent of the world's automobiles, compared to about 6 percent today. The United States commanded a similarly outsized share in other spheres of economic production, with three-quarters or more of world output of machine tools, electronics, chemicals, airplanes, and computers. The United States was energy self-sufficient then. US oilfields in 1950 accounted for over 50 percent of world oil production. American industry produced more than twice the goods and services of all European industry combined. US per capita production was 60 percent above Germany's, 70 percent above France's, and 80 percent above the United Kingdom's.

US GDP per capita was 4.52 times the average world GDP per capita in 1950. Total national output was more than three times that of the main rival of the United States—the late, not so great, Soviet Union.

How did we reach such an incredible "Great Prosperity," as F. A. Hayek dubbed the "unique 25-year period" of the postwar boom? One of the fond conceits of Keynesian partisans is the fallacy that massive deficit spending during World

War II—in which the United States spent money from an empty pocket—stimulated recovery from the lingering depression of the 1930s.

Not exactly.

Spoils of a "Good War"

World War II was a crucial factor in the mid-century prosperity of the United States, but outsized deficits didn't lay the foundation for mid-century prosperity. It was the full-fledged destruction of capital in the rest of the advanced world that made US industry so profitable in 1950. In the terms defined by Peter Taylor in *The Way the Modern World Works*, World War II was a "good war" for the United States.

Europe and Japan had been bombed to smithereens.

Only the United States and Canada escaped from World War II unscathed. Europe and Japan ended the war with their industrial capacity badly damaged and even ruined. The extensive destruction of capital restored the profitability of American business for a reason spelled out by Adam Smith in book 1, chapter 9 of *The Wealth of Nations*. As Smith explained, when many merchants compete in selling the same good, "their mutual competition naturally tends to lower its profit." The reciprocal of that is that when many competitors go out of business, the rate of profit for the remainder tends to go up.

Keynes's Recipe for Combating Deflation without Adjustment

Keynes saw the crisis of the 1930s as one of underconsumption.

His theory argued for increasing aggregate effective demand through budget deficits and sought to explain depression on the basis of slack demand, with the stipulation that wages were "sticky." But he offered no explanation of why wages happened to "stick" at one level rather than another.

Politically, of course, Keynes's argument comfortably fit the requirements of a stagnant, regulated economy. This harks back to the regulation of capitalist commerce in the thirteenth and fourteenth centuries, as characterized by Pirenne in *The*

Stages in the Social History of Capitalism. He wrote of the "most characteristic provisions" of statutes to "fix wages and regulate the conditions of work," and that they were "inspired by the desire to prevent operations that will unfavorably affect prices and the workman's wages."[4]

The great political appeal of Keynes's formula is obvious. He prescribed combating overproduction and underconsumption with the least possible inconvenience to either producers or workers. His recipe combatted deflation without adjustment.

That said, essentially every economist agrees that more competition reduces profits. And of course, when profits fall, this puts downward pressure on wages and employment.

"The Misdirection of Production"

The politically incorrect Austrian business cycle theory (ABCT) suggests that the crisis of profitability is accelerated and accentuated by central bank manipulation of interest rates. Unlike most theories of the effects of credit expansion on prices and output, the ABCT was not so much concerned with the effects of the total money supply on the price level or aggregate output and investment.

The Austrian economists, such as Ludwig von Mises and Friedrich von Hayek, identified business cycle bubbles as consequences of malinvestments, stimulated when credit expansion by central banks distorts intertemporal coordination of resources between capital and consumer goods (Hayek called it the "misdirection of investment"). This lengthens the structure of production beyond what can be supported by the underlying resource pool, or accumulation, given the time preferences of the various participants in the economy.

In the Austrian view, there is too little savings to support the lengthened structure of production. Time preferences are too short. People generally want to consume rather than save. As Hayek put it, this "can only lead to a much more severe crisis as soon as the credit expansion comes to an end."

Toward the end of his long life, Hayek fretted that the "Great Prosperity" had been exaggerated by the elimination of factors such as the gold standard and fixed rates of exchange. He believed an expansion of credit and open inflation created full, and even excessive, employment. Hayek regretted political efforts to prevent the coming of a depression in the 1970s, fearing that they would lead to an even worse eventual breakdown.

Bear this in mind as we go forward. It is crucial to understanding how politicians destroyed US prosperity and why their continued attempts to inflate bubbles only ensure more stagnation and ultimate collapse. There will be no new sustainable boom emerging until there is enough creative destruction of capital to restore profitability in a new surge of innovation.

More on "The Great Prosperity"

In 1950, this seemed far away. All the European allies owed vast amounts to the United States, which had emerged from the war with two-thirds of the world's gold reserves. The US dollar had become the world's reserve currency, and until the late '50s, it was the only fully convertible major currency not subject to exchange controls. In those days, the United States provided 85 percent of the world's direct foreign investment. And American management and marketing techniques became dominant practice in the other advanced economies.

So vast was the US lead in production, management, and marketing that competitors fretted that Americans would put everyone else out of business. This view was exemplified by French analyst J. J. Servan-Schreiber's 1968 international best seller, *The American Challenge*. He argued that the growing gap between American industry and the rest of the world posed problems that could lead to catastrophe.[5]

Of course, it turned out that Servan-Schreiber was quite wrong in imagining that the United States had mastered the challenge of universal education for continued prosperity. Nor did it turn out to be true that the United States' lead in productivity growth would continue to compound over the remaining years of the twentieth century causing a reduction in the workweek, due to automation. Servan-Schreiber expected that America would become a postindustrial society by the late '90s, with four seven-hour workdays per week, 39 workweeks per year, and 13 weeks of vacation. With weekends and holidays, that would have resulted in only 147 workdays a year.[6]

Sounds like fun. But it didn't work out that way.

Far from enjoying a life of leisure, Americans now work longer and take multiple jobs to make ends meet. As reported in the *Financial Times* in March 2015, the average American works 85,000 hours in a lifetime, 70 percent more— 35,000 additional hours—compared to the average Finn and 15,000 hours more than the average German.

In other words, Americans put in the equivalent of 32 years' worth of additional postindustrial 28-hour workweeks than imagined by Servan-Schreiber. Outside of Asia, Americans work longer than anyone else. Even the great majority of farm operators in America are now also employed in outside jobs.

As reported by C. E. Clark in a September 2015 *Hub-Pages* article—"Working 2 or More Jobs—Is This the New Normal?"—due to increased prices for goods and services and decreased salaries and wages, high-income earners are increasingly obliged to work multiple jobs in twenty-first-century America just to maintain their lifestyle.[7]

The United States was far and away the world's greatest creditor in 1950. Today, we have become the most indebted country in the history of the world. In 1950, the US national debt was about $257 billion. In the space of sixty-five years, the US national debt multiplied an astonishing seventyfold in nominal terms to rival the Death Star at $18.15 trillion.

In 1950, the average American earned $3,210 a year, when a dollar was worth much more than it is now. According to clearly corrupt government inflation data, a 1950 dollar is worth $9.53 today. The average cost of a new house then was $8,450 ($80,528 today according to the pretend government inflation statistics). In June 2013, according to the Census Bureau, the average sale price of a new home in the United States for June 2013 was $249,700.[8] The average family spent just 22 percent of its income on housing in 1950—50 percent less than today. The average cost of a new car in 1950 was $1,510 ($14,390 today if the official inflation adjustment were accurate). By contrast, the average transaction price for a new car in May 2013 was $30,978.

Another major difference between 1950 and today is that Americans used to live within their means. We were paid twice as much as Europeans with similar credentials so it wasn't a great hardship to do without credit cards. The first commercial credit card, the invention of Diner's Club founder Frank McNamara, was issued in 1950. American Express and Visa did not come along until eight years later, and Master Card began business in 1966. The original cardboard Diner's Club card was honored in twenty-seven restaurants in New York City. By 1951, there were 20,000 Diner's Club cards in use, or about one for every 7,500 Americans.

While the population of the United States has little more than doubled since 1950, the number of credit cards in circulation has gone up by about 30,500 times. US cardholders now have 609.8 million credit cards outstanding. Based on May 2013 statistics from the Federal Reserve, total US credit card debt was $856.5 billion, with the average household owing $15,325.

According to the Bureau of Labor Statistics, the average American, with or without the Diner's Club card, consumed 3,260 calories a day in 1950, about 600 calories more than the average man eats today, but not one of the 1950 vintage calories was composed of high fructose corn sweetener, an artificial food—and the largest source of calories in today's American diet—that was not invented until 1957.

Equally, while consumption of artificial trans fats was growing with the spreading popularity of margarine, most families in 1950 still used butter. Children in the 1950s vintage peanut gallery drank three times more milk than soda—the opposite of today, as children now drink three cups of soda for every cup of milk. And the milk they drank in 1950 was natural whole-fat milk—not the sugary no-fat concoction of lactose (milk sugars) that so many children imbibe today, which is a contributing factor to the fact that almost 19 percent of American kids, age six to eleven, are obese.

Yes, there were fat people in the 1950s. (Some of the maids employed by my mother and my aunt were real butterballs.) Yet as a child in that era myself, I can't remember ever seeing a fat kid—until I reached high school in the 1960s.

In that long-lost and innocent world, when no one worried about the Kardashians and their stretch marks, children may not have been precocious enough to calculate economic indicators, but they were economic indicators in themselves. The Baby Boom was a sign of good times.

I was one of these 77 million little statistics: the Baby Boomers. Bonnie Kavoussi put us in perspective in analyzing the contrary circumstances today in her article "Birth Rate Plummets, Young Americans Too Poor to Have Kids."[9] Kavoussi pointed out that countries with fewer jobs also typically have lower birthrates, which therefore act as an indicator of a nation's economic well-being.

Her summary of the reasons for the plunging birthrate in contemporary America show how far conditions have deteriorated since fertility per childbearing woman peaked at 3.7 live births in 1957. The decision by so many American families to have more children was itself a clear reflection of the good times in America. These advantages were squandered during the ensuing decades, resulting in the slowest population growth rate since the Great Depression, according to the US Census.

Raising kids is expensive—around $13,000 per year in a middle-income family, according to the Department of Agriculture—and today, younger Americans are experiencing lower wages, while 12.8 million Americans are out of work.

As a result, many college-educated men and women between the ages of twenty-three and twenty-nine are moving back in with their parents rather than becoming parents themselves.

"The Future Ain't What It Used to Be"–Yogi Berra

From the distance of six decades, it takes research and imagination to realize how optimistic Americans in 1950 were about the future, how gung-ho they were about technology, and how crazy they were about artificial foods and, yes, plastics. They fully expected to live in the future like *The Jetsons*, buzzing around the city of the future in flying cars.

As a prime example of our long lost expectations of a brighter future, consider a February 1950 article from *Popular Mechanics* by Waldemar Kaempffert, the then science editor of the *New York Times*. In "Miracles You'll See in the Next 50 Years," readers were told to "drop in by rocket plane on Totteneville (an imaginary town in Ohio), the sootless Garden City where you will live in scientific comfort in A.D. 2000."[10]

Kaempffert projected that the twenty-first-century American city would be built around new, rather than legacy, infrastructure, including a downtown airport with triple-decker highways radiating outward. Automobiles were to be powered with alcohol. The family helicopter pad would be on top of the garage. If you wished to visit Paris, you could travel there by supersonic rocket or jet plane or by atomic powered ocean liner. You would be cooking your meals with solar heat, and artificial foods made synthetically from sawdust and wood pulp were projected as staples of the twenty-first-century diet. The author also projected that soiled linen and used underwear would be recycled into candy.

As underscored in his article, he confined his predictions to processes and inventions that were then being hatched in American laboratories. Apparently, they were not only busy concocting high fructose corn syrup and trans fats galore in the 1950s; they were also working on ways to process the waste products of the lumber industry into your diet as a full range of artificial carbohydrates.

Note that researchers at Virginia Tech have recently succeeded in converting sawdust, tree bark, and grass into artificial carbs called "amylos"—more tasty treats in your future. Before long, the worst aspects of Kaempffert's projected future may come true. And you could find yourself munching pizza processed from sawdust.

Back to the Future . . .

Kaempffert went on to say that televisions would be ubiquitous and double as videophones. And housecleaning in the year 2000 was to be a cinch, because everything in the house would be waterproof, so all cleaning would be done with a hose.

Also, there was to be good news for the aging Baby Boomers by the year 2000. Doctors' understanding of diet and hormones would help them treat old age as a degenerative disease, increasing not only people's ability to maintain their youthful looks but also their life-spans.

The take away of the article was that everyone by the year 2000 was likely to enjoy a standardized life of luxury, and we should be glad of it. Little individuality was to be tolerated: "After all, is the standardization of life to be deplored if we can have a house like Joe Dobson's (Kaempffert's 'John Doe'), a standardized helicopter, luxurious standardized household appointments, and food that was out of the reach of any Roman emperor?" It was a view informed at a time by mass production, when one-size-fits-all uniformity was the ideal.

For my part, I find it hard to imagine food synthesized from sawdust being the envy of a Roman emperor. And don't get me started on the soiled linen and used underwear being recycled into candy. I know we eat some pretty vile artificial foods today, but I am glad that trend never got as far as the "best and the brightest" of 1950 anticipated.

The Disneyland of Rust and Ruin

Still, we have traveled a long way from the bright promise of "a standardized future," as envisioned in 1950, to the decline so evident today. Nowhere is that decline more starkly displayed than in the Disneyland of rust and ruin, Detroit. Fittingly, Ayn Rand, set her dystopian novel, *Atlas Shrugged,* about a future collapse in America in Detroit. Consider further this prophetic passage:

> A few houses still stood within the skeleton of what had once been an industrial town. Everything that could move, had moved away; but some human beings had remained. The empty structures were vertical rubble; they had been eaten, not by time, but by men: boards torn out at random, missing patches of roofs, holes left in gutted cellars. It looked as if blind hands had seized whatever fitted the need of the moment, with no concept of remaining in existence the next morning. The inhabited houses were scattered at random among the ruins; the smoke of their chimneys was the only movement visible in town. A shell of concrete, which had been a schoolhouse, stood on the outskirts; it looked like a skull, with the empty sockets of glassless windows, with a few strands of hair still clinging to it, in the shape of broken wires.
>
> Beyond the town, on a distant hill, stood the factory of the Twentieth Century Motor Company. its walls, roof lines and smokestacks looked trim, impregnable like a fortress. It would have seemed intact but for a silver water tank: the water tank was tipped sidewise.

They saw no trace of a road to the factory in the tangled miles of trees and hillsides. They drove to the door of the first house in sight that showed a feeble signal of rising smoke. The door was open. An old woman came shuffling out at the sound of the motor. She was bent and swollen, barefooted, dressed in a garment of flour sacking. She looked at the car without astonishment, without curiosity; it was the blank stare of a being who had lost the capacity to feel anything but exhaustion.

"Can you tell me the way to the factory?" asked Rearden.

The woman did not answer at once; she looked as if she would be unable to speak English. "What factory?" she asked.

Rearden pointed. "That one."

"It's closed."

Long the mecca of well-paying middle-class jobs for unskilled and semiskilled workers, Detroit was the richest large city in the world on a per capita basis in 1950. It was then home to the world's largest corporation, General Motors. As late as 1965, the combined profits of the top thirty European companies (the top ten each from Germany, Britain, and France) were $250 million less than the profit of General Motors alone.

"Ta ra-ra-Boom-de-ay"

In 1950, there were 295,000 factory jobs in Detroit. It is indicative of the difference between then and now that when GM was the largest employer in America, it paid its workers the equivalent of sixty dollars per hour in today's terms, compared to the average hourly pay of about ten dollars for nonsupervisory personnel at today's largest employer, Wal-Mart. A large fraction of Wal-Mart employees are on food stamps and other forms of public assistance.

In 1950, when it was "Howdy Doody Time," the lean, well-groomed middle-class children in the peanut gallery had good reason to look to the future with confidence. If they had been precocious enough to guess what the economy of the next quarter of a century would bring, they could well have applauded Buffalo Bob's promise of "a circus of fun for everyone."

To a large extent, the quarter of a century of Hayek's "Great Prosperity" really made for mass prosperity. Productivity rose by 97 percent and median wages rose by 95 percent. The incomes of the poorest fifth jumped by 42 percent, while incomes of the wealthiest 20 percent climbed by 8 percent. Then Nixon repudiated the gold reserve standard, facilitating the shift to financialization. In short order, "The Great Prosperity" came to a screeching halt. According to Harold Myerson's 2013 *American Prospect* article "The Forty-Year Slump," in 1973, the share of Americans living in poverty bottomed out at 11.1 percent.[11] The following year saw the first general wage decline in a quarter of a century. Wages fell by 2.1 percent, while median household income shrank by $1,500.

Not incidentally, this proved to be the peak in the income share of the bottom 90 percent of earners. Thereafter, productivity increased by 80 percent, but growth in median compensation stalled. Indeed, as reported by the *Washington Post* in December 2014's "Most Americans Best Days Are behind Them," income peaked in the last century in 81 percent of US counties. In 572 counties, income peaked in the 1970s.[12]

Notes

1   https://www.parkviewmc.com/ app/files/public/1484/2016 -Poverty-Level-Chart.pdf.

2   Rosiak, Luke, "Fathers Disappear from Households across America," *Washington Times*, December 25, 2012, http://www.washingtontimes .com/news/2012/dec/25/ fathers-disappear-from -households-across-america/ #ixzz2YtARqy6U.

3   Elliott, Michael, *The Day before Yesterday: Reconsidering America's Past, Rediscovering the Present* (New York: Simon & Schuster, 1996), 49.

4   Pirenne, Henri, "Stages in the Social History of Capitalism," in *Class, Status and Power*, ed. Richard Bendix and Seymour Martin Lipset (Glencoe: Free Press, 1953), 104.

5   Servan-Schreiber, J. J., *The American Challenge* (New York: Atheneum, 1968), 87–89.

6   Ibid.

7   See http://aufait.hubpages.com/hub/Working-2-or-More-Jobs.

8   http://www.housingwire.com/articles/25688-census-bureau-new-home-sales-inch-upward.

9   Kvoussi, Bonnie, "Birthrate Plummets, Young Americans Too Poor to Have Kids," *The Huffington Post*, March 27, 2012.

10 Kaempffert, W., "Miracles You'll See in the Next Fifty Years," *Popular Mechanics*, February 1950, 113–18, 364, 266, 270, 272.

11 Meyerson, Harold, "The Forty-Year Slump," *The American Prospect*, September/October 2013, 8.

12 Cameron, Darla, and Ted Mellnik, "Most Americans Best Days Are behind Them," *Washington Post*, December 12, 2014.

Chapter Six

Financial Cycles and the Dollar in the Twilight of Hegemony

The central banks are clearly destroying the monetary system that emerged after Nixon went to Camp David in August 1971. So here we are 45 years later and we are nearing the end of an unstable fiat central bank driven system and the alternative is fairly obvious—at some point going back to real money. I don't think governments will do that voluntarily, but certainly people trying to protect their wealth will. When that happens it will trigger a huge political crisis and hopefully an opportunity to change the regime and get back to some kind of viable and sound financial and monetary system.[1]

—David Stockman

The role of the dollar as the international reserve currency is an issue that has seemed of more pressing importance to investors than political economists. It is obvious why investors take an interest. The international standing of currencies forms a principal feature of the global monetary order, influencing a wide range of economic relationships. Despite the great impact of international currencies, however, political economists—with the notable exception of F. A. Hayek—have tended to neglect them. Perhaps this is because currencies are traded twenty-four hours a day, in view of which economists have found it wise to shy away from making heroic comments because of the nontrivial prospect of embarrassment by market movements.

This potential for embarrassment has been illustrated since June 2014, as the dollar rallied sharply in spite of many forecasts that it was destined to depreciate, even collapse, as the decay of US economic preponderance accelerated. If you look back as far as the 1960s, a flurry of investment commentary anticipating the demise of the dollar as the world reserve currency is stimulated each time the dollar has seemed poised to lose a lot of value.

William F. Rickenbacker's 1969 book, *Death of the Dollar*, is the sole example among the more prominent works in this category to have been written before Richard Nixon repudiated the dollar's link to gold. If you actually read this book, as I did almost half a century ago, you will be disappointed: it offers little insight into the current world monetary system and why it is flirting with collapse.

Rickenbacker made a name for himself pointing out that the industrial uses for silver made the metal too valuable to permit its continued use in coins at the low rates the US Treasury was willing to pay for it. *Death of the Dollar* was an extension of Rickenbacker's argument to gold, which he also found to be too valuable to permit its price to remain set at thirty-five dollars an ounce (as contemplated by the Bretton Woods agreements that spelled out the ground rules of US hegemony at the end of World War II).

Rickenbacker pointed out that the annual industrial consumption of gold had tripled from 1.46 million ounces in 1957 to 6.1 million ounces in 1966. By the end of the 1960s, industrial consumption was four times the annual US gold production. Therefore, Rickenbacker's conventional argument was that trends in supply and demand would make it difficult to achieve a sufficient deflation to preserve the dollar/gold peg at thirty-five dollars to the ounce. By implication, preserving fixed exchange would depend on a higher price for gold, and a devaluation of the dollar.

In that sense, *Death of the Dollar* was a very different kind of book than later volumes with similar titles; while Rickenbacker was writing it, during the final years of "The Great Prosperity," the signal crisis of US hegemony was still to come. Unlike today, the United States was still the world's greatest creditor nation. You may recall that the signal crisis begins with a negative judgment by capitalists on the possibility of continuing to profit from reinvestment in the material expansion of the economy. This isn't because they are pessimists—it is because they respond rationally to falling returns.

Return on US Capital Stock Plunges during the Late '60s

A crucial feature of the prelude to financialization in the 1970s was a 40 percent plunge in the rate of return on the capital stock of US manufacturers between 1965 and 1973, as reported by Giovanni Arrighi in *Adam Smith in Beijing*.[2] When Eisenhower left the White House, only a decade before Richard Nixon repudiated the dollar's link to gold, total US business investment was just a shade less than 50 percent of GDP, stronger even than what we have seen recently in China (46.4 percent in 2012) but without the artificial stimulus from a credit bubble. Eisenhower was no friend of easy money.

More recently, even in the wake of unprecedented monetary stimulus since 2008, US business investment was at the bottom of the tables at just 12.8 percent in 2012.

Over a longer period, the percentage of profits earned in manufacturing in the United States fell from over 50 percent in the early 1950s to just about 10 percent by 2001. Meanwhile, the percentage of profits accounted for by financial returns among so-called FIRE (finance, insurance, and real estate) companies, rose from about 10 percent to about 45 percent.

Equally startling, the ratio of financial revenues to operating cash flow for *nonfinancial* American firms rose from around 10 percent in 1950 to a five-year moving average of 50 percent by the turn of the century. By far the largest component of financial revenues was interest, reflecting the growing saturation of the US economy with debt while real income growth petered out.

The signal crisis represents the turn away from capital commitment to business assets in favor of financialization. As such, it is the prestage of a worsening crisis and the eventual collapse of the dominant regime in the terminal crisis of hegemony.

Growth of Financial Assets Vastly Outstrips Economic Growth

It should not be a surprise that long-term investment in the United States fell off a cliff as financial assets proliferated. London-based financial analyst Paul Mylchreest, of ADM Investor Services, reported in March 2015 that "the stock of globally traded financial assets has increased from US $7 trillion in 1980 to something approaching US $200 trillion."[3] This huge proliferation of financial claims growing at a compound annual rate of about 10 percent over thirty-five years, while the nominal growth of the economy was poking along at barely half that rate (5.33 percent), hints at greater crisis to come. Indeed, recent computations by the Bank for International Settlements show that total global debt was almost three times greater than the whole world economy in 2014.

It would be ominous enough that debt has been compounding at almost twice the rate of nominal GDP over three and a half decades. But the situation has become even more grim in recent years. Total public and private debt has grown by $60 trillion to 300 percent of GDP since the last financial crisis. The pace of total debt growth has increasingly diverged from the corresponding rate of economic growth. In fact, nominal GDP growth in the decade since 2007 has averaged just 2.92 percent. Part of the reason for the slowdown is the fact the economy is overburdened with debt. Other factors, explored elsewhere in this book, have also contributed to smothering economic growth—with ominous implications. The burden of debt is building toward *The Breaking Point*.

If the average interest rate were merely 2 percent, then a 300 percent debt-to-GDP ratio means that the economy needs to grow at a nominal rate of 6 percent to cover interest. With nominal GDP growth lagging, we're experiencing about a half trillion dollar annual shortfall in growth compared to what would be required to cover interest on outstanding debt. Far from growing out of the debt burden, the economy is sinking under it. The World Bank estimates that the ratio of nonperforming loans to total outstanding reached 4.3 in 2015. Compare that to 4.2 percent on the eve of the last financial crisis.[4]

A little-noted feature of the hypertrophy of debt in the fiat money system, where almost all our money is borrowed into existence as debt, is that the more money is borrowed, the stronger the deflationary trap is poised to snap shut. For one thing, debt drives production. Capitalists whose investments are financed by debt have incentives to continue expanding production, even at lower prices, to meet fixed debt payment obligations. When central banks encourage credit demand by slashing interest rates to invisibility, they stimulate a "cross-border carry trade" in which borrowers operating in countries with higher interest rates are tempted to borrow dollars at low interest rates. As of Q1 of 2015, according to the Bank for International Settlements, "nonfinancial" companies outside the United States had collectively borrowed $9 trillion. This is tantamount to a multi-trillion-dollar short position against the dollar. As the borrowers are obliged to buy dollars to repay their debt, the effect is equivalent to a short squeeze in currency markets.

When the Obama administration, with an eye on US elections in November 2014, amplified propaganda about a "vigorous recovery" in the late spring of 2014, an expectation of a coming interest rate rise in the United States helped compound a self-reinforcing rally in the dollar. The effect was to shrink demand for key commodities priced in dollars. Prices collapsed for a whole range of dollar-denominated commodities, undermining both cash flow and collateral, thus jeopardizing the ability of debtors to repay.

Also note that the ability of the real economy to support rapidly compounding financial claims (most of the financial assets are debt instruments) is exaggerated by looking at compound growth since 1980. Remember, from 1992 through 2000, reported US GDP growth only fell below 3 percent twice—in 1993 when it was 2.7 percent and in 1995 when it was 2.5 percent. But those days are past. More recent figures show that even by official accounts of growth it has dwindled to a standstill.

As David Stockman pointed out in his May 2015 article, "Wake-Up Call for B-Dud and the New York Fed Staff—This Isn't 'Transitory'," April 2015's number for manufacturing production represented a *0.33 percent annual growth rate* since December 2007.[5]

Debt and Money Destined to Be "Destroyed on a Truly Enormous Scale"

In other words, financial claims have been multiplying more than thirty times faster than industrial production since the onset of the last recession. This underscores Tim Morgan's thesis in his 2013 book, *Life after Growth*. Morgan states that "the total of financial claims has become vastly larger than anything that the real economy can deliver. . . . This divergence between real potential output and the scale of monetary claims helps explain why the world is mired in debts that cannot be repaid, and it also explains why the process of the destruction of the value of money is inevitable and is starting to gather pace." Morgan concludes, "What it means is the that financial and real economies can be reconciled only if financial claims (meaning both debt and money) are destroyed on a truly enormous scale." Unless you think like Obama in pretending that real economic growth is poised to surge, spiraling financial claims on a stagnant real economy imply an enormous wipeout of financial claims—hence my expectation of a coming "terminal crisis" of US hegemony.

The US government has become the world's greatest purveyor of economic lies since the Soviet Union. The government remorselessly overstates economic growth and exaggerates strength of the employment market. As pointed out by *Zero Hedge* in the May 2015 article "The Big Lie: Serial Downward Revisions Hide Ugly Truth," the level of US retail sales has been chronically exaggerated. Between 2010 and 2015, over 20 percent of the initial gains in retail sales were removed by serial downward revisions in later months. According to the article, "For over 65 percent of the time, a 'good' number prints, stocks rally, the everything-is-awesome meme is confirmed, and then a month later (or more) retail sales data is downwardly revised." (Along the same lines, the unemployment rate for April 2015, officially reported at 5.4 percent, is really 23 percent, as reported by Shadow Government Statistics, computed as Statistics Canada computes the unemployment rate in Canada.)

Then there is the dramatic 25 percent dollar rally that began around May 2014, which was triggered, in part, by the response of traders to statistical factoids that exaggerated the strength of the US economy. A stronger dollar, in turn, contributed to the systemic price reversal that cratered the price of oil and other economically sensitive commodities. These were second-order effects of China's monumental credit bubble.

There has been no lack of alarm about the fact that we are dependent on paper money that could quickly lose value—or perhaps suck your livelihood and fortune into a deflationary vortex. The current monetary system is unsustainable, and it's bound to collapse. To get a better perspective on this, let's take a step back. The US dollar and the world monetary system need to be understood in the broader context of fading US hegemony.

Rules from America's Days at the Summit of the World

The United States wrote the rules of the world economy when we were far and away the world's richest and most powerful economy. Today, our luster has faded. One of the puzzles we must decipher as investors is how, and under what conditions, the US dollar's role as a reserve currency is likely to end. Also, the current system should be understood as the culmination of a centuries-long process in the evolution of money and credit, as shaped by successive hegemonies. As Hayek pointed out in *New Studies in Philosophy, Politics, Economics and the History of Ideas,* the institutions of the moment are the latest attempt to cope with the demand for more, and cheaper, money—"a tradition of our civilization for centuries."[6]

A review of the past stages of hegemony shows several points to bear in mind now:

1. Banking has never been a truly free market activity. During each of the successive stages of hegemony over the past five centuries, the predominant power has sponsored an official or quasi-official bank that has determined the role of money and credit during that stage of the world's economic development.

2. As the scale of government has grown, there has been a loosening of restrictions that commodity-based money imposed on credit expansion, creating a general tendency for credit to become easier.

3. Debt crises have a way of coming to the fore during the twilight of hegemony. No matter the institutional framework of banking, the phase of financialization that follows the signal crisis of hegemony culminates in a terminal crisis of debt distress, often aggravated by the ruinous expenses of war.

4. Money and banking have evolved over the past half millennium to permit more promiscuous extension of credit. The US system of pure fiat money reflects the unprecedented scale of the US government as the largest the world has ever seen and the declining marginal returns (accelerating inefficiency) of a system that cannot pay its way. In this light, easy credit at

an unprecedented scale is the monetary reflection of scale diseconomies. The government needs to create trillions of dollars out of "thin air" to pay its otherwise unaffordable operating expenses. The terminal crisis of US hegemony may well prove to be the end of fiat money and fractional reserve banking, as the unstable fiat system collapses and money and banking devolve to a smaller and more efficient scale.

As Hall of Fame baseball genius, the late Yogi Berra is famous for pointing out, "You can observe a lot just by watching." What you can see if you look is that a distinctive feature of US hegemony in its twilight is the imposition of pure, fiat money throughout the globe. Although you can see some foreshadowing of the US monetary system in the period of British hegemony, no previous dominant regime had strayed far from commodity-based money. For perspective, let's take a quick historical tour of previous hegemonies over the past five centuries. You can see how money and banking have evolved through half a millennium to permit banks to create money "out of thin air," with the changes driven in large measure as expedients for financing ever-larger governments ever-more desperate for funds.

1. Genoan/Iberian Hegemony
La Casa delle compere e dei banchi di San Giorgio
Medieval Banking in Sixteenth-Century Dress

The financial hub of the first modern hegemony was Genoa, which specialized in finance capitalism, mainly extending credit to princes at a time when bankers did not create money, but only lent sums that already existed. How did that work?

You could learn a lot about banking in sixteenth-century Genoa by parsing the original name of Genoa's leading banking institution—"*La Casa delle compere e dei banchi di San Giorgio.*" This is usually translated as "The Bank of Saint George."

But a literal rendition of the Italian is "The House of public debts & 'banks' (plural) of Saint George." As Professor Giovanni Felloni elucidates, *casa* more or less approximates "corporation" as "it denotes a body with its own legal identity" that "survives the succession of those managing it."[7]

The affinity for Saint George probably also needs explaining. "It was the norm in medieval life to invoke the protection of a saint."[8] The creditors who funded Genoa's bank chose the warrior Saint George, whose cross not incidentally formed the design of the Genoan flag—essentially identical to that of England, as both incorporated the red Saint George's cross on a white field.

And *delle compere* refers to a type of public debt, the *compera*, that enabled Genoa's bankers to "finance the ambitions of foreign and local princes including the King of Spain." Part of the magic of the *compera* in its time was that it entitled buyers of sovereign debt to receive dedicated streams of income from the proceeds of specific taxes, thus circumventing prohibitions of the medieval church against "usury." Think of the contortions among Islamic banks today.

Note also that *dei banchi,* which literally means "the benches," is a medieval designation of "banks" (plural), so named because in the Middle Ages, Genoan bankers did not do business not from workshops, as did the craftsmen, but from behind a table, a flat surface a (*bancus*) set up in the market square. Note that *bancus* is not only the root of "banks" but also of "bankruptcy." The word *bancus* means "table or bench," and *ruptus* means "broken." When a merchant or banker could no longer honor his debts, his *bancus* or table in the market was broken to warn others not to conclude business with him.

Banchi is the plural form of *banco.* In late medieval and early modern Genoa, "*dei banchi di San Giorgio*" "signified 'bank counters,' since each banco had its own cash desk and set of accounts; the word in the plural form '*banchi*' indicated the existence of several bank counters at the same time and, in fact, there were 3 from 1408 to 1445, rising to 8 between 1531 and 1805." Among them were a gold bank, one that worked in silver and another in Spanish "real de a ocho" coins.[9]

The "real de a ocho," or the piece of eight (Spanish *peso de ocho*), was a silver coin, worth eight reales, that was minted in the Spanish Empire after 1598. It was conceived to correspond in value to the German thaler. The Spanish dollar was widely used by many countries as international currency because of its uniformity in standard and milling characteristics.

As you know, the Spanish dollar was the coin upon which the original US dollar was based, and it remained legal tender in the United States until the Coinage Act of 1857. It was also the origin of the "peso" currencies in use in many countries, as well as the Chinese yuan. Because it was widely used in Europe, the Americas, and the Far East, it became the first world currency.

In short, the first modern hegemony, the Genoan/Iberian regime, involved a continuation of medieval money and banking in the service of the new Iberian empires. It was all about the importation of gold and silver from the New World. Spanish and Portuguese banking was primitive, but as described above their coin was good. This formed the basis of a symbiotic relationship with the Most Serene Republic of Genoa, the small city-state that became the financial partner with the Iberian powers, in their period of hegemony in the sixteenth century.

"Up for Anything"

Most of the money that circulated in Genoa was minted by other states. But as discussed, Genoa did have a prominent and hyperactive financial institution, of medieval vintage, the Bank of Saint George, one of the oldest banks in the world. Run by Genoan oligarchs—who, like beer drinkers in the *Bud Light* commercial, were "up for anything"—the banks were major players in the slave trade and even administered their own colonies in Corsica, Gazaria in Crimea, and the Taman Peninsula on the Black Sea in present-day Russia.

Ferdinand and Isabella, as well as Christopher Columbus, maintained accounts at the Bank of St. George. The bank specialized in financing the Hapsburg sovereigns in anticipation of erratic shipment of silver from Peru. They lent especially vast sums to Spanish king Charles V, upon which Spain repeatedly defaulted—in 1557, 1560, 1575, and again in 1596—making it the first modern nation to default and signifying the signal crisis of Genoan/Iberian hegemony.

2. Hegemony of the United Provinces
Amsterdamsche Wisselbank (Bank of Amsterdam)
Pawn Shop for Debased Coin

The period of Dutch predominance began with an innovation during the rebellion against Spanish rule—the creation of the Bank of Amsterdam. Acting through the bank, the Dutch "provincial government minted and supported two good coinages, the guider (golden) and stuiver (silver)" worth one-twentieth of a guilder.

The Bank of Amsterdam served as a clearinghouse for currencies, acting much like a pawnshop for debased coins. It accepted deposits of any currency, or bullion, and then assessed the gold and silver content of such assets and gave the depositors an equivalent value in guilder and stuivers. This was important, because as Francis Turner put it, seventeenth-century "Europe was filled with coins of varying values, issued by governments of varying degrees of trustworthiness. To make it worse, each system had different ratios of the numbers of coins of one denomination that made up the next."[10] The Bank of Amsterdam became a financial clearinghouse. "The guilder and stuiver became the preferred currency for international exchange." Other currencies then in use were deposited in accounts of the Bank of Amsterdam and translated into the preferred "guilder and stuiver." In effect, the bank provided liquidity to debased currencies, crediting their holders with their precious metals content.

In short, the Bank of Amsterdam provided liquidity to any holder of gold and silver, even in the dilute form afforded in coinage of jurisdictions that seriously debased their currencies with base metal alloys. In so doing, the Bank of Amsterdam facilitated trade and encouraged in the inflow of funds to Bourse of Amsterdam.

Note that the Bank of Amsterdam practiced "warehouse" banking. Depositors paid the bank for the service of safekeeping their money rather than earning interest on deposits. This reflected the fact the Bank of Amsterdam was not engaged in fractional reserve banking—lending out some fraction of deposits, as goldsmiths had traditionally done and the banks we are familiar with do.

3. Hegemony of the United Kingdom
The Bank of England: Central Banking for Profit

The prime monetary innovation of British hegemony was the advent of central banking and legal sanction for the creation of money ex nihilo "out of thin air." The Bank of England received its Royal charter on July 27, 1694 (while Dutch hegemony was still in place), with the explicit purpose of creating money to fund the rebuilding of the English fleet.

England's Dutch King, William III, who was also Prince William of Orange, the hereditary "Stadtholder" of Holland, Zeeland, Utrecht, Gelderland, and Overijssel in the Dutch Republic, found the English Treasury bare when he invaded England and seized the throne from James II. Subsequently, the English Navy, along with the Dutch fleet had been decisively defeated by the French at the Battle of Beachy Head, an ill-advised encounter prompted by direct orders from Queen Mary, wife of King William who was away in Ireland at the time.

Without ready funds to rebuild the navy, you will not be shocked to know that some members of Parliament thought immediately of clipping coins—to raise funds by reducing the value of money. King William and his advisers preferred to raise funds by chartering a for-profit bank, two schemes for which were entertained. One that failed was for a "Land Bank," proposed mainly by the king's opponents, in which King William himself was to be the lead investor with a subscription of £5,000. But this plan was scrapped when only £7,500 was committed, whereas the Bank of England was chartered as a for-profit corporation, with an initial capital of £1,200,000, a sum that was raised in twelve days. Part of the reason for the king's enthusiasm for the new arrangement was that the Bank of England offered a mechanism for transferring the personal royal debt into a public debt controlled by the Parliament.

In return for creating a limited liability corporation, which would act as a bank for the government and have the right to issue banknotes, the shareholders of the Bank of England loaned the bank £1,200,000 at 8 percent interest. Of this sum, lent in turn to the government, half went immediately to fund a shipbuilding project for the Royal Navy. The Bank of England was also given a special dispensation to suspend conversion of its bank notes into gold.

This created the precedent for fiat money as the Bank of England notes circulated as undated debt instruments. Given the heavy debt load of the government, there was some push to early in the eighteenth century to dispense with the convertibility of banknotes into specie altogether. Treasury officials consulted Sir Isaac Newton, the great physicist, inventor of calculus, and Master of the Royal Mint.

That discussion is described by Isabel Paterson:

> Sir Isaac Newton was asked by the British Treasury officials and financiers of his day why the monetary pound had to be a fixed quantity of precious metal. Why, indeed, must it consist of precious metal, or have any objective reality? Since paper currency was already accepted, why could not notes be issued without ever being

redeemed? The reason they put the question supplies the answer; the government was heavily in debt, and they hoped to find a safe way of being dishonest. But Newton was asked as a mathematician, not as a moralist. He replied: "Gentlemen, in applied mathematics, you must describe your unit." Paper currency cannot be described mathematically as money.[11]

Preferring not to argue with one of the greatest geniuses who ever lived, the Treasury officials ratified Newton's plan, and Great Britain went on the gold standard in 1717.

By most accounts, the gold standard under British hegemony was a great success. It contributed to the peaceful order and prosperity that characterized the nineteenth century. Of course, some qualifications to those happy generalizations are in order. For one thing, *Pax Britannica* was not total. The late years of the eighteenth century and the early nineteenth century (through Napoleon's defeat at Waterloo, some two centuries ago on June 18, 1815) were a time of war.

Embroiled in the nineteenth-century approximation of world war, the British Treasury equivocated its commitment to the gold standard. When the financing requirements of the state escalated, the gold standard was suspended.

A Quarter of a Century Experiment with Fiat Money

The modern world's first successful fiat money regime, an era of an inconvertible pound, began on February 27, 1797, when the Bank of England stopped converting its deposit notes to gold specie in order to forestall a gathering run on its gold reserves. Among the factors at work were the facts that the Napoleonic Wars had been under way for some time and the Bank of England had permitted the supply of pound notes to grow to approximately twice its holdings of bullion. By the mid-1790s, there were notes for £14 million in circulation as compared to about £7 million in bullion reserves. Consequently, the market price of gold had risen above the mint price. And as you would expect, there were a lot of redemptions.

Initially, the suspension of cash payments, the so-called Bank Restriction Period, was an emergency measure to counter panic following rumors of a French invasion. The public expected the suspension to continue only for a few weeks, or at most, until the end of the Napoleonic Wars. But in fact, suspension of the gold standard lasted almost a quarter of a century until May 1, 1821.

When the war ended in 1815, the circulation of paper was so large that it was apparent that resumption of pound note conversion into gold could only take place after a "period of adjustment." This deflationary adjustment lasted for six years, at which point the gold standard was reestablished at the previous parity £3. 17s. 10½d an ounce. About which, the famous economist David Ricardo commented that "he should never advise a government to restore a currency which had been depreciated 30 percent to par."[12]

But the British went through the necessary deflation. Once reestablished, the gold standard remained successfully in effect until the outbreak of World War I, when conversion of the pound into gold was again suspended. Until 1916, when its gold reserves ran out, Britain was funding most of the Allies' war expenditures, including most of the empire's, all of Italy's, along with two-thirds of the war costs of France and Russia. Given these staggering costs, the money supply in Great Britain more than doubled while consumers experienced a 250 percent increase in prices.

When the Great War ended, it was again judged that a period of deflationary adjustment was required before specie conversion could be resumed. In the event, Britain went back on the gold standard in 1925 at prewar parity. Then the Great Depression hit, and Great Britain abandoned the gold standard in 1931. As Hayek noted, the British government abandoned the attempt to bring down costs by deflation just as it seemed near success. According to Professor James Morrison,

"Great Britain's abandonment of the gold standard in 1931 was one of the most significant and surprising policy shifts in the history of the international financial system."[13]

Another way of putting it would be to say that by going off the gold standard, Britain effectively abdicated its hegemony. Morrison attributes the collapse of the gold standard a "mistaken monetary policy" by the Bank of England, and deliberate action by Keynes to confuse the suggestible Prime Minister Ramsay MacDonald about staying on gold. But the gold standard did have a drawback from Keynes's interventionist perspective. As Elisa Newby, head of the market operations division of the Bank of Finland, spells out, "Under the gold standard the money growth rate cannot be regulated by governmental policy because the money stock can increase or decrease only if the commodity stock in monetary uses increases or decreases respectively."[14] In this sense, the gold standard was much more complementary to a laissez faire policy, which Britain came closer to following in the nineteenth century than in the depths of the Great Depression. That's not to say that the interventionist policies really constituted an improvement.

The last monetary policy innovation, in the twilight of British hegemony was, in Professor Morrison's words, "a flexible exchange rate regime," a "policy of cheap money"—meaning a monetary stimulus—"intended to combat depression."[15] That British innovation was one the United States was to follow with alacrity.

The example of the Bank of England exemplifies the high-level crony capitalism involved in the melding of for-profit banking with the financing of the hegemonic state. Bankers with the right to create money out of "thin air" can earn staggering profits. This was highly visible in the case of the Bank of England. It was a public company traded on the London stock market for 250 years. Its investors pocketed big profits over the centuries. A sum of £100 invested in Bank of England stock in 1694, assuming all dividends had been reinvested and without consideration of taxes, would have grown to £41,870,819 by 1945 when the Bank of England was nationalized.[16] It would be difficult to cite a comparable return in US banking because the gains in crony capitalist US banking have tended to be more veiled. But you will not be shocked at my suggestion that politically connected bankers make a lot of money.

4. Hegemony of the United States
The Reverse Midas Touch: Turning Gold into Paper

The monetary regime of US hegemony began after Bretton Woods in 1944, with the dollar as the denominator of international fixed exchange rates. Prior to World War II, during the twilight of British hegemony, gold had served as the anchor for fixed exchange rates. This meant each country guaranteed that its currency would be redeemed by its value in gold. After Bretton Woods, each member agreed to redeem its currency for dollars, not gold. The United States, in turn, agreed to redeem dollars for gold at the fixed price of thirty-five dollars to the ounce. At the time, the United States held three-quarters of the world's supply of gold. This was the respectable beginning of the dollar's role as the world's reserve currency—before the signal crisis of US hegemony tipped the system toward financialization.

The "Nixon Shock"

Richard Nixon was not called "Tricky Dick" for nothing. In 1984's *After Hegemony*, author Robert Keohane summarized the situation prior to the "Nixon Shock." Keohane explained that by 1970–71, confidence in US economic policy had become undermined and perceived as inflationary, resulting in a loss of confidence in the strength of the dollar. Faced with the prospect of trimming government spending before the 1972 presidential election, Nixon did not hesitate. He repudiated the gold reserve standard and defaulted on the US promise to redeem dollars at the rate 1/35th of an ounce of gold.[17]

I have no doubt that principled and effective leadership in 1970–71 could have preserved the gold reserve system, at least for a time, at the cost of negative political feedback from voters unwilling to tolerate spending cuts that would have been required to turn the budget deficit into a surplus. A politician with the intellect and character of Lee Kuan Yew could have pulled it off, resisting what Hayek identified as "the everpresent demand for more and cheaper money."

Richard Nixon was not the man for the job—Nixon was smart, but he lacked the self-assurance to save the gold reserve standard. He also had a limited and selfish perspective on monetary policy. Prior to the 1960 election, Arthur Burns, the first chairman of Eisenhower's Council of Economic Advisors, warned Nixon that he was likely to lose because the Federal Reserve, at Eisenhower's prodding, had tightened monetary policy, contributing to a recession that began in April 1960. In his memoirs, Nixon blamed tight money for his 1960 defeat. When he was finally elected in 1968, Nixon resolved to appoint Burns to chair the Federal Reserve Board at the first opportunity, which he did in 1970, on the understanding that Burns would assure that easy credit conditions prevailed for Nixon's reelection bid in 1972.

In the event, as recorded in Burns's diary, his relationship with Nixon proved rocky, as Nixon felt that Burns's monetary policy was inadequately inflationary. After a 1971 meeting with Nixon, for example, Burns made this startling note: "The President looked wild; talked like a desperate man; fulminated with hatred against the press; took some of us to task—apparently meaning me or [chairman of the Council of Economic Advisors, Paul] McCracken or both—for not putting a gay and optimistic face on every piece of economic news, however discouraging; propounded the theory that confidence can be best generated by appearing confident and coloring, if need be, the news."

In short, Nixon was far too insecure and obsessed with his reelection to have led the country into a deflationary retrenchment to forestall full-scale financialization. It may well have been true, as F. A. Hayek later contended, that retrenchment and deflation in the early '70s might have spared the world from a deeper and more convulsive crisis—the worst part of which still lies ahead.

The Inescapable Crisis

Speaking of the escape from fixed exchange rates, Hayek said that we should have no illusion that we can escape the consequences of our mistakes and that we had missed the opportunity to stop a depression from coming. He thought that we had used what he called our "newly gained freedom from institutional compulsion" (the dollar fix to gold) to act more stupidly than ever before, postponing an inevitable crisis and making things even worse in the long run. He confessed that he wished for the crisis to come soon.[18]

Thus Nixon unleashed what an early director of the Bank of England described as "the formidable weapon of unrestricted money creation." I suspect that he was more right than he knew to frame his discussion of pure fiat money in military terms. As we saw underscored by Great Britain's suspension of the gold standard, first in the Napoleonic Wars and second in World War I, the big impetus for fiat money was a strategic imperative to fund crucial war costs that apparently could not be met within the restraints of sound money. Equally, as Elisa Newby pointed out in her 2007 paper, "The Suspension of Cash Payments as a Monetary Regime," a key feature of the success of Britain's temporary abandonment of the gold standard during the Napoleonic Wars was the credible promise that the suspension of specie payment would, in fact, be temporary.[19]

As mentioned, the US system of fiat money reflects the unprecedented scale of the US government as the largest the world has ever seen and the declining marginal returns (accelerating inefficiency) of a system that cannot pay its way. Just as the British flirted with fiat money on two rare occasions—spaced about a century apart, when the survival of the state depended upon outlays that would have been more difficult to afford under ordinary conditions—the United States has evolved a pure fiat system of creating money out of thin air because that is the only expedient for paying its truly gargantuan operating expenses.

In the current case of the United States, vast military outlays in combination with welfare state spending at a historically unprecedented scale, compose the heaviest fiscal load the world has ever seen. There is compelling evidence in plain view that the US government does not pay its way. Proof of declining returns is evident in the fact that the US national debt grew by more than $1 trillion between September 2013 and September 2014. It surged from $16,738,183,526,697.32 to $17,742,108,970,073.37, reflecting an operating shortfall of more than $2.7 billion a day. Multiplying the increase in the official debt are the compounding accrual obligations of the United States of more than $200 trillion.

Furthermore, as computed according to Generally Accepted Accounting Principles (GAAP), the annual federal budget deficit runs in the trillions. For example, for 2012, the GAAP deficit was $6.9 trillion, 42.6 percent of nominal GDP.

Just as a survival imperative dictated the move to pure fiat money by the United States, so a similar imperative prohibited the smaller states operating at earlier stages in the sequence of hegemonies from attempting to employ fiat money. They could never have funded their debts or financed their militaries with cash created ex nihilo in earlier stages of economic development. These earlier stages took place before the introduction of fossil fuels increased the economic growth rate, permitting the real economy to support a larger sum of claims represented by money and debt. (As I endeavor to explain in a coming chapter, historically unprecedented economic growth propelled by exogenous hydrocarbon energy amounted to a hidden BTU content of fiat money.)

In this light, as Keohane shrewdly observed in *After Hegemony*, there has been a deficiency of hegemonic stability theory in accounting for change in the international monetary system that "insofar as it relies on GDP figures as indices of power resources, it *overpredicts* regime collapse."[20]

I believe that we are headed toward the terminal phase of the global financial system. What I doubt is that the reserve status of the US dollar can be displaced as an operating patch while business as usual proceeds in the global economy. To the contrary, the dollar will be displaced as part of Hayek's inescapable crisis. Market adjustments the sort envisioned in Exter's Inverted Pyramid will destroy money and debt on an enormous scale as a step toward the reconstitution of the global economy on a free market basis, probably incorporating the exchange of real money based on both silver and gold. These "barbarous relics" have the crucial feature of being assets that are not someone else's liabilities.

My expectation is that the eclipse of US hegemony will close the curtain on fiat money at center stage of the world monetary system. If it is seen again after the Breaking Point brings US hegemony to a close, it will be a relic of backward closed economies, such as in North Korea.

Financial Cycle Growths in Amplitude

Part of the dynamic that will propel this inescapable crisis is the increasing imbalance associated with the growing amplitude of the financial cycle. This cycle has arisen from the accelerating expansion of credit over the past three decades, corresponding with increases and decreases in private debt, relative to income, and the prices of assets financed by that debt, including real estate. Mathias Drehmann and Claudio Borio, economists working at the Bank for International Settlements, have pioneered the concept of the financial cycle in current terms. (See graph on page 19 of BIS report at http://www.bis.org/publ/work380.htm.) But similar thinking can be traced to Hyman Minsky and before that to Hayek's "Monetary Theory and the Trade Cycle" from the 1920s.

Measurement of the financial cycle is a challenge, but data compiled by the BIS economists shows that financial cycles can last as long as twenty years, with more pronounced swings of increasing amplitude over time. The imbalances accumulated and aggravated by rampant credit creation and the fuddling of price signals due to ZIRP threaten to crash the system as Hayek foresaw in the wake of the 1971 "Nixon Shock."

With this in mind, I recommend that you accumulate both silver and gold. As hedge fund billionaire Ray Dalio of Bridgeport Associates puts it, "If you don't own gold . . . there is no sensible reason other than you don't know history or you don't know the economics of it."

Notes

1 Stockman, David, "We Are Entering the Terminal Phase of the Global Financial System," *Zero Hedge*, May 18, 2015, http://www.zerohedge.com/news/2015-05-18/david-stockman-we-are-entering-terminal-phase-global-financial-system.

2 Arrighi, Giovanni, *Adam Smith in Beijing: Lineages of the Twenty-First Century* (London: Verso, 2007), 103.

3 Mylchreest, Paul, "Selling Time," *Equity & Commodity Strategy—Fulcanelli Report*, March 25, 2015, 4.

4 Das, Satyajit, "Can the World Deal with a New Bank Crisis?," *Bloomberg*, July 27, 2016.

5 Stockman, David, "Wake-Up Call for B-Dud and the New York Fed Staff—This Isn't 'Transitory,'" http://davidstockmanscontracorner.com/wake-up-call-for-b-dud-and-new-york-fed-staff-this-isnt-transitory/?utm_source=wysija&utm_medium=email&utm_campaign=Mailing+List+Sunday+10+AM.

6 Hayek, F. A., *New Studies in Philosophy, Politics, Economics and the History of Ideas* (London: Routledge & Kegan Paul, 1978), 213.

7 Felloni, Guiseppe, "A Profile of Genoa's 'Casa di San Giorgio' (1407–1805): A Turning Point in the History of Credit," 1. http://www.giuseppefelloni.it/rassegnastampa/A%20Profile%20of%20Genoa's%20Casa%20di%20San%20Giorgio.pdf.

8 Ibid.

9 Ibid., 7.

10 Turner, Francis, "Money and Exchange Rates in 1632."

11 Paterson, Isabel, *The God of the Machine*, quoted in http://www.anoopverma.com/2015/04/in-applied-mathematics-you-must-de.html.

12 David Ricardo to John Wheatley, September 18, 1821, quoted in Hayek, in *New Studies in Philosophy*, 199.

13 Morrison, James, "Keynessandra No More: JM Keynes, the 1931 Financial Crisis, and the Death of the Gold Standard in Britain," APSA 2010 Annual Meeting Paper. Available at SSRN: http://ssrn.com/abstract=1641715.

14 Newby, Elisa, "The Suspension of Cash Payments as a Monetary Regime," *Centre for Macroeconomic Analysis Working Paper Series*, June 2007, 4.

15 Morrison, "Keynessandra No More," 6.

16 https://www.globalfinancialdata.com/gfdblog/?p=942#sthash.gh8dSQB0.dpuf.

17 Keohane, Robert O., *After Hegemony: Cooperation and Discord in the World Political Economy* (Princeton: Princeton University Press, 1984), 208.

18 Hayek, *New Studies in Philosophy*, 205.

19 Newby, "The Suspension of Cash Payments as a Monetary Regime," 4.

20 Keohane, *After Hegemony*.

Chapter Seven

The "Great Degeneration"

From the Rule of Law to the Rule of a Law Professor

The madness of slavery is over, the time of liberty has been granted, English necks are free from the yoke.
—Gerald of Wales, 1215

On June 15, 2015, it had been 800 years since my swash-buckling ancestor Saire de Quincey, the Earl of Winchester, dressed in full battle armor, along with his cousin Baron Robert Fitzwalter and fellow conspirators, confronted King John at Runnymede Meadow and obliged him to sign the Magna Carta or, in Latin, the "Great Charter." As the saying goes, this was "the start of something big"—namely, the rule of law as exemplified by the Magna Carta's clause 39, which reads, "No free man shall be taken or imprisoned, or dispossessed or outlawed or exiled or in any way ruined, nor will we go or send against him except by the lawful judgement of his peers or by the law of the land."[1]

Clause 39 was inspired by the Magna Carta barons' out-rage over King John's treatment of the beautiful and cele-brated Matilda (Maud) de Braose, wife of the fourth Lord of Bramber. When King John sent officers to take Maud's son William into custody as hostage for payment of 5,000 marks, she told them she refused to deliver him to a king who had murdered his own nephew. (It was widely believed that John murdered Arthur, Duke of Brittany—son of his older brother, Geoffrey Plantagenet—to rid himself of a rival for the throne.) When King John heard that Maud had openly voiced the widely whispered view that he was a murderer, he dispatched an army to apprehend her. After a two-year pursuit through England, Wales, and Ireland, Maude and her son were captured by John's troops on the Antrim Coast of what is now Northern Ireland. They were brought back to England where John ordered them imprisoned, first at Windsor Castle, then at Corfe Castle in Dorset, where they were thrown into the dungeon without food. They starved to death.

King John was widely hated for the type of treatment that he imposed on Maud and William de Braose, and the Magna Carta was the barons' revenge on him. (It was not entirely expressed in clause 39.) Another "yippee moment" for Gerald of Wales was probably occasioned by clause 40, one of many that forbade the king from "selling" justice to the highest bidder or delaying it indefinitely: "To no one will we sell, to no one will we refuse or delay right or justice."

To follow the sequence a bit further, clause 41 also appeals to me as perhaps the pioneering encoded defense of free trade: "All merchants shall have safe and secure exit from England, and entry to England, with the right to tarry there and to move about as well by land as by water, for buying and selling by the ancient and right customs, quit from all evil tolls."

It has been a point of false pride that my remote ancestor played a leading role in establishing some principles that served the world well over the ensuing centuries:

- The power of the state is not absolute.
- Those in authority must obey the law.
- Even sovereign bankruptcy does not justify arbitrary taxation and the seizure of property without due process.

As the distinguished English jurist Lord Denning put it, the Magna Carta was "the greatest constitutional document of all times—the foundation of the freedom of the individual against the arbitrary authority of the despot."[2]

A number of thoughtful observers argue that the rule of law was crucial to the economic ascendancy of the West. Economic historian Douglas North has attributed the relative success of the United States and Canada to British institutions as being more conducive to growth. To the extent that he is right, much of the success of Australia and New Zealand could also be explained the same way, due to the observance of the rule of law in the former British settlement colonies. That being so, much credit goes to Saire de Quincey, his cousin Robert FitzWalter, and the other Magna Carta barons who forced a bankrupt king to observe the rights of subjects.

They were not unjustly bullying the king—they were otherwise conventional feudal lords motivated by resentment of excessive taxation and despotic governance.

Gigantic Shakedowns Evolve

The nature of predatory rule has evolved considerably in the 800 years since the Magna Carta. Bad actors no longer dispatch armed bailiffs to seize your children and hold them hostage for the payment of a steep ransom. Today, they deploy lobbyists in thousand-dollar suits who procure antimarket regulations backed by the coercive power of the state. As suggested in chapter 1, these departures from the free market cost you a vast amount (recall the credible estimate that puts the annual cost to you and every member of your family at $125,000 each). As pop philosopher Tavis Smiley, the holder of sixteen honorary doctorates, opined, "If you can't win the game, change the rules."[3] Unlike in the Middle Ages, the gigantic shakedowns of our time are mostly the consequence of efforts by powerful people to win big by changing the rules.

In the early thirteenth century when the Magna Carta was drafted, original thought, per se, was not as highly esteemed as it became in the modern world. In Saire de Quincey's time, copied ideas were more credible than creative thought—laws were not invented; they were remembered. It is interesting, therefore, that Saire de Quincey and his fellow conspirators had the ingenuity to reinforce custom by introducing a creative new element to the enumeration of customary rights and obligations.

King John seems to have been particularly incensed by the most original and longest clause in the Magna Carta, clause 61, in which the barons asserted the right to "choose any 25 barons of the realm they will, who with all their might are to observe, maintain and cause to be observed that peace and liberties which we have granted and confirmed to them by this our present charter."

In the event that the liberties were offended by the king's actions, clause 61 reserved the barons' right to seize the king's "castles, lands, and possessions, and in such other ways as they can . . . until in their judgment amends have been made." Can you imagine a charter for the enforcement of liberty today that gave taxpayers the right to seize Obama's bank accounts and other property?

The real essence of the Magna Carta, as German historian Max Friedrich Ludwig Hermann (a.k.a. "Fritz" Kern) noted, was not its reliance on the pen but the "sledgehammer."[4] It was this sledgehammer of resistance to the abuse of authority, not just pious words of protest, that informed the institutional developments that culminated in a tradition of the rule of law. Clause 61 was not a provision that was very popular with King John. He did his best to wiggle out of it.

As soon as the Magna Carta barons disbursed from London back to their homes, King John renounced the Magna Carta and persuaded his sometimes ally Pope Innocent III to release the king from his oath on grounds that it was imposed under duress. Saire de Quincey was subsequently excommunicated. He was later captured following a bloody battle with royal forces at Lincoln, after which he was imprisoned and his estates seized.

His property was only restored and his liberty granted when he agreed to leave England to join the Fifth Crusade, which he duly did. He died on November 3, 1219, aged sixty-four, on the road to Jerusalem, after surviving the Siege of Damietta in Egypt. He was buried in Acre, capital of the Kingdom of Jerusalem, but his heart was returned to England and interred at Garendon Abbey near Loughborough.

Alas, he went to a lot of trouble for nothing where we are concerned. Much of the legacy of the Magna Carta in establishing the rule of law in Anglo-Saxon countries, particularly the United States, has been frittered away and lost during my lifetime. Today, we live in an age of neofeudal debt serfdom, which puts us as much in need of a Magna Carta as Saire de Quincey and the other Magna Carta barons were.

Presidential Corruption Grows

The breakdown of the rule of law has many manifestations, both indirect and overt. Civil libertarians have documented a reversion to pre–Magna Carta authoritarian practices in the United States.

Among other things, Obama has asserted the right to use warrantless surveillance on his own say-so. But that is weak tea compared to Obama's assertion of the right to kill any US citizen without a charge, let alone a conviction, based on his sole authority. A leaked memo argues that the president has a right to kill a citizen even when he lacks "clear evidence of a specific attack" being planned. Not even the evil King John ever claimed the right to execute people without charge.[5]

The headlines have been full of details about the Obama administration secretly targeting the phone records of Associated Press reporters. There is evidence that those who dare to criticize the authorities have been smeared and targeted for arrest.

When Pulitzer Prize–winning journalist Chris Hedges sued the government in a challenge to the "indefinite detention of Americans," the government refused to promise that journalists like Hedges wouldn't be "thrown in a dungeon for the rest of their lives without any right to talk to a judge."

As Dana Milbank wrote in his May 2013 piece "Criminalizing Journalism" in the *Washington Post*, "To treat a reporter as a criminal for doing his job—seeking out information the government doesn't want made public—deprives Americans of the First Amendment freedom on which all other constitutional rights are based."[6] Note that the notion that freedom of the press is imperiled in the United States is not just Dana Millbank's eccentric opinion. The "World Press Freedom Index 2014," published annually by Reporters Without Borders, lists the United States as the country with the forty-sixth greatest amount of press freedom, just below Romania and above Haiti.[7]

Meanwhile, we have learned that conservative groups were targeted by Obama's IRS, but when Obama's brother applied for tax exempt status for the Barack Obama Foundation, he received a retroactive approval within a month—in pluperfect crony capitalist style. The Bush administration also used the IRS to target enemies.

Obama has taken this intrusion into our rights various steps forward. Press reports in April 2013 detailed IRS documents suggesting that the tax agency believes it can read your emails without a warrant. Files released pursuant to a Freedom of Information Act request quoted an internal IRS document claiming that the government did not need a warrant to obtain the contents of electronic communication that has been in storage for more than 180 days. Another file arbitrarily stated that the Fourth Amendment did not protect communications held in electronic storage, such as email messages stored on a server, because Internet users did not have a reasonable expectation of privacy. The IRS claims the right to read your emails without a warrant—a claim that was later modified in the face of a public outcry.[8]

Former judge and constitutional law professor Andrew Napolitano says that Obama's claim that he can indefinitely detain prisoners, even after they are acquitted of crimes, is a power that not even Hitler and Stalin ever claimed. So yes, we have strayed far from the rule of law: Americans no longer enjoy many of the rights that Gerald of Wales applauded when he said, "The time of liberty has been granted," when King John accepted the Magna Carta on June 15, 1215.[9]

Obama and his all-powerful centralized state have set the cause of civil liberties back 800 years. One expert who has been pointing the way toward understanding the deeper economic consequences of abandoning the rule of law is Niall Ferguson, the Laurence A. Tisch Professor of History at Harvard, senior fellow of the Hoover Institution at Stanford, and senior research fellow at Jesus College, Oxford.

"The Great Degeneration"

Ferguson laments what he calls "The Great Degeneration." In a 2013 book of that title, Ferguson argues that a great part of the problem facing the United States and other advanced economies is that we have abandoned the rule of law.[10]

He argues that one of the principal factors that makes nations strong is the guarantee that justice will be done. This is no longer the case. Ferguson sees four symptoms of the "Great Degeneration" of US institutions:

1. The breakdown of the contract between generations. He sees massive national debts and excessive entitlement spending that benefits older generations, at the expense of the young, as a departure from generational balance.
2. Excess regulation. This makes an already complex system more complex, thereby increasing instability. I argue that excess regulation is one of the key informing factors that accounts for the slowdown in economic growth. Despite the doubling of stock prices from 2011 to early 2015 (in conjunction with a debt-fueled outlay of $1.7 trillion by companies buying back their own

shares), overall commodity prices were flat in February 2015 since the recovery supposedly began. This is all symptomatic of a system more vulnerable to collapse than it was in 2008. Leverage has gone up, but by many measures, there has been no recovery and the authorities apparently have exhausted every remedy in their bag of tricks.

3. The rule of lawyers has replaced the rule of law. Ferguson points out that the United States has the highest cost of law of any country in the world—an ominous discount on the sustainability of the system. Instead of swift and speedy justice that cannot be sold, per clause 40 of the Magna Carta, we now have a twisted legal system that is gamed for self-serving needs. US universities graduate forty-one times more lawyers than engineers. It seems fitting that the endgame of such a corrupt system would be presided over by Barack Obama, a law professor.

4. The decline of civil society. According to Ferguson, the growing dependency on government to solve social issues has little economic benefit. The willingness to depend on government to solve problems turns every problem into a feeding frenzy for crony capitalists, thus slowing economic growth even further.

Ferguson has made a good start in pinpointing the eclipse of the rule of law as a major culprit contributing to the falling returns that unambiguously characterize so many aspects of American society and the US economy.

Moral Syndromes and "Monstrous Hybrids"

There are other more subtle consequences of the eclipse of the rule of law. A key to understanding some of these was provided by Jane Jacobs in her brilliant 1993 book, *Systems of Survival: A Dialogue on the Moral Foundations of Commerce and Politics*.[11] Jacobs makes the shrewd point that "two radically different," even contradictory systems of morals and values—what she terms "moral syndromes"—underpin our two different approaches to making a living. The first of these constellations of moral habits or ethical precepts—Moral Syndrome A, or the "commercial moral syndrome"—involves the following fifteen precepts:

1. Shun force
2. Come to voluntary agreements
3. Be honest
4. Collaborate easily with strangers and aliens
5. Compete
6. Respect contracts
7. Use initiative and enterprise
8. Be open to inventiveness and novelty
9. Be efficient
10. Promote comfort and convenience
11. Dissent for the sake of the task
12. Invest for productive purposes
13. Be industrious
14. Be thrifty
15. Be optimistic

Jacobs then lists fifteen additional closely observed but contradictory precepts that compose Moral Syndrome B, or the "guardian moral syndrome," which prevails in politics and jobs relating to government:

1. Shun trading
2. Exert prowess
3. Be obedient and disciplined
4. Adhere to tradition
5. Respect hierarchy
6. Be loyal
7. Take vengeance
8. Deceive for the sake of the task

9. Make rich use of leisure
10. Be ostentatious
11. Dispense largess
12. Be exclusive
13. Show fortitude
14. Be fatalistic
15. Treasure honor

Jacobs emphasizes that her lists were not conjured arbitrarily, but discovered after extensive research. She pored through biographies; business histories; and summaries of scandals, sociology, history, and cultural anthropology.

If you consider the inventory of the guardian precepts, they fairly comprehensively embrace those of Saire de Quincey, Robert FitzWalter, and the Magna Carta rebels. Apart from William Hardel, a wine merchant and urban property owner who was mayor of London, the authors and sureties of the Magna Carta were all feudal magnates. They exerted prowess, or obedience and discipline; adhered to tradition; respected hierarchy; and were loyal to one another and their cause, if not to King John. John's authoritarian rule, following similarly odious practices by his father King Henry II and his brother King Richard I, inspired the Magna Carta barons to seek vengeance, as exemplified by clause 39, for the many wrongs they had suffered.

Equally, clause 41, touching "the ancient and right custom" of all merchants to enjoy "safe and secure" entry and exit from the country without being burdened by "evil tolls," reiterated a range of precepts of the commercial moral syndrome. Among them were easy collaboration with strangers and aliens, competition, encouragement of initiative and enterprise, openness to inventiveness and novelty, investing for productive purposes, industriousness, thriftiness, and optimism.

The authors of the Magna Carta may have been mainly feudal aristocrats with prowess in warfare whose attitudes were largely informed by the guardian syndrome, but clause 40 shows their insistence on preserving the integrity of the commercial syndrome.

Although no one in 1215 was thinking in terms of the moral syndromes that serve as the ethical foundations of the two ways of making a living, Saire de Quincey, Robert Fitz Walter, and their comrades-in-arms apparently understood the fraught consequences when "guardians," such as King John, offered to peddle justice to the highest bidder ("To no one will we sell, to no one will be refuse or delay, right or justice"). Seen in the context of the thirteenth century, many of the other clauses of the Magna Carta were injunctions aimed at banning the trade of right or justice. For example, clause 36 stated, "Nothing in future shall be given or taken for a writ of inquisition of life or limbs, but freely it shall be granted."

The Magna Carta barons' labors to establish the rule of law were fruitful because they were reacting against a despotic sovereign who had challenged them with a comprehensive array of wrongs to be righted. King John and the other Angevin rulers had thoroughly compromised the ethical foundations of governance, turning the kingship into an example of what Jane Jacobs calls "a monstrous hybrid."

Her signal modern example of a monstrous hybrid is the late, unlamented Soviet Union. When commerce is organized according to guardian values, you get disaster. She writes that guardian economic planning leads to emphasis on guardian priorities. Because production and trade are not part of the syndrome, the commerce involved becomes corrupted, while its moral foundations are ruined. The consequences can be disastrous whether the economy is placed at the disposal of central planners at Gosplan (the USSR State Planning Commission), central planners at the Federal Reserve Board, or legions of private extortionists and crony capitalists.

Not the least difficulty arising from growing political domination of the economy is the fact that it is associated with increasingly pervasive dishonesty, as per the political precept "deceive for the sake of the task."

Make-Believe Well-Being

You can follow the statistical trail etched by increasing political domination of the US economy. It is manifested in the escalating corruption and data fiddling that understate inflation, overstate economic growth, and seriously undercount unemployment. There could hardly be a better, more succinct summary of the misreporting of US economic data today than that provided by Mikhail Gorbachev in a speech in the last days of the Soviet Union, in which he complained that "the world of day-to-day realities and that of make-believe well-being were increasingly parting ways."[12]

Lies, rather than truth, are precisely what you should expect when the political portion of a mixed economy becomes predominant. Honesty is a precept of the commercial syndrome. It is not solely a Western convention, as Jacobs reminds us, but a requirement for the success of commerce in every human culture.

Why do government statisticians lie and fabricate good news in an economy when growth has stalled? Because they are influenced by the governing guardian moral syndrome, where loyalty to the system and the willingness to "deceive for the sake of the task" are prized precepts. They lie to deceive you, to "simulate"—even if not necessarily to stimulate recovery—because political viability depends upon it. And the lies themselves have an effect on economic activity.

When you can be convinced that economic growth is accelerating, your job and business are secure, and prosperity will soon accelerate, you are more likely to spend and invest. The same can be said of others. Property developers will launch new projects. Retailers will accumulate inventories they expect to be purchased by newly solvent consumers. If politicians and their loyal lackeys in the Bureau of Labor Statistics can convince you that political management of the economy is more effective than it really is, the result is likely to be at least a temporary uptick in economic activity. People will spend more, borrow more, accumulate more inventories, and invest in more marginal undertakings than they would do if the president held a news conference and patiently explained that, no, there has been no real recovery from the Great Recession—it was all a statistical illusion fabricated by fiddling inflation measures.

The evolution of a heavily indebted centralized state with pure fiat money has led almost inevitably to a departure from the rule of law. Fiat money gives central bankers, like former chair of the Federal Reserve Ben Bernanke and current chair of the Federal Reserve Janet Yellen, almost unlimited power over your finances, including the power to dilute your future by counterfeiting trillions of dollars out of thin air, much of which is lavished on politically connected big banks that are "too big to fail."

That is OK where the authorities are concerned, because in their eyes you are just another neofeudal debt serf.

The Too-Big-to-Fail Metamessage

The breakdown of the rule of law could itself be a trigger of collapse. This is the metamessage inherent in "too-big-to-fail" crony capitalism. The authorities do not tell you overtly that we are close to collapse. But their policy of diluting your future, by spending trillions from an empty pocket to bail out leveraged "too-big-to-fail" institutions, speaks loudly. It tells you that the authorities believe the economy is so fragile that unless they indenture you to keep the gag going, at almost any price, it would collapse.

That is why they resort to financial repression, robbing you with near-zero interest rates, to subsidize banks and debt-driven consumption. As reported by Henny Sender in the *Financial Times*, a calculation by Swiss Re in 2015 suggested that US savers were robbed of $470 billion in interest income after the collapse of Lehman Brothers due to the Fed's ZIRP and financial repression.[13] They conjured tens of billions a month out of thin air to purchase Treasury issues to finance deficit spending that does not pay its way—the Keynesian pretense notwithstanding.

The more meager the results from ever-greater amounts of debt "stimulus," the more desperate they become. Since 2000, the explicit national debt has almost tripled to $17 trillion. But this is fine with the authorities. They want to "invest" more. They plan to double the debt again to keep the bogus measures of GDP inching higher. For what? The metastasizing debt has stimulated a meager $2.4 trillion growth in GDP from 2000 through 2013. And of course, even this meager growth rate of 1.5 percent is exaggerated.

Diluted Statistical Fantasies

We explore elsewhere how intentionally understated inflation exaggerates real GDP growth. Now the US Bureau of Economic Analysis (BEA) has outdone itself in proclaiming statistical fantasies. As part of its 2013 revision to the way it calculates GDP, the government will no longer tally pension funding as it is allocated to retirement accounts, which are included as "wages" in the GDP calculations. Instead of actual cash outlays, the BEA will now count corporate promises to someday, maybe, fund pensions.

What can you learn from the lies that the government tells you?

Don't throw up your hands and walk away. There is a meta-message hidden in the statistical fabrications. The authorities' anxieties to exaggerate GDP growth should not be overlooked. They tell you that the whole debt-financed system is predicated upon growth. Without GDP growth, the rapidly compounding debts and unfunded liabilities become unpayable. The whole system threatens to topple over like a bicycle reduced to crawl speed.

For a hint of how unstable the system is, you need only glance at the FY2012 US government budget deficit as calculated according to GAAP.[14] It hit $6.9 trillion that year against a GDP of $13.67 trillion. In other words, the federal government's GAAP deficit was just a bit above 50 percent of GDP. To truly balance the budget for the year would have required a tax hike of an impossible 50 percent of GDP. To grow out of the debt would require an equivalently impossible acceleration in the rate of growth. No major economy has ever grown as fast as the threshold growth rate required to approach solvency for the US government given its obligations.

Without growth, it becomes ever more obvious that people in the bottom 95 percent of the income distribution face a bleak future of neofeudal debt servitude. In a system where fiat money is borrowed into existence, slow growth is the other side of the coin to debt serfdom. The economy grows on expanding debt and cannot survive without it. Its prospects, and yours, certainly don't seem bright in a circumstance like now, in which powerful groups position themselves to grab the biggest possible slice of a shrinking economic pie.

No Recovery for the Middle Class

All the quantitative easing and other desperate measures to goose ever-diminishing returns to growth have amplified the gap between the owners of financial assets and the long-lost American middle class.

As Izabella Kaminska of the *Financial Times* wrote in the May 16, 2013, issue of *FT Alphaville*, even though housing and equities may have recovered, a large portion of the United States, specifically younger adults, has been disenfranchised from the economy.[15] QE propped up the financial sector, but for the economy to truly recover, much of the liquidity that's been created needs to be redirected to those people who have been frozen out of the economy.

What you see at work here is the shuffle and divide of people responding to a dying economy that is approaching peak consumption. The top 5 percent, the owners of the economy's financial and productive assets, continues to pursue the

American Dream of the good life. Meanwhile, increasing numbers among the bottom 95 percent have failed to keep pace by substituting debt for income in the attempt to maintain consumption. Now many are giving up. Suicide rates are higher than in the Great Depression. People are responding by the million to the demoralizing prospect of debt serfdom by dropping out.

Paradoxically, the first effect of mass dropouts from the labor force has been to reinforce the illusion of recovery. When the labor force shrivels, the authorities can pretend that the unemployment rate fell because fewer people were looking for work. But note that the long-term stability of the parasitic state, which depends upon taxes paid from the proceeds of debt-based growth, is called into question when the dropout rate rises too quickly. That is exactly what has been happening.

Since January 2009, ten people have dropped out for each person who was added to the labor force. In March 2013 alone, 663,000 persons left the labor force, bringing the total of working age adult Americans outside the workforce to an all-time high of 89,967,000.[16] That number has continued to soar.

This is why the average American adult spent just 3.57 hours out of every 24 on work and work-related activities, according to the Bureau of Labor Statistics American Time Survey. Americans as a group spend more than twice as much time sleeping as we do working. No wonder the US economy is crawling along at stall speed.

Part and parcel of an unprecedented decline in the labor force is a huge surge in the number of Americans claiming disability. Every month, 14 million people now get disability checks from the government. Since 2008, far more people have been placed on disability entitlements than in jobs. I see the surging labor force dropout rate, with millions claiming disability, mostly for back pain and mental illness—health problems that are the most subjective and easily fiddled—as rational responses by low-income people facing dead-end life prospects.

Should You Flee?

When the Roman Empire was in the throes of collapse, a question frequently asked of soothsayers by the newly impoverished was, "Should I flee?" They literally ran for the hills rather than stay put and go broke paying oppressive taxes. Today, there seems to be no place to flee, but millions have contrived to drop out by faking backaches and hallucinations. I see this as symptomatic of the breakdown of the rule of law and another trigger of the Breaking Point.

As Joseph A. Tainter reports in *The Collapse of Complex Societies*, a review of the historic record shows that complex social systems are prone to collapse when the marginal return on investments in complexity deteriorate. Tainter reviewed the collapse of seventeen past civilizations, with special focus on the Western Roman Empire. According to Tainter, after a complex society reaches a stage of declining marginal returns, the mathematical likelihood of collapse in due time increases. He pointed out that if Rome had not been taken over by Germanic tribes, another group would have eventually overthrown the city later on. While marginal returns on investment are growing, however, societies might be able to survive. His point is that societal collapse occurs under stress, when organizational change becomes a necessity. Therefore, collapse can be an economical alternative and is not intrinsically catastrophic—it is a rational process that may benefit a large portion of the population.

Rightly understood, the current crony capitalist system, embodying the dilution of your future through financial repression and QE, represents at least a perversion, if not the total abandonment, of the rule of law. Within the foreseeable future, the pronounced dropout trend will precipitate a crisis. Even if the authorities try to continue "kicking the can down the road," the road the United States has followed over the last half century is a dead end. That's why you need to be alert, stay safe, and prepare for the Breaking Point before the sweep of events makes that impossible.

Notes

1 http://www.bl.uk/magna-carta/articles/magna-carta-english-translation.

2 Heward, Edmund, *Lord Denning: A Biography* (London: George Weidenfeld & Nicolson, 1990), 10.

3 Comment by radio host Tavis Smiley, perhaps quoting the title of the book by Christine Mace and Mark Temkin.

4 Kern, Fritz, *Kingship and Law in the Middle Ages*, trans. S. B. Chrimes (Oxford, 1956), 127–29.

5 Turley, Jonathan, "Nixon Has Won Watergate: Barack Obama's Imperial Presidency Is Just What His Controversial Predecessor Wanted," *USA Today*, March 26, 2013.

6 Milbank, Dana, "In AP, Rosen Investigations, Government Makes Criminals of Reporters," *Washington Post*, May 21, 2013.

7 See http://rsf.org/index2014/en-index2014.php#.

8 See http://www.aclu.org/blog/technology-and-liberty-national-security/irs-says-it-will-respect-4th-amendment-regard-email.

9 http://www.globalresearch.ca/top-constitutional-experts-obama-is-worse-than-nixon/5335177.

10 See Ferguson, Niall, *The Great Degeneration: How Institutions Decay and Economies Die* (New York: Penguin, 2013).

11 Jacobs, Jane, *Systems of Survival: A Dialogue on the Moral Foundations of Commerce and Politics* (New York: Vintage Books, 1994).

12 Quoted in Jacobs, *Systems of Survival*, 99–100.

13 Sender, Henny, "Weak Growth Suggests QE Might Not Have Been Worth the Costs," *Financial Times*, April 12, 2015.

14 Williams, John, "ALERT GAAP-Based U.S. Budget Deficit," *Shadow Government Statistics* 496 (January 17, 2013).

15 http://ftalphaville.ft.com/2013/05/16/.

16 http://www.zerohedge.com/news/2013-04-05/people-not-labor-force-soar-663000-90-million-labor-force-participation-rate-1979-le.

Chapter Eight

FATCA, Dumb, and Happy

What the "Worst Law Most Americans Have Never Heard of" Means to You

Our ancestors . . . possessed a right, which nature has given to all men . . . of departing from the country in which chance, not choice, has placed them, of going in quest of new habitations, and of there establishing new societies, under such laws and regulations as, to them, shall seem . . . most likely to promote public happiness.
—Thomas Jefferson, 1774

As 2014 drew near, financial institutions around the world busied themselves closing the accounts of Americans. Know it or not, if you are an American, you are now among the lepers of world finance. Thanks to Obama's Foreign Account Tax Compliance Act (FATCA) enacted in 2010, by many accounts "the worst law most Americans have never heard of," it will henceforth be practically impossible for you to live or do business in any jurisdiction outside of the United States.[1]

CNN Money reported the story in September 2013, stating that, in light of the new act, banks around the world had begun telling their US customers to take their money elsewhere. The act aimed to recoup hundreds of billions of dollars that the United States lost each year from tax evasion, but many international banks decided they'd be better off losing US customers than having to comply with the new complicated law. The law would require every foreign financial institution in the world to contract directly with the IRS to supply detailed information on the accounts of US persons, with estimated costs of hundreds of millions of dollars each for a large financial institution (totaling up to $1 trillion worldwide). Some Canadian firms put the estimated aggregate compliance costs as high as $2 trillion, an estimate endorsed by the US Chamber of Commerce. "Estimates for implementing the information-collection measures demanded by FATCA run into hundreds of millions of dollars each for a large financial institution and in aggregate up to $1 trillion worldwide."[2]

A lot of money. Make no mistake about it, this is not just another installment in penny ante "financial repression." This is a full, East German–style lockdown. It is remarkable in many ways.

For one thing, FATCA applies to all foreign financial institutions everywhere on the globe. No valid legal theory has been advanced for applying US law in other jurisdictions. Also note, not a single provision of FATCA targets actual tax evasion activity. You might be tempted to suppose that this policy is targeted to ensnare ultrawealthy Americans who selfishly calculate that the costs they pay for the US government far exceed what it is worth. Not so.

By the way, I hasten to say that I am not one who makes the immense concession that people forfeit their rights by becoming successful. If FATCA were aimed only at billionaires or centimillionaires, it would still be a gross violation of human rights, as lucidly envisioned by Thomas Jefferson in the time when he was building up the courage to draft the Declaration of Independence. But FATCA is not aimed at billionaires. The government already knows who they are.

It is aimed at you.

You have heard demagogues in Congress fulminate about the rare instances where billionaires have renounced US citizenship and gained tremendous tax savings as a result. This was the case when Eduardo Saverin, a Brazilian-born entrepreneur immortalized in the movie *The Social Network*, renounced his

US citizenship after having moved to Singapore. (Many billionaires are only too keen to stay in the United States because that is the best way of conserving crony capitalist privileges—subsidies, contracts, and regulations—procured through investments in politics. Politicians don't want billionaires to flee the country because they would lose their best customers.)

Mr. Saverin, who cofounded Facebook, was never involved politically, beyond inspiring the rage of Democratic Senators Chuck Schumer and Bob Casey. Their apoplexy over Mr. Saverin's timely escape approached the intensity of the late East German president Walter Ulbricht's denunciations of "the moral backwardness and depravity" of unpatriotic East German emigrants who found their way over and around Ulbricht's "Anti-Fascist Protection Rampart," a.k.a. the Berlin Wall.[3]

Of course, Ulbricht was hardly renowned as a lucid economic analyst. In fact, the head of Stalin's secret police, Lavrentiy Beria, once described Ulbricht as "the greatest idiot that he had ever seen."[4] Beria never knew Senators Schumer and Casey.

Given that it is impractical for a bankrupt country to build an actual Berlin Wall, which would have to be 19,577 miles long to physically seal off US borders, Schumer and Casey want to create a virtual wall that makes it practically impossible for anyone to escape their clutches.

To that end, they announced a new bill called the Ex-PATRIOT Act, which would reimpose taxes on expatriates, like Saverin, even after they left the United States and began residing in another country. As *Forbes* reported in May 2012, the bill would presume that individuals with a net worth more than $2 million, or an average income tax liability of at least $148,000 over the last five years, are attempting to avoid taxes by renouncing their citizenship. These people would have to prove to the IRS that this was not the case or they would risk additional capital gains tax on future investment gains. That shows you what they think of the bargain they have created for US subjects.

The arrogance of these guys knows no bounds. They not only betray the principles of human rights so clearly articulated by Thomas Jefferson, frequently hailed as the founder of the Democratic Party, but they are apparently intent on repeating a policy that history shows has never worked. It didn't work for East Germany. It didn't work for the Roman Empire. It won't work for America, either.

It isn't enough that a man like Eduardo Saverin pays the US government hundreds of millions of dollars in taxes for which he receives literally nothing in exchange. The politicians know that no one in his right mind would shell out hundreds of millions of dollars for the pleasure of supporting their handiwork. That is why they favor an East German–style lockdown to make you the vassal of their superstate.

"Is My Flight to Be Stopped?"

FATCA, exit taxes, postexit taxes, and restrictions on expatriation are modern-day analogs to the tax reforms of Diocletian, the Roman emperor who ruled from AD 284 to AD 305. These reflected the unhappy fact that the Roman Empire had essentially declared bankruptcy and placed the burden of its inability to pay its debts on its citizens. Strangely, the Roman state grew even bigger and commanded larger military forces after it essentially went broke. The Empire imposed heavier taxes while conscripting citizens' labor and regulating their lives and occupations. This state's goal—beyond all else—was the survival of the state, and its leaders were willing to subdue individual interests and levy the empire's resources to this end.

While prosperity ebbed, and the people suffered, Diocletian escalated state spending tremendously. He increased the size of the army by as much as 50 percent, from 400,000 men when he took office to between 500,000 and 600,000. Diocletian also greatly expanded the bureaucracy, doubling it during his two decades in office. It merits mention that a contributing factor to the economic decline of the empire was natural cyclical cooling of the climate, which significantly reduced temperatures. Palaeoclimatic evidence reveals that average summer temperatures during the peak of the Roman Warm Period during the first century AD were on average 0.60 °C (1.08 °F) warmer relative to the current period (1951–1980 mean).[5] Warmer weather made for greater agricultural prosperity. The Roman economy was based 80 percent on farming, so warmer weather and the bumper crops it produced made it easier for Romans to pay high tax levies. But after the middle of the first century, the climate began to cool gradually, and agricultural production accordingly fell. This put farmers under great stress because they were taxed according to the productivity of their land during the earlier warm period. In many cases, the annual tax due exceeded the full value of the crop as yields fell by the end of the third century (the reign of Diocletian). Faced with ruinous taxes they could not pay, many small farmers sought to abandon their fields and run away. This prompted Diocletian to push the peasantry on the way toward feudalism by fastening people to their jobs. *The Cambridge Ancient History*, volume 12, first edition, explains:

> When things had gone so far, it was impossible to turn back; all that remained was to follow the road to the end. This meant guarding against a general flight, announcing compulsory labor, and binding all classes—or at least all who did not belong to a privileged caste—to their professions, the peasant farmer to his land and forced labor, the state employed worker to his workshop, the trader, including the *navicularius*, to his business or his Corporation, the small property-owner to his duties in connection with liturgies, a large property-owner to the curia, the soldier to his military service, and so on.[6]

Farmers, in particular, were prohibited from changing careers when confiscatory taxes made it ruinously unprofitable to stay in business. Those who tried to escape faced enslavement, even execution. Again, as reported in *The Cambridge Ancient History:*

> The full rigor of the law was let loose on the population. Soldiers acted as bailiffs or wandered as secret police through the land. Those who suffered most were, of course, the propertied class. . . . In connection with all this, compulsion and state-socialist regulation had established themselves more firmly. . . . Arrest, confiscation, and execution hung over their heads like a sword of Damocles . . . If the propertied classes buried their money, or sacrificed two-thirds of their estate to escape from a magistracy, or went so far as to give up their whole property in order to get free of the domains rent, and the non-propertied class ran away, the state replied by increasing the pressure. . . . In the petitions to the Emperor the threat of flight is the "ultimate refugium" and among the common questions which used to be put to an Oracle in Egypt three standard types were: "Am I to become a beggar?"[7]

As explained in *The Cambridge Ancient History*, volume 12, once the empire had gotten to a certain point, it became impossible to turn back. The state leaders felt a need to lock down a potentially fleeing population, and they therefore created a system of forced labor, binding people to their professions by law. Apart from members of the privileged castes, the peasant farmers were forced to stick to land and labor, the soldiers to the military, the traders to their businesses, and so on.[8]

Farmers, in particular, were prohibited from changing careers when confiscatory taxes made it ruinously unprofitable to stay in business. Those who tried to escape faced enslavement, even execution. Soldiers patrolled the land as bailiffs

and secret police. Those who suffered most were the prop-
ertied class, with arrest, confiscation, and execution hanging
over their heads. As the nonpropertied class ran away, the
state responded with increased pressure. Fears of destitution
caused many more to flee, and three common questions could
be heard throughout the land: "Am I to become a beggar?"
"Shall I take to flight?" and "Is my flight to be stopped?"

As was the case with ancient Rome, and more recently with
East Germany, the danger to the state intent upon squeezing
the population to the last drop does not turn on the escape of
a single tycoon. Yes, Obama and his commissariat, including
Senators Schumer and Casey, want to limit the freedom of
thirty-year-old billionaires like Eduardo Saverin, but it isn't
just billionaires they are after. They want every thirty-year-old
man to be a slave to Obamacare.

What has them scared is mounting evidence that Americans today are at least as smart as East Germans were half a
century ago. Ulbricht built the Berlin Wall after 3.5 million
East Germans had escaped. Obama started erecting his virtual Berlin Wall to imprison you with FATCA at the first hint
that large numbers of productive Americans were fleeing the
country.

You see, it is the millions of productive middle-class Americans who have recently escaped the United States, or are edging
toward the exits, that have the government most worried. While
the news has been full of reports for years about illegal immigration into the United States, the news media have been largely
silent about the growing exodus from the United States.

In the first decade of the twenty-first century, annual in-
migration into the United States from Mexico, both legal and
illegal, fell by more than 80 percent. And recent data show
that the number of Mexican migrants and their families returning to Mexico outnumbered those coming north into the
United States.

The many other Americans who have chosen to leave include legions of Anglo retirees decamping to a country where

their nest eggs go further. As reported in the July/August 2013 *Chartist* article, "Why So Many Americans Are Leaving the US in 1 Big Chart," seniors in the fortieth income percentile in the United States would be in the ninetieth income percentile in Mexico.[9]

The Association of Americans Resident Overseas suggests that there was a surge of persons leaving the United States after the onset of the Great Recession. This was implicitly confirmed by a State Department calculation that surfaced at about the time FATCA legislation was enacted. It concluded that some 1.34 million Americans had gone abroad and "fallen off the radar."[10] As one report put it, if Americans living abroad stopped paying their taxes, visiting the United States, and using embassy or counselor services, they would no longer be officially counted.

The "Great Escape"

Polling data show a startling surge in the number of Americans, especially younger Americans (aged twenty-five to thirty-four), who are planning to leave the United States. A 2011 survey conducted by Zogby found that an astonishing six million young Americans either had left the United States or were already packing their bags and planning to do so. Contrary to the myth that only billionaires could appreciate the logic of expatriating, the survey found that the largest percentage of those considering leaving was making $50,000 per year or less.

Is this really a surprise? Median American income earners do not need to read the fine print in the *New York Times* to realize that life in the United States has become a dead end for people like them. If they did read it, they would have seen in a fall 2012 article, "The Uncomfortable Truth about American Wages," that since 1970, the real earnings of the median male have declined by 19 percent—the median man in 2010 earned as much as the median man did in 1964. From 1970 to 2010, earnings for the median man with a high school diploma and no further schooling fell by 41 percent.[11]

Such is the pedigree of Obama's proletariat.

It is little wonder that millions of young American men are looking for opportunities elsewhere. The good news is that many have found success outside the United States. That is what Obama wants to stop.

Coley Hudgins wrote in "The Great American Migration," of his firsthand observations in Latin America that a steady influx of younger Americans were setting up shop, starting families, and having children. They weren't working for international businesses, nor were they even obtaining work visas. Instead, they were creating new jobs to fill niches lacking in their host countries or acting as consultants (who can work from anywhere with an Internet connection). Hudgins went on to point out that many foreign governments, recognizing the potential of this knowledge transfer, are now responding by easing immigration and residency policies for entrepreneurs and job creators. "What all of this demonstrates," Hudgins wrote, "is that even in bad times Americans' unquenchable appetite for risk, opportunity and economic freedom is the same as it's always been."[12]

Bob Adams, who has written about "The Great Escape" for *Barrons*, says that nearly 40 percent of young Americans (aged eighteen to twenty-four) are thinking about leaving the United States to seek opportunity abroad. An incredible 5.1 percent of Americans aged twenty-five to thirty-four are in the planning stages for relocation, including 3.1 percent of all American men. This represents more than a fivefold increase from 2009. Note also that 26.2 percent of Americans aged twenty-five to thirty-four are not working.[13] The *New York Times* put this in perspective in May 2013, stating that the United States' percentage of young adults without jobs had surpassed much of Europe's. Furthermore, among large, wealthy economies, between 2001 and 2013, the United States went from having the highest share of employed twenty-five- to thirty-four-year-olds to having among the lowest.[14]

As detailed by the Population Reference Bureau, by 2011, 5.9 million young adults in the United States had moved back home with their parents, including 18.6 percent of American men aged twenty-five to thirty-four.[15]

These are the people whom Obama wishes to lock down. He needs them to stay in the United States to subscribe to Obamacare. The fact that young men are more likely to depart than young women is particularly subversive of Obamacare. Obama needs all the men he can force under his thumb. They are crucial to the success of Obamacare. He needs them to buy expensive insurance cover for maternity care. Sounds like a joke, but it is true.

Contrary to the bland presumption that young people are enthusiastic partisans of Obama's corporatist Affordable Care Act, a survey conducted by Harvard University's Institute of Politics showed that 57 percent of young people between the ages of eighteen and twenty-nine disapprove of Obamacare, and large pluralities believe it will increase costs and worsen health care in the United States.[16] They are right.

It is notable that among the more popular destinations for American expatriates, Costa Rica enjoys higher life expectancy than the United States for both men and women. Yet per capita medical outlays in Costa Rica are just $1,197 annually. Even before Obamacare, US health care costs were $8,233 per capita—almost seven times higher than in Costa Rica, where private health insurance runs from $60 to $130 per month. (According to the IRS, it will cost a family of four a minimum of $20,000 a year for health insurance—$1,667 per month—not to mention the additional costs imposed by a minimum of twenty new taxes imposed by Obamacare.)[17]

I should mention that Costa Rica's distinction in enjoying a higher life expectancy than the United States is nothing special. I used the example of Costa Rica because as a resident of South Florida I am importuned with radio advertisements urging me to become a medical tourist in Costa Rica. Despite the fact that the United States spends incomparably more than anyone else on sick care, the United States ranks forty-third in the CIA's table of world life expectancy.[18]

Fifty years ago, the United States enjoyed the world's highest life expectancy by far. That was then. In the meantime, the triumph of corporatism left the United States with a health care system dedicated to the interests of insurance companies and the purveyors of pharmaceutical and medical devices rather than patients.

Note that the health care situation in the United States exquisitely illustrates what is meant by the phrase "fat, dumb, and happy." Fat, we are. According to a calculation published in *Forbes* in 2007, 74.1 percent of American adults are medically overweight or obese.[19] A 2012 report from the Trust for America's Health and the Robert Wood Johnson Foundation projected that unless Americans change their habits, half of US adults will be obese by 2030.[20] Considering that we are content to let ourselves be fleeced by one of the world's most expensive health care systems, we seem to be happy not being very smart.

It is perhaps no coincidence that apart from Japan, all of the areas with the very highest life expectancies—greater than eighty-two years—are city-states or minijurisdictions. Top of the list is the Principality of Monaco, with a composite life expectancy of 89.68 years. Also at the top of the table are Macau, Singapore, San Marino, Andorra, Guernsey, and Hong Kong. I see the fact that city-states are leading the world in both prosperity and life expectancy as a strong hint that when the US imperium finally comes to an end, the world system is destined to be reconfigured with city-states playing a leading role.

Meanwhile, an important new facet of the Costa Rican economy is medical tourism. Patients from the United States fly to Costa Rica for expensive dental procedures, such as implants. They also come for a whole range of surgical procedures in private Costa Rican hospitals. These are performed at an average of 70 percent cost savings as compared to the United States.

I don't suggest that such savings are available only in Costa Rica by some quirk of that country's health care system. An Organisation for Economic Co-operation and Development (OECD) report from 2008 concluded that the potential savings between US inpatient prices and other countries range from a 75 percent to 90 percent reduction in price depending on the type of the procedure and location.[21] The report also found that cost was not necessarily the main driver, suggesting that "availability and quality are the major factors for many medical tourists." This helps explain why many American retirees move to Costa Rica and elsewhere, notwithstanding the fact that Medicare benefits are restricted by an absurd requirement that they are not payable outside the United States (where costs are dramatically lower).

This restriction, like Obamacare itself, is a crony capitalist confection that guarantees you must pay the world's highest costs for medical care. It is also a barrier blocking the expatriation of retirees. Before FATCA, many of the private hospitals and dental practices in Costa Rica had been owned and managed by Americans. That law, however, had made it increasingly difficult for American entrepreneurs to operate or live abroad. I have found with my own humble entrepreneurial efforts that most foreign banks will no longer open accounts for companies with which I am affiliated, much less for my personal use.

For example, in the years since Obama has been in the White House, I have incorporated two private companies doing business in Brazil. The first of these became a public company. It took the better part of a year to assemble the "Know Your Customer" paperwork formalities to launch this enterprise. The second company began life as a joint venture with the largest insurance company in Brazil to provide safe transit within that country for incoming tourists and businesspeople. I thought the World Cup and the Olympics, following in 2016, created a great opportunity for such an enterprise. My German partner and I initially incorporated our enterprise in the British Virgin Islands, historically an excellent jurisdiction for companies that have no particular business nexus in the United States.

Ours was obviously a real company, formed by seasoned entrepreneurs in conjunction with a blue-chip, 7.7 billion reais ($4.3 billion) Brazilian company. Yet to my amazement, it took us almost all of 2013 to locate an offshore bank that would open a commercial account for our enterprise. We were repeatedly told that even if our business grew to be highly successful, opening an account for us could not be lucrative for banks—normal banking fees would not offset the exorbitant costs they expected to suffer due to harassment by the US government. This harassment was expected simply because I hold a US passport. (My German partner had no particular relish for subjecting our enterprise to US corporate taxation at some of the highest rates in the world when we did not even plan to conduct business in the United States.)

Bizarrely, a government that would be first in line with its hand out to seize a share of any profits I managed to make was preventing the business from getting off the ground in the first place. This reflects a sharp departure from the past. Through the end of the last century, it was relatively simple for an American to start a foreign business. I had experience in doing so as I helped launch about a dozen natural resource companies outside the United States. We did business all over the globe—from Africa, to South America, to Asia.

In those days, incorporating a company and opening a bank account could be done in a single day, in a matter of hours. No longer. Former president George W. Bush went a long way toward gumming up the channels of entrepreneurship with the so-called Patriot Act, one of the more pernicious pieces of legislation ever conceived.

Although ostensibly aimed to counter terrorism, it really marked a momentous shift in the nature of the American experience. From that point forward, you were guilty until proven innocent. The shift of the security state's focus away from defense against other states as enemies to nongovernmental organizations such as al-Qaeda—those that do not exercise a recognized monopoly of force over any territory—became a de facto death knell for freedom.

This was most evident when you traveled. Going through an airport, you were presumed to be a terrorist intent upon a suicidal act of sabotage until government agents scrutinized your laptop, your shoes, your belt, and every piece of lint in your pockets. The extremes to which the government has gone in the name of security have given the force of law to a lot of nonsense.

To the best of my knowledge, there is no record of any Episcopalian Baby Boomer like myself ever even attempting an act of terrorism. But this doesn't matter to a government intent on treating all of its own subjects as potential enemies. Even old ladies in walkers have been made to crawl through x-ray machines as if they were Osama bin Laden clones. I still chuckle when I recall my then eight-year-old daughter's remarks after she was taken aside for frisking as we went through an airport in 2002. "Dad, what is the matter with these people? Are they too stupid to see that I'm a child?"

Unfortunately, yes. The conceit that any and every American is equally likely to be a "terrorist" rationalizes the cancellation of your constitutional rights and your innate rights as a human being, as so brilliantly articulated by Thomas Jefferson (see the Declaration of Independence, as well as the passage quoted at the top of this chapter).

Big Brother Is Watching

Once upon a time, the United States was a free country. No longer. If you still think of the United States as a free country, it is time you updated your perceptions. Go to Amazon or the library (you can find it on Google Maps) and get a copy of George Orwell's classic 1949 novel, *Nineteen Eighty-Four*.

Set in a backwater province of a future superstate in a world of perpetual war and omnipresent government, *Nineteen Eighty-Four* details the story of an everyman character, Winston Smith, as he wriggles under the thumb of a dystopian tyrant, Big Brother. You'll see if you read the story again that Big Brother is almost a libertarian in comparison to Barack Obama.

According to a 2013 article in *The Guardian*, German Chancellor Angela Merkel told President Obama in a heated discussion that spying by NSA was similar to that undertaken by the Stasi, the secret police of the former East Germany.[22] Julia Angwin, who reports on security issues for the *Wall Street Journal*, went further. In a radio interview with WNYC, she said, "The US surveillance regime has more data on the average American than the Stasi ever did on East Germans."[23] In fact, the US government is compiling more information on you and other Americans than Stalin had on Russians, Hitler on German citizens, or any other government has ever collected on its people.

This includes the capture and storage of virtually every telephone call you make, records of all your purchases and savings down to the penny, email, text messages, Internet searches, social media communications, health details, employment history, travel, and student records. Everything. The government is spying on virtually everything you do.

According to the authoritative German magazine *Spiegel*, the National Security Agency (NSA) has a fifty-page catalog of "backdoor penetration techniques" that it employs to spy on you.[24] Digital security expert Jacob Applebaum, who helped *Spiegel* prepare its revelations, detailed how the NSA uses software known as "Dropout Jeep" to implant software on your Apple devices. This software enables the government to remotely retrieve your contact list, listen to your voicemail, locate you, capture your camera, retrieve your SMS files, and do dragnets on all your log-ins and passwords. They can turn on the microphone on your iPhone remotely and listen to any private conversation you hold in the vicinity of your cellphone, even if you are not making a call.

According to Bill Binney—a thirty-two-year veteran former top spy at the NSA who created the agency's mass surveillance program for digital information—the US government is collecting 100 billion emails per day and 20 trillion communications all told. As reported in an interview with Binney by the *WashingtonBlog* in 2013, if you land on the government's "enemies list," that stored information will be used to target you.[25] If the government decides it "doesn't like" you, it analyzes the collected data on you and your associates over the prior ten years to build a case against you.

More ominously, Binney explained that the NSA shares its collected information with federal, state, and local agencies that then use that information to prosecute petty crimes, such as drugs and taxes. The agencies are instructed by the NSA to claim they received this information in a more legitimate way while hiding its source from defense attorneys and judges. Binney concluded that the government use of data collected through spying is "a totalitarian process."[26]

All the data that are being collected on you are not just being stored for some potentially menacing use in the future. You wish. Some government bureau or agency could be targeting you right now.

And remember, if they decide they want to get you for something, they can.

You Unknowingly Committed Three Felonies Today

The number of laws and regulations in the United States is literally beyond counting. According to the *CCH Standard Federal Tax Reporter*, in 2013, it took 73,954 regular 8½ × 11 sheets of paper to spell out the US federal tax code. A 2011 report in the *Wall Street Journal*, "Many Failed Efforts to Count Nation's Federal Criminal Laws," estimated that there are 10,000 to 300,000 regulations that can carry the force of federal criminal law. Experts believe that if you are like the average adult, you unknowingly commit about three felonies a day.

The *Journal* also quoted John Baker, a retired Louisiana State University law professor who had tried counting the number of new federal crimes created in recent years, as saying, "There is no one in the United States over the age of 18 who cannot be indicted for some federal crime. That is not an exaggeration."

Lavrentiy Beria, the head of Stalin's secret police, famously bragged, "Show me the man and I will find the crime."[27] That is now easier for the US government since they have your every act recorded and filed away to use against you. If by some happy turn of fate, you were the rare person who could not be indicted and incarcerated for committing some infraction forbidden by the many unintelligible laws proliferated in the United States, the Obama administration has secured the legal authorization to jail you without charge, without trial, and without a day in court. The 2012 National Defense Authorization Act (NDAA), sections 1021 and 1022, authorizes the indefinite military detention of any person even suspected of an affiliation with terrorism.

The government under Obama has gone to great lengths to expand the definition of "terrorist"; it is no longer someone convicted of blowing up buildings or trying to sabotage airplanes in flight. The government's updated definition of "terrorism" includes anyone suspected of thinking for herself or himself—you for instance.

Multiple documents from the FBI, the Department of Homeland Security, the Department of Defense, and other agencies broaden the concept of terrorist to include people who are "reverent of individual liberty," "suspicious of centralized authority," and "anti-federalists."[28] Such individuals, like you, might be inclined to oppose whatever benighted measures the government intends to impose on the United States in the wake of the coming economic collapse.

If you've ever said anything in a telephone conversation or written anything in an email that betrays an inclination to think for yourself, you are a candidate for imprisonment without trial because the government can't be sure you will go along with the gag. And remember, they have been listening to all your conversations and reading all your emails, combing through them for keywords and phrases that hint you may be disgruntled with the status quo. If they found any, then you could be on Obama's list of undependable persons.

If you believe in anything enough to have mentioned it, you may be a target. If you were against the wars in Iraq or Afghanistan or expressed an opinion against bombing Syria, if you're a Constitutionalist or a Ron Paul supporter, if you are opposed to GMO foods, if you expressed sympathy for the Tea Party or Occupy Wall Street, whether Democrat or Republican—you could be on their terrorist list.

Believe it or not, complaining about the quality of your tap water could be interpreted as an act of terrorism. According to a June 2013 *Network World* article, when more than one hundred residents of Mount Pleasant, Tennessee, complained that children were becoming ill from drinking the local tap water, they were cautioned by Sherwin Smith, deputy director of Tennessee Department of Environment and Conservation's Division of Water Resources, "We take water quality very seriously. Very, very seriously. But you need to make sure that when you make water quality complaints you have a basis, because federally, if there's no water quality issues, that can be considered under Homeland Security an act of terrorism."[29]

In other words, almost any complaint "for the redress of grievances" can be construed under Obamaspeak as an act of terrorism. Have you spoken out against fracking, complained about the imperiling of bobcats in the Mojave, or questioned Obamacare? Are you a born-again Christian? Welcome to the club. And God forbid that you share the revolutionary beliefs of George Washington or Thomas Jefferson. Government files could classify you as a "person suspected of an affiliation with terrorism."

It doesn't matter whether that designation makes any sense or not. It would not necessarily have to be tested in court. The whole point of sections 1021 and 1022 of 2012's NDAA seems to be the suspension of the right of habeas corpus.

Why FATCA?

Notwithstanding the fact that they are already listening to all your phone conversations and reading all your emails, their surreptitious spying lacks one important feature that FATCA provides. Spying on your private life and your business may impose significant long-term costs on you by destroying the rule of law—while placing you under the economic yoke of the crony capitalists, their hired lackeys, and the useful idiots who run the government—but that would not immediately prohibit you from moving abroad and starting a new life.

FATCA does.

The lockdown FATCA regulations not only apply to some 7.5 million individual Americans already residing in foreign countries, who can no longer open bank or brokerage accounts, purchase insurance products, or obtain mortgages on foreign properties; they also impose disabling costs on foreign companies and businesses owned by Americans wherever they live. Any bank, brokerage, or insurance company that deals with a company or partnership operating outside the United States that is even 10 percent owned by an American is subject to all the costly bureaucratic reporting requirements imposed by FATCA.

Barack Obama and his FATCA program have compounded the obstacles, pioneered by George W. Bush, for Americans doing business in other countries.

European banks have quite reasonably concluded that having Americans as clients for financial services, even indirectly, is not worth the exorbitant costs of the heavy-handed extraterritorial regulation imposed by the US government.

Questions for Your Future

FATCA raises a host of questions. In one respect, it makes you scratch your head over the loss of freedom in the United States. Did we ever believe what we were taught a lifetime ago in high school civics class? Then America was said to be "the land of the free." The animating spirit of America, beautifully articulated by Thomas Jefferson, involved a keen appreciation for the natural rights of individuals to freely choose where to live, where to work, and presumably even where to bank. FATCA is an obvious contradiction of everything Jefferson thought the American Revolution stood for.

At another level, there is the puzzle about why foreign banks pay any heed at all to extraterritorial US regulations that threaten to impose costs of hundreds of millions on individual banks and total costs that could mount above $1 trillion. Why, indeed.

QE as a Surreptitious Subsidy of Foreign Banks

When you look carefully, you see a situation that is not what it seems. QE was at least partly an expedient for the surreptitious subsidy of foreign banks. A big part of the reason those banks play along with extraterritorial US laws like FATCA is that they have been paid to do so (particularly big foreign banks).

European banks have become the hirelings of the US government. Part of the desperate effort to preserve the US imperium, and maintain the US dollar as the world's reserve currency, involves back door bailouts and lavish subsidies to foreign banks that continue to deal in the last great manufactured product in which the United States retains a competitive advantage—the US dollar.

A hint about why banks everywhere feel obliged to kowtow to authoritarian US regulations is provided by the experience of banks dealing with Iran under US sanctions. While the United States accounts for only 12 percent of world trade, more than 35 percent of international transactions are conducted in dollars, including about $2.7 billion a day in dollar based derivative trades, many of which do not involve Americans or American firms.

Under these conditions, any foreign bank or financial institution that defies heavy-handed US regulations could have their access to the American banking system denied, just as those banks that violated US sanctions against Iran did. Under those conditions, the foreign bank would be unable to offer dollar accounts and dollar payments that rely on links to corresponding American banks. Because of the importance of the dollar, most banks, big and small, feel that they must do as the US dictates, particularly as they are paid to do so.

At a deeper level, FATCA raises questions of profound importance to you as an investor. What does FATCA tell you about the terminal crisis of US hegemony and how economies are likely to be reconfigured in the next stage of world capitalism?

Quite a bit.

There is a metamessage in "financial repression" in all its forms. It says that the system is fragile, and "the powers that be" dare not let you enjoy financial freedom lest the system collapse. That is the message of QE in its many guises.

Most investors are bewitched and bewildered over the prospect of tapering. It is a notion that presupposes that the system is strong enough to stand on its own if normal economic behavior set interest rates. It isn't.

Think of a clumsy man tottering on a tightrope high above the street. Will he cut the safety line that holds him aloft? Probably not. But if he makes a show of unfastening the line, he will do so tentatively, being sure to hold it close.

The real issue with QE is far from apparent to most investors, as is usually the case. I doubt 1 in 10,000 realizes that a major reason more than 80 percent of the high-powered money created by QE is not being leant to Main Street but gathering dust as excess reserves is because more than half of those reserves are held by foreign banks.

To better understand, roll back the clock to October 2008. At that time, the global financial system was in the process of collapsing as the "too-big-to-fail" banks held their collective bad breath over the challenge of covering the collapse of a $1.2 trillion subprime mortgage derivatives market (the most highly leveraged in an alphabet soup of dodgy mortgage exposure).

As you know, a lot of big banks, along with the world's largest insurance company, AIG, had written derivative contracts guaranteeing to make good on losses from subprime and other mortgage securities. Quite apart from the specific losses incurred on the various mortgage securities, the problem for the financial system was magnified by the fact that mortgage securities, previously rated AAA by credit agencies, were being used as collateral by investment banks like Lehman Brothers for the overnight borrowing that kept them in business. When that collateral fell to junk status, it triggered a wholesale run on the financial system.

As had become apparent by September 15, 2008, with the collapse of Lehman Brothers, banks had drastically underestimated the risks that they were incurring (largely because they weren't taking the risks—you were). They sold cheap insurance against an unraveling of the mortgage market in exchange for a gigantic liability they were cocksure they would never need to meet. In the disaster scenario that actually unfolded (one that I had highlighted in congressional testimony more than a decade earlier), mortgage-backed securities went from AAA credits to the rubbish bin almost overnight. There were no bids. Good or bad, the various mortgage securities all plunged together. The market understood what was going on; AIG stock plunged by 60 percent on September 16, 2008, alone.

The Federal Reserve stepped in with the first round of QE to save the big banks and insurance companies. They ginned up money out of thin air and improvised bids for mortgage-backed securities. The Fed spent $175 billion buying agency debt securities and $1.25 trillion of mortgage-backed securities.

This was all done in conjunction with other support from the Federal Reserve and Treasury, amounting to another $180 billion. As lavish as it was, it was not enough to keep AIG, the prime player in the derivatives market, from going belly up. Still, as financial analyst Daniel Amerman put it in a 2013 article for *Gold-Eagle*, "Absent quantitative easing, it was game over for the financial system."[30]

Naïvely, you might assume that having flirted with collapse, the US government would have made it a first priority to fix the system. Wrong.

Yes, Congress passed the Dodd-Frank Wall Street Reform and Consumer Protection Act—fourteen thousand pages of barely intelligible rules, many of which are still incomplete, compiled after one thousand meetings between regulators and the big banks. The surest effect of Dodd-Frank is to provide lucrative employment to legions of lawyers for deciphering its occult provisions.

$561 Trillion in Interest-Rate Derivatives

Dodd-Frank will not prevent a coming financial collapse. Think of it as the equivalent of climbing to a higher diving board. The irony is that while the first rounds of QE may have forestalled the terminal collapse of the US-led world financial system, the prolongation of QE over the years since 2008 has enlarged the problem.

The various installments of QE have held interest rates at artificially low levels and therefore made hedging against a rebound in rates to more normal levels a concern of the world's borrowers. As of November 2013, this had resulted in the accumulation of about $561 trillion of over-the-counter interest-rate derivatives—such as swaps, forward rate agreements, and options—according to the Bank for

International Settlements.[31] To be clear, banks have entered into derivative contracts, similar to those associated with mortgage-backed securities. The difference is that the new time bomb is almost 450 times the size of the subprime mortgage derivative market that almost overwhelmed the global financial system in 2008.

For reference, $561 trillion is almost thirty-six times the US GDP. Because much of the $561 trillion consists of liabilities of foreign banks, you may wonder if affects the United States. It does. The potential daisy chain of default would almost instantly leap over the oceans and open vast holes in the US financial system. That is why the Federal Reserve initiated QE in the first place. A 2010 Fed audit showed that of the $1.25 trillion of mortgage-backed securities the Fed bought in QE1, $442.7 billion were bought from foreign banks.

Believe it or not, the record shows that QE1 was the low water mark for the percentage of newly created money lavished on foreign banks.[32] Foreign banks were the biggest beneficiaries of the Fed's QE3 monthly $85 billion bond buying spree. They were also the biggest gainers from QE2. The Fed pumped $630 billion into foreign banks during that phase of its digital money-fabricating extravaganza. If you wonder why domestic banks are not lending more to Main Street, there is your reason. Most of the money the Fed created ended up in foreign banks. Barclays and Deutsche Bank are not big lenders in Nebraska. "Fat, dumb, and happy" US consumers and taxpayers are bailing out not only domestic US banks but big banks around the world.

In addition to directly shoveling money into the coffers of foreign banks, the Fed has been subsidizing them and buying their cooperation in another way—through the derivatives market. Unlike a normal options market, in which traders may be either long or short, the nature of interest-rate derivatives dictates that the banks will almost always be the party betting on stable or falling rates. The counterparty bet on rising rates will almost always be undertaken by borrowers seeking to hedge their exposure to higher rates. The highly correlated bets that have been placed by inadequately capitalized financial institutions basically doom the US-dominated world financial system.

To see why, consider that when interest rates rise, they will rise for every borrower. It makes perfect sense for real estate investors, for example, who depend upon borrowed money to finance their projects to seek a way of protecting their position against higher interest costs.

They can do this with forward rate agreements (FRAs). The usual structure of these derivatives is that the real estate investor would contract with a financial institution for an amount maturing sometime in the future according to the timeline of a project. The FRA is usually geared to the London Interbank Offered Rate or (LIBOR). The real estate investor is thus protected, at least on paper, to a predetermined amount as interest rates rise. The financial institution is short the FRA and stands to profit if interest rates remain stable or decrease.

Essentially the same thing happens with swaps. The structure and logic of the market dictate that it is always the bank, or other financial institution, that profits when interest rates fall or remain stable, while the other party (the borrower) gains from derivative contracts when interest rates rise. Obviously, borrowers of loans with adjustable rates have an incentive to hedge their exposure to the extra costs that would materialize if interest rates rise.

So the borrowers enter into derivative hedges against higher rates, while the banks take the opposite side of that trade. To the extent that interest rates remain stable or fall, as they have done since the Lehman collapse, these trades are very profitable for the banks. But if interest rates as expressed in LIBOR were to generally rise, the US-dollar-dominated banking system as a whole would be on the wrong side of that trade—and would therefore be even more insolvent than it is today. (Indeed, the protracted discussion by the Fed of its possible intention to raise rates modestly can be read as a hint to banks to let their bets against higher interest rates run off.)

Swap hedges aren't necessarily trivial or small transactions. This was clearly illustrated in 2008–9 in the wake of the subprime meltdown. At that time, news reports circulated documenting how municipalities, states, and other institutions lost billions buying their way out of swaps that turned sour when QE drove interest rates down from already low levels that prevailed on the eve of the crisis. A famous case was that of Harvard University, which spent a billion dollars to buy its way out of a losing swap trade with banks.

You see what this means for the current situation. It illuminates the mechanism through which QE shovels money into the pockets of banks, foreign as well as domestic. As long as the ZIRP remains in force, foreign banks get paid for going along with the gag and supporting Obama's lockdown of Americans through FATCA.

Over the longer term, one of the surer results to be expected is that interest rates will return to more normal levels. Looking back at the history of interest rates in the dominant economies of the past millennium, the current interest rates on US government securities have been set at a historically low extreme. In a 2013 article for *Business Insider*, Bryan Taylor pointed out that the United States continues to issue bonds to cover its expenses, despite bond yields reaching their lowest levels in history in 2012—below 1.5 percent. Taylor puts it this way in "How 3 Countries Lost Their Position as the World's Dominant Financial Power over the Last 800 Years":

> Over the past eight centuries, the locus of economic power has gradually shifted from Italy to Spain to the Netherlands to Great Britain and

> currently to the United States. The country at the center of the world's power and economy issues bonds to cover expenses. Investors in that country and abroad purchase the bonds because they represent the safest bonds that are available for investment . . . Between 1285 and the mid-1600s, yields on government bonds fluctuated between 6% and 10% and in some cases were around 20%. . . . Since the mid-1600s, the average yield on government bonds has been around 4% . . . Government bond yields reached their lowest levels in history in 2012, dropping below 1.50%.[33]

This trend continued into 2015.

Because the Federal Reserve has pushed interest rates down to the vanishing point, it is now almost impossible for them to go lower. The US government is insolvent according to any serious accounting of its assets and liabilities, but it won't go out of business quite yet. It may hang around in some shadow form, like the Holy Roman Empire, for centuries to come. But the time of the United States as a hegemonic power is drawing to a close in the current terminal crisis. The United States has already lost its manufacturing, and most of its commercial, predominance. It clings to a precarious predominance in finance. But that can't last long as chronic trade and budget deficits accumulate. And paradoxically, a sign of the end was the sharp rally of the dollar that presaged a systematic reversal in commodity prices.

More ominously, the US government has superseded the late Soviet Union as the globe's most implacable enemy of the free market. The United States has become an obstacle to capital mobility worldwide. This is reflected in FATCA and more. The US government is too big, costly, and complex. Its markets are the most heavily regulated on earth. As Joseph Tainter showed in *The Collapse of Complex Societies*, complexity inevitably leads to collapse as it engages the temptations of human creativity to find less complex and less costly ways of doing what needs to be done.

While US authorities may well have bribed the world banking establishment to continue trading in the dollar with QE—which funnels billions into their pockets through direct asset purchases and derivative trades—Obama has offset much of that incentive through his heavy-handed FATCA regulations. Megapolitical conditions now favor lower-scale operations. New technologies, as inadequately expressed in Bitcoin, already threaten the disintermediation of the dollar.

With the primary scope for dollar interest rate fluctuation to the upside, a concerted pause in QE could trigger a crisis event, like the subprime mortgage meltdown, but many times worse. With the nominal value of interest-rate derivatives now towering at 450 times the mortgage security derivatives that brought the financial system to death's door in 2008, it is obviously far beyond the scope of bankrupt nation-states to bail out the system when the next crisis inevitably hits.

They will do what scoundrels always do when faced with the loss of power: print money and repress the population. As reported by the Associated Press, the US Department of Homeland Security has contracts to purchase 1.6 billion rounds over the next five years, including hollow point ammunition—bullets that are banned by international law from use in war, along with massive quantities of bullets specialized for snipers. A March 2013 *Forbes* article explained that this amount of ammunition would be enough to sustain an active war in America for more than twenty years.[34]

In other words, the government is preparing for the collapse of the financial system. They expect to have to create trillions and trillions of new dollars to stuff into the black holes in the balance sheets of banks holding some of the $561 trillion in derivative bets against rising interest rates. Then if you don't like it, they'll shoot you.

Notes

1   http://www.internationalman
.com/articles/the-worst-law
-most-americans-have-never
-heard-of.

2   Prior, George, "Interview:
James Jatras, Lawyer and
Anti-FATCA Lobbyist,"
iExpats.com, December 28,
2012.

3   See http://www.ackselhaus
.de/berlin-wall/?hotel-berlin=
english.

4   http://www.historyinanhour
.com/2013/06/30/walter
-ulbricht-summary/.

5   Esper et al., *Journal of Global
and Planetary Change*, https://
wattsupwiththat.com/2012/
10/18/yet-another-paper
-demonstrates-warmer
-temperatures-1000-years
-ago-and-even-2000-years
-ago/.

6   Cook, S. A., et al., eds., *The
Cambridge Ancient History*,
XII, 1st ed. (Cambridge: Cambridge University Press, 1971),
268.

7   Ibid., 264–68.

8   Ibid., 268.

9   Peck, Don, "Why So Many
Americans Are Leaving
the U.S.—in 1 Big Chart,"
Chartist, July/August 2013.

10 http://www.csmonitor
.com/Business/The-Daily
-Reckoning/2010/0501/As
-illegal-immigration-falls-is
-America-in-decline.

11 Grennstone, Michael, and
Michael Loney, "The Uncomfortable Truth about American Wages," *New York Times*,
October 22, 2012.

12 See Hudgins, Colby, "The
Great American Migration,"
The Daily Caller, May 5, 2013,
http://dailycaller.com/2013/
05/05/the-great-american
-migration/#ixzz2mqYq14El.

13 Adams, Bob, "The Great Escape," *Barron's*, November 26,
2011.

14 Leonhardt, David, "The Idled
Young Americans," *New York
Times*, May 3, 2013.

15 http://www.nola.com/
business/index.ssf/2011/
09/census_numbers_show
_recession.html.

16 "Majority Disapprove of Health Care Law; Believe Their Costs Will Rise and Quality Will Fall," Institute of Politics, Harvard University, http://www.iop.harvard.edu/majority-disapprove-health-care-law-believe-their-costs-will-rise-and-quality-will-fall.

17 http://www.cnsnews.com/news/article/irs-cheapest-obamacare-plan-will-be-20000-family.

18 https://www.cia.gov/library/publications/the-world-factbook/rankorder/2102rank.html.

19 http://wondacharts.williamoneil.com/et/dfs/2008/910329/0001144204-08-015754/v107110_10k.htm.

20 https://srxawordonhealth.com/tag/robert-wood-johnson-foundation/.

21 See https://www.oecd.org/els/health-systems/48723982.pdf.

22 Traynor, Ian, and Paul Lewis, "Merkel Compared NSA to Stasi in Heated Encounter with Obama," *The Guardian*, December 17, 2013, https://www.theguardian.com/world/2013/dec/17/merkel-compares-nsa-stasi-obama.

23 WashingtonBlog, "Americans Are the Most Spied On People in World History," December 5, 2012; see also http://www.wnyc.org/story/241328-somebodys-watching-you/.

24 http://x22report.com/how-the-nsa-hacks-your-iphone/.

25 http://www.washingtonsblog.com/2013/12/former-top-nsa-official-now-police-state.html.

26 Ibid.

27 Slater, Dan, *Wall Street Journal Law Blog*, http://blogs.wsj.com/law/2008/03/13/alan-dershowitz-on-spitzergate-what-is-this-russia/.

28 http://www.wnd.com/2012/07/feds-label-liberty-lovers-terrorists-again/.

29 http://www.storyleak.com/official-complaining-tap-water-act-of-terrorism/.

30 http://danielamerman.com/articles/2013/QErealityD.html.

31 Gyntelberg, Jacob, and Christian Upper, "OTC Interest Rates Derivative Market in 2013," *BIS Quarterly Review*, December 2013, 70.

32 http://www.zerohedge.com/article/exclusive-feds-600-billion-stealth-bailout-foreign

-banks-continues-expense -domestic-economy.

33 Taylor, Bryan, "How 3 Countries Lost Their Position as the World's Dominant Financial Power over the Last 800 Years," *Business Insider*, December 8, 2013, http://www.businessinsider.com/700-years -of-government-bond-yields -2013-12#ixzz2nTRGGFBQ.

34 Benko, Robert, "1.6 Billion Rounds of Ammo for Homeland Security? It's Time for a National Conversation," *Forbes*, March 11, 2013.

Chapter Nine

Beyond Kondratiev

Secular Cycles and the Breaking Point

The Treasury opened up its window to help and pumped $105 billion into the system. And it quickly realized it could not stem the tide. We were having an electronic run on the banks. They decided to close down the operation . . . to close down the money accounts . . . If they had not done so, in their estimation, by 2 p.m. that day $5.5 trillion would have been withdrawn . . . Within 24 hours, the world economy would have collapsed . . . People who say we would have gone back to the 16th century were being optimistic.
—Former Representative Paul Kanjorski (D) of Pennsylvania's Eleventh Congressional District, on the 2008 financial crisis

The notion of secular cycles is one of the more promising keys for interpreting history since Nikolai Kondratiev discovered long cycles of economic conjecture in 1926. His long cycles last an average of fifty-five years. The Secular Cycle is a much longer two- to three-century expression of the "fractal nature of historical dynamics," in which history repeats itself in cycles that look very similar, if not identical, over telescoping time scales.

The pattern traced by basis point fluctuations in the price of a large-cap stock like Apple, subject to high-frequency algorithmic trading, closely resembles a graph of the fluctuations in the social structure of the top strata of magnates in medieval

England from 1150 to 1450. The persistence of "fractal geometry" as we zoom in and out over so many scales in economic life, from milliseconds to centuries, seems to confirm mathematician Benoît Mandelbrot's suggestion that the more we examine, the more we find the same patterns varying endlessly, up and down.[1]

The famous economist Joseph A. Schumpeter, who highlighted the importance of creative destruction, also left his mark by identifying and naming three economic cycles of varying lengths in his 1939 book, *Business Cycles*: the Kitchin is an inventory cycle of three to four years, the Juglar is an investment cycle of seven to ten years, and the Kondratiev is a long wave cycle of forty-five to sixty years.[2]

Beyond all these is the Secular Cycle, which is not only an economic cycle; it also traces the waxing and waning of demographic and political factors. It describes and explains "the rise and decline of nations," a phrase I use deliberately in homage to the late Mancur Olson (a mentor of mine who wrote a brilliant book of that title).

Olson spelled out a theory about economic growth, stagflation, and social rigidities based on the logic of choice. His argument is a rational exposition of why "distributional coalitions," a.k.a. crony capitalists and special interests, have a strong advantage over the general interest in securing the spoils of politics. Olson explained why perverse policies are likely to prevail at the expense of economic growth when societies are stable for a sufficient time to make lobbying economically profitable, especially in large economies. As Olson put it, the resulting policy "stupidities, rigidities, and instabilities" are usually quite enough to explain the failures of economies to grow. The "perverse policy syndrome" he identified promotes inefficiency, stagnation, and inequality.

From my perspective, part of the charm of *The Rise and Decline of Nations* is the fact that Olson abandoned the conceit that politicians and governments were educable and sincere—one that prevailed in the economics profession for most of the last century. The economists generally pretended that policies adopted by government were not the result of pressures, bribery, and back-scratching largely orchestrated behind the scenes, but wise, well-meaning attempts to promote the public interest. To the contrary, Olson stated that organized groups usually create policies favoring themselves while working against the interests of larger unorganized groups in society, causing an unequal distribution of income.[3]

The Secular Cycle entails a different take on the rise and decline of nations. It has less to do with the organizational advantages accruing to groups of different sizes as they maneuver to control the state for their own advantage and more to do with the waxing and waning of population as a whole. The Secular Cycle is dynamic and includes demographic, as well as political and economic, dimensions.

For a theory that is pregnant with implications for your future, however, the Secular Cycle has remained almost deliberately obscure. Before now, you could only study it in fragments and piece them together like bits of a spilled jigsaw puzzle. To my knowledge, there has never been a coherent expression of these long-term oscillations. You would look in vain for a comprehensive overview of the big picture.

What do I mean? Simply this: You can't be expected to get the "big picture" from a few unassembled bits of colored cardboard. Fragments and partial truths about the dynamics of growth and disintegration abound in academic literature and the blogosphere, but what do they mean? Putting them in perspective has been difficult because they have not been fully pieced together.

"Don't Know Much about History"

An obvious reason for the partial view is that there are greater rewards from studying growth than disintegration. Also, ignorance should not be overlooked as an explanation for inadequate understanding of the past. "Don't know much about history," is not only a refrain from Sam Cooke's iconic ballad "Wonderful World"; it is also an accurate characterization of current knowledge, notwithstanding the trillions lavished on education.[4] The weak grasp of history today tends to foreshorten perspective. It is hard for people who really "don't know much about history" to discern its patterns.

Further to that, the experience of developed economies over the past two centuries has been one of unprecedented growth, interrupted by occasional spasms of depression. Only an outlying country—Argentina—among economies that became rich in the modern era seems to have experienced the disintegrative phase, highlighted by long periods of negative compound growth and political instability. By and large, however, there has been little attention paid to the prospect that modern economies could follow the same downhill trajectory that historians have documented in so many instances in the past.

Pieces of the Secular Cycle jigsaw puzzle were identified by Jack Goldstone in his 1991 book, *Revolution and Rebellion in the Early Modern World*. Employing what he describes as "a demographic/structural approach," Goldstone argues that population growth tended to cause overwhelming fiscal problems for the state, including destabilizing intra-elite competition and popular unrest.[5] Put simply, Goldstone is a sophisticated neo-Malthusian.[6]

Almost two centuries earlier, in 1798, Thomas Malthus published *An Essay on the Principle of Population*, the leading modern text on population and the economy. Two centuries before that, in 1588, the sixteenth-century Jesuit scholar Giovanni Botero had anticipated most of the Malthusian perspective on population in *On the Cause of the Greatness of Cities*. Malthus's, Goldstone's, and Botero's argument is one that seems to reemerge from the footnotes to be discovered anew every two centuries, perhaps because the underlying Secular Cycle is more in evidence on that schedule.

Malthus was famous for pointing out that the tendency of population to increase geometrically meant that it was prone to escalate faster than the means of subsistence—hence the danger of a Malthusian crisis in which food prices increase, real income declines, and consumption among the poor drops. The resulting economic distress, sometimes compounded by plague and war, results in lower birth rates and higher mortality. This stabilizes or reduces population, easing the pressures on the means of subsistence. After an adjustment period, often involving political reorganization, food prices fall, real wages rise, population growth resumes, and the cycle repeats itself.

Enter Peter Turchin, an ecologist and evolutionary biologist, and Sergey Nefedov, of the Institute of History and Archaeology of the Russian Academy of Sciences. Using Goldstone and Malthus as their points of departure, Turchin and Nefedov wrote *Secular Cycles*. Their book focuses on multicentury oscillations in economic and political dynamics ("Secular Cycles") that they argue have characterized agrarian economies over the last two millennia.[7]

Turchin and Nefedov make an effort to specify common stages of past civilizations as they rise and decline. The so-called expansion phase peters out in stagflation, the first stage of the disintegrative phase, where the economy declines toward crisis and depression, often culminating in the collapse of the state. They explain that the stagflation phase is typically characterized by a high level of social inequality and an oppression of society's productive segments. Population growth leads to larger armies and bureaucracies, which result in more government spending. But tax revenues fail to keep up with mushrooming outlays. Despite increased taxation, the state still enters a fiscal crisis, giving way to bankruptcy, loss of military control, rebellion, and the breakdown of central authority.

Turchin and Nefedov present startling details of the dramatic oscillations in population correlated with the Secular Cycle, documenting the disintegrative phase of the Secular Cycle. In medieval England, for example, the population rose from about 2 million in 1086 to a high of

6.52 million in 1292, only to fall back dramatically to about 2 million by 1450.

Their argument suggests that many of today's seemingly unique problems, such as mounting economic inequality, and the inability of the sclerotic political system to come to grips with the looming prospect of state bankruptcy, may simply be the latest manifestations of a centuries-long Secular Cycle dating far into the past.

Turchin and Nefedov have added colorful detail, but not enough of the jigsaw puzzle to give you a clear view of the big picture.

Climate as a Megapolitical Driver

It fell to a reviewer of *Secular Cycles*, Bryan J. L. Berry of the University of Texas, an expert in long waves, to develop the most interesting interpretive analysis of the Secular Cycle. (Berry is the author of *Long-Wave Rhythms in Economic Development and Political Behavior*.) Whether we "like it or not," he warns, "our lives appears to be embedded in a higher order of complexity." He argues that longer-term cycles are "more than a figment of some overactive imagination."[8]

Berry points to a megapolitical basis for the population oscillations and accompanying crises that characterize the Secular Cycle. Population doesn't just surge because people all of a sudden randomly decide to have more children. They make such decisions in clusters when real income rises, as reflected in the famous postwar Baby Boom generation. Fluctuations in climate have also been obvious drivers in the waxing and waning of prosperity. Berry summarizes the climate fluctuations that drove history:

> Global warmists notwithstanding there have been long cycles of solar activity and global temperatures that correlate with the alleged secular cycles. Rome's ascendancy was in a warm period that preceded the Dark Ages' cold., Followed by

the medieval warm period that reached its maximum between 1110 to 1250 and then descended to a low, the Wolf minimum (1280–1350), at the end of which the Black Death ravaged Europe (1347–50). Temperatures abated for a century as Europe was reshaped in response to massive depopulation before declining to the Sporer Minimum between 1460 and 1515, rose for another century and then descended to the depths of the Little Ice Age in the Maunder minimum (1645–1715), during which time the bubonic plague returned. Each epoch of declining temperatures would have been sufficient to cut yields, reducing fertility as marriages were delayed and the proportions never married increased while death-inexperienced populations were ravaged by plague. Each epoch of increasing temperatures brought increased agricultural productivity and population increase. The crisis phase of the Plantagenet and Capetian cycles occurred in the Wolf minimum and their terminal depressions during the Sporer minimum. The Tudor-Stuart and the Valois and Muscovy cycles foundered during the Maunder minimum.[9]

Berry underscores points that we take up in this volume. If you think about it, you can see the danger inherent in one of today's false narratives—the pretense that the planet is warming due to human-caused carbon dioxide emissions. What could otherwise seem merely a cynical rationale for an assortment of power grabs and crony capitalist rip-offs is something much worse. The remorseless pretense that humans are causing global warming masks a more ominous turn in the solar cycles that have heretofore driven history.

The implications of the current decline in solar irradiance are sweeping. It could parallel the way that natural climate cycles drove productivity and political cycles in the preindustrial organic economy, which operated upon the energy of sunlight as converted by plants through photosynthesis. You could be challenged by the disintegrative phase of the Secular Cycle as another solar minimum wreaks havoc on unprepared global populations that have swollen by tenfold since the last Little Ice Age.

This would be less challenging if the earth really were warming, as Al Gore and his accomplices never tire of telling you. Unfortunately, global warming is a hoax—little more than a crony capitalist rationalization for a multi-trillion-dollar rip-off. Rather than getting warmer, the Earth has actually been getting colder for the past eighteen years (up to 2015), with the government wasting billions of your dollars annually on bogus climate research, designed to reach a forgone conclusion. They have turned out thousands of pages with all sorts of alarms about why global warming is a serious problem notwithstanding eighteen years of falling temperatures. Mostly, what they have succeeded in doing is providing an updated validation of Upton Sinclair's classic observation: "It is difficult to get a man to understand something, when his salary depends on his not understanding it."[10]

But not everyone is fooled. One of the more concise summaries of the dangers arising from solar hibernation is the argument from *Dark Winter*, a book by John L. Casey, a former White House national space policy advisor, NASA headquarters consultant, and space shuttle engineer. Casey echoes my belief that the world is at the threshold of a climate period similar to the Little Ice Age. In *Dark Winter*, Casey tells the truth about ominous changes taking place in the climate. Among other things, he predicts crop-destroying cold, food shortages, and riots around the world, including in the United States. Among his original insights, Casey argues that there is a high probability of record earthquakes and volcanic eruptions, which are more prevalent in periods of colder climate for unknown reasons.

The Secular Cycle is a template for understanding one of the more unexpected developments of modern history: the destabilizing onset of protracted cold. Indeed, it has probably already begun. I base my apparently crazy forecast of a coming Little Ice Age on the research of solar physicists such as Dr. Habibullo Abdussamatov, and the late Dr. Theodor Landscheidt, who detected a pattern of declining solar irradiance years ago and warned that another Little Ice Age could begin in the first half of this century.

You need only have flown across the continent as I did while writing this book to see that most of North America was buried in a deep carpet of snow then. Temperatures ran 15 °F to 20 °F below normal. Talking heads on CNBC blamed a sequence of weak economic statistics on the surprisingly cold winter. Does that work for you?

You have been conditioned by decades of nattering about global warming to expect a much warmer climate over the foreseeable future. This just shows again why you need an independent source of information and judgment like *Newsmax* and *Strategic Investment*. The normal news and information channels in American society are totally bent under the weight of false narratives. You can trust their reports on today's date, but that's about it. You certainly can't trust what they tell you about the weather, except perhaps the current temperature reading. If you believe Al Gore, anthropogenic global warming, redubbed "climate change," is supposedly responsible for putting most of North America in a deep freeze. Huh?

As I write, National Weather Service forecasts that another blast of arctic air could push temperatures in the Midwest from 30 °F below normal to 50 °F below normal. This is global warming? What a joke. You have been misled by self-serving propaganda, ginned up at your expense, exactly the type of abuse President Eisenhower warned against in his prescient farewell speech to the nation on January 17, 1961. He spelled out exactly why you cannot blindly trust government-funded research. Crony capitalists like Al Gore lie remorselessly about climate change because it pays for them to do so.

Gore "Richer than Romney" from Crony Capitalist Scams

A *New York* magazine profile, "Al Gore's Golden Years," reports that the former vice president "is now richer than Mitt Romney."[11] A Google search on the subject of Gore's wealth turns up a treasure trove of information about the apparently not-so-secret inner workings of crony capitalism.

A November 3, 2009, article in London's *Telegraph* reported that Al Gore could become world's first "carbon billionaire."[12] The article details Gore's "profiteering from government policies he supports that would direct billions of dollars to the business ventures in which he invested." In particular, the *Telegraph* mentions Silver Spring Networks and Gore's other green energy companies that profited from billions of Department of Energy grants.

A 2012 article in the *Washington Post*, "Al Gore Has Thrived as Green Tech Investor,"[13] provides more details of his profiteering from hysteria about global warming, ginned out of government-funded research to build support for reducing your standard of living and siphoning away billions of tax dollars. According to the piece, fourteen green-tech firms that Gore has invested in received or benefited from over $2.5 billion in loans, grants, and tax breaks—part of Obama's push to use public money to support a renewable-energy industry in the United States.

Turning Back the Clock to the Inquisition

Global warming is a geocentric theory of climate change, proposing that human actions on earth are the largest factors determining climate. According to global warming fanatics, heliocentric factors such as patterns of solar irradiance have little or no bearing on the earth's climate. The fact that Gore and his followers are taken seriously at all shows how far rational scientific thought has receded today. Indeed, Gore and company seem to have done more to revive geocentrism than even Cardinal Bellarmino and the fires of the Inquisition. Of course Pope Francis has taken up the cause of geocentricism where Cardinal Bellarmino left off, issuing a papal bull in support of the view that humans cause temperature fluctuations on earth.

Heliocentrism, Then and Now

On February 17, 1600, Giordano Bruno was brought to the Campo de' Fiori (Field of Flowers) plaza in Rome, "his tongue in prison because of his wicked words," and burned at the stake as an unrepentant heretic.[14] Among the "dangerous" views that cost Bruno his life was his strongly stated conviction that the Sun, not the Earth, was the center of the Solar System. His heliocentrism was even more offensive to theological orthodoxy because Bruno was a pioneer in insisting on a high value for what is now called the Drake equation, a probabilistic formula for estimating the number of stars supporting intelligent life. Bruno declared that there was an infinite number of worlds like ours circulating around stars like our sun.

Contemplating Bruno's fate makes me grateful for the relatively meager progress toward freedom of thought that has been eked out over the past four centuries. It is a particular blessing that Al Gore, today's leading proponent of the earth-centered view of climate, lacks the gravitas of Cardinal Bellarmino, the Grand Inquisitor, who sentenced Bruno to be burned at the stake and later condemned Galileo to life in prison after Galileo was referred to the Inquisition in 1615. (Galileo got off with a light sentence because he recanted his heretical view that the Earth revolves around the Sun.) Unlike Cardinal Bellarmino, Gore cannot speak Greek, and his enforcement of the consensus views of the day about the importance of the Earth over the Sun is not backed up by the fires of the Inquisition. Even for a man with the equivocal intellectual integrity of Gore, there is a limit to how hypocritical he could be. It is hard to imagine Gore supporting the open air burning of heretics, as humans are a carbon-based life form, and the auto-de-fé no doubt released a lot of CO_2.

Gore may not favor the public burning of heretics, but he is all in with the Inquisition's mode of argument against heliocentrism. Cardinal Bellarmino, the Grand Inquisitor declared, "You will find all agreeing in the literal interpretation that the sun is in heaven and turns around the earth with great speed, and that the earth is very far from heaven and sits motionless at the center of the world."[15]

Gore is equally pleased to tell you that climate variation originates on Earth, not the Sun. You have no doubt heard his mantra, updated for verisimilitude, like the vote tallies in a North Korean election results: "97 percent of climate experts agree humans are causing global warming."[16] In strict logic, 97 percent of experts is a smaller majority than the 100 percent ("all") experts Cardinal Bellarmino thought were in agreement with the geocentric consensus 400 years ago. You could say that Gore was slipping compared to the Inquisition, but given that science has progressed, and people today are at least ostensibly free to think for themselves, it is startling that manipulators like Gore have achieved the success they have in advancing an inherently implausible theory that anthropogenic global warming threatens a host of horrible consequences for the climate.

If you listen to Gore, you might suppose that CO_2 made up a big proportion of the total atmosphere and was put there recently by humans burning oil and coal to power a lavish modern standard of living. Wrong. CO_2 comprises just 1/10,000th more of the atmosphere today than it did in 1750 before the Industrial Revolution. It has always been unlikely that this tiny margin of increase in CO_2 could have greater influence on Earth's climate than the sun.

About 186 billion tons of CO_2 enter the atmosphere annually. Only about 6 billion tons of that amount, or 3.3 percent, is attributable to human activity apart from breathing. The breaths exhaled by humans and animals account for about 71 billion tons of CO_2—more than ten times the CO_2 attributable to the economic activity that Gore wants to squelch.

There is nothing excessive or frightening about current atmospheric carbon levels. They have previously been twenty-five to one hundred times higher than now, with no evidence that this caused runaway greenhouse effects, nor any of the other horrifying hypotheticals that Gore and the remorseless liars at the Intergovernmental Panel on Climate Change (IPCC) of the UN pretend to be so indignant about.

Evidence that climate on earth is informed mainly by the Sun, rather than by humans releasing trivial amounts of CO_2 in the atmosphere, is so compelling that even some leading ecologists have begun to defect from the Anthropogenic Global Warming (AGW) camp. For example, Patrick Moore, the Canadian ecologist who cofounded Greenpeace, told the US Senate Environment and Public Works Committee on February 25, 2014, that the fact that there were higher temperatures and an ice age at a time when CO_2 emissions were ten times higher than today contradicts the "certainty that human-caused CO_2 emissions are the main cause of global warming."[17]

People with their wits about them should be able to see that both elements of the global warming faith are misguided. First, in light of geological history, it is extremely unlikely that human-caused CO_2 emissions could heat the planet to a cinder when an Ice Age occurred with CO_2 concentrations ten times higher than today. Second, it is far from obvious that we should wish to make the planet colder if we could. Nor should the positive impact of higher atmospheric CO_2 on plant productivity be ignored. As Matt Ridley points out, the fact that there are benefits of higher carbon dioxide emissions is not even controversial in scientific circles. Among other authorities, Freeman Dyson, professor emeritus of mathematical physics and astrophysics at the Institute of Advanced Study at Princeton, has declared that the nonclimatic effects of carbon dioxide are "enormously beneficial."

Unfortunately, that is an argument the world is unwilling to hear. In the coming months and years, I believe we will have an expensive and painful tutorial reminding us, as Professor Berry suggests, that each time period of declining temperatures seems to have coincided with the disintegrative phase of the Secular Cycle. This implies national bankruptcy amid a scramble for diminished supplies of food and energy resources like the world has never seen. Think of a game of musical chairs with death awaiting the losers. There will be a lot of losers. Current US Census Bureau forecasts project that the population of the earth will rise to 9.306 billion people by 2050. If Dr. Abdussamatov, John Casey, and others, including yours truly, are correct in projecting that another Little Ice Age will cool the planet for decades to come, you can be sure that the actual population of the earth in 2050 will fall well short of the Census Bureau estimate.

Of course, there is more to be said about Secular Cycles and whether the disintegrative phase of crisis, depression, and collapse is likely to be played out in state breakdown in industrial societies as it was in the agrarian societies documented by Turchin and Nefedov. For his part, Jack Goldstone argues that the threat of collapse is still with us, as we repeat behavior patterns that have led to unwelcome consequences in the past.

Stay tuned. How the Secular Cycle might play out under conditions of another Little Ice Age is a matter we explore further.

Notes

1 Mandelbrot, B. B., "Fractal Geometry: What Is It, and What Does It Do?," *Proceedings of the Royal Society A* 423, no. 3–16 (1989), 4.

2 Schumpter, Joseph A., *Business Cycles: A Theoretical, Historical and Statistical Analysis of the Capitalist Process* (New York: McGraw-Hill, 1939).

3 Olson, Mancur, *The Rise and Decline of Nations: Economic Growth, Stagflation, and Social Rigidities* (New Haven, CT: Yale University Press, 1982), 170.

4 http://www.azlyrics.com/lyrics/samcooke/wonderfulworld.html.

5 Goldstone, Jack A., *Revolution and Rebellion in the Early Modern World* (Berkeley: University of California Press, 1991).

6 Dunning, Chester, "Does Jack Goldstone's Model of Early Model State Crisis Apply to Russia?," *Comparative Studies in Society and History* 39, no. 3 (July 1997), 572.

7 Turchin, Peter, and Sergey A. Nefedov, *Secular Cycles* (Princeton: Princeton University Press, 2009).

8 Berry, Bryan J. L., *Long-Wave Rhythms in Economic Development and Political Behavior* (Baltimore: Johns Hopkins University Press, 1991).

9 From the review of *Secular Cycles* by Bryan J. L. Berry, *The American Journal of Sociology* 116, no. 2 (September 2010), 708.

10 Sinclair, Upton, *I, Candidate for Governor: And How I Got Licked*, repr. (University of California Press, 1994), 109.

11 http://nymag.com/news/features/al-gore-2013-5/.

12 http://www.telegraph.co.uk/news/earth/energy/6491195/Al-Gore-could-become-worlds-first-carbon-billionaire.html.

13 https://www.washingtonpost.com/politics/decision2012/al-gore-has-thrived-as-green-tech-investor/2012/10/10/1dfaa5b0-0b11-11e2-bd1a-b868e65d57eb_story.htmlprovides.

14 See http://www.gutenberg.org/ebooks/46901?msg=welcome_stranger.

15 Cardinal Bellarmine's letter to Paolo Antonio Foscarini, April 12, 1615, http://www

.historyguide.org/earlymod/
foscarini.html.

16 http://www.forbes.com/sites/
alexepstein/2015/01/06/97-of
-climate-scientists-agree-is
-100-wrong/#3045dd467187.

17 http://www.climatedepot
.com/2014/02/25/greenpeace
-co-founder-tells-u-s-senate
-earths-geologic-history
-fundamentally-contradicts
-co2-climate-fears-we-had
-both-higher-temps-and-an
-ice-age-at-a-time-when
-co2-emissions-were-10
-times/.

Chapter Ten

Ecofascism and the Natural Causes of Climate Disruptions

The "End of History" Becomes a Dead End

One of the tantalizing themes of the last quarter of the twentieth century was the notion that history had come to an end, and the combination of capitalism and liberal democracy would allow people everywhere to enjoy the material prosperity characteristic of the American middle class. But there was a problem with this vision. The biophysical limits to resources implied dramatic increases in the prices of crucial inputs, particularly petroleum, in order for the whole world to live like the American middle class.

Of course, it turned out that a good part of the surge in natural resource prices experienced in the first decade and a half of the twenty-first century was attributable to history's greatest artificial credit bubble in China, rather than demand from the growth of broad-based consumption among the new emerging market middle class. In any event, commodity prices surged, underscoring the natural limits to growth.

Peter J. Taylor shrewdly noted in *The Way the Modern World Works: World Hegemony to World Impasse* that the invention of "ecocatastrophe" can be understood as a way for the rich to maintain their dominant status in society.[1] He described the selfish interest of those wishing to reserve the good life for themselves as requiring a justification that would be seen as a logical, sensible reaction to a world in crisis.

Hence the invention of the global warming hoax. It may be bad science, riddled with obvious shortcomings, but it offered a path forward for those among the rich and powerful who want to "conserve their acquired capital while denying capital accumulation to others."

The far-fetched proposition that driving your automobile threatens to destroy the planet provides a rationalization for retracting the promise of American-style middle-class prosperity for billions of people in emerging economies. There are still "huddled masses yearning to breathe free," but not only has the Statue of Liberty's welcome mat been retracted; Gore and the other climate bullies now say the huddled masses can't be allowed to drive. Anywhere. All their billions of little cars would get in the way of the limousine traffic and pump up CO_2 levels.

What is more, global warming alarmism threatens to retract the promise of American middle-class prosperity for most of the American middle class. By mandating the use of costly low-density alternative energies, Gore and the global warming vigilantes could achieve a no-growth economy through the back door, pricing the bottom 90 percent of the American income distribution out of access to the good life.

This amounts to what Taylor describes as "ecofascism." It is a policy that augurs ill for independent capital accumulation, but it perfectly suits Al Gore's world of crony capitalism. It also seems set to trigger a big reduction in consumption, not to mention famine, on a large scale.

Don't make the mistake of supposing that the global warming hoax is an innocent misunderstanding, merely a matter of misprogrammed computer models or a failed excursion into the thin air of theoretical physics. It is really a matter of life and death. While we have been living longer, adding an average of three months to life expectancy every year in Western countries, the agenda of ecofascism is not survival for all. To the contrary, it means death to the many with the promise of a comfortable survival for the few—Al Gore and his privileged pals.

Taylor foresees the ecofascist world system as involving two zones: a rich zone in which capital accumulation will cease, conserving the good life, and a poor zone in which capital accumulation will be prevented through coercion. Add the end of an interstate system to this lack of capital accumulation and capitalism will be replaced by a "postmodern global apartheid," or "neo-fascist world system" ostensibly dedicated to saving the Earth.

Al Gore and his fellow prophets of ecofascism were shrewd enough to recognize that a simple no-growth economy would not enable them to long board the benefits of a modern standard of living. Why? Because in the modern economy, more than 99 percent of all activity is powered by exogenous energy and only 0.7 percent is powered by somatic energy, or muscle power. This means that the no-growth modern economy could not be the stationary state, as described by Adam Smith. Not for long. To the contrary, it should be thought of as a hovercraft. Without fuel, it would crash and burn. That is why the ecofascist project requires the cartelization of hydrocarbon energy. The ruling elite requires the preservation of a sufficient energy reserve to fuel a high standard of living for itself—but no one else.

Of course, the Earth really doesn't need saving, especially from CO_2. The long paleoclimatic record correlating CO_2 to temperature shows that high amounts of atmospheric CO_2 are transient phenomena. Contrary to Gore and company, there is no tendency for runaway CO_2 concentrations to increase and cause detrimental climate change. Far from it. Past increases in CO_2 emissions due to volcanic eruptions dwarf those now attributable to human activity. Notwithstanding claims by the Intergovernmental Panel on Climate Change (IPCC) that high atmospheric CO_2 persists, carbon dioxide is naturally recycled by the Earth. In fact, concentrations of atmospheric

CO_2 have decreased dramatically over the past 545 million years as the Earth has efficiently sequestered CO_2, mainly by growing forests.

Remember that there is compelling evidence showing that CO_2 is not a pollutant but an important life-giving atmospheric component, as any greenhouse operator can confirm. CO_2 is an important contributor to the organic capture of solar energy through photosynthesis. That is why an efficient greenhouse operation will triple ambient CO_2 of about 400 parts per million (ppm) to 1,300 ppm during the day by pumping in extra CO_2. They would not do that if CO_2 were really a pollutant.

One of the recurrent features of episodes of deep cold that increase glaciation is that they result in a reduction in CO_2. It can drop below 200 ppm, perilously close to the 150 ppm level where plants can no longer grow. During the Little Ice Age, glaciation began to expand after 1550, following ninety years of the Spörer Minimum. During the colder Maunder Minimum, glaciation increased again—alpine glaciers extended over valley farmland, and Arctic sea ice extended farther to the south.

Indisputable Natural Solar Cycles

As a matter of logic, there is a glaring deficiency to the theory of anthropogenic global warming: it disregards a well-documented historical record showing that climate on Earth has repeatedly warmed and cooled for centuries and millennia before humans built industrial factories or drove automobiles. For example, anthropogenic global warming could not have caused the Roman Warm Period.

For more details on the history of climate, review the Blytt-Sernander sequence, a series of climate phases identified from the study of peat bogs in Northern Europe. These divisions, defined by radiocarbon dating, show that the warmest phase of the current Holocene interglacial period, the Atlantic, happened long ago, occurring between five thousand and eight thousand years after the end of the last ice age. Obviously, if the warmest period in history was thousands of years ago, long before the Industrial Revolution, that ancient episode of global warming must have been driven by something other than human emissions of greenhouse gases like CO_2.

It was.

Like all current and past phases of climate on Earth, it was driven by natural variations in the emission and absorption of radiation from the Sun. This, in turn, raises an obvious question: What determines variations in solar irradiance? They could be almost totally random, though this is unlikely because proxy records and historical evidence strongly establish a quasi-bicentennial cycle of colder climate. Alternatively, climate cycles could be driven by imponderable fluctuations in the solar dynamo. But it is also possible that the cycles in solar output may be predictable.

Planetary Alignments and Climate Variability

The late Dr. Theodor Landscheide, of the Schroeter Institute for Research in Cycles of Solar Activity, linked climate variability to planetary alignments, in a way that has nothing to do with astrology. This led him to predict a "New Little Ice Age Instead of Global Warming."[2] In 1989, Landscheide foresaw a sunspot minimum whose timing he correlated to "an 83-year cycle in the change of the rotary force driving the Sun's oscillatory motion about the center of mass of the Solar System." Stating that the future course of this cycle could be computed, he expected that a severe cooling of the Earth, similar to the Maunder Minimum type, was inevitable at around 2030 and again around 2200. Landscheide was a pioneer. His quest to identify cycles of solar activity has been taken up and sophisticated since his death.

Solar-planetary theorist Ken McCracken, working with Jurg Beer and Friedhelm Steinhilber, claims that the paleoclimatic record over the last 9,400 years reveals twenty-six Grand

Minima similar to the Maunder Minimum. McCracken, Beer, and Steinhilber claim that the Grand Minima in the Holocene, including the Maunder Minimum, all occurred during disordered phases of the Sun's motions. Most of these Grand Minima appeared in clusters of two to seven Grand Minima in sequence, with intervals of up to 1,200 years in which there were no Grand Minima.[3] They marshal evidence from Carbon-14 and Beryllium-10 galactic cosmic ray proxies documenting variations in cosmic ray intensity and solar activity. They find four strong correlations with the motions of the Jovian planets. Assessing these together, they calculate the probability of them occurring by chance at less than one in 100,000.

McCracken, Beer, and Steinhilber report that Helio cosmic ray intensity decreases during the first sixty years of the approximately 172-year Jose Cycle and increases in the remaining 112 years "in association with Barycentric anomalies in the distance between the Sun and the center of mass of the Solar System."[4]

Barycenter Anomalies and Solar Inertial Motion
Note that low cosmic ray intensity is associated with higher solar activity and warmer temperatures, while a high flux of cosmic radiation occurs when there is an inactive Sun and climate is cooler.

Low cosmic ray intensity was measured when Uranus and Neptune were in superior conjunction (mutual cancellation), while high intensities (lower solar activity) occurred when Uranus and Neptune "were in inferior conjunction" (additive effects).[5]

To better understand the argument for planetary forcing of variations in solar output, consider that the commonplace observation that the Earth orbits around the Sun is not precisely true. In fact, the Earth (as well as the Sun itself) orbits the "barycenter," or center of mass, of the Solar System. This center of mass sometimes lies within the Sun, and sometimes is outside its surface, depending on the alignment of the giant Jovian planets, particularly Jupiter (318 times the mass of the Earth).

The center of mass of the Sun and Jupiter lies just above the surface of the Sun at 1.07 solar radii (462,743 miles) from the center. The center of mass of the Sun and Saturn is 0.58 solar radii (250,833 miles) from the Sun's center. Therefore, when you have a "syzygy"—an out-of-town word (from the Greek *syzygos*—"yoked together") that refers to a straight-line configuration of three or more celestial bodies—with Jupiter and Saturn on the same side of the Sun, the center of mass is 1.65 solar radii (713,575 miles) from the Sun's center. Add Uranus (0.18 radii) and Neptune (0.32 radii), and the center of mass of the Solar System can be offset by as much as 2.15 solar radii (929,810 miles) from the Sun's center.

The four Jovian planets that exert the greatest gravitational pull in moving the center of mass (barycenter) of the Solar System only return to the same position (within two degrees) every 4,267.25 years. However, there are many shorter cycles that some astronomers associate with more frequently occurring barycenter anomalies. As they see it, all solar Grand Minima as recorded in climate and paleoclimatic records during the current Holocene Epoch coincide with planetary alignment-caused angular momentum perturbations of the Sun.

Focusing first on the grand planetary realignment cycle, it is notable that solar physicists have correlated proxy climate records (dendrochronology: Carbon-14 and Beryllium-10 solar activity proxies from the Arctic and Antarctic) with the Jet Propulsion Laboratory's tabulation of the barycenter coordinates of the Sun, the eight major planets, and Pluto.

These records show that the Solar System is indeed a "system" that involves complex planetary synchronization. The plot of planetary alignments coincides with repeating, sometimes almost identical, patterns of climate change as reflected in the solar activity proxies.[6]

Data from the Little Ice Age (LIA) that followed the Medieval Warm Period offer a powerful "tell" if you wish to understand climate. The LIA—one of the colder Grand Minima of the Holocene climate epoch that began 11,700 years ago— had a "twin." Proxy records, centered on a period around 3500 BC, show almost identical solar radiation patterns. When the two series are overlaid, the difference in the curves is practically imperceptible.[7]

What accounts for this? The precise answer is still unclear. As the planets move in different configurations in their counterclockwise orbits around the Sun, the barycenter oscillates in a range of repeating trefoil patterns. It seems evident that certain planetary alignments coincide with barycentric anomalies that disrupt normal solar radiation. Solar theorist Geoff Sharp states that those associated with Grand Minima entail a disordered Solar System barycenter. "Large excursions of the inner loop are required for significant solar disruption."[8] Is he right? The world's governments really don't want to know. An authoritative answer might disrupt their plans to combat a trumped-up climate catastrophe.

A powerful graphic representation of the correlation between solar inertial motion and solar-terrestrial climate cycles was published by Czech astrophysicist, Ivanka Charvatova. She writes:

> The solar inertial motion (SIM) (motion of the Sun around the mass Centre of the Solar System) is caused by the varying positions, predominantly of the giant planets (José, 1965). The varying positions of the giant planets (Jupiter (J), Saturn (S), Uranus (U), Neptune (N)) force the Sun to move inside a circular area which has a diameter of 0.02 AU (astronomical unit) or 3.10^6 km or 4.3 solar radii. The SIM is computable in advance, a great advantage that opens up a possibility of establishing predictive assessments.[9]

It Even Eluded Newton

Stick with me here. This analysis can easily be introduced on the basis of a college astrophysics class. But a fully comprehensive explanation of the mechanism by which the various planetary configurations perturb the Sun's dynamo, as well as the way this perturbation informs changes in Earth's climate, remains the province of one or more high-performance solar physicists. It is beyond me. It even eluded Sir Isaac Newton, in his 1678 *Principia.* Newton unrealistically failed to account for the elliptical orbits of the planets; according to Newton's third law, "all bodies must attract each other."[10] Yet Newton only hinted at a solution to what is now known in celestial mechanics as the "n-body problem," the problem of the mutual gravitational attraction of three or more celestial bodies.

Another point of note, Newton worked on the *Principia* during the Maunder Minimum, a period when sunspot activity was negligible. This was hardly a propitious time to analyze the impact of planetary alignment on the Sun's dynamo. Its most visible manifestation was not readily apparent then, from 1645 to 1710. Also Newton worked long before Herschel discovered Uranus and almost two centuries before Neptune was discovered on September 23, 1846. As you may know, Neptune is the densest of the massive Jovian planets, and the third largest by mass.

Astronomer Geoff Sharp has identified a planetary configuration with Jupiter, Neptune, and Uranus within fifteen degrees of alignment on one side of the Sun and Saturn opposite that is associated with solar cycle slow down or shutdown that occurs in every case. When Uranus and Neptune are close together, there is an average of three chances for Jupiter and Saturn to form this configuration, which will happen around every 208 years. This is a complex, rather than a simple, oscillation that includes periods of retrograde motion. As the Sun orbits around the center of mass of the Solar System, it loops back on itself, causing it to move through to its own previously generated magnetic fields. This affects the Sun's angular momentum, which sometimes turns negative. For reasons of basic physics, angular momentum is transferred to the Sun's internal rotation. Australian astrophysicist Ian Wilson and colleagues proposed that changes in this rotation rate are synchronized with changes in the Sun's orbital motion about the barycenter.[11]

Conservation of angular momentum is an absolute symmetry of nature. The Sun exists in a plasma state and behaves like a very heavy fluid undergoing thermonuclear reactions—the perturbations of angular momentum appear to be sufficient to disturb the normal patterns of solar radiation. Wilson suggests that the perturbations of angular momentum mainly affect the outer layers of the Sun's convective zone.[12]

Among the reasons that recurring Grand Minima of solar activity associated with planetary forcing have not been widely recognized is that the grand planetary realignment cycle stretches much further into the past than does human recognition of the extent of the Solar System. There are no instrument-monitored records dating that far back.

Obviously, no one was correlating bad weather with the planetary alignments of Neptune and Uranus 4,267.25 years ago. Neptune was only discovered 168 years ago. Further to that, due to orbital drift, the return of the four outer planets to the same position every 4,267.25 years is not identical, and the accuracy of proxy records is not precise enough to confirm whether the planetary alignment return falls within two degrees each cycle.

Note that Steve Desch, an astrophysicist at Arizona State University, argued in the *Astrophysical Journal* that Neptune and Uranus used to be twice as close to the Sun as they currently are and actually changed places about four billion years ago.[13] The astrophysical arguments about the formation of the gas giants are not immediately crucial to our inquiry, but Professor Desch's argument does underscore the issue of orbital drift that helps disguise the recurring patterns of solar Grand Minima.

$100 Billion for Climate Research Propaganda

The ongoing quest for understanding the natural causes of solar cycles highlights the bogus nature of the $100 billion, or more, invested by the world's governments, purportedly for climate research, but actually for propaganda to rationalize the institution of an ecofascist world system. If they were actually interested in cultivating better understanding of the drivers of climate, an allocation of even 20 percent of the resources squandered on global warming propaganda could have gone a long way toward illuminating the natural basis of solar cycles. But the IPCC explicitly limits its inquiries to consideration of only human-caused global warming—incredible intellectual dishonesty.

The irony is that the invention of ecocatastrophe as "a subterfuge" for the rich to maintain their dominant status was only of interest to the powers-that-be if the catastrophe was hypothetical, not genuine. A bogus catastrophe, like anthropogenic global warming, could serve to rationalize political cartelization of precious hydrocarbon energy. An actual ecocatastrophe, such as another Little Ice Age that some solar physicists believe could soon begin, would have the opposite effect.

It would kill the whole bogus enterprise of controlling anthropogenic global warming by clarifying that climate change is determined by the rhythms of nature, not by political diktat. In a real ecocatastrophe, the $1 billion a day being spent to combat global warming by reducing CO_2 emissions would have to be undone. Laws and treaties to the contrary, mothballed coal-fired plants would have to be reopened in an effort to raise ambient CO_2 levels to facilitate the growth of crops in a suddenly colder world.

Notes

1   Taylor, Peter J., *The Way the Modern World Works: World Hegemony to World Impasse* (Chichester: John Wiley & Sons, 1996), 216.

2   https://www.scribd.com/document/16745228/New-Little-Ice-Age-Instead-of-Global-Warming.

3   McCracken, K. G., J. Beer, and F. Steihilber, "Evidence for Planetary Forcing of the Cosmic Ray Intensity and Solar Activity throughout the Past 9400 Years," *Solar Physics* 289 (March 20, 2014): 3207–29.

4   Ibid.

5   Ibid.

6   Ibid.

7   Sharp, Geoff, "Calibrating the Dendrochronology and Carbon Dating Record via Astronomical Alignments," February 10, 2014, http://www.landscheidt.info/?q=node/323.

8   Ibid.

9   Charatova, Ivanka, "The Cycle of 2402 Years in Solar Motion and Its Response in Proxy Records," *GeoLines* 11 (2000), http://geolines.gli.cas.cz/fileadmin/volumes/volume11/G11-012.pdf.

10 Newton, Sir Isaac, *The Principia: Mathematical Principles of Natural Philosophy*, trans. Andrew Motte (New York: Danieal Adee, 1846).

11 Wilson, I. R. G., et al., "Does a Spin-Orbit Coupling between the Sun and the Jovian Planets Govern the Solar Cycle?," *Publications of the Astronomical Society of Australia* 25 (2008), 85.

12 Ibid., 91.

13 See http://www.space.com/4755-trading-cosmic-places-neptune-uranus-swapped-spots.html.

Chapter Eleven

Deconstructing the "Greatest Lie Ever Told"

40 million people are now already at risk of severe coastal flooding. That number could well triple within the next half-century or so. Even wealthier countries are not immune to the impacts. In the United States, for example, particularly vulnerable areas are: Miami Beach, the Chesapeake region, coastal Louisiana, and coastal Texas . . . This will have implications that extend right up to the steps of our nation's Capitol. A recent study found that sea level rise of only a tenth of a meter would lead to $2 billion in property damage and affect almost 68,000 people in Washington, D.C.

—Al Gore, 1993

You have heard this sad story umpteen times before. Even if you were not tuned in to see Al Gore on the *Today Show* on May 24, 2006, you have a pretty good idea of what he told Katie Couric. He said then that if his global warming carbon abatement agenda were not enacted, within fifteen to twenty years, "Yes, in fact the World Trade Center memorial site would be underwater." In short, this is the cartoon version of *The Day After Tomorrow*, Roland Emmerich's 2004 climate disaster movie, but without the sex appeal of Emmy Rossum.

The scenario of melting polar ice caps flooding the world is an impossible exaggeration that meshes with Al Gore's other efforts to Hollywoodize your understanding of climate. Remember the catchy graphics in Al Gore's film, *An Inconvenient*

Truth, showing all of South Florida and much of San Francisco disappearing under water? This geophysical counterfactual provides one of the prime rationalizations for the campaign to spend tens of trillions of dollars—of which Gore stands to pocket many millions—to prevent global warming supposedly caused by carbon dioxide emissions.

The idea that we face a disastrous rise in sea levels was propagated so that you would not resist efforts to have our pockets picked under the guise of "saving the planet." You were told that the Antarctic and Greenland ice caps were destined to melt and that warmer oceans would expand with catastrophic results, threatening shore dwellers the world over, particularly around important areas of the United States where rich people live and among poor, low-lying island nations.

Without a doubt, inundation by rising sea levels has become the catastrophe of choice in the twenty-first century. Not the least reason is that rising sea levels are to this point an almost entirely hypothetical menace. In a 2007 report, the UN's Intergovernmental Panel on Climate Change (IPCC) said that by the 2080s, many millions more people than today are projected to experience floods every year due to sea level rise, particularly those in densely populated and low-lying megadeltas of Asia and Africa, along with those on small islands.[1]

If you are going to be smitten by catastrophe, it is more rewarding and convenient to have your million-dollar oceanfront villa in Hilton Head—much less your two-bit tropical country—forecasted to be swamped by rising sea levels some sixty or seventy years in the future than it is to fall prey to an actual hurricane, much less an earthquake or a volcano, today. For one thing, hurricanes, earthquakes, and volcanoes are dangerous. They kill people. And cleaning up after them involves lots of work. Your car could be washed away or buried in ash. Volcanoes spew out gases like sulfur dioxide, carbon monoxide, methane, hydrogen fluoride, and even mists of hydrochloric acid. Clouds of these gases, emitted by actual volcanoes, sometimes settle in low-lying areas and asphyxiate people and livestock.

By comparison, inundation by rising sea levels is tidy. No one has to breathe noxious gases, or even get wet. It is all a matter of computer simulations, like a video game. That is why the president of the Maldives and the prime minister of Tuvalu, among others, have opted to be victimized by rising sea levels experienced through computer simulations rather than wait for some actual catastrophe that might justify supplication for compensation from wealthy countries.

"Sheer Nonsense"

Professor Niels-Axel Mörner, the former head of the Institute for Paleogeophysics and Geodynamics at Stockholm University, a world expert on sea level changes and coastal evolution, reports that, in recent years, former Maldivian president Mohamed Nasheed maintained that the Maldives would be submerged under the sea. Mörner refers to this claim as "sheer nonsense."[2] A decade ago, while Mörner was the president of the INQUA commission on Sea Level Changes and Coastal Evolution, he conducted a sea level research project in the Maldives, finding that the sea level was not rising and had been stable for the last thirty to forty years. He stated that the 1970s sea level even fell by approximately twenty centimeters.

Former president Nasheed is not alone in seeking to win compensation for a projected rise in sea levels. In a July 2014 interview with CNN, Anote Tong, the former president of Kiribati, stated that rising sea levels, due to global warming, would lead to the total annihilation of the thirty-three coral islands in the Central Pacifica that make up Kiribati.[3]

Part of the explanation for the eagerness of the leaders of small island countries to proclaim that they have no future is that they are responding to the promise of lots of money to say so. According to the Climate Policy Initiative, global North-South climate cash flows were estimated at between $39 billion and $62 billion as of October 2013.[4] In addition, they were promised up to $30 billion more at the Copenhagen and Cancun climate talks in exchange for backing for international treaties to completely revamp world energy markets. As reported in the *Guardian*, details of this bribe were included among the revelations released by WikiLeaks. One tantalizing tidbit said that the accord promised $30 billion in aid for the poorest nations hit by global warming they had not caused. Within two weeks of the Copenhagen meeting, the Maldives foreign minister wrote to US Secretary of State Hillary Clinton, expressing the country's eagerness to back the plan.[5] Strangely, for a country whose leaders believed it had no future, the Maldives are now planning to build sixty-four resorts, at an estimated cost of $40 million each, along with eleven new airports.

Not to be outdone in the competition for victimhood, Ian Fry, the delegate of Tuvalu to the 2009 United Nations Climate Change Conference in Copenhagen, gave a tearful speech suggesting that Tuvalu needed to be saved from rising sea levels. In the speech, he said, *"I woke this morning, and I was crying, and that's not easy for a grown man to admit. The fate of my country rests in your hands."*[6] Sincerity is the key in this type of presentation. As they say, if you can fake that you've got it made. (Fry is actually an Australian who lives in Canberra.)

Darwin Debunks Hysteria about Disappearing Coral Islands

Lest you waste any tears over low-lying island nations whose leaders are all worked up over the computer-simulated threat of inundation due to carbon dioxide emissions, causing sea levels to rise, the fact that this is a nonthreat was clearly explained by Charles Darwin in *The Voyage of the Beagle* (1839).[7] He saw that rising sea levels created and expanded coral atolls. It did not destroy them. Notwithstanding the fact that they never reach much above about one foot in height, coral atolls have survived a sea level rise of more than 330 feet over the last 20,000 years. As Darwin showed, they rise up higher when water levels rise. So there is no danger to the many island nations that are maneuvering to get on the global warming gravy train.

In his autobiography, Darwin explained that his insight into the geology of barrier reefs and atolls was one of his proudest scientific accomplishments, developed on the west coast of South America before he had ever even seen a coral reef. He then wrote, "No other work of mine was begun in so deductive a spirit as this; for the whole theory was thought out on the west coast of S. America before I had even seen a true coral reef. I had therefore only to verify and extend my views by a careful examination of living reefs. But it should be observed that I had during the two previous years been incessantly attending to the effects on the shores of S. America of the intermittent elevation of the land, together with its denudation and deposition of sediment. This necessarily led me to reflect much on the effects of subsidence, and it was easy to replace in imagination the continued deposition of sediment by the upward growth of coral. To do this was to form my theory of the formation of barrier reefs and atolls."[8]

Darwin could see 175 years ago that there was no danger of rising sea levels destroying low-lying atolls. But of course, Darwin was an actual thinking scientist, whose research was financed by his father, not by government grants. Darwin was thinking for himself, not pimping for the global warming gravy train, and more recent research confirms his insight.[9]

Notwithstanding the logic clearly spelled out by Darwin, Tuvalu officials claim that their islands are being flooded. Where is the evidence? There is none. Professor Mörner reports that there is a clear indication of stability over the last thirty years.[10]

Australia's National Tide Facility (NTF) reported that the historical record shows "no visual evidence of any acceleration in sea level trends." Nonetheless, in 2010, former Tuvalu Prime Minister Koloa Talake (who actually lives in Tuvalu), announced that Tuvalu, Kiribati, and the Maldives were planning legal action in the International Court of Justice against Western nations emitting carbon dioxide, claiming they are raising the sea level in the Pacific.

The Right Honorable Koloa Talake did not wish to be out-distanced in the scramble for carbon abatement billions by the Federated States of Micronesia's lawsuit against the Czech Republic. The Micronesian environment minister confessed in an interview with a Czech business newspaper that his government had been put up to suing the Czech Republic by Greenpeace, which provided details of a plan to retrofit two inefficient, Communist-era, coal-powered generating plants at Prunerov, in North Bohemia, the largest electricity suppliers in the country. Even if everything claimed by global warming alarmists about CO_2 emissions were true, the Prunerov power stations could account for no more than a couple of microns of sea rise in Micronesia.

Greenpeace bravely solicited a number of low-lying countries to sue Western nations as a publicity stunt over carbon emissions. Meanwhile, it is interesting to note that neither Greenpeace nor the island governments apparently so agitated over CO_2 would dream of importuning India and China, where 900 new coal-fired power plants are in the planning stages or already under construction.[11]

Furthermore, you would think that if the Tuvalu government actually believed that CO_2 emissions were causing the atmosphere to heat, resulting in their country sinking beneath the waves, they would not be adding to CO_2 emissions themselves. But they have neglected alternative energy and are almost entirely dependent on burning foreign oil. Their policy seems to be to take money for whatever purpose from wherever they can get it. Among their successes, they got money from Japan to import new diesel generators in 2006. You can bet they won't sue themselves over CO_2 emissions.

Professor Mörner detects the same fake hysteria about rising sea levels in Vanuatu, where the tide gauge indicates a stable sea level over the last fourteen years.[12] Vanuatu is claiming compensation on the global warming gravy train based on a prediction that there will be no one living on the main island of the Maskylines by the year 2090.

Professor Mörner characterizes the notion that sea levels are rapidly rising due to global warming as the "greatest lie ever told."[13] "The sea is not rising," he tells everyone. "It hasn't risen in 50 years." Professor Mörner is an unusual researcher in this respect. He is willing to give voice to politically incorrect sentiments. As he says, "You have to say sea level is rising to get money and get published."

Of course, Professor Mörner has two advantages that have enabled him to critique the official view that sea level is rising due to climate change caused by CO_2 emissions from burning hydrocarbon fuels. As the retired head of the Institute for Paleogeophysics and Geodynamics at Stockholm University, Mörner was a distinguished scholar who had the standing to speak out. And because he was born in 1938, and was nearing the end of his career, he was not held hostage by his ambition to the corrupt considerations of government funding for his work.

Thinking citizens will note that there is strong evidence that sea levels have risen by about 390 feet since the last ice age. But by about five thousand to six thousand years ago, glacial melting in temperate zones had more or less ceased. The balance between sea and land has been essentially stable since the low-altitude glaciers in the Earth's temperate zones finished melting. (Remember, in the last ice age, Detroit, Glasgow, and Stockholm were buried beneath a mile of ice.)

There is good reason to doubt that there has been any substantial shift in "eustatic" sea levels—levels due to greater volumes of water as compared to displacement by falling land—in the past several thousand years. Eustatic sea levels were formerly thought to be global as compared to local sea levels. But it is now understood that they are local or regional. Contrary to what you have been told, the uncertainties of sea level measurement are greater than the supposed margins of change over just about any time interval during the past few thousand years.

Let's look at it more closely.

In the first place, it is misleading to think of sea level as a singular noun. It should be recognized that there are many sea levels. If you are like most people and your geophysical intuition was informed by experiences in a body of water no larger than a bathtub, you have probably formed the wrong idea that there is a sea level that is a simple surface. Not true.

The globe on your desk is a sphere. The world is not. This has long been recognized. In Sir Isaac Newton's 1687 *Principia*, he spelled out his laws of motion, including a proof that a rotating fluid body takes the form of an "oblate ellipsoid of revolution" which he termed "an oblate spheroid."

Then there are "reference ellipsoids." As the name implies, reference ellipsoids are mathematical models of the Earth in rotation that geodesists have used as a reference frame for recording geophysical information. Mean sea level (MSL) can be calculated from reference ellipsoids. In the old days, MSL was calculated from tide gauges as the arithmetic mean of hourly water elevations observed over a nineteen-year cycle in reference to some fixed benchmark. Contrary to what you might suppose, sea level calculated in Amsterdam was not the same zero elevation as sea level calculated in Miami. Sea level measured in Rio de Janeiro was yet another value, as were those from Mumbai and Hong Kong. There was not one sea level. There were many.

Among the many reference ellipsoids that have been calculated, perhaps the most important is the World Geodetic System 1984 (WGS 84) ellipsoid. That one is incorporated as the default datum in the Global Positioning System (GPS) that enables you to find your way around unfamiliar neighborhoods. In most places in North America, GPS is accurate enough for driving instructions. But it would not enable you to measure even the upper range of projected sea level rise at 3.2 mm per year if you drove onto a ferry today and again twelve months later.

Your GPS receiver uses the reference ellipsoid model of sea level, so the number you see on the screen is the elevation above the model and not the real sea level. The shape of the ellipsoid is a smooth squished sphere, but the shape of real sea surface is riddled with irregularities.

You can get a hint of the error margin from the fact that GPS elevation calculations diverge significantly for areas on land shown on accurate topographic maps. Geodesist Witold Fraczek reports that his office in California is shown on topographic quadrangle maps and high-resolution digital elevation models at 1,312 feet above MSL. But the GPS reading is 1,207 feet—a 105 foot difference.[14] The reason for the discrepancy is the irregular shape of the Earth that is only approximated by the WGS 84 ellipsoid.

To improve accuracy, geodesists employ another reference frame for the shape of the Earth: the geoid. The geoid approximates MSL. And get ready for it: the geoid is defined as "the hypothetical, equipotential gravitational surface" that the Earth would assume if it were covered entirely by water.[15] Because the Earth's mass is not evenly distributed, different parts of the Earth's surface are subject to stronger gravitational forces than others.

The geoid was calculated to reflect the gravitational force variation over the surface of the Earth. The geoid is usually depicted as a contour chart using approximately sixteen feet contour intervals to depict deviations from the ellipsoid. In other words, think of the geoid as a lumpy gravity map. While the geoid is a more realistic approximation of the real shape of the Earth, incorporating irregular features, it is only an approximation. Its accuracy is limited and varies according to latitude. The absolute error at well-surveyed satellite sites is approximately plus or minus 3.3 feet to 6.5 feet.

The takeaways from this detour into the rough waters of geophysics are several:

1. It shows that calculations that purport to measure global MSL to a precision of millimeters are hypothetical approximations only. Nothing more. The applied math geeks say the geoid model is only accurate

to plus or minus 3.3 feet to 6.5 feet. So how do they get away with claiming MSL rise measured in millimeters and fractions thereof? You don't have to be a geophysicist to see that they are dealing in insignificant figures whose reliability is suspect.

2. Sea level is more accurately understood as a local or regional geophysical quantity rather than a uniform global one.
3. The irregularities in the surface of the sea controlled by the gravitational potential of the Earth are an order of magnitude greater than experts thought.

The surface of the sea, even at its calmest, is not level. Now read that sentence again, because judging by the reaction of other readers, you are may have misunderstood it. I do not mean merely that the bottom of the sea is uneven. The reality is more interesting. Both the bottom of the ocean and its surface—the sea level—are marked by big hills and deep valleys. The deepest valley on the surface of the ocean is off the coast of India where the geoid descends 344.5 feet below the ellipsoid. In other words, you could say that in that part of the Indian Ocean, MSL is 629.9 feet lower than it is in the Indonesian Archipelago, where the biggest known hill in the ocean rises about 285 feet above the ellipsoid.

Clearly, sea level is more complicated than Nobel Prize–winner Al Gore lets on. Given the fact that there are many different sea levels, few of which have ever been measured, there are manifold opportunities for cherry picking or distorting data to present any trend you are paid to show (especially when the rate of change is a matter of millimeters). The global warming vigilantes are drawing heroic conclusions compounded from an array of insignificant figures.

CO_2 or Basic and Ultrabasic Rocks?

Note that gravitational highs that can raise sea levels by hundreds of feet occur where masses of basic and ultrabasic rocks form in an upwelling of magma onto the seafloor. Basic and ultrabasic rocks that have the highest gravitational attraction form in regions of undersea volcanic activity, such as in the Indonesian archipelago. The significance of ultra-basic rocks like dunite and peridotite, which are very low in silica and rich in iron and magnesium, is that they exert strong gravitational attraction. Equally, sedimentary basins account for gravity lows. So it seems plausible that sea levels are influenced more by developments on the sea floor than by the atmosphere. The constant shifting of tectonic plates should be expected to alter local sea levels far more than any possible effect of CO_2 emissions from the power plants at Prunerov, much less your car.

Not only do gravity variations reflect variations in the Earth's crust and mantle, but in many areas where global warming activists complain that rising sea levels are a big issue, such as Venice, the real problem is not the sea get-ting higher, but subsidence—the land getting lower. Fur-thermore, the normal year-to-year variation of climate in any given locale is far greater than any overall trend due to global warming. Therefore, you would expect that global warming would be undetectable in the climate record of any given location.

It is also well established that sea level varies according to barometric pressure and shifts in ocean currents. The consid-erations outlined above capture some of the complexity and uncertainty in attempting to calculate and measure trends in average global sea level to a resolution of a millimeter. Given that much of the sea has not been measured in the past, and many of the areas where tide gauges were deployed, such as the North Sea, are characterized by tectonic subsidence, the selection criteria for picking which tide gauge records to count, and how to integrate them with satellite altimetry data, are far from obvious.

As Professor Mörner points out, clear observational field measurements indicate that sea levels are not rising in the

Maldives, Bangladesh, Tuvalu, Vanuatu, or French Guiana.[16] The IPCC and its associates, however, name these as key sites in the debate on sea level and have predicted terrible flooding in these areas, despite the reality being different than the IPCC's claims.[17] Professor Mörner further states that the satellite altimetry group undertook reinterpretation of the raw data in order to obtain results they desired, opining that the "global sea level factor" is never clear and trustworthy, but rather a matter of opinion.[18]

This is where Al Gore might object and tell us again as he told the Senate Environment Committee on March 21, 2007, "The science is settled."[19] And he further said that carbon dioxide emissions, if left unchecked, "could lead to a drastic change in the weather, sea levels, and other aspects of the environment."

Francis Bacon on Al Gore

This is where Sir Francis Bacon and I would say in unison, "What rubbish." OK, Sir Francis Bacon, the father of the Scientific Revolution, would not say, "What rubbish," but only because he's been dead for the better part of 400 years. But in 1620, when very much alive, Bacon rubbished Al Gore's views about "settled science," which strangely echo the view of the medieval Scholastics who opposed free inquiry and the scientific method. In the preface to the *Novum Organum Scientiarum*,[20] Bacon wrote: "Those who've taken upon them to lay down the law of nature as a thing already searched out and understood, whether they have spoken in simple assurance or professional affectation, have therein done philosophy and the sciences great injury. Whereas they have been successful in inducing belief, so they have been effective in quenching and stopping inquiry; and have done more harm by spoiling and putting an end to other men's efforts than good by their own."

Al Gore's "settled science" is not really science at all. Programming a syllogism into a computer does not make it science. He and the other global warming vigilantes are merely brandishing a computer-aided syllogism of the sort that Bacon sought to transcend:

- **Major premise**: carbon dioxide emissions raise atmospheric temperatures.
- **Minor premise:** warmer temperatures melt ice sheets and expand seawater.
- **Conclusion**: CO_2 emissions will raise sea level.

While it is true that the melting of major land stores of glacial ice would result in a significant rise in sea levels, contrary to Al Gore, there is little, if any, prospect that the World Trade Center memorial site would be underwater seven to twelve years from now, as he told you in 2006. The "settled" opinion of oceanographers is that sea levels have risen at an average rate of no more than three millimeters per year. The ground floor of the World Trade Center memorial site is twelve feet above sea level. For it to be underwater, as Gore predicted, by 2026, much less 2021, would require that sea levels rise by one foot per year.

That is ten times faster than the outside estimates of the historic rise of sea levels. Even during the most rapid meltwater pulse following the end of the Ice Age about 14,200 years ago, evidence suggests that the sea level rose about sixty-six feet over a 500-year period. Gore is telling you that sea levels will rise more than 7.5 times faster than they did during the most rapid phase of major sheet ice melting after the last Ice Age.

That is nonsense. The depth of the permafrost and the altitude of the ice fields in both Greenland and Antarctica mean that the temperature of the Earth would have to rise much higher than any forecast effect of higher atmospheric concentrations of CO_2 could explain. Greenland Summit is approximately 10,500 feet above sea level. The average annual temperature there is -25.6 °F. Global warming alarmists project an increase in global temperatures of 7.2 °F. Permafrost is safe. You won't need a kayak to navigate the area around Wall Street. The current hysteria over a projection of an ongoing dramatic rise in sea levels from melting glaciers is remote from the facts.

As the austral winter came to an end on October 7, 2014, Antarctic sea ice, far from melting away, had set a new high record of 7.76 million square miles—about 2.750 million square miles greater than had ever been recorded by satellites since they began tracking sea ice in 1979.[21] At that point, CO_2 was measured at 336 ppm. Meanwhile, atmospheric carbon dioxide has risen by 20 percent globally. According to scholastic Al's syllogism, that sea ice shouldn't be there.

But don't worry. You don't have to study the philosophy of science or slog through Geophysics 101 to figure out that rising sea levels are not an imminent threat. All you have to do is watch Al Gore. Look at how he spent some of the outsized fortune he pocketed as the chief crony capitalist on the global warming gravy train: He plopped down $8.875 million to buy a villa on the Pacific Ocean in swanky Montecito, Santa Barbara County, California.

That is the metamessage to take to heart.

Notes

1   *Climate Change 2007: Synthesis Report* WGII 6.4, 6.5, Table 6.11, SPM.

2   Mörner, Niels-Axel, "Sea Level Is Not Rising." See https://www.scribd.com/doc/54200036/Sea-Level-is-Not-Rising-by-Professor-Nils-Axel-Morner.

3   Watts, Anthony, "Remember the Threat of Flooded Atolls and Climate Refugees Due to Sea Level Rise? Never Mind," http://wattsupwiththat.com/

2014/07/31/remember-the
-threat-of-flooded-atolls
-and-climate-refugees-due
-to-sea-level-rise-never
-mind/.

4 http://matzav.com/world
-spending-1-billion-per-day
-to-tackle-global-warming/.

5 "WikiLeaks Cables Reveal
How US Manipulated Cli-
mate Accord," see https://
www.theguardian.com/
environment/2010/dec/03/
wikileaks-us-manipulated
-climate-accord.

6 Johnson, Brad, "Tuvalu to
Obama and the Senate: The
Fate of My Country Rests in
Your Hands," http://grist.org/
article/2009-12-14-tuvalu-to
-obama-and-the-senate-the
-fate-of-my-country/.

7 See Darwin, Charles, *The Voyage of the Beagle* (Hertford-
shire: Wordsworth Editions,
1997).

8 Darwin, Charles, *Autobiography* (1887), 98–99.

9 See Oskin, Becky, "Was
Darwin Wrong about Coral
Atolls?," *LiveScience,* May 13,
2013, http://www.livescience
.com/31975-how-coral-atolls
-form.html.

10 Mörner, "Sea Level Is Not
Rising."

11 Carrington, Damian, "More
than 1,000 New Coal Plants
Planned Worldwide, Figures
Show," *The Guardian*, November 19, 2012.

12 Mörner, "Sea Level Is Not
Rising."

13 See Mörner, Niels-Axel,
"The Greatest Lie Ever Told"
(available from morner@pog
.nu), http://www.lavoisier
.com.au/articles/greenhouse
-science/sea-levels/ollier2007
-26.php.

14 Fracczek, Witold, "Mean Sea
Level, GPS and the Geoid," Ar-
cUser Online (July–September
2003). See http://www.esri
.com/news/arcuser/0703/
geoid1of3.html.

15 https://recedingseas
.wordpress.com/2015/07/19/
mean-sea-level-gps-and-the
-geoid/.

16 Mörner, "Sea Level Is Not
Rising," 8.

17 Ibid.

18 Ibid., 13.

19 For a colorful introduction to
Gore's testimony, see http://
drtimball.com/2013/is-al
-gore-the-latter-day-pardoner
-carbon-credits-are-modern
-indulgences/.

20 Bacon, Sir Francis, *Novum
Organum Scientiarum*, trans.

G. W. Kitchin (Oxford: Oxford University Press, 1855).

21 "Antarctic Sea Ice Reaches New Record Maximum," *NASA Science News*, October 7, 2014, http://science.nasa.gov/science-news/science-at-nasa/2014/07oct_antarcticseaice/.

Chapter Twelve

Can Food Crises Trigger Collapse?

The Pakistan Economy Watch (PEW) on Tuesday asked the government to take serious steps to ensure food security in the country as an international food crisis can engulf the world soon ... Dr. Murtaza Mughal said that the vulnerable and the poor would be hardest hit who spend as much as 60 to 75 per cent of their income on food. He said that situation at home is far from encouraging; flawed policies have left almost all the federal and provincial departments related to agriculture as dysfunctional ... The matter should not be taken lightly as during the last crisis 30 countries witnessed food riots while many governments were sent packing.
—*Pakistan Today*, July 25, 2012

In 2013, when I told my *Strategic Investment* readers that an unexpected turn toward colder weather could precipitate a range of economic challenges, colder weather had already begun to affect the economy. Ironically, as John Williams showed in *Shadow Government Statistics*, the first impact of extraordinarily cold weather was to artificially inflate the government's defective economic statistics through a spike in utility usage, and related industrial production, in each month of the first quarter of 2013.[1]

The proximate effect of a colder climate is deflationary. It increases heat load, thus magnifying power requirements for a modern economy. Colder winters mean greater energy consumption, ramping up utility usage. Colder climate makes you poorer as you have to pay more to heat your homes, body, and car. Colder climate makes life's necessities more expensive. It reduces purchasing power and contracts real income, contributing to recession.

Coldest Year since 1883

Looking ahead, the question is how adverse could the consequences be if, as some solar physicists suggest, the recent spate of colder weather deepens into another Little Ice Age?

As reported in *Der Speigel*, March of 2013 was the coldest it had been in Germany since 1883.[2] Yet 2013 was the solar maximum for Solar Cycle 24. The cycle is so named because it is the twenty-fourth eleven-year Schwab cycle since scientists began counting these cycles of solar activity from the eighteenth century until the present.

Proxies for Solar Irradiance

There is fairly complete sunspot data going back to 1610. Generally speaking, higher sunspot activity is associated with warmer weather. This has been known since long before the seventeenth century.

Observation and recording of sunspots by Imperial Chinese astronomers began during the Shang Dynasty (1700 BC to 1027 BC). The Chinese kept detailed sunspot records for thousands of years. They observed that more sunspots were correlated with warmer weather. *Feng,* or abundance, was associated with the *Dou,* one of seven words for "sunspot."[3]

William Herschel, the German-born, British polymath who coined the term "asteroid," discovered some 2,400 heavenly objects, including the planet Uranus, along with two of its major moons, Oberon and Titania, as well as two moons of Saturn and distant nebulae. In addition to taking an interest in sunspots and the link between solar activity and terrestrial climate, he was also a professional violinist and oboist who composed twenty-four symphonies.

In 1801, just about a year after he discovered infrared radiation, Herschel published his *Observations Tending to Investigate the Matters of the Sun, in Order to Find the Causes or Symptoms of Its Variable Emission of Light and Heat.*[4] He reasoned that fewer sunspots meant less light and heat from the Sun and thus poor harvests. Herschel correlated sunspot records with the price of wheat, observing that the price of wheat soared when there were fewer sunspots.

More recently, two Israeli researchers, Lev A. Putilnik of the Israel Space Agency and Gregory Yom Din of the Golan Research Institute, have confirmed Herschel's insight by analyzing the direct link between wheat prices and solar activity in the seventeenth century. They concluded that history shows—not surprisingly—rising food costs during solar minima, or times of low solar output.[5]

Solar physicists distinguish between two types of solar minimum: regular oscillation type and the more dramatic Grand Minimum of the Maunder type, such as that marking the Little Ice Age. During the 1890s, English astronomer William Maunder published two papers associating colder weather during the seventeenth-century nadir of the Little Ice Age with an almost total absence of sunspot activity. For one thirty-year span within the Maunder Minimum, only fifty sunspots were observed, whereas during the recent period of global warming 40,000 to 50,000 sunspots would have been typical.

Interest in Sunspots Wanes

Notwithstanding the strong intellectual pedigree for observations linking sunspots to climate stretching back for thousands of years, the appreciation of this link was far stronger at the end of the nineteenth century than it has been lately. Herschel and Maunder believed there was a strong link between sunspots and climate. Al Gore doesn't.

The astronomers and solar physicists of the earlier days lived before the triumph of crony capitalism. King George III may have caused the founding fathers' heartburn, but he didn't put political pressure on Herschel to deny that climate on Earth is informed by the radiance of the Sun.

By contrast, today's climate researchers have been bribed by government grants totaling more than \$100 billion to argue that human CO_2 emissions are fostering rapid global warming. When politicians discovered an imperative for linking CO_2 emissions to global warming, appreciation for the Sun's role in climate drastically receded. With all the pressure to make the Earth, rather than the Sun, the center of the climate mechanism, it is hardly surprising that the UN's IPCC claimed in its 2007 report that only 7 percent of the change in temperatures over time could be attributed to the Sun.

This orthodoxy began to wobble ever so slightly in May 2012 when the *Journal of Atmospheric and Solar-Terrestrial Physics* published research by Norwegian scientists who found a strong correlation between the length of the solar sunspot cycle and the earth's temperature during a specific cycle. While the Norwegians did not argue that solar output is the only driver of climate variability, they did suggest that its importance is as much as a magnitude (a factor of ten) greater than the IPCC would have you believe.[6]

Notwithstanding all the lures, financial incentives, and political pressures for climate researchers to go along with the global warming gag, a surprising number of independent scholars have continued to think for themselves, including a number who have forecast a forthcoming Grand Minimum of solar activity, perhaps comparable to that of the Maunder Minimum that seems to have caused the last Little Ice Age. Two of them are Silvia Duhau, professor of physics at the University of Buenos Aires, and Cornelis de Jager, of the Royal Netherlands Institute for Sea Research. Both have published a series of papers in recent years analyzing solar variability.

Of particular interest is "The Forthcoming Grand Minimum of Solar Activity." In this 2010 paper, they conclude that solar variability is entering into a long Grand Minimum that will last for at least a century. They show that the Solar System has been in a transition phase since the turn of the millennium that should have ended by 2014. We are transitioning from the Grand Maximum of the twentieth century to a Grand Minimum that should bring sharply colder temperatures.[7]

This raises an important question for your investments, your business, and your family: Do you want to trust your future to the inventor of the Internet, Al Gore? Or should you take a contrarian view? Or at least draw up some contingency plans in the event that thousands of years of experience correlating high solar activity with prosperity and low solar activity with economic depression, dearth, devolution, and collapse—in other words, the Dark Ages—might still carry value as you harness your intuitions about the future? As you ponder that, bear in mind that it isn't only obscure Argentine and Dutch researchers who are focusing on solar activity.

NASA's National Oceanic and Atmospheric Administration (NOAA) Solar Cycle Prediction Panel is a group of solar physicists assembled periodically under the auspices of the US government. They, too, identify the solar maximum for Cycle 24 as having occurred in 2013.

Based on what we have come to consider normal patterns of solar activity, 2013 should have been a warmer year than normal. But low temperature records were broken around the globe. If this was a solar maximum, it implies that the next solar minimum could bring bitterly cold weather—quite the opposite of Al Gore's much-hyped global warming.

In other words, frigid weather during a solar maximum, when we should be warmer, is a portent of much colder weather to come. As astrophysicist Piers Corbyn of WeatherAction.com points out, solar activity has been generally very low, providing further evidence of an inevitable shift toward a new mini ice age. Corbyn states that the emphasis on CO_2's effect on climate has pointed the world in the wrong direction. According to Piers Corbyn, brother of British Labor Party leader

Jeremy Corbyn, "man-made climate change does not exist and the arguments for it are not based on science."[8]

He suggests that global cooling is now "locked in." His predictions of a soon-beginning deep freeze match those of other solar physicists, like the late Dr. Theodor Landscheidt of the Schroeter Institute for Research in Cycles of Solar Activity, Dr. Victor Manuel Velasco Herrera of the University of Mexico, and Dr. Habibullo Abdussamatov, a prominent Russian solar physicist.

There is general agreement within the scientific community that the current Holocene interglacial warming will be followed sometime before the crack of doom by another full-fledged Ice Age. Of more immediate concern is the prospect of another Little Ice Age. In my view, the indisputable fact that the world is cooling while CO_2 emissions continue to rise lends credibility to predictions of another Little Ice Age.

It is not immaterial to the thinking person that the contrarian forecasts of solar physicists deciphering cycles of the Sun have proven more reliable than predictions of global warming due to CO_2 emissions. Because of the huge, lavishly funded global warming bureaucracy embedded in governments and UN agencies employed full-time to gin up scarce stories to stampede you into supporting draconian measures to reduce CO_2 emissions, the public record is replete with official predictions of unstoppable warming. These have proven spectacularly wrong.

In fact, they have been so wide of the mark that it is embarrassing. I have in my notes about twenty pages of single-spaced links to articles citing research and peer-reviewed studies disproving and debunking climate forecasts extrapolating catastrophic consequences from the increase in man-made CO_2 emissions in the atmosphere.

These included suggestions that polar bears were threatened with extinction due to heatstroke. Yet an aerial survey released by the Government of Nunavut showed that the polar bear population was flourishing, having grown by up to 66 percent.[9]

You may also remember global warming alarms about the melting of glaciers in the Himalayas and Greenland. Don't forget how that melting was supposed to flood New York City. This was just one gaudy detail in a parade of horrors involving the rapid rise of sea levels. And along with the hysteria over flooding, you also supposedly faced an epidemic of wildfires. These predictions are little better than bunk.

In 2005, the IPCC projected that "by 2010 the world will need to cope" with a stampede of 50 million climate refugees who purportedly would flee their homes due to the flooding of coastal cities and the rapid expansion of deserts. The UN even posted helpful maps on their websites to alert residents of the supposedly endangered locales that they might wish to flee.

As you know, 2010 has come and gone. Is there any sign of the 50 million (some global warming alarmists said 200 million) climate refugees clamoring for asylum in the uplands of the world?

No. Not a trace.

If you review the old maps where the UN projected catastrophic flooding and update the population figures for these supposedly vulnerable areas, there is no evidence of even 50 climate refugees, let alone 50 million. As Gavin Atkins pointed out, a very cursory look at the first available evidence seems to show that those places identified as most at risk of having climate refugees are actually among the fastest growing regions in the world. A map on the United Nations Environment Program (UNEP) website highlighting the so-called environmental danger zones was taken down.

You can't blame the climate Nazis for being embarrassed. Their intellectual position is less respectable than that of the Ptolemaic consensus that opposed Galileo's heresy that the Sun is the center of the Solar System. The global warming propagandists claim that human action in emitting CO_2 is more important as a driver of climate than the Sun.

On the face of it, this claim was always unlikely because the Sun is the prime source of warmth in this neighborhood of the galaxy, and human CO_2 emissions are a tiny fraction of naturally occurring CO_2.

While admitting that human CO_2 is small compared to naturally occurring CO_2, global warming alarmists pop champagne corks and claim that the natural CO_2 is absorbed in the carbon cycle, while stating that, for various mysterious reasons, the natural carbon cycle supposedly cannot absorb the relatively tiny increment added by human use of hydrocarbon fuels. Therefore, unlike naturally occurring CO_2, the human CO_2 is supposed to be cumulative, thus creating a devastating greenhouse effect warming the planet.

The global warming alarmists virtually ignore fluctuations in the Sun's output as factors informing the weather. And their claim that the natural carbon cycle cannot absorb the tiny additional increment of human generated CO_2 is mysterious in light of the fact that man-made CO_2 is chemically indistinguishable from the billions of tons of carbon suspended in the oceans, and naturally part of the atmosphere.

As S. Fred Singer and Dennis T. Avery write in *Unstoppable Global Warming: Every 1,500 Years*,[10] evidence calls the greenhouse theory into doubt. According to Singer and Avery, the human-generated greenhouse effect must be so small that it presents little threat to the planet. They state that this is especially true because each additional unit of CO_2 causes less warming than the previous unit. Data confirm that the lower atmosphere is not trapping much additional heat due to higher CO_2 concentrations.

Remote Sensing Systems (RSS) on satellites that measure global midtropospheric temperatures show that notwithstanding an increase in CO_2 emissions, from 364 ppm in July 1997 to 395 ppm in July 2012, global temperatures declined. The global atmosphere cooled from the end of the last Super El Niño that began with a low in April 1997.

The computer models beloved by global warming proponents forecast rapid increases in temperature since 1997 that have not materialized. The disconnect between the dire predictions and the actual record of falling temperatures in the twenty-first century calls the whole global warming hysteria into question.

To my way of thinking, some of the most persuasive evidence that climate is driven primarily by solar activity was presented by the Russian solar physicist Habibullo Abdussamatov in *National Geographic News* in February 2007.[11] Abdussamatov, head of space research at St. Petersburg's Pulkovo Astronomical Observatory, argued that fluctuations in the Sun's activity are responsible for any warming on the Earth with parallel effects on other planets, particularly Mars.

Abdussamatov's provocative argument that fluctuations in solar output account for heating and cooling of the planets led to observations that other heavenly bodies—including faraway Pluto; Neptune's moon, Triton; and Jupiter—could also be experiencing climate change. According to the blog *Strata-Sphere*, this "has some [scientists] scratching their heads over what could possibly be in common with the warming of all these planets . . . Could there be something in common with all the planets in our solar system that might cause them all to warm at the same time?"

Duh. It is not as if Abdussamatov were keeping it a secret. He told everyone quite clearly what is responsible. (This is so obvious that I assume *Strata-Sphere* was joking.) If you have read this far, you know that one thing all the planets and moons in our Solar System have in common is the Sun.

The Retrial of Galileo

It is hardly a surprise that Abdussamatov has been viciously attacked by the guardians of global warming orthodoxy. He has been dismissed as "crazy" and a "nutter" for arguing that solar irradiance, rather than human action on Earth, controls Earth's climate.

It is a good thing for Abdussamatov, Piers Corbyn, Silvia Duhau, Cornelius de Jaeger, and other solar physicists that the high priests of global warming can only ridicule and ostracize those with the temerity to put the Sun back at the center of the Solar System. Ironically, it has been 500 years since Galileo attracted the attention of the Inquisition with the publication of his *Letters on Sunspots* in 1613.

It is arguable that Abdussamatov is, for the moment, a more important heretic then Galileo. Not that I suggest his dissent from global warming dogma rivals Galileo's achievements as the "Father of Modern Science," but Abdussamatov's heliocentric message could be of more urgent concern to you than Galileo's. Abdussamatov claims that the prelude to the next Little Ice Age began as early as 2014. Suppose the solar physicists are right. Would that be enough to tip societies in an already-troubled economic environment into collapse?

That is one of the more important questions that you, as an investor and a human being, have to answer as you look ahead at the conditions you are likely to face in the foreseeable future. As we have explored, protracted turns toward colder weather in the past have been associated with periods of economic decline and devolution, often characterized as dark ages.

There is little doubt that past dark ages were almost exclusively triggered by episodes of colder climate. In his authoritative analysis, *The Collapse of Complex Societies*, Joseph Tainter lists seventeen examples of complex societies that have collapsed—cities "buried by drifting sands or tangled jungle, ruin and desolation where once there were people and abundance."[12]

Some of the examples he cites are fairly obscure, such as the Hohokam (American Indian dwellers of the southern Arizona desert who built a sophisticated economy around irrigated agriculture), the Chacoans (Pueblo builders who formerly inhabited the arid San Juan Basin in northwestern New Mexico), and the Kachin societies (from the region where Highland Burma borders China and India). (Tainter does not specify the date of the specific Kachin collapse he has in mind, so I cannot correlate it to any specific climate change.)

Nonetheless, contrary to Al Gore, I have found no instance of the collapse of a complex society triggered by warmer weather, whereas the record abounds with examples of collapses associated with colder weather.

As previously explained, a turn toward colder weather is frequently manifested by disturbances in the upper atmosphere leading to drought. It is easy enough to imagine how colder climate, manifested in drought and shorter growing seasons, could have been a catastrophe for economies based on agriculture in the past.

Remember, for example, that the ancient Roman economy was 85 percent to 90 percent based on agriculture. Rigid and draconian taxes, based upon output during the heyday of the Roman Warm Period, became unpayable as farm production fell, first during the cold weather crisis in the half-century from AD 235 to 284. During that time, at least twenty-seven recognized emperors, along with at least twice as many usurpers, struggled to repel repeated and ruinous barbarian incursions that almost destroyed the empire.

That final collapse came 200 years later during the fifth century, when another period of terrible cold inspired barbarian tribes, including the Vandals, to head south. The land they invaded was already bankrupt and practically illiterate.

Unlike the Chinese Empire at the time, the Western Roman Empire had become so illiterate and innumerate that it is difficult for historians to quantify sunspot activity. So far as we know, no Romans were directly observing sunspots, although there may have been scattered observation of aurora borealis.

The best guess is that there were two grand minima in the waning centuries of the Roman Empire, much like the Little Ice Age of the following millennium.

It's important to note that two recent grand maxima were both immediately followed by grand minima—the Dark Ages Cold Period and the Little Ice Age. It is this regularity—verified by proxy records for temperature through oxygen isotopes from mollusk shells—rather than a simple annual periodicity that also lends credibility to Abdussamatov's forecast of another Little Ice Age beginning within thirty years.[13]

Certainly, the dramatically colder weather experienced around the world during what should have been a solar maximum, as well as the notoriously colder winter that characterized the early months of 2014, remind thinking people that the mechanisms of climate are more complicated than the simpleminded assertion that higher CO_2 emissions are bound to drive up temperatures.

I would be the first to agree that a few days, or weeks, of uncharacteristically cold or warm temperatures do not compose a new climate reality. Still, the unmistakable evidence of bitter cold slowing the economy in North America in Q1 2013 and 2014 adds credibility to the notion that the world could be in store for even colder weather.

As the satellite data on atmospheric temperatures confirm, we've been seeing a gradual cooling since the late 1990s. These have produced strong signals of cooling. Europe is an icebox. A blizzard in North Africa, the first snow there in more than thirty years, claimed 300 lives in 2013. And after not seeing snow for the better part of the twentieth century, the southern states of Brazil have had snowfall in two or three of the past five years. If you open your eyes, the evidence is here.

Going into a new Little Ice Age does not mean there will no longer be heat waves. But the variability of weather will increase with a cooler bent overall. You can expect lower winter lows, later spring frosts, and earlier fall frosts—all of which have an adverse effect on crops.

Will You Be Swept Up in a Secular Cycle?

The question is whether a lapse into colder weather could be grave enough to trigger significant regime collapse, as documented by Turchin and Nefedov in *Secular Cycles*. If so, how might this be transmitted? Clearly, agriculture represents only a tiny fraction of the GDP of the advanced economies: about

1 percent for the United States, United Kingdom, Canada, Germany, Ireland, and Japan; 2 percent in Australia, Italy, France, Holland, Portugal, and Sweden; and 3 percent in Spain.

The ratios are higher in the BRIC countries: 10 percent in China, 18 percent in India, 4 percent in Russia, and 5 percent in Brazil—notwithstanding the fact that Brazil is now the world's largest exporter of five major internationally traded foods, including coffee, sugar, beef, and chicken, and number two in soybeans and corn.

But the percentage of GDP derived from agriculture is not the crucial issue. In a world with 7 billion mouths to feed, the important measure of stability is the percentage of household consumption expenditures devoted to food. According to the USDA Economic Research Service, this is 33.9 percent in China. India's is 35.8 percent. In Egypt, it's 38.3 percent, while in Iran it's 26.3 percent. Perhaps most worryingly, in Pakistan, it's 45.4 percent.

As indicated by the comment quoted at the top of this report, agriculture in Pakistan is dysfunctional. Almost half of Pakistani per capita annual income is spent on food. That would be a recipe for instability even in the absence of other factors that make Pakistan a tinderbox.

Don't forget that Pakistan is a failing state with 150 hydrogen bombs. It has already engaged in three wars with India, also a nuclear power, since the bloody partition of British India in 1947.

Ostensibly, the Pakistani-India conflict is based on religion. But even if there were no religious distinctions between India and Pakistan there would be a geopolitical rift arising from India's control of Kashmir, a Muslim state of India that is more notably the highland region, which gives India control over water flowing downstream to Pakistani farmers.

India has recently been busy constructing two hydroelectric dams on the upper reaches of the Indus River. The forty-five megawatt, 190-foot-tall Nimoo-Bazgo dam, dedicated in 2014, and the Kishanganga Hydroelectric Plant, due to come online in 2016, have the capacity of storing up to 4.23 billion cubic feet of water. They will almost certainly reduce the flow of the Indus River toward Pakistan, violating the terms of the bilateral 1960 Indus Water Treaty. This is why Pakistan appealed to the International Court of Arbitration in the Hague to halt construction of the Kishanganga dam. Fully 90 percent of Pakistani agriculture depends on irrigation from the Indus River. India won a qualified victory with a final award specifying that 318 cubic feet per second of natural flow of water must be maintained in the Kishanganga River at all times to preserve Pakistan's rights to the water downstream.

Perhaps as a consequence of the global turn toward cooler weather over the past fifteen years, water flows into Pakistan are already down 30 percent from what had been considered normal levels. If a deepening Maunder Minimum–like fall in solar irradiance disrupted currents in the ocean and upper atmosphere, as typically happens, this could disrupt the monsoon rainfalls that account for a large portion of precipitation in Pakistan, thus making the flashpoints for conflict with India over irrigation water from the Indus River even more combustible.

Late Pakistan Trust chairman Majid Nizami, a powerful man who had close ties to the Pakistani military, gave a speech proclaiming that war with India is inevitable. He declared that "Indian hostilities and conspiracies against the country will never end until she is taught a lesson."[14]

Note that Pakistan and China have declared mutual support for one another, while India and China, which fought a war in October 1962 over their disputed Himalayan border, continue to squabble over Arunachal Pradesh, an Indian state that China claims is part of Tibet.

Given the history of food rioting in Pakistan, and a very high percentage of household expenditures required by people to eat, it is easy to foresee that sharply colder weather could trigger dire consequences.

Also note that a high percentage of the world's food exports originate in regions of the northern hemisphere where agricultural productivity is subject to a steep drop with the advent of a colder climate.

There is a whole swath of unstable nation-states (future failed-states) from North Africa through the Middle East and to Afghanistan and Pakistan. Imports of grain worldwide increased more than fivefold between 1960 and 2013. This placed more than one-third of the world's nation-states in the vulnerable position of depending on imports for one-quarter or more of the staple grains they consume. In sixty-two countries, the area of farmland is inadequate to supply domestic consumption. In about one-third of those countries, twenty-two to be exact, agricultural products consumed require more freshwater than is available.

A turn to colder weather that reduced or eliminated grain surpluses in the exporting countries would have devastating consequence for those countries in North Africa and the Middle East most dependent on grain imports. For a hint of how severe the impact of declining temperatures could be on carrying capacity, dust off the 1974 CIA working paper "A Study on Climatological Research as It Pertains to Intelligence Problems."[15]

If you look at this report, as I have, you will see that the climate science of forty years ago was less blinkered and more evidence-driven than today's global warming hysteria. The excellent 1974 CIA summary states that it was likely that the Earth would revert to a neoboreal climate like that of the Little Ice Age, which predominated through most of the 400 years after 1600, with the happy exception of some decades in the middle of the twentieth century (and we now know the last quarter of the twentieth century).

The CIA report reminds us that the neoboreal climate was "characterized by broad strips of excess and deficit rainfall in the middle latitudes and extensive failure of the monsoon."[16] The fact that there was extensive failure of the monsoon in the Indian subcontinent in the cooler conditions of the nineteenth century underscores the potential dangers of deteriorating weather triggering nuclear conflict between India and Pakistan. While both countries have recently been exporting grain, the balance of their surpluses could rapidly erode in cooler conditions. The CIA report reminds us that even in the early '70s, when weather turned colder, Pakistan adopted plans to import US grain in March 1973 because of crop failure due to drought. What would happen if the exportable grain surplus from the Northern United States and Canada were sharply curtailed due to colder climate contracting the growing season? That is not at all unlikely.

The CIA report underscores how tenuous the carrying capacity of world agriculture actually is: "As an example, Europe presently, with an annual mean temperature of 12 degrees C (about 53 degrees F), supports three persons per arable hectare. If, however, the temperature declines 1 degree C only a little over two persons per hectare could be supported and more than 20 percent of the population could not be fed from domestic sources. China now supports over seven persons per arable hectare; a shift of 1 degree C would mean it could only support four persons per arable hectare—a drop of over 43 percent."[17]

Of course, it is reasonable to infer that the vulnerability highlighted in the mid-1970s has intensified with the passage of four decades, as Europe's population has increased by about 70 million persons in the intervening years. And China's population has soared by about 487 million persons. At the same time, fertile land has been lost to development in both Europe and China, while freshwater resources in China have declined due to increased pollution and depletion of fossil aquifers.

In short, there is an unprecedented hostage to fortune in the hands of the climate gods—in a world that has been rendered ever more crisis-prone.

Notes

1   http://www.shadowstats
.com/article/no-517-gold
-update-march-cpi-industrial
-production-housing-starts
.pdf.

2   http://www.spiegel.de/
international/europe/cold
-german-winter-refuses
-to-warm-up-for-easter-a
-891468.html.

3   Zhentao, Xu, "Solar Obser-
vations in Ancient China and
Solar Variability," *Philosophical
Transactions of the Royal Soci-
ety of London. Series A, Math-
ematical and Physical Sciences*
330, no. 1615, "The Earth's
Climate and Variability of the
Sun over Recent Millennia:
Geophysical, Astronomical
and Archaeological Aspect"
(April 24, 1990), 513–16.

4   http://longstreet.typepad.com/
thesciencebookstore/2012/02/
william-herschel-adam-smith
-sunspots-and-wheat.html.

5   http://link.springer.com/
article/10.1007/s11207-004
-5356-5.

6   Solheim, Jan-Erik, et al.,
"The Long Sunspot Cycle 23
Predicts a Significant Temperature Decrease in Cycle
24," *Journal of Atmospheric*

*and Solar-Terrestrial Phys-
ics* 80 (May 2012), 267–84,
http://www.sciencedirect
.com/science/article/pii/
S1364682612000417.

7   http://www.cdejager.com/wp
-content/uploads/2008/09/
2010-Grand-Min-JCosm-8
-19832.pdf.

8   See http://www.weatheraction
.com.

9   http://www.theglobeandmail
.com/news/national/
healthy-polar-bear-count
-confounds-doomsayers/
article4099460/.

10 Singer, Fred S., and Dennis
T. Avery, *Unstoppable Global
Warming: Every 1,500 Years*
(Lanham, MD: Rowman &
Littlefield, 2007).

11 See Ravilous, Kate, "Mars
Melt Hints at Solar, Not
Human, Cause for Warm-
ing, Scientist Says," *National Geographic News*,
February 28, 2007, http://
news.nationalgeographic.com/
news/2007/02/070228-mars
-warming.html.

12 Tainter, Joseph, *The Collapse of
Complex Societies* (Cambridge:
Cambridge University Press,
1990).

13 http://hockeyschtick.blogspot
    .com/2013/12/new-paper
    -predicts-another-little-ice
    .html.

14 http://www.safehaven.com/
    article/25038/is-a-water-war
    -between-india-and-pakistan
    -imminent.

15 http://www.governmentattic
    .org/18docs/CIAclimate
    ResearchIntellProbs_1974
    .pdf.

16 "A Study on Climatological
    Research as It Pertains to In-
    telligence Problems," 25.

17 Ibid., 24.

Chapter Thirteen

The Deep State

Crony Capitalists with Guns

There is another government concealed behind the one that is visible at either end of Pennsylvania Avenue, a hybrid entity of public and private institutions ruling the country according to consistent patterns in season and out, connected to, but only intermittently controlled by, the visible state whose leaders we choose.

—Mike Lofgren, "Anatomy of the Deep State"

In case you missed it, former Capitol Hill staffer Mike Lofgren created a sensation with his essay "Anatomy of the Deep State,"[1] delineating the contours of the Deep State. Bill Moyers devoted an entire program to discussing Lofgren's account of "the big story of our time" on February 21, 2014. Literally dozens of articles have appeared since then analyzing some aspect of Lofgren's argument.

He says that a hybrid entity of public and private institutions—a latter-day version of President Eisenhower's military-industrial complex—"is effectively able to govern the United States without reference to the consent of the governed as expressed through the formal political process." The Deep State has carved out an autonomous orbit apart from the checks and balances of constitutional government.

As reported by the *Washington Times* in 2006, when National Security Agency (NSA) whistleblower Russell Tice offered to testify before Congress on unconstitutional and unlawful spying on American citizens, the NSA sent him a letter stating that while he had the right to testify before Congress, the intelligence committees that he wanted to testify to were not cleared for the programs he wanted to discuss. Absurdly, the NSA considers its programs too top secret to be divulged to Congress.[2]

But meanwhile, consulting firm Booz Allen Hamilton brags on the third page of its 2012 annual report that 49 percent of its 25,000 employees hold "top secret or higher" security clearances. Booz Allen Hamilton is paid billions of dollars to know all about the NSA's secret programs, even to design and implement them, but members of Congress only know what the Deep State cares to tell them.

In 2007, Jay Rockefeller, former chairman of the Senate Intelligence Committee, explained that despite his position in the Senate Intelligence Committee, he only received the information that "they" allowed. As he put it, "Don't you understand the way Intelligence works? Do you think that because I'm chairman of the Intelligence Committee that I just say I want it and they give it to me? They control it. All of it. All of it. All the time. I only get—and my committee only gets what they want to give me."[3]

Equally, Tea Party stalwart Congressman Justin Amash (Republican Michigan) says of the NSA: "You don't have any idea what kind of things are going on. So you have to start just spitting off random questions. Does the government have a moon base? Does the government have a talking bear? Does the government have a cyborg army? You don't know what kind of things the government might have, you just have to guess and it becomes a totally ridiculous game of 20 questions."

Whether You Like It or Not . . .

But that is not all. As my beautiful wife puts it, elected officials only ostensibly run the visible government, as outlined in Civics 101. She says they are merely Muppets who do the bidding of the Deep State, the people George W. Bush referred to as "the deciders"—a fascinating phrase from a former president who was twice elected by voters who naïvely assumed that Mr. Bush would be the "decider" so long as he inhabited the Oval Office.

Apparently not.

As a Washington insider, Lofgren has never met my wife, but he is well placed to document the truth about the Deep State. He came to Capitol Hill in 1983 as an aid to Republican John Kasich, a rising star in the House of Representatives. Lofgren stayed on with Congress for twenty-eight years, ending his career in 2011 as the chief Republican analyst for military spending on the Senate Budget Committee.

From that vantage, Lofgren was able to report as a matter of fact that the Deep State has first dibs on your money. In his "Anatomy of the Deep State" essay, he describes how the government spent $1.7 billion since 2007 to construct a building in Utah, the size of seventeen football fields, in which the NSA plans to store a yottabyte—the largest numerical designator computer scientists have yet coined—of information. This massive storage capacity has been implemented to archive every single trace of our electronic lives. Of course, there are many more illustrations of the primacy of the Deep State in spending the resources siphoned out of your pocket.

The *Washington Post* quoted George S. Hawkins, general manager of the Washington, DC, Water and Sewer Authority, lamenting the deterioration of the infrastructure under the streets of the nation's capital. He presides over a "decrepit system" of 1,300 miles of water pipe and 1,800 miles of nineteenth-century sewers.[4] Leaky pipes lose an average of 25 percent of drinking water before it reaches the faucet. And every year, Washington's sewage system, built in 1889, flushes three billion gallons of raw sewage into the Potomac River and its estuaries.

Yuck.

Emergency crews are busy around-the-clock patching an average of 450 breaks a year. "All the big cities have these problems, and to me it's the unseen catastrophe," Hawkins said. There is no money to repair or upgrade the water and sewage systems in Washington and the other 771 US cities with water infrastructure on its last legs. But the Deep State had no trouble coming up with $7 billion to rebuild the sewers of Baghdad.

Lofgren points out that Washington, DC, is the geographic headquarters of the Deep State. A partial explanation for the apparently puzzling fact that the denizens of the Deep State would prefer to spend $7 billion making sure that the toilets flush in Baghdad rather than in their own hometown is that they are only incidentally in the infrastructure business.

George S. Hawkins may play a crucial role in keeping Washington functioning, but he probably doesn't have a top-secret security clearance. If some of the trillions that are lavished on national security budgets were reallocated to repair decrepit infrastructure in the United States, Hawkins's days and nights would pass more easily, but the 854,000 contract personnel with top-secret clearances who feast on taxpayer largess would do less feasting.

For one thing, an appropriation of $1 trillion or more to repair and upgrade domestic water and sewer systems would necessarily be open to more competition than Deep State firms faced in Baghdad. Every construction and civil engineering firm in the United States would be eligible to participate, along with many large international firms, such as MACE of Abu Dhabi and Muna Noor Engineering & Contracting of Muscat, Oman. Such firms, experienced in building water projects in the desert, would be far more difficult to exclude from the bidding process if top-secret clearance was not required as a condition for participating.

Seen in this light, the secret clearance required to cash in on Deep State contracts is an effective crony capitalist mechanism for minimizing competition and controlling markets.

And that is not all.

Because there would be more competition over the tenders for civilian water and sewer projects, profits would be lower. The firms winning the contracts would also be subject to more exacting completion standards than they faced in the chaos of Baghdad.

James Glanz summarized what happened in Iraq in a 2007 *New York Times* article, "Bechtel Meets Goals on Fewer than Half of Its Iraqi Rebuilding Projects."[5] Quoting an Inspector General's report, Glanz wrote that the new audit revealed landfills that were never dug, fiber-optic networks that were never completed, and sewage treatment facilities that never worked as planned.

With civilian contracts to build water and sewage facilities in the United States there would be no chance for contractors to collect millions while just going through the motions and failing to complete facilities and other major infrastructure projects.

Lofgren highlights another telling aspect of the rule over America by the Deep State: when President Barack Obama does the bidding of the deciders, he has more or less free reign to completely ignore the Constitution. The tattered remnants of constitutional checks and balances, however, were briefly strong enough to bind Obama and frustrate his wish to appoint Dr. Vivek H. Murthy as US Surgeon General. He could tell the generals in the Pentagon to kill almost anyone on the globe on his own say-so, but he barely had the power to install his own candidate in the ceremonial office of Surgeon General.

I offer four observations:

1. There is little hint that recent political leaders heeded the prophetic warning against the dangers of subordinating the United States to the Deep State that President Eisenhower articulated in his farewell address to the nation on January 17, 1961. Lofgren tells us that

apart from "gadfly Senator Rand Paul of Kentucky," congressional Republicans have been largely silent about the rise of misplaced power that Eisenhower feared.

2. Equally, there is no evidence that the Deep State deciders are directly dictating public policy in realms other than national security. For example, there seems to be no Deep State line on whether Tesla should be banned from bypassing dealer networks and selling cars directly to consumers. Nor is there apparently a Deep State diktat on Obamacare, high fructose corn syrup, or sugar subsidies. And notwithstanding the importance of preserving the dollar's status as the world's reserve currency, there appears to be only an uneasy alliance between the Deep State and the bankers lobby that controls US monetary policy.

In the meantime, be aware that "the subsurface part of the Deep State iceberg" has mostly been content to float along on the ocean of red ink that is the consequence of the deciders' own efforts, and those of others, to spend uncounted trillions out of an empty pocket.

3. Mancur Olson's argument in *The Rise and Decline of Nations* is directly relevant to the triumph of the Deep State.[6] The emergence of its leaders as the deciders, who pull the puppet strings controlling the Muppets, accords with the logic of Olson's argument. In any stable human society with settled borders, he said, distributional coalitions and lobbies tend to accumulate over time, with parasitic intentions. He believed that groups with the organizational incentives and coherence to capture the state for their own profit would not stop short in their plunder until they had totally destroyed a country's economic vitality.

Unfortunately, Olson died in 1998, long before the Tea Party was ever heard of. Yet he could not have imagined a circumstance where powerful special interest lobbies, like those comprising the Deep State, would share the interest of some citizens in reforming government finance. He doubted that those groups with the power to enact policies and programs that benefit themselves at the general expense would forgo any benefit they might otherwise have won out of public-spirited concern for the solvency of future generations.

In fact, Olson personally told me in the 1980s, while I was laboring to enact a balanced-budget requirement in the US Constitution, that even if I succeeded, I would fail. In his view, the desire of special interest lobbies to benefit from runaway deficit spending was stronger than the Constitution.

He cautioned that "the scarce resource of respect for the Constitution" would be swept away by the powerful groups who would pay no more attention to a restriction on their ability to empty your pocket than they have to constitutional niceties that ostensibly prohibit the government from tapping your phone or reading your email word-for-word without a warrant.

4. Olson's argument explains why the Deep State puppet masters have no interest in, or respect for, upholding the general interests that all citizens share. It also explains, however, why they might be obliged to take account of and heed the interests of other smaller "privileged" groups. Olson's "privileged" groups are privileged in an organizational sense. They are groups in which members have an incentive to see that the collective good of their group is provided and that it will be obtained, even without any group organization or coordination. In other words, unlike the encompassing general interest, which Olson tells us will not

find representation in the political process, smaller privileged groups will be represented.

So if a burdensome tax is proposed that will reduce the real living standards of millions of people by $100 each, Olson tells us that those millions will be unable to organize in order to achieve the collective good of defeating that tax. By contrast, if burdensome taxes were proposed that would cost one hundred people millions of dollars apiece, the smaller, privileged group of one hundred multimillionaires or billionaires would probably be able to defeat the tax. Unlike the encompassing general interest, smaller privileged groups will be represented in the political process, even if there is no obvious organization or explicit coordination undertaken on their behalf.

So whose interests would you expect to be represented, or at least accommodated, by the denizens of the Deep State?

Certainly not the general interests that you share with other citizens, common human betterment or even the survival of civilization itself. In Olson's *The Logic of Collective Action*, he discusses the ideas of George C. Homans, author of *The Human Group*. Homans tells us that past civilizations, and perhaps even our own, might have been saved if large-scale cooperation could have been organized with the same cohesion found in small groups. Yet Olson tells us this can't happen. He writes, "It does not follow that because the small group has historically been more effective, the very large group can prevent failure by copying its methods."[7]

If you are one of millions poised to lose $100 to an annoying new tax, for example, you cannot thwart its enactment by pretending that you are a billionaire and personally hiring a battery of influential lobbyists. Billionaires can prevent themselves from being taxed on that basis. You can't. That is why an accumulation of antimarket distortions could cost you and every member of your family $125,000 in lost income annually.

Equally, if you assume that the Deep State deciders have no political ideology whatever, apart from a commitment to prying as much loot as possible from the political process in the guise of national security, the most logical way for them to go about it is to see that the cost of their appropriations is passed on to you and not to those with a greater capacity to fight them.

It would make no sense for the Deep State to risk antagonizing other privileged groups that possess the incentives and resources to rival their political power. Consequently, they tend not to pick fights with other vested interests. The deciders more or less leave other privileged groups to scramble for whatever dollars they can squeeze out of a nearly bankrupt political system.

That is not to say, however, that the deciders of the Deep State may not lend support to policies and programs of other vested interests in cases where doing so seems to increase the resources the Deep State can capture.

This logic helps explain why there tends to be a single economic orthodoxy ruling America—a not always logical amalgam of arguments and rationales favored by the various privileged groups of crony capitalists that control the political process. Even before Richard Nixon proclaimed, "We are all Keynesians now," military Keynesianism had fattened the coffers of the Deep State.[8]

The United States now spends more than every other country combined on the military. And our stated expenditures comprise only about half the real costs. Hundreds of billions in annual military outlays are hidden in the budgets of the Departments of Energy, Homeland Security, State, and Veterans Affairs.

But enough is never enough. There are massive new weapons systems on the Pentagon's drawing board that would add trillions more, such as the Littoral Combat Ship and the F-35 Joint Strike Fighter. the F-35 alone is expected to cost $1.5 trillion—enough to cover Russia's entire military budget at current levels for the next thirty-seven years. David Crawley helps explain why military equipment costs so much:

> I worked for a company that sold a microchip to the military for more than $2k per chip. This chip would have sold to a civilian contract for about 30 cents, but we never sold it to civilians as it was such an old technology (about 20 years old) that no civilian wanted to buy it . . .
>
> The cost to re-qualify to a lower cost part was about half a billion dollars (all that paperwork remember). We were just one of thousands of line items of parts that were too small for congress to notice. So we absolutely price gouged like crazy. Contrary to what other people answering this question might claim the part was not more reliable, or somehow magically better, it was actually quite a lot worse than alternatives. Imagine that happening thousands of times over on millions of small parts that make up hundreds of big contracts and you can see why the American military is the most expensive in the world by far.[9]

As the agenda of the Deep State is all about government spending, its leaders are only too glad to profit from neo-Keynesian arguments that government spending should be increased. It is a measure of the success of the Deep State that the twenty-five biggest military contractors sell $235 billion per year of weapons and security services to the US government.

Equally, the policy of financial repression that robs middle-class savers with a regime of invisibly low interest rates not only subsidizes too-big-to-fail banks; it also facilitates greater government spending. As I write, net outlays for interest payments on the national debt are a bare fraction of what they would be in a normal interest rate environment.

In mid-1995, the Fed funds rate—the interest rate banks charge other banks when they lend each other cash—was as high as 6 percent, and all other interest rates were comparably higher. The total net interest paid to service the national debt then was $232.1 billion—more than 15 percent of federal outlays. At that time the national debt was $4.974 trillion, which was just 29 percent of its level at the end of fiscal year 2013 ($16.738 trillion). In 2013, with the Fed funds rate at 0.25 percent, debt service took 6 percent of federal outlays, or $222.8 billion—$9.3 billion less than in 1995.

History reminds us that extremely low interest rates will ultimately rebound to more normal levels. That would mean a jump in magnitude of the Fed funds rate. It would not be 0.25 percent—the historic average for the Fed funds rate is 4 percent. Obviously, the historically low interest rates secured by the too-big-to-fail banks also conveyed substantial benefits to the Deep State by permitting government spending for line items other than debt service to be higher than it would have been otherwise.

The national debt has more than tripled since 1995: total federal outlays have risen by 244 percent, yet thanks to QE and financial repression that drains the savings of America's middle class, net interest payments on the national debt are lower than they were in the mid-1990s.

When interest rates rebound, the carrying costs of past deficits will balloon, crowding out other spending in the federal budget. This will likely lead to the emergence of more intense intra-elite competition, a factor identified by Peter Turchin and Sergey Nefedov as characteristic of the disintegrate phase of the Secular Cycle.

Deep State Disses the Tea Party

As Lofgren reminds us, the Deep State is crucially dependent on the appropriations process:

> While it seems to float above the constitutional state, its essentially parasitic, extractive nature means that it is still tethered to the formal proceedings of governance. The Deep State thrives when there is tolerable functionality in the day-to-day operations of the federal government. As long as appropriations bills get passed on time, promotion lists get confirmed, black (i.e., secret) budgets get rubber-stamped, special tax subsidies for certain corporations are approved without controversy, as long as too many awkward questions are not asked, the gears of the hybrid state will mesh noiselessly. But when one house of Congress is taken over by tea party, life for the ruling class becomes more trying.

This highlights a puzzling contradiction in Lofgren's thinking. He issues a clarion call to awaken the public to the dangers posed by the Deep State to "the visible, constitutional state . . . envisaged by Madison and the other Founders," yet he paradoxically adopts a snarky attitude toward "the Tea Party," the only effective expression of constitutional politics to yet pinch the Deep State's siphon on the jugular of the body politic. Lofgren became a vitriolic critic of the Tea Party, likening it to "Frankenstein's monster," and deriding the tactics of fiscal brinksmanship that have threatened default on the national debt, and led to sequestration, and thus a partial defunding of the Deep State.

Which is it? Is he more alarmed by the dangers posed by the Deep State? Or, rather is he more piqued by the disruptions the Tea Party has imposed on the "functionality in the day-to-day operations of the federal government"? He tells us himself that the Tea Party has made life more trying for the Deep State (and also presumably for senior budget analysts who process national security appropriations). Lofgren says, "If there is anything the Deep State requires it is silent, uninterrupted cash flow and the confidence that things will go on as they have in the past. It is even willing to tolerate a degree of gridlock: Partisan mud wrestling over cultural issues may be a useful distraction from its agenda. But recent congressional antics involving sequestration, the government shutdown and the threat of default over the debt ceiling extension have been disrupting that equilibrium."

On the one hand, Lofgren tells us that the status quo "equilibrium" should be disrupted. On the other, he has the Deep State insider's contempt for the simple citizens who have gradually come to realize—a quarter of the century after the death of the Soviet Union—that the national security state has become an expensive scam they can no longer afford.

Lofgren's unresolved cognitive dissonance is reflected in his confusions about where the Deep State ends and other elite interests begin. Let's examine these more closely as they point to the likely emergence of more intense intra-elite competition, a factor identified by Peter Turchin and Sergey Nefedov, as characteristic of the disintegrate phase of the Secular Cycle. They argue that as states break down and bankruptcy approaches, the interests of various elite groups tend to diverge, leading to factional battles between patron-client groups.

Of course, so long as government spending capability was sufficiently abundant, the Deep State has good reason to avoid conflict with other privileged groups with the incentives and resources to effectively represent themselves politically. This explains the compliance of the Deep State with the prevailing economic orthodoxy. And it alone could account for the fact that the Deep State was content to allow the bankers lobby to control monetary policy. Further to that, the Deep State profited tremendously from the increase in government spending capacity achieved through quantitative easing.

It does not follow, however, that every consequence of current economic policy expresses the will or the interests of the Deep State (which should be understood as shorthand for crony capitalists with guns). And according to Olson's trenchant analysis of the logic of group action, it is unlikely for a group as sprawling as the Deep State to formulate coherent policy perspectives in opposition to those adopted by other groups, whose perspective is adopted by the establishment of the moment, given that these are an amalgam of the self-interested viewpoints of the leading organizationally privileged groups in different areas.

Lofgren mistakes this "get along to go along" orthodoxy for evidence of a genuine ideology binding the denizens of the Deep State with Wall Street and Silicon Valley in a quasi-official ruling class. He suggests that they are deeply dyed in the hue of the official ideology of the governing class, an ideology that is neither specifically Democrat nor Republican. Domestically, whatever they might privately believe about essentially diversionary social issues, such as abortion or gay marriage, they almost invariably believe in the Washington Consensus: financialization, outsourcing, privatization, deregulation, and the commodifying of labor. "Internationally, they espouse twenty-first-century American exceptionalism: the right and duty of the United States to meddle in every region of the world with coercive diplomacy and boots on the ground and to ignore civilized behavior."

In case you're not up to date with your Marxist jargon, "commodifying of labor" is a concept Marx developed in *The Communist Manifesto*, where he decried "the callous cash payment" that transforms the labor of workers into just another cost of the production process.[10] For my part, I've never understood what the fuss was about. It seems to me that recognition that labor is a cost of the production process is not so much an ideological artifact as it is rudimentary accounting. No economic system could fail to take it into consideration. And as to the "callous cash payment," most people think of that as the good part.

The fact that Lofgren lists "commodifying of labor" as a key feature "of the official ideology of the governing class," tells us more about his discontents than it does about the views and postures of the elite. As we look more carefully, you can see the potential for looming, intra-elite conflict.

Such is all but assured by the fundamental divergence of interests between the "essentially parasitic, extractive nature" of the Deep State (tax consumers) and the entrepreneurial focus of the more productive (tax paying) segments of the fabled 1 percent.

The utter impossibility of meeting all financial claims on future production in a flat line economy will be ever more obvious as we totter toward the Breaking Point. And this will trigger a more acrimonious intra-elite conflict along the lines delineated below.

Is the Deep State Working with Russia?

In an eerie echo of the Cold War, the conflict of interest likely to trigger intra-elite fighting arises from an anachronistic ambition that the Deep State shares with Russia's strongman, Vladimir Putin.

Both the Deep State and Putin want to nationalize their elites. Putin is utilizing sanctions handed to him by the Deep State over the crisis in Ukraine to ring-fence Russia's tycoons. These sanctions will help keep Russian money bottled up within the borders of the country rather than chasing opportunities across the whole global economy, as Russia's richest billionaire, Alisher Usmanov, has famously done with major stakes in Apple, Facebook, and Alibaba.

Equally, the Deep State's prosperity is threatened by the globalization of America's investment elites. As authoritarian policies like FATCA show, the Deep State wants to close off options for Americans to live and build businesses outside the borders of the United States. This entails a major conflict with the interests of a considerable portion of the 1 percent who embrace the technologically driven globalization of industry and services. They don't want to keep losing business because customers of American technology products don't want the Deep State spying on everything they do. As reported in the *New York Times*, revelations about Deep State spying have already cost American technology companies billions.

Maria Rankka, CEO of the Stockholm Chamber of Commerce, says the balkanization of the World Wide Web, in response to US data surveillance policies, threatens to destroy "the borderless character of the digital economy," jeopardizing between $4 trillion and $11 trillion in gains to the global economy by 2025.[11]

As globalization has developed, many markets around the world have come to be dominated by transnational companies, the top one hundred of which are 85 percent owned by American shareholders. As examples such as the Apple iPhone, iPod, and iPad so vividly demonstrate, even much of China's growing industrial production is deployed in the service of American companies.

In a February 2014 *Politico* article, Sean Starrs, a PhD student at York University in Toronto, pointed out that despite China becoming the largest PC market in the world, American firms still command 84 percent of the profit share in computer hardware and software.[12] It is not only the tech sector that knows it can make higher profits by operating across jurisdictions. The whole market-oriented contingent of investors and high earners are unlikely to welcome Deep State efforts to perpetuate international conflicts and the declining marginal returns they engender.

But this is a story that will more fully unfold tomorrow.

QE Forestalls Intra-Elite Conflict?

Meanwhile, a little-noted consequence of QE has been to temporarily forestall the endgame intra-elite conflict by conveying substantial gains to both the Deep State and the larger, more globalized segments of the vaunted 1 percent.

The key to understanding how QE defers intra-elite conflict is to recognize that the Federal Reserve's choice to divert the savings returns of middle-class Americans, to fatten the balance sheets of banks, was a desperate measure to preserve a status quo, one dependent on rising debt to fund government deficits at a scale that private savings could not support. It was not altogether an accident that this fattened the balance sheets of the 1 percent as well. The central bankers were hoping to stimulate a wealth effect. As Dallas Fed president Richard W. Fisher was widely credited with saying, "QE was a massive gift intended to boost wealth."

When the Fed essentially monetizes stock indices, the owners of stocks tend to get richer. This is true quite apart from whether they mainly own stock in firms that prosper in the crucible of market competition or they've invested in crony capitalist ventures that profit from government contracts and favors.

That this wealth effect tended not to trickle very far down the income distribution to reach the bottom 80 percent of the population reflects the fact that middle-class finances have already been hollowed out since the signal crisis of US hegemony in the 1970s. Due to the tendency of the middle class to invest in housing stock in preference to corporate stock, middle-class families were much more adversely affected by the subprime mortgage bust than were wealthier persons. In the housing bubble of the last decade, home prices rose sharply due to the abracadabra of cheap money conjured out of thin air by the Federal Reserve. In response, median households with stagnant income drew down their housing equity by extracting an average of $1 trillion annually, in excess of closing costs and satisfaction of previous mortgages, between 2001 and 2005.

You don't need to be a Nobel prize–winning economist to see that going deeply into debt on the basis of inflated values spells trouble. As Joseph Stiglitz argued in a January 2013 *New York Times* piece, the growth in the decade before the crisis was unsustainable, reliant on the bottom 80 percent consuming about 110 percent of their income.[13] The excess consumption was financed by "free cash" mortgage refinance as described above.

When the housing bubble burst, household net worth in the United States fell by $16 trillion. Because middle-class households were seven times more exposed to housing, which comprised two-thirds of their wealth before the bust, they were much more adversely affected than the 1 percent with more diversified portfolios. The 1 percent held 90 percent of their assets in stocks, securities, and business equity rather than in homes.

When the penultimate bubble burst, the bottom 80 percent lost, on average, 39.1 percent of their net worth between 2007 and 2010. By contrast, the top 20 percent lost an average of just 14 percent of their net worth. They made this up, and more, from gains in the stock market. While housing prices only began to rebound in 2012, the S&P 500 rose 60 percent between March 2009 and the end of 2010 alone. As the much-maligned top 1 percent owned 50.9 percent of the stocks in America, they made a lot of money from the bull market stimulated by QE, pocketing, according to David Cay Johnston, 95 cents out of every dollar of income growth from 2009 through 2012.

So while by some estimates household net worth has rebounded by $16 trillion since 2008, most of it rebounded to the top 1 percent, who owned most of the stock that soared in value. But if you're one of the top 1 percent yourself, you may recognize that's not all it's cracked up to be.

As Phil DeMuth explored in *The Terrible Tragedy of Income Inequality among the 1%*, you may be part of the 1 percent without being a fabled tycoon like Warren Buffet, George Soros, Peter Thiel, or Donald Trump.[14] In fact, DeMuth points out that about half of the 1 percent are small business owners and professional practitioners, such as doctors and lawyers. Still, according to DeMuth, even the bottom ranks of the 1 percent hold, on average, about $1.5 million in liquid assets.

To really achieve what my friend Bill Bonner calls "financial escape velocity," you need to be, at a minimum in the top one-tenth of 1 percent. DeMuth puts it this way: once you achieve an annual income of $1.9 million, then you "start to escape earth's monetary gravitational field." Even then, you won't be "Hollywood rich" until you reach the top one-hundredth of the 1 percent, making at least $10.2 million per year.

Apart from the president of the United States, very few government employees would qualify for even the lower ranks of the 1 percent. And that may be part of what irks Lofgren about the Deep State: he was a firsthand witness to the "revolving door" deals that reward government operatives with a second career, lucrative beyond their dreams. He jumps to the conclusion that because money is available to grease the wheels of this lucrative revolving door, Wall Street must be "the ultimate owner of the Deep State and its strategies."

I don't think so.

It isn't really Wall Street that funds the Deep State. That money is drained from your pockets and those of the US citizenry through the political process. Wall Street merely capitalizes the income streams that pour into Deep State companies. Almost without exception, the twenty-five biggest defense contractors are public companies. Their CEOs and other executives earn salaries that, in most cases, put them high into the upper rungs of the 1 percent. And the public listings offer added options for lucrative Deep State rewards.

The antics of the Deep State are among the hardest to parse and decipher in the contemporary world of crony capitalism, as they are shrouded in a gauze of secrecy; this makes it all but impossible for you to know with how many groups the war on terror is being fought (that number is top secret), much less the names of these groups.

Edward Snowden, a computer geek and high school dropout earned $200,000 a year at Booz Allen Hamilton (NYSE: BAH) (enough to place him in the top 5 percent of the income distribution), pulled back the curtain and revealed some of these details.

He showed that BAH, with a market cap of $3.25 billion, seems to have designed much of the strategy and tactics of the war on terror. BAH even originated and helped implement the National Security Agency's plan to spy without a warrant on all your conversations, read your emails, and record every detail of your electronic life—or as Snowden put it in his sensational revelations, "to hack into the entire world."

Thanks to Snowden, we now know that BAH, a firm that draws 99 percent of its $5.76 billion annual revenues from government contracts, was one of the primary deciders of the Deep State. In that role, it was in a position to perpetuate and increase its profits by perpetuating and broadening the war on terror.

Deep State Proclaims Diseconomies to Scale

Hungry dogs are famous for believing only in meat.

BAH specifically shilled and lobbied for a cyberwar program to "re-engineer the Internet" to eliminate any vestige of privacy you might enjoy. As BAH puts it, the firm is oriented to "improving public safety with analytics." That included writing speeches for politicians—BAH quite literally put words in their mouths. Talk about muppets.

BAH's EBITA of $529 million pales compared to some of the other big military contractors such as United Technologies, Raytheon, General Dynamics, Northrop Grumman, and Lockheed Martin. Still, Booz Allen Hamilton contributes its share of employees to the top one-tenth of the 1 percent. Public filing show that five of its executives earned $3.5 million or more in 2013, topped by the $4,659,255 paid to John M. McConnell, executive vice president and former NSA director. McConnell was also the director of national intelligence under former president George W. Bush. He worked for BAH before taking that job and returned to the firm after leaving it. The company website reports that McConnell is responsible for its "rapidly expanding cyber business."

Talk about crony capitalism. As commentator Glenn Greenwald put it in a March 2010 *Salon* article, "McConnell's behavior is the classic never-ending 'revolving door' syndrome: public officials serve private interests while in office and are then lavishly rewarded by those same interests once they leave."[15] Greenwald pointed out that McConnell's main role at Booz Allen is the same as it was in public office: outsourcing US intelligence and surveillance to private corporations. These private companies' activities are even more shielded than normal from all accountability and oversight, while they generate massive profit at the expense of the public.

McConnell has been a straight-out advocate of authoritarian control over the Internet and cyberspace. He wants the US government and the for-profit Deep State firms to be able to monitor and control every message and transaction that goes over the Internet anywhere in the world.

In strict logic, McConnell's proposed crackdown on cyberspace reflects the plunging scale at which violence can be organized in the Information Age. Unlike the situation through most of the modern period, where violence was almost entirely monopolized by nation states operating at ever-larger scale, violence in the twenty-first century can, in principle, be organized even at the individual level.

This means there is almost an infinite set of potential enemies or "terrorists" involving every living human in manifold combinations with every other individual.

In the paranoid world of the Deep State, anyone could be an enemy; indeed, as you learn anew whenever you go through the screening process to board an airplane, everyone is an enemy until proven otherwise in real time. You could be conspiring with one or more of 2,500 passengers with whom you once took a cruise to disable a utility network. That's ridiculous, of course. But they won't take your word for it.

And that makes for a huge problem. Quite apart from the usual difficulties that stand in the way of proving a negative, the ambition on the part of the Deep State to monitor and control every message and transaction on earth underscores the growing diseconomies inherent in a government attempting to control an economy at a continent-wide scale. Speaking for the Deep State, McConnell warns that an enemy could disrupt America's financial and accounting transactions, equities and bond markets, and even retail commerce, resulting in chaos. US power grids, transportation, water-filtration systems, and telecommunications are also at risk.

A moment's reflection shows that these vulnerabilities highlighted by McConnell reflect falling returns to the architecture of those large-scale systems. As Amory and Hunter Lovins detailed in their 1982 book, *Brittle Power*, a highly centralized energy-distribution system for electricity, oil, gas, and so on is vulnerable in the way that a distributed, decentralized system would not be.[16] Clearly, the answer is to reconfigure the highly centralized systems' architecture into a less vulnerable decentralized system.

If operating an economy on a continent-wide basis requires that an all-powerful state monitor every trace of human life on a real-time basis, then the cost and complexity this entails will inevitably drive down the scale at which economies function. Or to put the same conclusion in other words, the Deep State version of the command economy is bound to fail.

The attempt to hitch an evermore complex economy to a life-support system comprising serial asset bubbles in combination with politicians, a.k.a. Muppets, spending trillions upon trillions out of an empty pocket will end in tears. Equally, as in the last days of Rome, fighting expensive and pointless wars may enrich Deep State power, but it does little or nothing to enhance US security or long-term prosperity.

Taking the long view, the trashing of the Constitution by a Deep State desperate to increase national security funding should be viewed as a risk that accompanies the passing of an old order. As you read the news, it brims with stories that hint of the end of the American imperium. Typically, hegemonic systems collapse first at the periphery. That is happening now in Argentina, Venezuela, Thailand, Ukraine, Egypt, Libya, Yemen, Syria, Turkey, Greece, and throughout the Middle East. And the governments of Southern Europe are also bankrupt. As the terminal crisis moves from periphery to the center, all bets will be off.

Notes

1 Now published in book form: Lofgren, Mike, *The Deep State: The Fall of the Constitution and the Rise of a Shadow Government* (New York: Viking, 2016).

2 See "Ex-Official Warned against Testifying on NSA Programs," *Washington Times*, January 11, 2006.

3 http://www.zerohedge.com/contributed/2014-03-25/quote-chair-senate-intelligence-committee-proves-intelligence-agencies-are-co.

4 Halsey, Ashley, III, "Billions Needed to Upgrade America's Leaky Water Infrastructure," *Washington Post*, http://www.washingtonpost.com/local/billions-needed-to-upgrade-americas-leaky-water-infrastructure/2011/12/22/gIQAdsE0WP_story.html.

5 http://www.nytimes.com/2007/07/26/world/middleeast/26reconstruct.html?_r=0.

6 Olson, Mancur, *The Rise and Decline of Nations: Economic Growth, Stagflation, and Social Rigidities* (New Haven, CT: Yale University Press, 1982).

7 Olson, *Logic of Collective Action*, 49–50.

8 http://www.forbes.com/global/1999/0222/0204077a.html.

9 https://www.quora.com/Why-does-military-equipment-cost-so-much-compared-to-comparable-civilian-equipment.

10 See Marx, Karl, and Frederick Engels, *The Communist Manifesto* (Moscow: Progress Publishers, 1969), first published 1848, trans. Samuel Moore in cooperation with Frederick

Engels, 1888; ch. 1: Bourgeois and Proletarians, 2.

11 Rankka, Maria, et al., "We Shouldn't Take the 'World' Out of the 'World Wide Web,'" *Financial Times*, March 27, 2014, 8.

12 Ibid.

13 See https://www.equitymaster.com/dailyreckoning/detail.asp?date=01/23/2013&story=8&title=Is-inequality-holding-back-recovery.

14 http://www.forbes.com/sites/phildemuth/2013/11/25/are-you-rich-enough-the-terrible-tragedy-of-income-inequality-among-the-1/#41589a4f1bb1.

15 Greenwald, Glenn, "Mike McConnell, the WashPost & the Dangers of Sleazy Corporatism: A Former Bush Director Uses the Washington Post to Advocate Dangerous Policies He Would Personally Profit From," *Salon*, March 29, 2010, http://www.salon.com/2010/03/29/mcconnell_3/.

16 Lovins, Amory B., and L. Hunter Lovins, *Brittle Power: Energy Strategy for National Security* (Lawrence, MA: Brick House, 1982).

Chapter Fourteen

The Domino Effect

Crony Capitalism, Diminishing Returns, and the Theft of Middle-Class Wealth

What are these arguments? They are the arguments that kings have made for enslaving the people in all ages of the world . . . the same old serpent that says you work and I eat, you toil and I will enjoy the fruits of it.

—Abraham Lincoln

A few months ago, I got a rare tutorial on what ails America from a fellow passenger on a Delta flight from Atlanta to Palm Beach. It is not usual that economic concepts can be spotted out the window from ten thousand feet. But it was a clear night with a bright moon, and I knew exactly to what the anonymous expert referred. The network of irrigation canals that crisscross Southern and Central Florida is well known to anyone who lives there. Such a canal crosses the back boundary of my property. Other than taking care that my wife's Pomeranian doesn't dive in to swim with the alligators, I seldom give it much attention.

On this particular evening, however, we were too close to landing for me to dig through the book bag for another read. I had just finished *Every Bitter Thing,* a dark novel by the late Leighton Gage, so I was already ruminating about corruption and injustice, but with attention to spare for the comments of my seatmate, a civil engineer traveling to Palm Beach with an eye to landing a lucrative contract with the South Florida Water Management District (SFWMD).

With about 2,000 miles of canals, another 2,800 miles of levees or berms, nearly 70 pump stations and more than 650 water control structures and 700 culverts, SFWMD has a lot of expensive infrastructure to maintain. And they are 50/50 partners with the federal government in a $20-billion, thirty-year project to rework the whole water infrastructure of South Florida.

As we discussed his ambitions, I asked the engineer to educate me on the purpose of the ubiquitous canals. I expected him to spout some politically correct assurances about protecting and restoring ecosystems. But he didn't.

"Oh, that's easy," he said. "They are part of a gigantic subsidy to sugar farmers."

I was taken aback. As Emerson reminds us in his "Essay on Compensation," quoting Edmund Burke, "No man had ever a point of pride that was not injurious to him." Or as my father preferred to put it, "Every point of pride is a point of weakness."

I confess: I have tended to pride myself on mindfulness and a sometimes-acute ability to observe what others miss. But here I was clearly in a daze. Having grown up in Maryland, where the landscape had not changed appreciably since my ancestors arrived there in the seventeenth century, I was simply taking solid ground for granted, unaware that my house in Wellington, and indeed, the whole neighborhood where I live, are sitting on ground reclaimed from the Everglades. Bedding down not fifty yards from an irrigation canal, I should have realized that I was an interloper living on former swampland.

After all, I had read a number of Carl Hiaasen novels some years ago, beginning with *Strip Tease,* which I received as a present from the lovely Morgan Fairchild, an intelligent woman with whom I used to pal around. The opposite of a "dumb blonde," Morgan was, and probably still is, a keen fan of mystery novels and Hiaasen in particular. This was years before I moved to Florida. Now that I am installed here, I can see that some of Hiaasen's stock characters—the corrupt congressman, murderous political fixers and lobbyists, and yes, greedy sugar barons who despoil the environment—are more true to life than I imagined on first reading.

Obviously, I must have rushed my reading of *Strip Tease*, or I would have been less taken aback to be reminded that the true stories of the great rip-offs in twenty-first-century America are indeed stranger than fiction. And so simple, as seen by an expert in water infrastructure. Not so simple, as seen out the back window by the typical Florida homeowner. I may not share the same perspective as the "typical Florida homeowner," but immediately when the engineer told me the irrigation canal in my backyard was part of a sweet deal to plutocrats in the sugar industry, I saw some familiar landscape in a wholly new light.

Further research showed that the expected, politically correct assurance that South Florida's massive water projects actually are about restoring ecosystems would have been marginally true but misleading. The tens of billions now to be spent are all about restoring damage done by previous water projects, particularly by sugar farming that only became possible because of massive civil engineering boondoggles undertaken at public expense.

I should perhaps explain that heretofore, I was not entirely uninformed about the unpalatable antics of Sugar Daddies in profiting at our expense through politics. But I was only aware in a limited accounting sense. I had known since my lost youth as a campaigner for the forgotten taxpayer in Washington that sugar farmers pocket some of the most lavish subsidies that crony capitalism affords. On several occasions, my colleagues and I at the National Taxpayers Union had tried to forward legislative proposals to roll back the annual tribute paid to the sugar barons. We did not try very hard, however, as we soon found this was impossible. The sweet deal for Sugar Daddies was one of the more sacred line items of the federal budget.

Perhaps because real life members of Congress from both parties, like the fictional Congressman Dilbeck is in *Strip Tease*, were showered with contributions from sugar barons, it was literally unimaginable that Congress would curtail the flow of money from your pocket to theirs. According to the Audobon Society, Big Sugar donated more money to politicians and political parties than General Motors. (And look at all the billions GM got back on their political investments.) Even though it does not make the headlines, Big Sugar has done as well or better. In December 2013, the *Washington Post* quoted a leading lobbyist: "The sugar guys win votes because they are better at politics than anyone else." Note the way the system works: the game is won not by those who are better at doing business, or serving consumers, but by those who are "better at politics than anyone else."[1]

I was well aware that the sugar barons had succeeded through politics in requiring you to pay two to three times the world price for sugar. In fact, if you know anything about commodity trading, you know there are two different futures markets for sugar: World Sugar No. 11 and US Sugar No. 16. There is no chemical difference between the two, but there is a price discrepancy—a result of fat subsidies and a tariff program that supports US sugar farmers.

A sweet deal for them, if not for you. The *Washington Post* reports that government and academic studies have estimated that elevated prices cost food makers and consumers at least $1.9 billion a year. A lowball estimate.

That much I had known for years. What I had not fully realized until I talked to the anonymous water engineer, was that the Sugar Daddies did not stop short at ripping off you and other taxpayers and consumers for a couple of billion dollars a year. Their sights were set much higher. In fact, the whole landscape of South Florida, with its thousands of miles of canals and levees is an expensive monument to the triumph of crony capitalism. Even though the US climate is not well suited for growing sugar—and it's cheaper to do so in countries like Brazil and India that have better climates for sugar cultivation—the US government provides a lucrative price for US sugar producers, while limiting imports.[2]

Taxpayer subsidies were an essential prerequisite for the launch of the Florida sugar industry in the first place. It got its start early in the twentieth century courtesy of Everglades Drainage District, a tax-funded initiative of Governor Napoleon Bonaparte Broward, who promised "to drain that abominable pestilence-ridden swamp" for agricultural use.[3] As you may infer from Governor Broward's comment, it dates from a time before the Democratic Party was in thrall to environmentalism, a long time ago—1904.

In those days, sugar farming in Florida was confined to small plots of dry land on the southernmost tip of the Florida Peninsula. A few hardy pioneers planted cane in Flamingo on Cape Sable, an area made famous in the late nineteenth century for its hellish infestation of insects. (Naturalist Leverett White Brownell reported that he had seen an oil lamp in Flamingo extinguished by a cloud of mosquitoes.) By comparison, the sugar farming farther north on Florida's west coast seemed almost civilized.

The 1910 census reported that 144 people were living in the southwest communities of Everglades Township and Chokoloskee Island, in Collier County near Naples, where they primarily engaged in labor-intensive farming of sugarcane. But even the most adept farmers had to fish and hunt to make a living. In those hardscrabble conditions, there was no sugar lobby any more than there was an asparagus lobby or an eggplant lobby—just small farmers trying to scratch out a living.

Yet even when sugarcane production in the United States was negligible, the sugar beet lobby was busy rigging markets, with mischievous effects, at the end of the nineteenth century and early in the twentieth.

It is a little known fact that Cuba would have become a US state in the wake of the Spanish-American War if not for the fierce opposition of Western sugar beet farmers. Cuba had become the chief sugar producer in the world after 1860. Following the Spanish-American War, the Treaty of Paris assumed the United States would occupy Cuba. As a result of US occupation, tariffs on Cuban sugar were reduced by 52 percent. This exposed Western sugar beet farmers to competition, to which they proved predictably allergic. Not to worry: Senator Henry Teller of Colorado had proposed and enacted the Teller Amendment prohibiting the annexation of Cuba, out of fear that annexation would open the inefficient US sugar market to competition.[4]

Teller's scheme was only partly successful. As the twentieth century unfolded, Americans invested in Cuban sugar production. By 1920, there were ninety-six Cuban sugar refineries, sixty-two of which were owned by Americans. Up to three-quarters of Cuban sugar was shipped to the United States, and with significant US ownership, Cuban sugar was soon exempted from tariffs. Even after the Great Depression revived protectionism, the infamous Smoot-Hawley Tariff imposed only a 14 percent rate for sugar, compared with an average of 69 percent for all agricultural products.

By mid-century, before Castro took over Cuba, the US government was paying a sugar trade subsidy of two cents per pound above the world price to Cuban producers. This price premium was worth $500 million a year to Cuban producers, and 54.8 percent of Cuba's sugar trade was with the United States.

Then Came Castro

Fidel Castro overturned the Cuban sugar market and, in the process, turned Senator Teller's bad dream of a US sugar market dominated by Cubans into a different kind of nightmare. When Fidel Castro took over the Cuban sugar industry from Julio Lobo and the Fanjul Gomez-Mena family, enough of the Everglades had been drained so that 47,000 acres in Florida were planted in sugarcane. At this crucial juncture, with the preponderance of Cuban sugar still in the hands of US investors, Lobo declined a personal invitation from Che Guevara to become Minister of Sugar in Castro's government. Subsequently, he fled to Spain and retired on his $200 million fortune, worth at least $1.5 billion in today's dollars. But after having dominated Cuban sugar production since 1850, the Fanjuls were not ready to retire. They, too, fled Cuba with "a hefty financial portfolio," some fine paintings, and a mastery of the occult art of freebooting in a corrupt economy—knowledge they would soon put to expert use in both the United States and the Dominican Republic.

To understand what happened next, you have to appreciate the luminously corrupt way that business was conducted in pre-Castro Cuba. If influence peddling had been an Olympic sport, Cubans would have been gold medalists in those days. As the leading sugar planters in mid-century Cuba, the Fanjuls had honed their political skills in dealing with a corrupt government whose leaders were only too keen to enrich the few at the expense of the many, especially when they could rake off a piece of the action for their pains.

Remember, Cuba's penultimate dictator before Castro, the kleptocrat Fulgencio Batista, governed in conjunction with Mafia kingpins Meyer Lansky, Charles "Lucky" Luciano, and Santo Trafficante. Indeed, it was reported that Lansky offered then Cuban president Carlos Prío Socarrás a bribe of $250,000 in 1952 to vacate the presidency to facilitate Batista's return to power. In the event, Socarrás was deposed by Batista in a military coup four months before a scheduled election. Socarrás had been alerted to the impending coup but boarded a plane and flew to exile rather than taking steps to counter it. You can only guess whether he took Meyer Lansky's retirement bonus with him.

The Mafia bosses preferred to do business with Batista even though, in some cases, he literally required daily payoffs. It was well known that Batista's bagmen would call every night on Trafficante's casinos, including the iconic Tropicana Club, to collect 10 percent of the day's take.

You probably don't know the Fanjuls, unless you see them lording around Palm Beach, as I sometimes do. The *New York Times* describes the Fanjul brothers as "Florida's Cuban-American reigning sugar barons who preside over Palm Beach's yacht-owning society."[5] But even in the unlikely event that you keep a yacht in Palm Beach and you see Pepe Fanjul when you stop by the yacht club for a drink, that still wouldn't give you much of perspective on America's reigning sugar barons. The way they work is that Alfy contributes heavily to the Democrats and Pepe covers the bases by contributing heavily to Republicans.

Close readers of the Starr Report got an intimate peek at these Sugar Daddies' high-level connections at work. In the report, Monica Lewinsky stated that on President's Day in 1996, she was with former president Bill Clinton when he spoke by phone with a Florida sugar grower who turned out to be Alfonso Fanjul.[6] It was nothing unusual for Alfy Fanjul to bend the president's ear about the sugar business. In this case, Fanjul, who was cochair of Clinton's 1992 Florida campaign, called to persuade the president to oppose a proposed tax on sugar growers to pay for the cleanup of the Everglades. Fanjul reportedly said that he and other growers opposed such a tax because it would cost them millions.

Years later, after he saw the Starr Report and learned that the president was multitasking during their conversation, Fanjul observed, "I heard no heavy breathing or nothing."

Part of the Fanjuls business model is to maintain a low profile. Their private holding company Flo-Sun is out of the public eye. But if you are a consumer in the United States, or even elsewhere in the world, you will know one or more of the Fanjuls' many subsidized sugar brands: Florida Crystals, CNH Sugar, Redpath Sugar, Tate & Lyle Sugars (the leading sugarcane refiner in the European Union), Lyle's Golden Syrup, and the iconic Domino Sugar, which pioneered the individual serving of sugar in 1916.

The "Domino Effect" has meant diminishing returns in many areas of the economy. We hear a lot of complaint and discussion these days about the 1 percent, who are said to be unfairly hogging prosperity. For my part, I don't begrudge billionaires any money they can make fairly and honestly in the free market. But I do begrudge those who profit through unfair advantage and the misuse of power through crony capitalism. As the free market has been left behind, so have the fortunes of most Americans.

American prosperity has been in a stall for half a century. A big part of the problem is the success of modern-day snake charmers, like the Fanjuls, who have again unleashed the "same old serpent that says you work and I eat, you toil and I will enjoy the fruits of it." The fact that they have been able to profit by taking billions out of the pockets of the bottom 90 percent of the income distribution accounts for large efficiency losses and the destruction of tens of thousands of jobs that might have otherwise provided for middle-class livelihoods.

The Fanjuls recognized, more readily than most, that crony capitalism, not the free market, rules the world. The Fanjuls left Havana to exercise their well-honed skills in crony capitalism in Florida and the Dominican Republic.[7] They came at an opportune time to take advantage of the US embargo on Cuban sugar. And even though the United States was ill suited as a setting for rebuilding their sugar empire, they jumped at the opportunity provided by the federal government's absent-minded Florida swamp-draining boondoggle.

They set up shop in Florida, buying swampland and politicians for a pittance; then they got their swamplands drained at your expense. As if by magic, the Fanjuls benefited from the US Army Corps of Engineers' projects to drain more of the Everglades for agricultural use—a tax-funded initiative that turned swampland into farmland and made large-scale sugar farming in Florida possible.

Today, more than 420,000 Florida acres are planted in sugarcane, and according to CNN, the Fanjuls farm an estimated 180,000 of those acres in the Everglades.[8] Thanks to US government intervention that compels you and other consumers to pay artificially high prices for sugar, the Fanjuls pocket tens of millions of dollars annually in artificial profits. Because they control about 43 percent of Florida's sugarcane production, CNN reports, they collect at least $60 million a year in subsidies.[9]

With their control over the US sugar market, the Fanjuls saw to it that the sugar subsidies were structured to keep the price of sugar high. For one thing, sugar loans are usually granted directly to the sugar processors like the Fanjuls instead of to farmers. So from the Fanjuls' perspective, none of the free money is wasted on some poor wretch trying to scratch out a living from twenty acres of sugarcane in Loxahatchee. A consequence of directing the subsidies to the processors rather than directly to the farmers is that it reinforces cartel pricing. There is no chance of a farmer undercutting the cartel price when he could maximize his income by selling more at a lower price.

And note this sweet twist.

If the proceeds from the harvest yield more than the cost of the loan, the Fanjuls and other big shot sugar operators repay the loans and realize the profit in cash. Otherwise, they can repay the loans in sugar.

Another not inconsiderable benefit of these politically favored nonrecourse loans is the fact that they come with highly subsidized interest rates. Domino and other sugar processors borrow money from the Treasury at rates that are sometimes lower than the government pays to finance its deficit. As the *Wall Street Journal* reported in 2013, over the previous nine years, the United States lent sugar processors $8.8 billion. The loans in 2012 were granted with 1.125 percent to 1.25 percent interest rates.[10] By comparison, the average rate paid by the US government on interest-bearing debt in 2012 varied from 2.791 percent in January to 2.523 percent in December of that year. So the government borrowed billions at up to 2.5 times the interest rate it received on sweetheart loans to billionaires.[11]

During that same period, the interest rates on student loans (graduate and undergraduate Stafford loans) ranged between 3.4 percent and 6.8 percent.[12] Also note that unlike the nonrecourse loans to Domino, student loans are total recourse—they cannot even be discharged in bankruptcy. Student borrowers are indentured for life. Evidently, enriching the Fanjul family is not only more crucial than US fiscal solvency; it is up to six times more important than financing the educations of young Americans.

Yet another sour taste associated with the Domino Effect is that when the cash prices on sugar fall to a point that would otherwise make the subsidized loans unprofitable, Domino and other sugar processors can repay their loans with sugar instead of cash. That is like allowing young people to repay their student loans by delivering their class notes and used textbooks to the Department of Education. I can easily imagine that the 53 percent of recent college grads who are jobless or underemployed would like to use Domino's approach to satisfying their federal loans.

The comparison is unrealistic, I grant.

For one thing, unlike young people trying to use student loans to find their way in a bankrupt world, the Fanjuls need not account for how they use the proceeds of their federal loans in the first place. While the website of the Department of Education's Office of Inspector General details a long list of persons indicted or jailed for misuse of student loans, there is no such thing as misusing sugar loans. They are truly sweetheart loans—just another packet of free money donated at your expense to the Sugar Daddies.

The Fanjuls could not have been named "the first family of corporate welfare" in the United States by both CNN and the *New York Times* if they were not really proficient at picking your pocket.[13] Believe me, they are. They have found so many ways to rig markets and live at your expense that it would take a platoon of forensic accountants months to decipher and quantify them all.

When you compile a tally, don't forget to take into account the millions they pocket gaming the sugar import quota system. Through a subsidiary, the Fanjuls grow sugar in, and export it from, the Dominican Republic as well. Whether they sell their sugar from the Everglades or from the Dominican, they are guaranteed a US price that is more than double anywhere else in the world. The *New York Times* explains: "The sugar exporters who are able to sell to the United States also benefit from those astronomical prices. The Dominican Republic is the largest quota holder." And as reported by CNN, the Fanjuls are "the largest private exporter of Dominican sugar. . . . Through a subsidiary, Central Romana Limited, the brothers grow sugarcane and operate the world's largest sugar mill there . . . Whether they sell sugar from their holdings in the Everglades or from their mill in the Caribbean, the Fanjuls are guaranteed a US price that is more than double anywhere else in the world."[14]

They rigged the markets so that American consumers and taxpayers had to lavishly subsidize them. The CNN/GAO estimate that rigged sugar markets put about $60 million a year into the Fanjuls' bank accounts is really a gross underestimation. It counts only the portion of budgeted federal outlays that experts claim end up with the Fanjuls. The total costs are much higher than that. Economists put the dead weight loss to consumers from inflated sugar prices at $3.5 billion annually.[15] And that doesn't count the follow-on costs.

In the process of growing their subsidized sugar, the Fanjuls imperiled a fragile Everglades ecosystem with biochemical discharge and agricultural runoff. As a result, populations of wading birds in the Everglades have declined by 90 percent since the Fanjuls arrived in Florida. Fertilizer runoff and excessive draining for agriculture have seriously imperiled water quality. The Everglades, the source of most drinking water in South Florida, has been found to contain excessive amounts of phosphorus and sulfate-mercury, a serious poison. Both are the result of discharge from sugar production. That is why Big Sugar fought lengthy court battles in the 1980s and '90s in an attempt to block studies of water quality in the Everglades.

This is not the place to recite the whole tangled tale of research and documentation of the ecological damage done. The Everglades Foundation's "Polluter Pays Study," which looked only at phosphorus pollution, not sulfate mercury pollution (which becomes methyl mercury poisoning), concluded that taxpayers were subsidizing "50 percent of Big Sugar's pollution cleanup costs."

Notwithstanding Article II, Section 7 of the Florida Constitution, the "polluter pays" amendment, the sugar barons convinced politicians to make taxpayers absorb the lion's share of the costs for cleaning up the mess they made. The State of Florida's Everglades Forever Act of 1994 has already cost at least $1.8 billion—of which, according to CNN, the Fanjuls pay $4.5 million a year.[16]

On the federal level, a 1997 analysis places the annual spending by the Army Corps of Engineers to regulate water flow in Central and South Florida at $63 million, of which the Corps estimates that $52 million subsidizes agriculture, mainly sugarcane farming in the Everglades. By implication, 43 percent of that, or another $22 million a year, subsidizes the Fanjuls.

Another $20 Billion in Domino Effect

But this is small change compared to the outlays entailed in the larger Comprehensive Everglades Restoration Plan (CERP). It is this massive project—a joint undertaking between the Army Corps of Engineers and the SFWMD—that had my anonymous seatmate drooling. According to the *Washington Independent*, federal projections put the cost of CERP at just under $20 billion.[17]

Think about it. You would be filthy rich, too, if you could rig a market as large as the sugar one, requiring everyone in the United States to pay you a multiple of the world free market price. From 1990 through 2009, US prices for raw sugar averaged almost exactly double the global average—21.56 cents per pound, compared to 10.85 cents per pound in the rest of the world.

As I write, the current closing price for US Sugar No. 16 is 24.83 cents per pound—a hefty 43 percent premium to world prices but mercifully smaller than the usual markup (as reported by the Intercontinental Exchange, a center of global trading in soft commodities).

The system is rigged to make the sugar market the personal fiefdom of the Fanjuls. This has not only cost you and other citizens untold billions, but the subsidies have also resulted in the loss of twenty thousand jobs in the confectionery industry each year due to the higher prices of sugar in the United States. So said the Department of Commerce in a 2006 report.[18] This implies that crony capitalist domination of the sugar market has cost more than 100,000 Americans the opportunity to enjoy a middle class livelihood since the collapse of the subprime bubble in 2008.

There a lot of thirtysomethings sleeping on their parents couches who might have jobs if not for the Domino Effect. This is exemplified by the fact that iconic US confection brands, such as Life Savers and Hershey Foods, closed production facilities in Chicago, Pennsylvania, Colorado, and California and moved to Canada, where the cost of sugar is half that in the United States.

The Domino Effect on Your Diet

That is one substitution effect. Another involves the substitution of high fructose corn syrup (HFCS), a cheap artificial sweetener that has been adopted in soft drinks, baked goods, sweetened fruit drinks, condiments, and almost everything else you can think of in the American diet. Americans eat more of this vile product than any other people on earth. You also pay your share of some $40 billion in subsidies doled out to corn farmers. And it is a big reason why the United States has the highest incidence of obesity and type 2 diabetes in the world.

Dr. Joseph Mercola, who draws on the research of Dr. Robert Lustig, professor of endocrinology at the University of California, reports that HFCS consumption contributes far more to obesity and insulin resistance than simple table sugar—the kind the Fanjuls have made needlessly expensive. HFCS leads to the following:

1. Insulin resistance
2. Impaired glucose tolerance
3. High insulin levels
4. High triglycerides
5. High blood pressure

Studies show that consumption of high fructose corn syrup in the United States has skyrocketed since 1970.[19] So have rates of obesity and type 2 diabetes. Demographic analysis at the University of Utah shows that the obesity epidemic in the United States intensified after the 1970s and that each cohort has successively higher rates of obesity at every stage of life. Note that one in ten Americans now has diabetes, which entails an average increase in medical spending by $7,402 per year compared to nondiabetics. Treatment of diabetics accounts for some 32 percent of all Medicare spending, or roughly $171.5 billion in 2012.

It would take some elaborate forensic accounting to determine what large fraction of those tens of billions, soon to be hundreds of billions, of dollars a year should be attributed to the Domino Effect. But clearly, sweetheart deals to the Sugar Daddies cost you a lot of money.

Notes

1 Wallsten, Peter, and Tom Hamburger, "Sugar Protections Prove Easy to Swallow for Lawmakers across the Spectrum," *Washington Post*, December 7, 2013.

2 Kowalski, Chuck, "The Two Sugar Markets—US Sugar and World Sugar," *About.com Commodities*, http://commodities.about.com/od/researchcommodities/a/The-Two-Sugar-Markets-Us-Sugar-And-World-Sugar.htm.

3 http://www.mnn.com/earth-matters/translating-uncle-sam/stories/what-happened-to-the-everglades.

4 Herring, George C., *From Colony to Superpower: U.S. Foreign Relations since 1776* (Oxford: Oxford University Press, 2008).

5 http://www.nytimes.com/2003/11/29/opinion/america-s-sugar-daddies.html.

6 Pooley, Eric, "High Crimes? Or Just a Sex Cover-Up? Starr Shows All the Ways Clinton Tried to Keep Monica Quiet," http://www.cnn.com/ALLPOLITICS/time/1998/09/14/high.crimes.html.

7 Haney, Rich, "The Cruel War on Innocent Cubans," *Cubaninsider*, http://cubaninsider.blogspot.com/2013/09/the-cruel-war-on-innocent-cubans.html.

8 Bartlett, Donald L., and James B. Steele, "Sweet Deal: Why Are These Men Smiling? The Reason Is in Your Sugar Bowl," *CNN.com*, November 23, 1998.

9 Ibid.

10 Wexler, Alexandra, "Bulk of U.S. Sugar Loans Went to Three Companies," *Wall Street Journal*, June 26, 2013.

11 https://www.treasurydirect.gov/govt/rates/pd/avg/2012/2012.htm.

12 See http://www.asa.org/basics/loans/interest-rates/student-loan-interest-rates.aspx.

13 See Bartlett and Steele, "Sweet Deal," *CNN.com*, November 23, 1998; and "America's Sugar Daddies," *New York Times*, November 21, 2003.

14 Ibid.

15 Maneka, Bilal, "U.S Sugar Subsidies and the Caribbean's Sugar Economies" Council on Hemispheric Affairs, July 2013.

16 http://www.cnn.com/
    ALLPOLITICS/time/1998/
    11/16/sweet.deal.html.

17 Daly, Kyle, "Sugar Industry,
    Fanjuls Cash in while Taxpayers
    Foot Bill for Everglades, Etha-
    nol Research," *The Washington
    Independent*, April 14, 2011.

18 http://www.sweetenerusers
    .org/ Sugar%20Program
    %20Costs%20Jobs%20-%20
    %20Oct%2020071.pdf.

19 http://www.naturalnews.com/
    026468_sugar_corn_corn
    _syrup.html.

Chapter Fifteen

The Big Fat Lie

Why $3.8 Trillion Year Won't Cure Baumol's Disease

Procter & Gamble's claims about Crisco touching the lives
of every American proved eerily prescient. The substance
(like many of its imitators) was 50 percent trans fat, and it
wasn't until the 1990s that its health risks were understood.
It is estimated that for every two percent increase in
consumption of trans fat (still found in many processed and
fast foods) the risk of heart disease increases by 23 percent.
—Dr. Drew Ramsey and Tyler Graham, "How Vegetable
Oils Replaced Animal Fats in the American Diet"

I admit it.

As I assembled my notes to write this, I went to the freezer
and scooped out a big bowl of Ben & Jerry's Vanilla Ice Cream,
consisting of 40 percent saturated fat.

Yum. I feel a subversive pleasure in savoring the spoonfuls
of creamy goodness—tempered, of course, by recognition that
the twenty grams of sugar in each serving are a virtual poison.
(I would have been much better advised to eat coconut oil,
which is roughly 63 percent saturated fat, one of the highest
percentages of any food.)

My embrace of saturated fats probably shows that I make more
use of the Internet than the average person. No doubt among
the three billion pieces of intelligence that Big Brother monitors
on Americans each month are details of my online searches for

accounts of the updated meta-analysis of the recovered data from the Sydney Diet Heart Study and accounts of Dr. William Castelli's puzzled observations about the people who ate the most saturated fat in the Framingham Heart Study.

This information confirms another dimension of the defining problem of our time: the status quo is an engineering marvel, a dishonest confection built on half-truths and propaganda through which every effort is made to confound you, mislead you, and keep you too busy consuming to think for yourself.

More than you might imagine, this is all epitomized by the vexed topic of saturated fats.

Your Job as an Alimentary Canal

You see, first and foremost, your contribution to the system is that of an alimentary canal. Don't forget it. You are meant to consume, avidly and without hesitation, whatever designer rations of modern commerce that the nanny state determines suit you. And of course, the bureaucrats are not just randomly pulling suggestions out of a hat. They are designing the official diet based on what best-connected lobbyists and political contributors want.

What is good for you, your health or your purse, is of little consequence.

And of course, if you can't afford to pay for these delicacies, as is the case with one in five American families, the nanny state will issue you entitlements, SNAP food stamps, so that you can consume and make your contribution to the GDP. And if the "evo-deviant" diet they have prepared for you has morbid effects, so much the better. Your miseries will have contributed some additional stimulus to the lagging GDP. The world's most expensive health care (or sick care) system, running at an annual tab of $3.8 trillion, can enjoy some more prosperity by ministering to your ruined health.

It is crony capitalism at its finest.

America's Big Problem

When more resources are force-fed into sectors with declining returns, like health care, education, and the military, the result is not really economic stimulus rightly understood, but a particularly malignant version of Baumol's Disease—a condition where the least productive sectors grow more costly over time.

As government diverts more resources into low productivity sectors and reduces the overall growth of the economy through efficiency losses, the politicians also paradoxically increase employment in the parasitic sectors. That is why health care jobs continue to grow faster than the US economy. If you don't think closely, you could easily draw the false conclusion that growing sick care costs were actually stimulating the sick economy.

Not so.

In November 2012, the Altarum Institute, a health care consulting company, reported that since the recession began in December 2007, the health sector added 1.4 million jobs—a cumulative growth of 10.1 percent—while non-health employment fell by 5.6 million jobs—a cumulative decline of 4.6 percent.

I have no reason to dispute the figures from the Altarum Institute. In fact, they are just what you should expect—a measure of the increased misallocation of resources. The extra trillions paid for health care in recent decades meant prosperity for that sector, while other innovative sectors with rising marginal returns starved for resources.

So while health care added jobs, more productive sectors shed 5.6 million jobs.

Not good.

Don't mistake this for a moment. The obesity bubble is no free market phenomenon, any more than the subprime bubble was anything other than a regulated catastrophe. We never would have lost trillions building McMansions for persons with bad credit if the Federal Reserve and the leaders of government had not gone along with the gag and encouraged the banks to play fast and loose with your money.

Equally, the "Big Fat Lie," which has destroyed the health of millions to ensure the prosperity of a few, is a corrupt exploitation of centralized power presided over through the FDA and other agencies of the Big Government corporatocracy. The food industry, Big Pharma, and the mainstream medical industry have successfully manipulated the system to promote the obesity epidemic at your expense. And the government is their not-so-silent partner.

If you have heeded the dietary guidelines promulgated by the US Department of Health and Human Services (HHS) and the US Department of Agriculture (USDA), then your health has been compromised by eating the official government diet. It is not a coincidence that obesity in America has surged fiftyfold over the last century, mostly since the nanny state issued its first dietary guidelines extolling the high-carb, low-fat (i.e., trans fat) diet. In a startling coincidence, the corporate state almost invariably endorsed whatever fandango of cheap artificial ingredients the food industry found most profitable to improvise and purvey.

As Mary Enig, the PhD biochemist and nutritionist who first blew the whistle on the dangers of trans fats put it, organizations such as the American Soybean Association (ASA), Ingredion (formerly Corn Products International), and the Center for Science in the Public Interest (CSPI) have all been economically motivated to promulgate dietary misinformation. They are also aided by the FDA, many of whose key personnel come from, and later return to, the vegetable oil industry.

And in an even more startling coincidence, the mass media will have conditioned you to want whatever processed approximation of food that industry was prepared to sell you. For example, you have probably been led to believe that you should avoid "artery-clogging saturated fats." Try Googling that phrase in quotes. When I tried it, I got 428,000 hits—clear proof that "artery-clogging saturated fats" has become a pervasive cliché of our culture. If you do not feel that saturated fats are bad for you, you must be either of independent mind or oblivious. Thanks to the Internet, it is now much easier to be of independent mind. You can now search for evidence showing that saturated fats are good for you.

There is plenty of it.

What you will find helps illuminate what could otherwise be a perplexing puzzle—how the traditional human diet came to be demonized in our culture within my lifetime. It involved an impressive, if not noble, campaign of propaganda that enlisted all the organs of authority—from the government, to the medical establishment, to an equally self-interested pharmaceutical industry and the compliant mass media—to misinform you about the nature of heart health and rational dietary choices.

In this respect, I think it illuminating to focus on saturated fats as the soft underbelly of crony capitalism. It brings another dimension to the problem of sclerosis that fascinated my late friend and mentor, Mancur Olson. He argued in *The Rise and Decline of Nations* that the longer societies remain stable the more likely it is that powerful special-interest lobbies will collude to twist the rules of the economy to their own ends and your detriment. Olson shrewdly recognized that special interest groups can change "the direction of social evolution." But little research has been devoted to the efforts by special interests with strong incentives to inform popular views on important subjects by clogging information channels with officially sanctioned propaganda and lies. If you understand how this corrupt system works, you would not be surprised to learn that the biggest sponsors of dietitians' conventions and trade shows are junk food makers.

The demonization of saturated fats provides an excellent case study of how crony capitalists mislead you for their own profit on health issues. This came about as a proximate consequence of the eclipse of the family farm and the emergence of a potentially vast market for cheap artificial ingredients that could be profitably processed into palatable form.

The sad truth was recognized early on by *Popular Science* magazine, commenting on the waste products of cotton farming, with the observation that what ended up on your table "was garbage in 1860." The garbage quotient grew exponentially after food processors learned to process corn oil with extreme heat, nickel, emulsifiers, bleach, and artificial flavors and coloring to fabricate food-like products that would not make consumers gag. After the garbage fats became palatable, they were to be processed into Wonder Bread, cakes, Pringles, doughnuts, Oreos, moon pies, Twinkies, Girl Scout Cookies, Kentucky Fried Chicken, french fries, and other trans fat–laden staples of suburban culture.

When I was a child in the 1950s, however, most foods were still prepared the old-fashioned way—at home with eggs, butter, cream, cheese, and (dare I mention it?) lard. But this entailed major drawbacks from the perspective of the food industry:

1. Butter, cream, and other natural saturated fats are expensive to produce, transport, and store. The food industry was looking to substitute cheaper ingredients to widen profit margins and make production more scalable.

2. Foods prepared with natural saturated fats like butter, eggs, and cream vary in taste and consistency from batch to batch, depending on the diet of the animals that produced the fat. The food industry preferred to deal with synthetic or processed fats that would yield products with a standardized appearance, taste, and texture that could be mass-produced.

3. Traditional foods were almost always consumed immediately upon preparation. The natural saturated fats employed in most recipes could go rancid if left unrefrigerated for even a few hours. The food industry wanted products with the shelf life of a mop handle.

Big Fat Lies

Given these considerations, the food industry had a stake in weaning the public away from the natural saturated fats that had formed an important component of the healthy human diet from hunting and gathering times forward. For 200,000 years, biologically modern humans had thrived eating saturated fats. But suddenly, in the last century, one of the boldest episodes of crony capitalist manipulation ever attempted succeeded in convincing a distracted and gullible public to change their diet in health-threatening ways.

How did they do it? They resorted to the time-tested methods of shaping public opinion: scare tactics and the big lie. J. Walter Thompson, America's first full-service Madison Avenue advertising agency, pointed the way. One of the eight alternative marketing strategies they concocted for the launch of Procter & Gamble's pioneering artificial fat product, Crisco, was based on the unsubstantiated pretense that it was "a healthier alternative to cooking with animal fats."

Another milestone in establishing the Big Fat Lie was achieved three-quarters of a century later by one-time Democratic presidential candidate George McGovern. McGovern built his Senate career in thrall to the grain farmers for whom he advocated lavish subsidies. But he really went overboard as the chairman of the United States Senate Select Committee on Nutrition and Human Needs.

McGovern pushed the federal government to embrace the imaginary health benefits of the low-fat, high-carb diet. These were incorporated into federal nutritional guidelines. This special-interest recipe for ill health was soon foisted on innocent children through the school lunch program.

The inescapable corollary of reducing calories from saturated fats was to increase the ingestion of the cheapest substitute ingredients. The result was a tilt in the American diet away from consuming natural and satisfying saturated fats toward carbohydrate convections laced with toxic trans fats and artificial high fructose corn sugars.

High Fructose Poison

The overrepresentation of HFCS on the American table was a follow-on consequence of the Big Fat Lie, driven by the fact that HFCS is sweeter and cheaper than cane sugar. Experts on sugar metabolism, like Dr. Robert Lustig, argue that there are major differences in how your body processes different types of sugars. Any cell in your body can use glucose, but virtually the entire metabolic burden of fructose rests with your liver, where unlike glucose, it tends to get stored as fat.

Dr. Lustig argues that the fatty acids created during fructose metabolism cause insulin resistance and nonalcoholic fatty liver disease, which have skyrocketed in the United States since the high-carb, low-fat diet was adopted.

And don't forget, the pharmaceutical industry was waiting in the wings to enjoy windfall profits from all the damage that low-fat diets did to human health.

Cholesterol Confusion

The whole notion that saturated fat is bad for you began with an intellectually dishonest twentieth-century medical experiment undertaken by Nikolaj Nikolajewitsch Anitschkow in which large amounts of dietary cholesterol were cruelly fed to rabbits. If your knowledge of zoology extends even so far as having seen "Bugs Bunny's Thanksgiving Diet" on television, you know that Bugs is always nibbling on a carrot, not a sausage.

Rabbits don't eat meat.

Little wonder then that when rabbits were force-fed dietary cholesterol it literally did "clog" their arteries. But to say that this proved dietary cholesterol is bad for humans is like pretending you have proven that tuna fish can't swim by dumping a hundred rabbits overboard in the middle of the ocean. The fact that rabbits cannot process dietary cholesterol says nothing about how omnivores like humans are affected by eating saturated fats.

Without delving too deeply into all the intellectual frauds entailed in the demonization of saturated fat, The Big Fat Lie gained growing traction during my childhood as companies marketed artificial trans fats in margarine and other processed vegetable oils as healthy (and cheaper) alternatives to butter (also known as "the 70 cents spread"). They even concocted "non-dairy creamers" loaded with trans fats that required no refrigeration.

Margarine: Edible Wax?

This switch from natural butter to artificial trans fats in margarine took advantage of a patent formulated by the German chemist Wilhelm Normann in 1902. Normann invented a process whereby liquid oils could be hydrogenated and turned into solids. Initially, he intended the artificial hydrogenated fats to substitute for wax and tallow in the production of candles.

But when the candle market crashed due to the spread of electricity, Procter & Gamble found a more profitable use for Normann's invention. They acquired rights to the patent and began producing a trans fat product for human consumption called Crisco, composed of partially hydrogenated cottonseed oil. Like candles, but unlike traditional shortening, Crisco never went rancid sitting on the shelf.

Many consumers embraced the convenience of fake foods that didn't spoil. They also tended to enjoy the fact that margarine, unlike butter, did not need to be kept well chilled in the refrigerator. So there was no need to soften margarine before spreading it on bread.

But undoubtedly the biggest driver of the move away from butter and cream toward a diet low in saturated fats was the Big Fat Lie—the carefully cultivated conviction that saturated fat is bad for the heart and unsaturated fats, particularly polyunsaturated omega-6 fatty acids, were a much healthier alternative.

Lies from Down Under

A crucial study that seemed to support that view was conducted in Australia on men between the ages of thirty and fifty-nine who had already had a heart attack or had been diagnosed with heart disease. Decades ago, when the study was conducted, its outcome was falsely construed to support the idea that increasing your intake of polyunsaturated omega-6 fatty acids and lowering dietary saturated fat would improve heart health.

But guess what? The conclusion in support of eating polyunsaturated omega-6 fatty acids was contradicted by underlying data allegedly supporting the reported conclusion. It proved to be as bogus as the claim by the Obama administration that the US economy has recovered. Equally, when a team of researchers reopened and reanalyzed the data from the Sydney Diet Heart Study, they found that it was categorically untrue that subjects who consumed more omega-6 fatty acids and less saturated fat were healthier. To the contrary, those in the polyunsaturated fat group had significantly higher rates of death than those consuming traditional, saturated fat.[1]

It wasn't even close—the omega-6 group experienced a 50 percent higher death rate from all causes. (OK, let me not exaggerate: the overall death rate was 49.15 percent higher.) The polyunsaturated fat group experienced a 56.4 percent higher death rate from cardiovascular disease, and they died at a 61.4 percent higher rate from coronary heart disease. In short, the conventionally accepted conclusion that more polyunsaturated vegetable oils were a healthier alternative to eating saturated animal or vegetable fat was remote from the facts.

Setting aside these spectacularly faulty conclusions drawn from the initial Sydney Diet Heart Study, there is other solid evidence that people in cultures with the highest percentage of saturated fats in their diet have the lowest risk of heart disease. Consider the Inuit Eskimos who live in Greenland and the Canadian Arctic. Their diets, comprised mostly of whale meat and blubber, derive approximately 75 percent of calories from saturated fat. They are almost entirely free of heart disease and cancer.

Equally, the Maasai tribe in Kenya thrive on a diet of meat, the blood of cattle, and a fatty milk comparable to half and half. It may not sound very appetizing, but the Maasai have no heart disease.

You don't need to travel to the ends of the earth to find remote groups with traditional diets who thrive on high saturated fats. The French have the highest fat consumption in Europe but the lowest rate of death from heart disease, according to European Cardiovascular Disease Statistics.[2] In other words, the "French paradox" may have less to do with drinking red wine than with eating lots of butter, Béarnaise sauce, triple cream brie, and Époisses de Bourgogne.

They Really Don't Want to Know

In 1948, the US government funded a longitudinal lifestyle study of 5,209 healthy men and women aged from thirty to sixty-two in Framingham, Massachusetts, to see who developed coronary heart disease. Along the way, more than one thousand medical papers have been published detailing findings from the Framingham study.

For example, by the 1960s, it had become evident that smoking cigarettes increases the risk of heart disease. Researchers also determined that exercise decreases risk and obesity elevates it. The study also seemed to support the demonization of cholesterol, with the proviso that high levels of HDL ("good") cholesterol reduce risk of heart disease. But look more closely and you see that the Framingham study actually undercuts rather than confirms the Big Fat Lie.

In an analysis that many found puzzling, Dr. William Castelli, the third director of the Framingham study, reported in the *Archives of Internal Medicine* in 1992 that those eating the most saturated fat were the healthiest.[3] Castelli wrote, "In Framingham, Massachusetts, the more saturated fat one ate, the more cholesterol one ate, the more calories one ate, the lower people's serum cholesterol. The opposite of what . . . Keys et al would predict . . . We found that the people who ate the most cholesterol, ate the most saturated fat, ate the most calories weighed the least and were the most physically active."

Castelli's remarks are sensational. They point to the truths about the Big Fat Lie. It turns out that the cliché about "artery-clogging saturated fats" repeated 428,000 times in my Google search may not be the word of God after all. Dr. Castelli's revelations point in precisely the opposite direction. Little wonder that they have been played down by those with a stake in maintaining the cholesterol theory of heart disease. Notwithstanding a remarkably muted response by the establishment, Dr. Castelli's observations have not been entirely overlooked by ordinary persons interested in their health. They even merit a discussion page on the online encyclopedia Wikipedia.[4]

Dr. Castelli's remarks are more interesting when you carefully analyze their context. On the face of it, when a leading cardiologist like Dr. Castelli acknowledges that people eating the most saturated fat in the long-running Framingham heart study had lower serum cholesterol and weighed the least, he is effectively repudiating the Big Fat Lie.

It is as if Benjamin Bernanke were to write an article stating that QE is actually a deflationary policy that contracts the economy and promotes unemployment—all of which may be true. But it is practically impossible for top establishment figures to consciously admit that the whole premises to which they have devoted their lives are wrong.

Cognitive Dissonance

In the case of the Big Fat Lie, Dr. Castelli seems to have shied away from the obvious conclusion: the modern American diet is rationalized upon a faulty hypothesis about saturated fat. As I parse his comments, my impression is that he still doesn't get it—he is perplexed because the data doesn't fit with mainstream medicine's conviction that saturated fat *should be* bad for you, and it doesn't confirm the Big Fat Lie.

What is more amazing, given the totally bent information channels that inundate you with propaganda demonizing cholesterol, are the results of peer-reviewed research showing that high cholesterol is good for your health. Yes, you read that properly. High cholesterol has been wrongly demonized.

A 1994 study from Yale University by Dr. Harlan M. Krumholz et al., titled "Lack of Association Between Cholesterol and Coronary Heart Disease Mortality and Morbidity and All-Cause Mortality in Persons Older than 70 Years," showed that people with low cholesterol had nearly twice as many heart attacks as those with high cholesterol.[5] But that's not all.

A separate ten-year study, reported in the *Lancet*, showed that people with higher cholesterol had a lower risk of death from all causes.[6] Of course, I doubt that high cholesterol protects against traffic accidents or stray bullets, but the inverse correlation with natural causes of death is contrary to what you have been told.

Even more compelling, in a study of 17,791 heart disease patients, researchers reporting in the *American Heart Journal* found that lower serum cholesterol actually is predictive of increased mortality. Patients with the supposedly healthy cholesterol readings of 150 mg/dl were at a 48 percent greater risk of death than patients with allegedly "dangerous" cholesterol levels of 250 mg/dl. *Indeed, each 10-mg/dL increase in TC level was associated with a 4 percent decreased risk of in-hospital mortality.*[7] Surprised? Don't be. The system is designed to fleece you, not to keep you healthy. One in four Americans over the age of forty-five takes cholesterol-lowering drugs, as did 46 percent of the patients in the *American Heart Journal* study. The fact that these much-prescribed drugs take a heavy toll on health could be considered an innocent coincidence or a cruel hoax. Take your pick.

The fact that you are left to decipher this doesn't perplex me at all. It is only perplexing to someone who is invested in validating a dietary and health theory that gained credence in the twentieth century because of the big government corporatocracy. Big government is manipulating an antimarket to reward powerful interests like food companies and pharmaceutical companies, among whose biggest products are statin drugs.

Let's Pretend

Think about it. Everyone who matters wants to keep up the appearance that the Big Fat Lie is true. The food industry does, for obvious reasons. Their margins from selling processed, fake foods that are cheaper to produce, totally scalable, and don't require refrigeration are incomparably higher than what they could earn selling real foods with natural, saturated fats subject to rapid spoilage.

Although it may seem strange, even the dairy industry has adapted and found a way to profit from the "fat makes you fat" lie. They became complicit in that hoax through the aggressive marketing of nonfat milk as a supposedly healthier alternative to whole milk. What rubbish. The obvious corollary to this is that dairies get to sell the milk fat separately. As I write, the most recent closing price for a pound of butter fat on the Chicago Mercantile Exchange was $1.7025. The price differential, if any, between fat-free milk and whole milk is always skinnier than the approximately $.50 a gallon the dairies gain by selling the butterfat separately from the milk. Fat-free milk is marketed not to make you healthier but to profit from your gullibility.

But if you ever find yourself drinking that stuff, remember the pig farmers are grateful. The ready availability of nonfat milk makes it easier for them to fatten their hogs. Nonfat milk has the same effect on the metabolism of pigs as it has on yours. It makes them fat, which is why it is commonly used by pig farmers to fatten their swine.

(If you think I'm joking, follow this link that reports on three studies that found drinking skim milk makes children fatter: http://www.npr.org/blogs/thesalt/2013/03/19/174739752/

whole-milk-or-skim-study-links-fattier-milk-to-slimmer-kids. It links to an NPR story from March 20, 2013: "Whole Milk or Skim? Study Links Fattier Milk to Slimmer Kids.")

As a blog from the Butter Believer succinctly put it, "Were our ancestors eating fat-free sour cream, cholesterol-free 'buttery spreads' or skim milk? Of course not. Dairy had always been consumed in its whole, full-fat form before the industrialization of foods began. And no one had heart disease. The field of medical cardiology didn't even exist until the advent of industrial seed oils packed with toxic polyunsaturated fat."[8]

The fact that the Big Fat Lie is indeed a lie is perversely one of its charms to the crony capitalist corporatocracy. If the high-carb diet loaded with polyunsaturated omega-6 fats of the dietary guidelines really were conducive to good health, much of the support for such a diet would vanish. It is precisely the fact that the government's official diet has ruined the health of tens of millions of Americans and brought on an epidemic of obesity, type 2 diabetes, and coronary heart disease that accounts for the widespread willingness among so many vested interests to go along with the gag.

They are happy to pretend that it is good for you to eat gobs of polyunsaturated omega-6 fatty acids laced with artificial trans fats—so long as it really isn't. If it really were good for you that would mean a startling collapse in demand for a whole range of industries.

The Big Fat Lie's Beneficiaries

At the beginning of the twentieth century, when everyone was eating saturated fats, obesity was exceedingly rare. And so was coronary heart disease. Of course, I would not pretend that the disturbance of metabolism arising from the introduction of fake fats in the American diet was the sole cause of the surge in obesity. It is certainly true that the proliferation of laborsaving devices and the movement away from physical work have reduced the caloric burden of everyday living. That said, many of these developments took effect in the second half of the nineteenth century without precipitating a surge of obesity.

It is also pertinent that a recent study of calorie expenditure by a surviving hunter-gatherer population, the Hanza, of Northern Tanzania, showed no significant difference in total energy expenditure between the Hanza who procure their own food and sedentary modern office workers. So contrary to what you might expect, the labor-saving devices that we employ but the Hanza don't apparently can't be blamed for the fact that so many of us are obese.[9]

Energy requirements may wax and wane, but the fact that so many persons have found it difficult or impossible to adjust their diets accordingly, through the natural regulatory mechanisms of appetite, suggests to me that those mechanisms had been deranged, most probably by the introduction of fake foods, particularly fake fats.

Before fake fats destroyed the balance between nutrition and energy exertion, heart disease was too rare to even require a medical specialty. The first coronary catheterization was not even performed until 1929. The lucrative field of interventional cardiology has emerged since then, greatly expanding since the late 1970s when Big Brother's Big Fat Lie was officially incorporated in the US government's dietary guidelines.

There were only 500 practicing cardiologists in the United States in 1950. That number has ballooned almost fiftyfold since then, while the population has only a bit more than doubled. In 2014, 1,954,000 cardiac operations were performed, making work for lots of surgeons and helping amortize expensive surgical theaters and operating rooms in hospitals throughout the United States.[10]

Seen from the perspective of the self-interest of vested groups, a lot of the US economy is predicated upon your continued embrace of the Big Fat Lie. Not only does the food industry profit, but the prosperity of cardiologists and weight-loss clinics is directly linked to the willingness of the American people to swallow the lies they've been told—and the food that goes with it.

America's Fat Epidemic

When the twentieth century began, only 1 in 150 Americans was obese. By 1950, as the first generation exposed to trans fats in Crisco reached middle age, the number of obese soared to 10 percent of the population. By the mid-'70s, 15 percent of Americans were obese. Data from 2012 shows that two-thirds of Americans were overweight, of whom 35.7 percent were obese with grim consequences for health.[11]

The pervasive consumption of trans fats represents a major departure from past practices when obesity was rare. Animal studies suggest that contrary to what you have been told, obesity is not merely a function of calories ingested, but weight gain varies dramatically with the composition of calories in the diet. The junk food industry would have you swallow another dietary myth: the simpleminded conviction that weight gain is merely a matter of burning fewer calories than you ingest. They would have you believe that all calories count equally as contributions to obesity.

Wrong.

Accelerated weight gain is a direct consequence of eating artificial, partially hydrogenated polyunsaturated oils. In a long-term study lasting six years, scientists fed one group of monkeys a diet containing trans fats, while another luckier group of monkeys got a diet without them.[12] Both diets were identical in total fat content and the number of calories. But the weight gain was not identical. The trans-fat monkeys gained 400 percent more weight than the trans-fat-free monkeys, although both consumed the same number of calories.

It isn't just the food industry and cardiologists that make a living off of the big fat lie; oncologists have gotten their share of new business as well. A seven-year study conducted in France, as part of the European Prospective Investigation into Cancer and Nutrition, tracked twenty thousand women with complete diet histories and blood samples. This showed that trans fat consumption was associated with a 75 percent increase in invasive breast cancer. And the overall incidence of cancer has soared as the percentage of calories in the diet from saturated fats has declined. According to the Centers for Disease Control and Prevention, about one-third of all cancers are directly related to obesity.

Consider the weight loss and diet industry, whose market depends almost entirely on the big fat lie. The research firm Marketdata estimates that the total US weight loss market enjoyed revenues of $60.9 billion in 2010. What would that market have been worth if Americans were still eating the traditional diet high in saturated fat our ancestors consumed a century ago, when only 1 person out of 150 was obese?

Big Pharma Cashes In

And of course, the pharmaceutical industry now has at least 29 billion reasons to lie about cholesterol. That is the amount of money they pocket annually by selling statin drugs designed to reduce serum cholesterol. And the FDA that pretends to be looking out for you is doing its best to make sure you are taking expensive statins (expensive in more sense than one). Doctors are now being told to no longer adhere to rigid clinical guidelines that trigger the use of a statin when cholesterol levels reach a certain threshold. Even if your cholesterol is not "too high" according to the former metrics, your doctor will be encouraged by the government's official pill-pimper to put you on a regime of statins. As Chris Kesser of *Let's Take Back Your Health* lucidly explained, 92 percent of people taking statins are healthy.[13] The FDA has approved the prescription of these drugs to people at low risk for heart disease and stroke and who don't even have high cholesterol.

Of course, it is only a happy coincidence from the perspective of the drug companies that their lucrative sales of statin drugs have, among other side effects, the likelihood of increasing lucrative sales of diabetes drugs. As reported by Alice Park in a March 2013 *Time* article, "Statins May Seriously Increase Diabetes Risk," a study published in *Diabetologia* reported a finding by Finnish scientists that men prescribed statins had a 46 percent greater chance of developing diabetes after six years compared to those had not been prescribed the drug.[14] Furthermore, the risk of diabetes increased with the higher the dose of the statin and the longer the patients took them.

Doesn't sound good for the patients, but as they say, it is a foul wind that blows no one any good. Big Pharma's most lucrative class of drugs is diabetes medicine. The market for such drugs is currently about $30 billion annually and rising rapidly as another American is diagnosed with diabetes every twenty-three seconds.[15]

Apart from its impact in contributing to diabetes by causing obesity, scientists have linked trans fatty acids to type 2 diabetes because of their effect in hampering proper function of the insulin receptor. Meanwhile, a Brazilian study showed that rats fed diets that included partially hydrogenated oils (trans fats) had higher than normal blood glucose as they matured.[16] Because of the multiple morbidities associated with diabetes, it creates lots of business for various specialties in health care.

Diabetes is one of the top two causes of blindness, requiring at least annual visits to ophthalmologists. Diabetics have eighteen times greater risk for kidney failure, thereby employing many renal specialists. It is also the leading cause of lower limb amputation, employing surgeons and creating a bigger market for wheelchairs and artificial prostheses.

You see how it works.

Between 40 percent to 50 percent of type 2 diabetics require regular insulin, and most of the others are users of prescription hypoglycemic agents, like the controversial drug Avandia, whose makers appear to have rigged scientific data and fibbed about its safety record. Despite having caused over 83,000 heart attacks, according to the Senate Finance Committee, Avandia is still being prescribed.[17]

Regardless of the drug used, almost all diabetics require daily glucose monitoring. The US glucose monitoring market is worth $2.5 billion annually. According to the *Center for Disease Control (CDC)*, 9.3 percent of Americans now have diabetes.[18]

The overwhelming evidence that the health of Americans has been compromised by eating a low-fat, high-carb diet laden with fake but economical ingredients with long shelf lives adds an important perspective to the dramatically declining marginal returns in sick care.

In 1980, health economist H. E. French III, PhD, wrote a study for the American Enterprise Institute, "The Long-Lost Free Market in Health Care: Government and Professional Regulation of Medicine," in which he stated that the United States spends far more on health care than most other nations, but its health status remained below most industrialized nations. He also pointed out that even though the costs of medical care in the United States had been rising rapidly, health status had not noticeably risen in the same time period. US health care had, however, been characterized by increasing extensive regulation.[19]

In the thirty-five years since French wrote his indictment of the poor cost/benefit performance of the American health care system, the nominal costs of medical care in the United States have skyrocketed more than ten times over. We now spend $3.8 trillion a year—greater than the whole GDP of Germany—to be less healthy than we were three decades ago.[20]

The Real Reason Health Care Is So Expensive

Economists have failed to agree on why this is the case. What are the main factors contributing to the plunging marginal returns in health care?

Different theories have been offered.

In 1967, economist William Baumol advanced a hypothesis in an *American Economic Review* article, "Macroeconomics of Unbalanced Growth: The Anatomy of Urban Crisis." His explanation was that productivity in other areas of the economy was rising so much faster than in health care that increases in the incomes of health-care workers would inevitably exceed productivity growth. Therefore, the relative cost of health care was destined to continuously rise—a phenomenon that became known as Baumol's Disease.

There is no lack of evidence for the continual escalation of health care costs, but in my view, Baumol's Disease is only a partial explanation. Part of the problem, as H. E. French suggested at the time of the Obamacare debate, is deteriorating health due to lifestyle choices. Seen another way, it is all part of the "absurd tax," to quote Adam Smith, that we pay for the sins of crony capitalism.

The medical profession has been inventing patients for decades by its collusion with junk food makers, Big Pharma, the insurance companies, professional dietitians, the FDA, and the whole round robin of corrupt crony capitalists who have conspired to feed you the Big Fat Lie.

Why You Can't Trust Mainstream Medicine

At the very least, the abysmal failure of the medical community to make even the slightest inroad into the obesity epidemic opens the door to legitimate questions about whether they sincerely want you to be healthy. This was driven home to me by an exchange I had with a pediatrician when my youngest child required a health certification to enter kindergarten.

I took Arthur to a doctor reputed to be the best pediatrician in Palm Beach County. She duly examined him, stuck him with a few shots, and then sat me down for a lecture on the importance of a sound diet to promote his health, particularly to avoid obesity. I was flabbergasted when she proceeded to tell me that Arthur should never be permitted to drink whole milk, only the fat-free stuff.

At the time of this interview, I was already well aware that the indictment of saturated fats in the diet was based on misinformation. Studies disproving the value of skim and nonfat milk were readily available, so I found it strange that they would be unknown to an apparently intelligent doctor.

To disabuse her of the misimpression, I duly sent the good doctor the results of a Harvard study of 12,829 children ages nine to fourteen that had been published in the *Archives of Pediatrics and Adolescent Medicine*. It showed, as did the other studies referenced earlier in this chapter, that drinking skim milk, not whole milk, led to weight gain. As reported in the peer-reviewed article, "Contrary to our hypotheses, dietary calcium and skim and 1% milk were associated with weight gain, but dairy fat was not."

Astonishingly, the pediatrician told me that "it didn't matter" whether it was true that drinking skim milk would reduce the chance of my child becoming obese. She was obliged to advise us to follow that recommendation anyway. She said, "As board certified pediatricians, we follow the dietary recommendations set by the American Academy of Pediatrics."

Unbelievable.

I concluded at that moment that the mainstream medical establishment was consciously dispensing perverse recommendations designed to create patients. Thanks to this bogus propaganda, childhood obesity has skyrocketed by 300 percent over the past thirty years: one in three American children, between the ages of ten and seventeen, is now overweight or obese.

And while I am bashing pediatricians, who must all be married to cardiologists, I must point out another absurd recommendation that should weigh on their consciences if they have any. The American Academy of Pediatricians actually recommended that statins be prescribed for kids as young as eight years old.

Long after these little fatties have outgrown the equivocal attentions of their pediatricians, they'll be buying new
Mercedes for cardiologists and oncologists, along with the
nephrologists, ophthalmologists, and sawbones who will minister to the morbidities of diabetes.

This seemingly cynical view accords with that expressed by
Mancur Olson in *A New Approach to the Economics of Health-
care*. He wrote: "Why should such a wasteful and expensive
system be adopted? Who is responsible for proposing and supporting it? As a hardened economist, I believe that those who
profit from the arrangement are the ones who sought it. This
belief grows not only out of the lore of my craft but also out of
the history of the arrangement at issue, which goes back to a
time when the government did not have much to do with the
health care system."[21]

Today, and for many decades, government has had a lot to
do with the health care system. I would say that the government has long colluded with the food industry and the mainstream medical establishment to encourage Americans to
adopt an unhealthful diet that literally creates patients whose
miseries must be treated at lavish expense. Pharmaceutical
companies are only too delighted to treat the populations poi-
soned by an unhealthy diet with more poisons that compound
the damage.

As a result, we experience plunging marginal returns on
health care spending, along with another danger Olson highlighted in *The Rise and Decline of Nations*—namely, an increase
in *"the complexity of understandings."*[22] Because you can't trust
your doctor or dietitian to recommend a wholesome diet, and
you certainly can't trust the FDA or the junk food companies,
you have to figure it out for yourself if you hope for a healthy
life for your family.

The Obamacare program of mandatory health insurance to
funnel still more trillions into the sick care maw is another
long stride in the wrong direction. It rewards the crony capitalists who have sacrificed your health for their own profit.

In light of Joseph A. Tainter's thesis in *The Collapse of Complex Societies* that collapse occurs due to declining marginal returns, the plunging returns in health care alone could trigger national bankruptcy. Force-feeding more money into the system through Obamacare just continues the Big Fat Lie and brings us that much closer to collapse.

Notes

1 http://drnevillewilson.com/2013/03/04/lost-and-found-the-fat-facts/.

2 http://www.dietdoctor.com/stunning-saturated-fat-and-the-european-paradox.

3 http://www.ncbi.nlm.nih.gov/pubmed?term=%22Archives+of+internal+medicine%22%5BJour%5D+AND+1371%5Bpage%5D+AND+1992%5Bpdat%5D&cmd=detailssearch.

4 See http://en.wikipedia.org/wiki/Framingham_Heart_Study.

5 Krunholz, Harlan M., MD, and Teresa E. Seeman, PhD, et al., *Journal of the American Medical Association* 272, no. 17 (November 2, 1994).

6 Weverling-Rijnsberger, Annalies W. E., MD, "Total Cholesterol and Risk of Mortality in the Oldest Old," *The Lancet* 350, no. 9086 (October 18, 1997).

7 Horwich, T. B., A. F. Hernandez, D. Dai, C. W. Yancy, and G. C. Fonarow, "Cholesterol Levels and In-Hospital Mortality in Patients with Acute Decompensated Heart Failure," *American Heart Journal* 156, no. 6 (December 2008), 1170–76. doi: 10.1016/j.ahj.2008.07.004. Epub 2008 Sep 9.

8 *The Butter Believer*, September 6, 2012, http://butterbeliever.com/fat-free-dairy-skim-milk-secrets/.

9 See http://www.telegraph.co.uk/news/health/news/9426588/Office-workers-burn-as-many-calories-as-hunter-gatherers.html.

10 http://www.cdc.gov/nchs/fastats/inpatient-surgery.htm.

11 https://www.niddk.nih.gov/health-information/health-statistics/Pages/overweight-obesity-statistics.aspx.

12 http://www.wakehealth.edu/News-Releases/2006/Trans

_Fat_Leads_To_Weight_Gain_Even_on_Same_Total_Calories,_Animal_Study_Shows.htm.

13 http://chriskresser.com/the-hidden-truth-about-statins/.

14 http://time.com/3732605/statins-may-seriously-increase-diabetes-risk/.

15 http://www.diabetes.org/diabetes-basics/statistics/.

16 http://www.foodandnutritionresearch.net/index.php/fnr/article/view/28536.

17 http://www.avandia-heart-lawyers.com/news/pringle_010908.php.

18 http://www.cdc.gov/diabetes/pubs/statsreport14/national-diabetes-report-web.pdf.

19 French, F. E., III, "The Long-Lost Free Market in Health Care: Government and Professional Regulation of Medicine," in *A New Approach to the Economics of Health Care,* ed. Mancur Olson (Washington, DC: American Enterprise Institute, 1981), 44.

20 Munro, Dan, "Annual U.S. Healthcare Spending Hits $3.8 Trillion," *Forbes,* February 14, 2014, http://www.forbes.com/sites/danmunro/2014/02/02/annual-u-s-healthcare-spending-hits-3-8-trillion/.

21 Olson, Mancur, ed., *A New Approach to the Economics of Health Care* (Washington, DC: American Enterprise Institute, 1981), 8.

22 Olson, Mancur, *The Rise and Decline of Nations: Economic Growth, Stagflation, and Social Rigidities* (New Haven, CT: Yale University Press, 1982), 73.

Chapter Sixteen

The Hidden BTU Content
of Fiat Money

*Fundamentally, debt is a claim on future money but, since
money is itself a claim on the real economy, and hence on energy,
debt really amounts to a claim on the energy economy of the
future. . . . Energy returns have been declining for a long time,
and I believe that growth in the real economy ceased quite some
years ago. . . . [T]he, financial 'shadow' economy of money and
debt has continued to expand, opening up a huge gap between,
on the one hand, the economic claims incorporated in the
financial system and, on the other, the actual potential of the
real economy . . . What it means is that the financial and real
economies can be reconciled only if financial claims (meaning
both debt and money) are destroyed on a truly enormous scale.[1]*

—Tim Morgan, *Life after Growth*

I don't usually make paranormal claims. But it seemed that
perhaps the simplest way of introducing Dr. Tim Morgan is
to tell you that he could be the reincarnation of Frederick
Soddy.

Of course, that's not exactly like telling you that he is Polly
Styrene's serious older brother. He isn't. But probably more
people recognize Polly Styrene, the late British punk rocker,
than know Frederick Soddy, a Nobel Prize winner and pioneer of atomic energy who explained radioactive decay and
developed the theory of isotopes. A crater on the far side of the
moon was named for him.

More to the point, Soddy was also a pioneer of biophysical economics and a critic of fractional reserve banking who was among the first to argue that compound interest contradicts the laws of thermodynamics.

"The ruling passion of the age," Soddy proclaimed in the 1920s, "is to convert wealth into debt—to exchange a thing with present-day real value (a thing that could be stolen, or broken, or rust or rot before you can manage to use it) for something immutable and unchanging, a claim on wealth that has yet to be made. Money facilitates the exchange; it is," he argued, "the nothing you get for something before you can get anything."[2]

There is an irony here. Soddy was an actual scientist who tried to import concepts from physics to sharpen the understanding of economic problems—his work had virtually no effect on mainstream economics. The discipline had veered off in another direction where physics was concerned. When the so-called social sciences were under development in the late nineteenth century, Leon Walrus and Vilfredo Pareto, economists from the Lausanne School, sometimes referred to as the Mathematical School, introduced complex mathematical notation to economics to make it seem more like theoretical physics. Yet the assumptions they introduced to make the equations work made economic theorizing less realistic. Soddy's ambition was not to make economics more mathematical but to ground it more realistically in the laws of thermodynamics. He thought, and I agree, that a major problem with economics was that it relied too much upon mathematical truths that were divorced from the laws of physics.

> Debts are subject to the laws of mathematics rather than physics. Unlike wealth, which is subject to the laws of thermodynamics, debts do not rot with old age and are not consumed in the process of living. On the contrary, they grow at so much percent per annum, by the well-known

mathematical laws of simple and compound interest . . . For sufficient reason, the process of compounding is physically impossible, though the process of compound decrement is physically common enough. Because the former leads with passage of time ever more and more rapidly to infinity, which, like minus one, is not a physical but a mathematical quantity, whereas the later leads always more slowly towards zero, which is, as we have seen, the lower limit of physical quantities.[3]

Basking "Flamboyantly" in the "Stored Sunlight of Paleozoic Summers"

Put simply, the first and second laws of thermodynamics mean that perpetual motion is impossible. No scheme or machine can create energy out of nothing or recycle it forever. Before the Industrial Revolution, Soddy tells us, people lived on the energy revenue captured from sunlight by plants, "the original capitalists." Since then, humankind has augmented photosynthesis by consuming "energy capital" or coal (and oil), which he refers to as the "stored sunlight of Paleozoic summers."

The modern "flamboyant period" of using up the capital stock of fossil fuels was perceived by Soddy as a very passing phase, destined to give way to a period when the constraints on energy revenue would be acutely felt. Soddy criticized the conventional belief that the economy is a de facto perpetual motion machine capable of growing to generate infinite wealth. Indeed, he lampooned the very idea of compounding over a long period. As he put it, "If Christ, whose views on the folly of laying up treasures on earth are well known, had put by a pound at this rate, it should now be worth an Octillion, and Tariff Reform would be of little help to provide that, even if you colonized the entire stellar universe. . . . It is this absurdity which inverts society, turns good into evil and makes orthodox economics the laughing stock of science. If the consequences were not the familiar atmosphere of our daily lives they would be deemed beyond the legitimate bounds of the most extravagant comic opera."[4] This is a criticism echoed in a more measured way by Dr. Tim Morgan—an intellectual heir, who, however, gives no hint in *Life after Growth* of ever having heard of Soddy.

I wonder if he ever heard of Polly Styrene? I suppose it is entirely possible that Morgan could have rediscovered Soddy's themes without having encountered his work. I started writing about the drag on growth from higher energy prices years before I ever read Soddy's prescient economic analyses that tie energy depletion and "entropy" back to the laws of thermodynamics.

Of course, I am more interested in intellectual history than your average punk rock fan. Soddy is interesting for tossing pebbles at the high priests' windows, while Morgan is interesting for the detail that he marshaled illustrating the radical collapse in Energy Return on Energy Invested (EROEI).

Now that I have introduced Soddy and Morgan, please put them in your "Favorites" list. There is always a chance you might get a call from Dr. Tim Morgan. Soddy, not so much. But their ideas will be crucial in informing the Breaking Point.

Labor Theory of Value: An Energy Theory of Value

Morgan also inadvertently refreshed my understanding of that vexed topic—the labor theory of value—to which Adam Smith, David Ricardo, and Karl Marx all subscribed but which proved so much more incendiary in Marx's treatment. Tim Morgan suggests that the labor theory of value is really an "energy" theory of economic value. He writes, "Human effort is energy, and that energy is in turn derived from the food that we eat, which itself is another form of energy. The nutritional content of food can be measured in calories (a unit of heat), and human labor can be quantified in Watts, a unit more commonly used to measure electricity."

If we are smart about it, we can see that the equation of human somatic muscle energy with exogenous energy dramatically overvalues human effort. There is no conceivable way that the great majority of work done in a modern economy could be performed by human labor alone. Morgan offers a compelling example: put one gallon of gasoline in a car, drive it until the fuel runs out, and then pay someone to push it back to the starting point. This illustrates the major difference between the price of energy and its value in terms of work done.[5]

A Gallon of Gas Worth $6,420 in Work Equivalent

It is a stark illustration. A (US) gallon of gasoline equates to 124,238 BTU of energy, which in turn corresponds to 36.4 kWh. "Since one hour of human physical labor corresponds to between 74 and 100 W, the labor-equivalent of the gasoline is in the range 364 to 492 hours of work. Taking the average of these parameters (428 hours) and assuming that the individual is paid $15 per hour for the strenuous and tedious activity, it would cost $6420 to get the car back to the start-point. On this rough approximation, then, a gallon of fuel costing $3,50 generates work equivalent to between $5,460 and $7,380 of human labor."[6]

This cost mismatch reflects the fact that human muscle power is very inefficient and inadequate in comparison to the work that is done for us by hydrocarbon fuels on a daily basis.

If you are still not convinced, Morgan invites you to employ "workers pedaling dynamo-connected exercise bicycles to generate the energy used by electrical appliances in a typical Western home." He guesses, and so do I, that the cost of powering the home that way would be many magnitudes higher than "the average electricity bill."

More Energy Deployed since 1900 than in All of Previous Human History

This is why the challenge to economic growth poised by the plunging EROEI is so serious. Unlike in the past, when almost all physical work was powered by human and animal somatic energy, most work today is powered by exogenous sources. Morgan writes, "Of the energy—a term coterminous with 'work'—consumed in Western developed societies, well over 99% comes from exogenous sources, and probably less than 0.7% from human labor."[7]

Leslie A. White put the meager yield from human energy (labor) in perspective in the 1940s:

> The first source of energy exploited by the earliest cultural systems was, of course, the energy of the human organism itself. The original cultures were activated by human energy and by this source and form alone. The amount of power that an average adult man can generate is small, about 1/10 of one horsepower. When women and children, the sick, aged, and feeble are considered, the average power resources of the earliest cultural systems might be reckoned at about 1/20 hp per capita. Since the degree of cultural development—the amount of human need-serving goods and services produced per capita—is proportional to the amount of energy harnessed and put to work per capita per year, other factors remaining constant, these earliest cultures of mankind, dependent as they were upon the meager energy resources of the human body, were simple, meager and crude, as indeed they had to be. No cultural system, activated by human energy alone, can develop very far.[8]

For most of recorded history, economic growth was negligible. Historian J. R. McNeill states the obvious: "The economic growth of the last two centuries, and the population growth too, would have been quite impossible within the confines of the somatic energy regime."[9] Those confines were first stretched by the use of coal to replace wood in the early days of the Industrial Revolution.

In *Something New Under the Sun*, McNeil estimates that energy use worldwide increased by threefold during the nineteenth century.[10] That process of accelerating energy conversion increased even more dramatically during the twentieth century, when global oil production compounded at an annual growth rate of 5.73 percent. This represents a truly astounding departure from the past. McNeill points out that humans have probably deployed more energy since 1900 than in all of human history before 1900. "My very rough calculation suggests that the world in the twentieth century used ten times as much energy as in the thousand years before AD 1900 and in the hundred centuries between the dawn of agriculture and 1900, people used only about two-thirds as much energy as in the twentieth century."[11]

A "Very Passing Phase"

Little wonder that the material standard of prosperity in the advanced countries, those that harnessed the most energy, in the twentieth century reached unprecedented heights. If McNeil can be believed, twentieth-century prosperity was supported by one-third more work than had been accomplished through the whole of human experience back to the dawn of agriculture. We live better than our ancestors because so much more work has been done on our behalf. It is the situation that Soddy described as a "very passing phase" of augmenting our energy income of current sunshine by consuming "energy capital" or coal (and oil), comprising the "stored sunlight of Paleozoic summers."

According to Soddy, the "flamboyant period of high consumption of energy capital was bound to end soon." How soon? Soddy doesn't say, except to imply that we have enjoyed what can only be a limited and passing phase of prosperity based on using up the energy that capital stored over hundreds of millions of years.

Morgan suggests that this phase is already over. He asks whether you as an investor can confidently expect global oil output to double again in the next seven to eight years. By implication, that is what would be required to return to the twentieth-century growth rate in living standards. Morgan tells us that the answer turns on EROEI. I prefer to think in terms of EROEI rather than "peak oil" because peak oil has become entwined with, and confused by, the whole corporatist green energy agenda. It is easier to misconstrue the assertion that the world is running shy of oil into a rationalization for crony capitalist rip-offs, like Solara and corn-based ethanol, than it is to fabricate subsidies on the basis of EROEI.

In fact, the last thing the corn lobby wants to hear is an analysis of their biofuels in energy budgeting terms. Tim Morgan comments: "Biofuel EROEIs seldom exceed 2:1, and some are negative, meaning that the energy extracted from producing so-called 'green' fuels is actually less than the energy put into the process in the first place! In the energy budgeting terms in which we are going to have to calculate our decisions in the future, producing such fuels is value-destructive, and is about as rational as putting barrels of oil into rockets and blasting them into space."[12]

Morgan argues that critics of Peak Oil "have provided the right answer to *the wrong question*. Cornucopians needs tell us that there is nothing to worry about, because reserves of oil (and of other fossil fuels) remain abundant. This *completely misses the point* . . . Because the real issue is not absolute volumes of energy at all, but surplus energy (that is the difference between the gross amount of energy produced and the energy consumed in the extraction process)."[13]

Another virtue of analyzing energy prospects in terms of EROEI enables you to better calculate the crisis horizon. In principle, a peak in oil production could be compatible with a long, gradual falloff in output. Other things being equal, a peak only implies higher oil prices (or insufficiently high prices to justify rapidly escalating capital investment to produce ever-more-elusive barrels of oil). It doesn't tell you when energy returns reach the cliff's edge, where the capture of surplus energy plunges so far that neither the real economy as we have known it nor the shadow economy of money and debt remains viable.

Net Energy Is Key

Both Morgan and Soddy insist that the economy is a physical system vitally dependent on surplus energy. Soddy's was an abstract argument. Morgan's analysis in *Life after Growth* is built on an impressive array of detail documenting the ongoing drastic decline in the availability of surplus energy. Morgan is a former top analyst for London-based interdealer Tullett Prebon, which specializes in wholesale trading in energy markets. He has a market insider's view of energy. Among other things, he deflates the collective delusion that shale gas and oil, which can be extracted through fracturing techniques, or "fracking," represent a quick fix that governments and their populations might like to suppose.[14]

To the contrary, he explains that the critical EROEI equation is still very low. For one thing, drilling costs for extracting oil from tight sands are very high. For another, the rate of production decline from initial levels tends to be astonishingly rapid: "Compared with an annual decline rate of about 7–10% from 'traditional' oil wells, decline rates for production in the Bakken Shale play in the United States have been put at as much as 69% in the first year."[15] In fact, the economic return from these wells has been so sketchy that the promoters who develop them have to maintain large lines of bank credit or float junk bonds to stay in business.

The *Financial Times* quotes research by David Einhorn of Greenlight Capital in which he found that, since 2006, large shale producers had spent $80 billion more in acquiring and developing shale reserves than they had made from actually selling oil, and they stayed in business only through a constant inflow of capital.[16] Cash flow from production has generally proven insufficient to finance drilling of expensive additional wells, as well as meet the costs for remediating and replacing the large quantities of water required in fracking.

As recently as the 1930s, oil discoveries tended to have EROEIs in excess of one hundred to one. By the 1970s, this ratio had declined to about thirty to one and has continued to plunge. As costs have risen, few current discoveries offer EROEIs greater than ten to one. Average field sizes have also declined. Morgan claims that the overall EROEI of the North Sea today may be no higher than about five to one. "Tight sands" production from shale offer "EROEIs of barely 5:1 (if that)."[17]

More ominously, the "EROEIs of surface-mined tar sands is probably little better than 3:1 (if that), and those sands (accounting for about 4/5 of the total) which cannot be surface-mined can only be extracted using massively energy intensive techniques such as SAGD (steam-assisted gravity drive), such that EROEIs are minimal, or even negative."[18] (Think of microwaving a mountain.)

Obviously, the overall EROEI is a composite of that from new oil production combined with the EROEIs from legacy fields, such as the giant Al Ghawar in Saudi Arabia, which has been producing millions of barrels of oil a day since 1951. Unless major new fields with EROEIs equivalent to Al Ghawar are discovered soon, a most unlikely prospect, the composite EROEI for the world economy will continue to dwindle. Morgan draws the indicated conclusion: "It is that the economy as we have known it for more than two centuries, is entering a potentially terminal phase unless some means can be found to stabilize the overall surplus return on energy invested. At some point between EROEIs of perhaps 8:1 and 4:1, the economy would cease to be viable at all."[19]

Ecofascism

Hence the shrewd observation by Peter J. Taylor noted in *The Way the Modern World Works: World Hegemony to World Impasse*, about the invention of "eco-catastrophe" and "Eco-Fascism" as its putative solution. Taylor sees that some among the rich and powerful have reconstrued the threat to prosperity arising from depletion of hydrocarbon energy resources into an ecological crisis. The marker of this crisis is hysteria over the level of ambient carbon dioxide emissions in parts per million. A doomsday alarm over "climate change" due to the accumulation of trace amounts of a gas that is crucial to photosynthesis, and thus the earth's annual "income from sunshine," would be funny, were it not so threatening to your well-being and that of billions of persons.

As Taylor tells us, "Eco-Fascism" can be understood as "a subterfuge of the rich to maintain their dominant status." He describes the selfish interest of those wishing to reserve the good life for themselves as requiring "a cover of legitimization, a justification that defines the new politics as a logical and sensible reaction to a world in crisis."[20] A coming chapter analyzes the "Eco-Fascist" program for cartelizing world energy supplies and the added dangers it entails in an age when solar irradiance is falling.

Here it is worthwhile to recall Soddy's forecast that the final stage of the "flamboyant period" of energy capital consumption would be distinguished by war over scarce resources in which "imperialism marks its final bid for survival." This was a deduction, not an observation. Dick Chaney and George Bush were school boys when Soddy died in 1956.

Of course, those who deny that the economy is a physical system informed by a surplus energy equation dismiss the problem by saying that the sums spent on purchasing energy account for "only about 8% of global GDP," and therefore "energy inputs are somehow 'too small to matter.'" Really? According to Morgan, this view is "one of the most irritating aspects of ill-informed debate." One could just as easily say that since a human heart seldom weighs more than 10.5 ounces, even in a 250-pound man, removing the heart could not count for much, as at less than two-thirds of 1 percent of body weight it is "too small to matter." Of course, the heart is so central to the human energy system that without it the rest of the body would be no more than dead weight.

Equally, as Morgan emphasizes, "The reality is that energy is completely central to all forms of activity, so the threat posed by a sharp decline in net energy availability extends into every aspect of the economy, and will affect supplies of food and water, access to other resources, and structures of government and law."[21] I go further and argue that any discontinuity—either a surge or a slowdown in net energy uptake in the economy—will not only alter the growth rate but also alter the nature of money.

This is a view that I explored in an earlier book, *Brazil Is the New America*. As you may not have read it, it is based on the deduction that the collapse of growth occasioned by the disappearance of cheap energy will have a more devastating impact in the US economy than that of Brazil.

Distorted in a Green Prism?

In the rare cases when economists reflect on the implications of fossil fuels on economic growth, their thoughts tend to flow along a few well-worn channels. Especially over the past half-century, many have turned discussion of the impact of energy inputs and growth rates into consideration of aspects of entropy and materials throughput, with a heavy emphasis on environmental degradation.

It is much easier to find research linking high rates of economic growth to soil erosion—or complaints, echoing Marx, that consumer society is entering a terminal phase—than to uncover analyses exploring the links between economic growth and the nature of money and debt. Even where you can find such tidbits, they tend to be tinged with indelible coloration from "the far green side of the political spectrum," to quote Roger K. Brown, of the blog *The World Is Finite*.[22]

I have found that the fluctuations in hydrocarbon energy conversion are important megapolitical variables. I identified a shift in the nature of money, and the proliferation of debt, among the changes informed by the impact of cheap oil and implicitly undone by its disappearance.

Money and Power

Manipulation of money has been integral to the exercise of power ever since money was first invented. As David Glasner wrote in "An Evolutionary Theory of the State Monopoly over Money," "The history of money virtually coincides with a history of the debasement, depreciation, and devaluation of the currency by the state. . . . Thus, coinage and tyranny seem to have emerged together, a confluence which is borne out by the experience of the ancient world. Both coinage and tyranny originated in Lydia. Gyges, the Lydian king of the seventh century BC to whom the term tyrant was first applied (Durrant 1939, 122), is also credited with having made coining 'the prerogative of the state after he had first used it to obtain supreme power.'"[23]

The sudden emergence of economic growth at previously unprecedented rates after the Industrial Revolution created new opportunities for exploitation of money—including the chance to franchise the vast seigniorage profits of fiat money.

Rapid growth enlarged expectations of future production, thus generally enhancing the collateral value of the shadow economy of money and debt that represents claims on future wealth. Naturally, the lien on future income tended to rise with its apparent value. Surging growth also implies at least mild price deflation, another factor that creates an opening for exploitation of the public: in this case, through inflation.

For example, during the late nineteenth century, the high-water mark of the gold standard, and the progress of production, led to a general fall in prices in the United States by 1 percent on average each year. (Prices fell about 20 percent over twenty-three years.) As Murray Rothbard wrote in his 1998 essay, "The Gold Exchange Standard in the Interwar Years," the phenomenal advance of productivity led to falling prices. As he states, "With productivity outpacing the new supply of gold, prices had to fall in terms of gold during that period."[24] This gradual decline in the price level increased incentives to save, as each dollar that remained unspent would be worth more in the future.

Of course, it is probably not a coincidence that at about this time, the very notion of thrift came under attack as contributing to economic distress. In particular, the famous mountaineer A. F. Mummery and economist J. A. Hobson published an influential book in 1889: *The Physiology of Industry: Being an Exposure of Certain Fallacies in Existing Theories of Economics*.[25] In this proto-Keynesian volume, they lambasted thrift, arguing that underconsumption was responsible was the cause of the slowdown in late nineteenth-century growth. Although it was not conceived as such, *The Physiology of Industry* can be viewed as a kind of unconscious plea for fiat money, which goes to show that the intellectual fads tend to fall in line with the underlying physical basis of the economy.

The corollary to this is that the amount by which prices would otherwise have fallen in a noninflationary economy was available to be pocketed by bankers and their accomplices in a more or less undetectable theft. This proved to be an irresistible temptation that was to be gratified by the creation of monopoly central banks to constantly expand currency in partnership with commercial banks.

There is a big difference between borrowing money from a bank and borrowing money from, say, your father-in-law. If he wants to lend you $10,000, he must come up with the whole swag himself. He can only lend you money he has saved from other uses. It costs him $10,000 to lend you $10,000. But through the abracadabra of fractional reserve banking, the bank can lend you $10,000 at a negligible cost. The bankers' only risk is that to the extent that you fail to repay the loan, with interest, they must charge the unpaid balance against their capital. The money they lend to you never existed before they wrote the check. That is what is known in technical terms as "inflation."

There has been a lot of inflation in the United States in the past century. I write some little while after the banker's party celebrating the one-hundredth anniversary of the founding of the Federal Reserve System. Although the Fed was allegedly created to "control inflation," during its first century of existence, the supply of money in the United States (M2) multiplied 665 times from $15.78 billion in 1913 to $10.952 trillion in 2013.

For perspective, the M2 money supply multiplied at the slower pace of just a little over twelve times in the half-century before the Federal Reserve was instituted. It was by no means true that there was a free market in banking prior to 1913. The National Bank Act of 1864 was one among a crazy quilt of federal and state laws that regulated banks and the issuance of money prior to creation of the Federal Reserve.

Among other things, national banks were prohibited from making mortgages on real estate. This therefore limited their capacity to compete in rural areas, while intensifying banking competition in cities. As a result, the fading farm sector faced high interest rates, while intense banking competition resulted in lower interest rates in urban areas. Although the United States was ostensibly employing gold and silver money, in the half-century prior to 1913 the M2 money supply grew at an annual rate of 5.61 percent.

By contrast, M2 grew at an annual average rate of 6.76 percent—20 percent faster—after the Federal Reserve came into existence. Overall, the M2 money supply grew almost twenty-nine times more than the Consumer Price Index (CPI). According to official statistics, an item that cost $20 in 1913 would have cost $470.85 in 2013, not $13,300—a factoid that reflects two unheralded truths:

1. The government has lied about the inflation rate, especially over the last quarter of a century.
2. The greater part of inflation, rightly understood as expansion of the money supply, affected a redistribution of income and wealth rather than showing up primarily as higher consumer prices. (This is exactly what you should expect, as there is no particular advantage to anyone in adding almost $11 trillion to the money supply if the only effect of doing so were to proportionately tack zeros on the price of everything.)

During that same one-hundred-year period, real GDP per capita, calculated in 2009 dollars, multiplied just sevenfold: from $6663.85 per capita in 1913 to $49,226.16 in 2012. Notwithstanding the greatest surge of energy inputs in history, that is a compound growth rate of just a little more than 2 percent. So contrary to the pretense inherent in QE, there is no compelling evidence that monetary expansion over the long term stimulates real growth. But without a doubt, the overlay of fractional reserve banking with pure fiat money created one of the greatest realms for crony capitalist exploitation ever devised. The dilution of the dollar inherent in the 665-fold multiplication of the money supply redistributed income and wealth from the poor to the rich.

What triggered the shift away from gold and silver to a pure fiat money? Economic historians tend to blame disruptions in the wake of World War I and other unfavorable winds. But I see it in more simple terms. The shift away from gold and silver to fiat money was a follow-on consequence to the unprecedented surge in per capita energy use from about the middle of the nineteenth century forward.

Short-Term Growth Accelerated by Fiat Debt Expansion

The economy is inevitably informed by the physical resources that underlie it. When the introduction of hydrocarbon energy dramatically lifted growth rates, it also introduced an almost hydraulic pressure to restructure money. When real growth rates rose, as energy inputs expanded, this implicitly enlarged the energy economy of the future, permitting, as Tim Morgan put it, the "financial 'shadow' economy of money and debt" to expand. But the gold standard constricted the expansion of the financial shadow economy of money and debt, so it had to go.

Fiat money entailed temporary advantages in a rapidly growing economy. Among them were the seigniorage profits from creating money out of thin air, enjoyed by commercial banks. Another was the impact of credit inflation in temporarily lifting nominal asset prices, increasing stock prices, and enlarging tax receipts, while facilitating the illusion that the government could offer voters benefits that were worth more than they paid for them.

Put simply, the introduction of fossil fuels increased the economic growth rate, permitting the real economy to support a larger sum of claims represented by money and debt. In effect, historically unprecedented economic growth propelled by exogenous hydrocarbon energy amounted to a hidden BTU content of fiat money.

The virtual rivers of oil that the United States obtained at minimal cost precipitated a transformation of the monetary system in a direction that accorded with the interests of bankers, their best customers, and those running governments. Yale politics professor Douglas W. Rae has sought to quantify the increase in energy conversion. His *A Short History of American Horsepower* highlights a jump in energy production in the United States from 8,495,000 horsepower in 1850 to 34.958 billion horsepower in 1990.[26]

An apparent drawback of commodity-based money in a high-growth environment is the fact that supplies of gold and silver are inelastic. As Elisa Newby, head of the Market Operations Division of the Bank of Finland, spells out: "Under the gold standard the money growth rate cannot be regulated by governmental policy because the money stock can increase or decrease only if the commodity stock in monetary uses increases or decreases respectively."[27]

Therefore, because governments and central banks are not alchemists capable of creating gold out of thin air, credit cannot be expanded as readily under a gold standard as under a fiat regime. As growth rates accelerated in the twentieth century, fueled by compounding use of hydrocarbon energy, authorities in one economy after another moved to replace commodity-based money that incorporated limitations on the extension of credit—which tended to limit the nominal GDP growth—in favor of a pure fiat money borrowed into existence through fractional reserve banking.

It was no drawback that fiat money facilitated the enrichment of governments, enabling them to garner more resources, fight more wars, and create the illusion of democratic consensus through deficit spending to buy votes, as they could not do so readily when hampered by the restrictions of a gold standard.

The availability of an elastic supply of credit permitted at least a temporary acceleration of growth. Part of this linkage derives from the fact that fiat money is borrowed into existence, allowing consumers, companies, and governments to spend and invest without first earning and saving the requisite amounts—as envisioned by Adam Smith. In *The Wealth of Nations*, he tells us that "the accumulation of stock (capital) is previously necessary."[28] The apparent ability of an elastic system of fiat money to short-circuit the need to earn profits and save them offered at least a temporary expedient for accelerating growth. A *growing* economy allows room for interest payments without necessarily constraining other outlays. This provides the leverage to growth through the credit system.

A rapid increase in the amount of money and debt outstanding, at least in its early stages, permits consumers to make purchases beyond what their cash flow would otherwise permit and without having to save. Extra money adds to purchasing power through extra credit created out of thin air, creating demand that otherwise would not exist. The same goes for business investments in which companies can borrow money to expand. Rapid growth in the real economy is a crucial factor in the equation in that it permits the process to continue.

Falling Short of Perpetual Motion

It verges in the direction of perpetual motion, except for the fact that the amount of the mortgage on future revenues that can be supported by future sunshine falls far short of infinity. As Soddy emphasizes, debt is a purely mathematical abstraction that can follow the law of compound interest. But the real energy revenue from future sunshine cannot. As a matter of fact, it is only because the deficient energy revenues from annual sunshine can be subsidized by the consumption of energy capital, accumulated from the stored sunlight of Paleozoic summers, that the debt liens are even temporarily sustainable. In the long run, they are not. The energy capital upon which the system depends for viability is limited, and it has become more difficult to access as EROEI has plunged.

Just as fiat money can be created out of thin air through credit expansion, so it can also vanish into thin air through debt default. With fiat money in an environment of rising energy inputs, businesses and consumers could make outlays that spur growth in the current period without first restraining their budgets to accumulate savings—and not incidentally. Just as economic growth spurred the hypertrophy of predatory government, so it opened an opportunity for bankers to appropriate a hefty increment of the growth. In other words, the spur to growth, provided by the oil-powered economy, created an almost irresistible inducement to revamp the monetary system. This resulted, almost inevitably, in a debt-ridden economy.

The unprecedented surge in the amount of energy employed, and therefore the amount of work undertaken per capita, had far-reaching consequences in revolutionizing money. Rapid growth provided cover for predatory diversion of the value of money, financializing the economy while creating great profits for bankers and the government. Rapid money growth also made it easier for a majority of enterprises to profit and stock prices to rise.

Fiat Money Lifts Stock Prices

The connection between monetary expansion and higher stock prices, so clearly in evidence since 2008 due to the extreme practice of quantitative easing, has always been in play with fiat money. As Austrian economist Fritz Machlup put it in his 1940 book, *The Stock Market, Credit, and Capital Formation*, "In the absence of inflationary credit the funds available for lending to the public for security purchases would soon be exhausted, since even a large supply is ultimately limited . . . Only if the credit organization of the banks (by means of inflationary credit) or large-scale dishoarding by the public make the supply of loanable funds highly elastic, can a lasting boom develop . . . A rise on the securities market cannot last any length of time unless the public is both willing and able to make increased purchases."[29]

Of course, if you are one of those to whom the government has directed profits by encouraging the proliferation of fiat money, and thus raising stock prices, remember that you are expected to pay for this privilege by bearing a lopsided tax burden. The way the game works is that the politicians want to make you rich so they can tax your money away and use it to provide benefits to hordes of needy voters that seem to be worth more than they paid for them. Neither the politicians nor the voters particularly care whether you like it or not.

The Transitory Advantage of Fiat Money

The introduction of hydrocarbon energy began a process that changed money and banking. But it has been little appreciated, then or now, that the system of fiat money that emerged in response to rapid growth, fueled by the surge of BTUs derived from hydrocarbon energy, could only be of transitory advantage. This is true for at least two fundamental reasons, both of which argue against an indefinite continuation of rapid growth:

1. The marginal returns from the early applications of hydrocarbon energy in the economy were bound to fall as energy inputs rose.
2. Due to the "magic" of compounding, an indefinite expansion of the economy called for prodigious increases of energy inputs to what has proven to be an unrealistic degree. As Kenneth Boulding famously quipped, "Anyone who believes that exponential growth can go on forever in a finite world is either a madman or an economist." More on that to come.

Declining Returns from Energy Inputs

People following the normal economic imperatives tended to first invest newly available energy in areas of greatest return, generally where inadequate somatic energy capacity was a bottleneck to production. For example, the productivity gain from replacing a mule-drawn plow with a tractor was tremendous. But deploying a comparable quantity of BTUs to air condition the farmer's house arguably contributed less dramatic gains. By the very nature of things, it tended to become harder to achieve robust productivity gains by increasing energy use as the supply of exogenous hydrocarbon energy expanded.

This is borne out by the record. If you compare economic growth through the twentieth century with the growth in energy inputs, there is clear evidence of diminishing returns. Energy analyst Gail Tverberg comments in a May 2015 article, "Why We Have an Oversupply of Almost Everything (Oil, Labor, Capital, Etc.)," that "adding one percentage point of growth in energy usage tends to add less and less GDP growth over time . . . This means that if we want to have, for example, a constant 4 percent growth in world GDP for the period 1969 to 2013, we would need to gradually increase the rate of growth in energy consumption from about 1.8 percent (= 4.0 percent—2.2 percent) growth in energy consumption in 1969 to 2.8 percent (= 4.0 percent—1.2 percent) growth in energy consumption in 2013. This need for continued growth in energy use, to produce the same amount of economic growth, is happening despite all of our efforts toward efficiency and becoming more of a 'service' economy."[30]

Jevons and Compounding Energy Inputs

Perhaps more crucially, there is the daunting problem of compounding that so vexed Soddy, identified in a different context by William Stanley Jevons, in his classic 1865 essay, "The Coal Question: An Inquiry Concerning the Progress of the Nation, and the Probable Exhaustion of Our Coal-Mines."

Jevons, as you may recall, was an important figure in the history of economics as one of the originators of the marginal revolution that put an end to the labor theory of value. He emphasized that "value depends entirely upon utility."[31] If no one knew the difference, a house conjured out of a top hat by a magician would be worth the same as an apparently identical house cobbled together by brigades of union carpenters, masons, and joiners. (And of course, if people did know the difference, the house created by magic would undoubtedly be worth more because of the novelty factor.)

Escaping "the Laborious Poverty of Early Times"

Writing only a few years after the launch of the petroleum industry in 1859, Jevons naturally focused his attention on coal, as it was the primary hydrocarbon fuel in use in his day. Jevons saw that energy was the "mainspring of modern material civilization . . . the source at once of mechanical motion and of chemical change." He believed that, with it, almost any feat was possible, but without it, we would be "thrown back into the laborious poverty of early times."[32]

Jevons drew on records of historical coal production to show that over the eighty years prior to 1865, production had grown at a relatively consistent rate of 3.5 percent per year, or 41 percent per decade. He also recognized the logic of this compounding: for that growth rate to continue, it meant coal production would have to climb from about 100 million tons in 1865 to more than 2.6 billion tons 100 years later. Jevons then calculated that if that were to happen, the country would produce approximately 100 billion tons within this period. Jevons recognized that known resources were insufficient for such compound growth over even 100 years. Long before the century mark was reached, the growth rate, which was the measure of prosperity, would inevitably decline. The decline of growth associated with dwindling energy inputs is a matter I analyze further in the next chapter.

Notes

1   Morgan, Tim, *Life after Growth* (Hampshire: Harriman House, 2013).

2   Soddy, Frederick, *The Role of Money: What It Should Be, Contrasted with What It Has Become* (London: Routledge, 1934), 24.

3   Soddy, Frederick, *Wealth, Virtual Wealth and Debt* (London: George Allen & Unwin, 1926), 70.

4   See Daly, Herman, "The Economic Thought of Frederick Soddy," *History of Political Economy* 12, no. 4 (1980), 469–88; Soddy, Frederick, *The Inversion of Science* (London: Henderson, 1924), 17.

5   Morgan, *Life after Growth*, 11.

6   Morgan, Tim, *Perfect Storm: Energy, Finance and the End of Growth* (London: Tylett Prebon, 2013), 60.

7   Ibid., 12.

8   Quoted in Henrietta L. Moore and Todd Sanders, *Anthropology in Theory, Issues and Epistemology*, 2nd ed. (Hoboken: John Wiley & Sons, 2013), 112.

9   McNeill, J. R., *Something New under the Sun: An Environmental History of the Twentieth-Century World* (New York: W. W. Norton, 2000), 15.

10 Ibid.

11 Ibid.

12 Morgan, *Life after Growth*, 61, 62.

13 Ibid., 55.

14 Ibid., 63.

15 Ibid., 64.

16 Crooks, Ed, "Shale Looks More like Dotcom Boom than Lehman Debt Bubble," *Financial Times*, May 7, 2015.

17 Morgan, *Life after Growth*, 61.

18 Ibid., 63.

19 Ibid., 66.

20 Taylor, Peter J., *The Way the Modern World Works: World Hegemony to World Impasse* (Chichester: John Wiley & Sons, 1996), 216.

21 Morgan, *Life after Growth*, 69.

22 See Brown, Roger K., "It's about a Reasonable Standard of Consumption: People Are Starting to Get It," http://www.theworldisfinite.com/.

23 Glasner, David, "An Evolutionary Theory of the State Monopoly over Money," in *Money and the Nation State*, ed. Kevin Dowd and Richard H. Timberlake Jr. (New Brunswick: Transaction, 1998), 21–24.

24 Rothbard, Murray, "The Gold Exchange Standard in the Interwar Years," in *Money and the Nation State*, ed. Kevin Dowd and Richard H. Timberlake Jr. (New Brunswick: Transaction, 1998), 132.

25 Mummery, A. F., and J. A. Hobson, *The Physiology of Industry: Being an Exposure of Certain Fallacies in Existing Theories of Economics* (London: John Murray, 1889).

26 Rae, Douglas W., "Vacratic America: Plessy on Foot v. Brown on Wheels," *Annual Review of Political Science* 4 (June 2001): 417–38.

27 Newby, Elisa, "The Suspension of Cash Payments as a Monetary Regime," *Centre for Macroeconomic Analysis Working Paper Series*, June 2007, 4.

28 Smith, Adam, *The Wealth of Nations* (Chicago: University

of Chicago Press, 1976), book 1, 292.

29 Machlup, Fritz, *The Stock Market, Credit and Capital Formation* (New York: Macmillan, 1940), 78, 90, 92.

30 Tverberg, Gail, "Why We Have an Oversupply of Almost Everything (Oil, Labor, Capital, Etc.)," *Our Finite World*, May 6, 2015.

31 Jevons, William Stanley, *The Theory of Political Economy* (London: Macmillan, 1871), ch. 1, par. 2.

32 Jevons, *The Theory of Political Economy*.

Chapter Seventeen

The Great Slowdown

Updating Secular Stagnation and the Stationary State in Light of *The Coal Question*

Today's general level of understanding about how the economy works, and energy's relationship to the economy, is dismally low. Economics has generally denied that energy has more than a very indirect relationship to the economy. Since 1800, world population has grown from 1 billion to more than 7 billion, thanks to the use of fossil fuels for increased food production and medicines, among other things. Yet environmentalists often believe that the world economy can somehow continue as today, without fossil fuels. There is a possibility that with a financial crash, we will need to start over, with new local economies based on the use of local resources. In such a scenario, it is doubtful that we can maintain a world population of even 1 billion.

—Gail Tverberg

This chapter analyzes the dire consequences of the continuing decline in energy intensity manifested in the twenty-first century. Among other things, this presages a widening mismatch between the growth of the real economy and the metastasizing claims embodied in the shadow economy of money and debt. The default response of the bankrupt nation-state to the collapse of growth, and the revenue shortfalls that accompany it, is to expand, rather than constrain, debt. This widens the chasm between the rapidly compounding claims of the shadow economy and the stagnant real economy upon which they are a lien.

The miseries of Greece are a case in point, where reported real GDP has declined at a compound negative rate of -4.86 percent since 2008, while the effective average interest rate on Greek government debt was 2.4 percent in 2015. At that rate, in about the time it takes the compounding debt to double, the economy will shrink by 41 percent, as energy-constrained economies struggle to grow.

In recent years, attention has often been called to the drastic fall in Energy Return on Energy Invested (EROEI). Yet that said, there is so little understanding of the crucial role of hydrocarbon energy inputs in fueling economic growth since the Industrial Revolution that we start from behind in trying to tease out the consequences of a hydrocarbon shortfall for the future. Among them, I discuss secular stagnation and the darker possibilities foreseen by Adam Smith in his analysis of the stationary state, culminating in the declining state, with special relevance to understanding the Breaking Point, as I elaborate in the next chapter.

The Three Economic States of Adam Smith

It is little noted today that Adam Smith wrote of three distinct economic states: the "progressive state," what we would today describe as a growing economy; the "stationary state," or a stagnant steady state economy; and the "declining state" that moves backward, as in Jevon's retrograde economy.[1]

At first glance, these would appear to be relatively simple, straightforward analytical categories. Not quite. As I explain below, Smith's concept of the "stationary state" needs to be updated in biophysical context. Adam Smith and the classical economists thought in terms of an organic economy where growth was limited by the productivity of the land. So in that sense, the economy operated within an energy limit—the energy capacity of photosynthesis. But over the past couple of centuries, we have escaped from the traditional limits on growth by incorporating vast amounts of hydrocarbon energy to perform the work of the economy. This has profound implications for understanding all the economic states.

The meanderings of economic thought since Adam Smith's day have also helped displace consideration of the biophysical context of the economy. The fashion for equilibrium analysis has helped confuse matters considerably. In his 1973 essay, "The Shadow of the Stationary State," poet and economist Kenneth E. Boulding discussed the idea that any society must be "progressing, stationary, or declining." He went on to say that the progressing state and the declining state "were thought of as self-limiting, in the sense that in each the rate of progress or of decline would diminish until it was zero and the stationary state was reached."[2]

It is apparent that Boulding is using the term, "stationary state," in a confused sense. He was talking about two different equilibrium states: a high-level equilibrium attained, however briefly, when the trend rate of economic growth in the progressing state slows to zero and another very different economy, in which a low-level equilibrium is reached when the rate of decline in a declining state economy peters out at the economic equivalent of absolute zero. In other words, in Boulding's low-level stationary state you're talking about going as low as you can go. Rock bottom.

This differs from Adam Smith's view.

Among more than 500 pages in *The Wealth of Nations*, Adam Smith devotes only a few pages to the stationary state and scarcely more than a few sentences to the declining state. He alerts us to the fact that they are analytical possibilities, without delving too deeply into their characteristic features. Smith devoted most of his attentions in *The Wealth of Nations* to exploring the "progressive state." He writes:

> It deserves to be remarked, perhaps, that it is in the progressive state, while society is advancing

> to further acquisition, rather than when it has acquired its full complement of riches, that the condition of the laboring poor, of the great body of the people, seems to be the happiest and the most comfortable. It is hard in the stationary, and miserable in the declining state. The progressive state is in reality the cheerful and hearty state to all the different orders of the society. The stationary is dull; the declining melancholy.[3]

It is apparent, however, that in Smith's terms, the stationary state entails a higher level of opulence than the declining state.

Coal Heavers and Prostitutes

There is little to indicate that Adam Smith recognized the importance of the growing use of coal in the British economy of his time. In an odd digression in *The Wealth of Nations*, Smith suggests that "coal-heavers" could be paired with prostitutes as "the strongest men and the most beautiful women perhaps in the British dominions," owing to their tendency to eat a lot of potatoes.[4] In a more extended analysis of the economics of coal, he declares erroneously that "coals are a less agreeable fewel than wood," and therefore cheaper. He also suggests that coal is hardly worth mining because the profits from doing so are supposedly so scanty that "they can be wrought advantageously by nobody but the landlord."[5]

Clearly, Smith was not alert to the importance of the higher BTU content of coal, or the growing dependence of the British economy on the propulsive force fueled by growing quantities of coal. Nor, apparently, did Smith fathom the distinction between the traditional organic economy where wood prices varied with the state of agriculture, much like the price of cattle, he tells us, and the new industrial economy based on fossil fuels that was taking shape in his time.[6]

Apart from the lack of attention to the productive potential arising from the higher BTU content of coal, it is evident from what Adam Smith said, speaking of a "full complement of riches," that he was analyzing an organic economy—one where the sole source of energy was the conversion of sunlight through photosynthesis.

The Organic Economy and Limits to Growth

E. A. "Tony" Wrigley, longtime professor of economic history at Cambridge University, notes in a 2011 essay, "Opening Pandora's Box: A New Look at the Industrial Revolution," that the classical economists Adam Smith, Thomas Malthus, and David Ricardo dismissed the potential for prolonged growth before the Industrial Revolution since organic economies were limited by the "productive powers of the land."

Smith wrote during the takeoff phase of the Industrial Revolution and was hard at work collecting notes for what was to become *The Wealth of Nations* in 1761, when Francis Egerton, Third Duke of Bridgewater, opened the famous canal that made him the richest noble in England, ferrying coal from his mines in Worsley, Lancashire, to Manchester, the flourishing new center of industrial England.

Adam Smith was an economist, not an entrepreneur. He apparently did not grasp the importance of the growing incorporation of hydrocarbon energy from coal in the production process as readily as did the Duke of Bridgewater. Of course, few did. The duke died in 1803 with a fortune worth in the vicinity of £20 billion in today's money.

In any event, the fact that Adam Smith, along with the early generations of classical economists, did not "get it" where exogenous energy is concerned, means that their treatments of the stationary and declining states are now dated and need revision.

The Constraints of an Organic Economy

Meanwhile, when I say that there is little understanding of the role of hydrocarbon energy in fueling economic growth since the Industrial Revolution, I do not mean to downplay the work of economic historians like Tony Wrigley, who convincingly documented that the Industrial Revolution was an energy revolution. In *Energy and the English Industrial Revolution*, Wrigley explains that the Industrial Revolution was an "escape from the constraints of an organic economy."[7]

Of course, when Tony Wrigley speaks of an organic economy, he does not mean an economy where everyone eats crunchy granola from Whole Foods. A better description of the organic economy is that it depends primarily on photosynthesis for energy. The consumption of energy is integral to any productive process, and in an organic economy, everything relies on the productivity of the land. Wrigley tells us that the breakout from the constraints of the organic economy came with the capture of exogenous hydrocarbon energy from coal.

Wrigley offers a vivid measurement quantifying the vast increase in energy conversion achieved through the use of coal, as compared to the traditional deployment of somatic energy by men and draught animals in the organic economy. Drawing on the 1851 British census, Wrigley reports that there were 128,086 coal miners in England and Wales in 1851, while 1,135,833 men engaged in agriculture. He further reports that each coal miner, on average, produced thirteen terajoules of energy annually, while the average energy consumption of each man in agriculture was 0.10 terajoules.

It is not hard to credit that people deploying 1,300 times more energy were responsible for a huge surge in the amount of useful work done. Remember, the details that Wrigley marshals are from a century and a half ago. If the paramount importance of energy were in doubt in the middle of the nineteenth century, it should not be now. The only reason there was an Industrial Revolution—and hence, growth in material production that was both prolonged and exponential, leading to the high-living standards enjoyed today—is because hydrocarbon energy, initially in the form of coal, supplanted wood as the main fuel in powering the economy.

The Defective Mainstream Narrative

Strangely, while the crucial role of energy in launching the Industrial Revolution is well established as a matter of economic history, its logical corollary—that a slowdown or decline in energy inputs will be reflected by a slowdown, or reversal, in economic growth—seems to have no place in the contemporary mainstream narrative.

In fact, the only mainstream economist I can think of who wrote something illuminating on the topic is long dead. William Stanley Jevons sounded an alarm in his classic 1865 essay, "The Coal Question: An Inquiry Concerning the Progress of the Nation, and the Probable Exhaustion of Our Coal-Mines."

Running Faster and Faster to Stay in the Same Place

Seeing that modern material civilization depended on hydrocarbon energy, Jevons reminds us that continued economic growth depended upon a daunting problem of compounding that threatened to shorten and darken the prospects for the future, much as it has shortened and darkened the prospects for Greece, Puerto Rico, Italy, and elsewhere.

Jevons worried that we faced diminishing returns in the quest to continue expanding hydrocarbon energy inputs that power economic growth. He showed that energy inputs had been multiplying "in a uniform ratio" of 3.5 percent per annum over the eight decades before he wrote. But he warned that long-term continued progress was impossible due to changes around the world and the eventual failure of mines, which would cause a stationary condition.[8]

Jevons used "stationary condition" as shorthand for the "sufferings and dangers" entailed in economic decline, but he made it clear that the crucial, if altogether impossible, task of maintaining high compound growth in hydrocarbon energy inputs was essential to preserving modern prosperity.

Jevons tells us that diminishing returns block the doubling of any type of physical output ad infinitum. And this has definite implications for our future use of hydrocarbon fuels. At some point, production would simply hit a peak, which suggested dire consequences for economic growth.[9] (Where British coal production was concerned, Jevons was right. It peaked on the eve of World War I in 1913.) Jevons was not anticipating a flattening out of prosperity at a high level, but a retrograde situation that would bring the economy back to a lower level of prosperity. Jevon's lucid ruminations in *The Coal Question* mark one of the more closely argued attempts to specify why a growing economy might peter out into a stationary state, or even a declining state in the terms anticipated by Adam Smith. Jevons's analysis pinpoints a slowdown in the growth of energy inputs as an exogenous supply constraint that reduces GDP growth.[10]

More than that, Jevons sees the crucial difference between stationary organic agricultural economy and an industrial economy dependent on dwindling energy reserves—a point that modern economics has failed to fully grasp.[11]

The Impossibility of an Industrial Stationary State

John Stuart Mill, whose working life and that of Jevons overlapped, wrote of the stationary state in 1848. But unlike Jevons, Mill seems to have presumed that the stationary state for an industrial society could actually be stationary.

He believed it was impossible to ultimately avoid the stationary state. This irresistible necessity—that the stream of human industry should finally spread itself out into an apparently stagnant sea—must have been, to the political economists of the last two generations, an unpleasing and discouraging prospect. The tone and tendency of their speculations goes completely to identify all that is economically desirable with the progressive state, and with that alone.

"Adam Smith always assumes that the condition of the mass of the people, though it may not be positively distressed, must be pinched and stinted in a stationary condition of wealth, and can only be satisfactory in a progressive state. The doctrine that, to however distant a time incessant struggling may put off our doom, the progress of society must 'end in shallows and in miseries,' far from being, as many people still believe, a wicked invention of Mr. Malthus, was either expressly or tacitly affirmed by his most distinguished predecessors."[12]

Hoping to Park on a Steady-State Hovercraft?

While Mill seems to have a more positive view of the stationary state than Adam Smith, it may be because his view was less realistic than that of Jevons. Mill does not specifically mention energy resources as crucial, as Jevons does. Mill comes close to endorsing an early version of the current limits to growth green paradigm that supposes we can enjoy a stationary, steady state economy forever. (To confirm for yourself that my characterization of this perspective does not amount to tackling a straw man, see the website of the Center for the Advancement of the Steady State Economy [CASSE].)

Neither J. S. Mill nor the green enthusiasts for CASSE seem to have recognized that the stationary state for organic agricultural economies, powered by somatic energy, does not translate to a steady state industrial economy—unless it were powered entirely by solar energy. Otherwise, anticipating or longing for a steady state industrial economy is nonsense. It is like calling for a steady state hovercraft, ignoring the fact that the hovercraft cannot levitate without fuel.

The energy shortfall that collapses the progressive growth economy is equally subversive of the no-growth steady state economy. In this sense, the distinction between the two is without a difference: the depletion of oil reserves implies collapse, whether or not the aim is to grow GDP or keep it flat in a steady state.

Mill ignored the biophysical constraints that could conceivably make for the stationary state. These require an economy living within the energy budget of current sunshine, without augmenting it through the consumption of energy capital.

Mill says, "At the end of what they term the progressive state lies the stationary state."

Not today.

I would suggest that, as seen in the Great Slowdown of the twenty-first century, at the end of the progressive state industrial economy is not the stationary state, but rather the retrograde or declining state. Unlike the circumstance imagined by the classical economists, there are not three states of an industrial economy, but only two: the progressive state (a growing economy) and the declining state (a retrograde economy) headed for the Breaking Point.

Declining Marginal Returns

Remember Baumol's Disease, the condition in which the costs of the least productive sectors multiply faster than the economy grows? This affliction, which leads to low productivity activities absorbing an ever-greater share of resources, fatally complicates the fantasy of achieving a steady state economy.

Here's why. The US economy is afflicted with a number of sectors with chronically declining returns. These include the extractive industries, including oil and hard rock mining—sectors in which returns are diminishing primarily because we encounter natural limits as resources in the most easily accessed locations and concentrations have been depleted. In addition, there are also declining returns in sectors dominated by corporatist and crony capitalist distortions, such as medical care, education, and the military.

The trend is for these radically inefficient sectors to require escalating energy inputs whether or not the deficient GDP measures expand or contract. Therefore the growth of the productive economy may be even more constricted by low energy inputs than a casual data scan would suggest.

A great deal of energy is being wasted on unproductive activities.

Education: An Ever-Less-Efficient Sector

Consider the case of education. In principle, education improves productivity and should, therefore, pay its way. Once upon a time, it did. Now, not so much. In fact, I suspect that the slowdown in income growth after about 1973—itself reflecting the falloff in cheap oil inputs—stimulated a misguided attempt to improve economic prospects for nonelite workers at the bottom of the income ladder by prescribing a college education for everyone. As a result, the number of Americans going to college surged absurdly from 10 percent of high school graduates prior to World War II to about 70 percent in the twenty-first century. Not surprisingly, college tuition costs skyrocketed by 1,200 percent over the thirty years from 1984 to 2014.

All told, as of 2014, Americans owed $1.2 trillion in student loans, with an average of $26,000 per borrower. With 3.8 percent interest, this translates to a monthly payment of $320. Lauren Asher, president of the Institute for College Access and Success, commented in a 2013 *Forbes* article, "Debt costs you time in savings, pushes back when and whether you can buy a home, start a family, open a small business or access capital."[13] Meanwhile, the returns on the investment in college have been declining. A report by Elise Gould for the Economic Policy Institute, "Even the Most Educated Workers Have Declining Wages," details the fact that between 2013 and 2014, the greatest real wage losses were among people with a college or advanced degree. And over a longer period from 2007 through 2014, all education categories showed flat or declining real average hourly wages.[14]

In short, the escalating costs of college education, while categorized as an investment, have begun to evidence sharply falling returns. They take a huge slug of inputs, including cash flow and energy, out of the economy, without returning as much as smaller outlays might. They well illustrate how inefficient sectors grow, absorbing more workers and resources, including crucial energy resources, without a commensurate return.

Past the Threshold of Diminishing Returns

We have reached and exceeded the point of diminishing returns in which the rapid depletion of readily found and produced cheap oil has created a conundrum of commercial practicability, as envisioned by Jevons. The lack of demand for high cost energy has led to falling prices, leading ahead to a potentially devastating lack of supply. Put simply, with low oil prices, oil companies cannot afford to commit to capital expenditure (CapEx) investment at a scale sufficient to keep global oil production expanding as a matter of "ever-increasing difficulty," to quote Jevons.[15] And this is not a problem that central banks can remedy. In the uncharacteristically sage words of Benjamin Bernanke, "Unfortunately, we can't print oil."[16]

A century and a half ago, a mainstream economist clearly saw the economic importance of maintaining the growth in energy inputs. Today, his argument has fallen into a memory hole. This raises a number of issues for your attention:

1. The evolution of views about the economy does not necessarily follow a logical progression. Every proposition that passes for received wisdom needs to be examined and reexamined for validity. In too many cases, what appears to be a "commonsense" truth is really bogus: a widely circulated misconception that gains currency because it flatters the ambitions or enhances the interests of powerful groups.

2. Among those powerful groups, none is more powerful than the bankrupt nation-state itself. And you know it is bankrupt because none of the leading advanced nation-states can afford to pay legitimate normalized rates of interest on their huge sovereign debts. Nation-states have massive sovereign debts because they have outlived the conditions that gave rise to their growth and they no longer pay their way. Bankrupt or not, however, the government continues its traditional role in subvening the economics profession. As the scale of

government grew, along with energy inputs, since the middle of the nineteenth century, the government became a major source of funds for bribing economists to rationalize and celebrate whatever politicians chose to do.[17]

3. Our response to crises has an embedded pattern. Panic is followed by evermore extreme gestures at creating more fiduciary credit ("fictitious capital"). As economic growth has slowed, governments have become more eager, even desperate, to cultivate support for deficit spending and higher debt levels. Indeed, bailouts are no longer discrete events. They are chronic, structural interventions, involving the continuous creation of money out of thin air to preserve the feeble vital signs of a prostrate economy. Like a coma patient on life support, permanently attached to an IV drip, the economy survives only so long as the interventions continue. Leaving it to its own devices would be equivalent to pulling the plug—it would expire in a heartbeat.

4. Apart from official concern about preserving and extending the debt supercycle, another factor distorting the mainstream narrative is civic myth. The conceit that government grew as a result of deliberate and informed popular choice, not as a second-order effect of geological accidents and the proficiency of petroleum engineers, blocks full appreciation of the role of energy in the economy.

5. The long experience of exponential economic growth extending over many generations has contributed to an informal conviction that relatively rapid growth is the natural result to be expected. The expectation that growth at a twentieth-century pace can resume and continue indefinitely is taken for granted. Of course, this frames a paradox. If Jevons's thesis is correct, as I believe, then the longer the period of high growth

incorporating rising energy inputs continues, the more, rather than less, likely it is that growth will soon come to an end.

In any event, I believe the declining energy intensity of the economy is indeed implicated in the financial stresses, debt defaults, recession, and the Great Slowdown, now construed as secular stagnation.

Secular Stagnation

The notion of secular stagnation—a condition in a market-based economy in which there is little to no economic growth—is another name for the stationary state, as reformulated in the 1930s by Alvin Hansen. It provides the servants of the establishment—like Larry Summers, the former treasury secretary and president emeritus of Harvard University—with yet another intellectual landmark on which to erect a billboard advertising a case that more government debt is required to re-ignite growth. Summers argues in a *Business Economics* article, "U.S. Economic Prospects: Secular Stagnation, Hysteresis, and the Zero Lower Bound," that there has been a "decline in the equilibrium or normal real rate of interest that is associated with full employment." The solution, Summers tells us, is (what else?) more government spending financed by debt.[18]

A Surplus Energy Equation, Not a Monetary One

Summers postulates an "inverse Say's Law: Lack of demand creates over time lack of supply." I believe that something akin to this is indeed involved in the decline of the economy. But not in the way that Summers argues. Specifically, the problem is not monetary in nature, but biophysical. In Tim Morgan's words, "The economy is a surplus energy equation, not a monetary one, and growth in output (and in the global population) since the Industrial Revolution has resulted from the harnessing of ever-greater quantities of energy. But the critical relationship between energy production and the energy cost of extraction is now deteriorating so rapidly that the economy as we have known it for more than two centuries is beginning to unravel."[19]

The problem of long-term stagnation arises not from a lack of bank reserves but from insufficient reserves of cheap energy that make it practically impossible to double oil output again in the next seven to eight years (as Morgan tells us would be required to return to twentieth-century growth rates).

What's App?

Of course, there are different ideas about the causes of secular stagnation. Summers frets that savings are too high relative to investment opportunities. He points particularly to WhatsApp and what he considers to be the alarming fact that it developed a greater market value than Sony with almost no capital investment.[20] This takes us rather far away from what Adam Smith tells us in *The Wealth of Nations*, where the success of an entrepreneur's efforts is "generally in proportion to the extent of his stock (capital)," implying that lower capital requirements would make for more success, not less. Smith also gives voice to the old-fashioned capitalist prejudice that funds for investment need to be previously accumulated— saved, that is, and not borrowed.

The logic of Smith's argument is that a declining requirement for investment should make for the more effective deployment of capital, not less. The investor who wishes to employ his capital with maximum effectiveness presumably prefers a situation like today's in which significant new ventures can be seeded for magnitudes less capital than was required generations ago. While declining capital requirements might not please bankers, because they vitiate collateral and reduce the demand for credit, they should please entrepreneurs.

You might argue that the surge of hundreds of billions in credit demand to finance stock buybacks is a partial response to a decline in perceived opportunities for large-scale investment in the physical expansion of industry and trade. But this only directs our attention to the next question: Why have opportunities for large-scale business investment receded?

Witness the progression of Caterpillar's stock buybacks in relation to capital expenditures. In Q1 2013, Caterpillar invested about $800 million, with no share buybacks. But by Q3 2014, in the midst of thirty-one consecutive months of declining retails sales, Caterpillar share buybacks took $2.5 billion and the company's CapEx had dwindled to less than $500 million. Buybacks now exceed CapEx by five to one for this industrial bellwether. Where there is no growth, financial manipulation through share buybacks pays better than investment in industrial capacity.

"Is US Economic Growth Over?"

Professor Robert Gordon, who helped renew interest in secular stagnation in the wake of the subprime crisis, asked important questions in his 2012 paper "Is U.S. Economic Growth Over? Faltering Innovation Confronts the Six Headwinds."[21] For an establishment economist, Gordon took a contrarian, or at least old-fashioned, view in respect to the well-conditioned expectation that economic growth is a continuous process that will persist indefinitely. Gordon wrote that there was "virtually no growth" before 1750 and there is no guarantee that growth will persist forever. He further stated that the "rapid progress made over the past 250 years could well turn out to be a unique episode in human history."

Gordon deserves credit for challenging the taken-for-granted assumption that economic growth is inevitable, yet you would look in vain in his analysis for a compelling explanation of the growth slowdown. Instead, Gordon blames "faltering innovation" and "six headwinds," a collage of clichés that offers little in the way of insight into why economic growth might suddenly have stalled after two and a half centuries. While recognizing that there was no growth before

1750, Gordon stops short of utilizing that insight to explain the twenty-first century's Great Slowdown.

Accounting for Growth

If you are a fan of econometric modeling, you will be interested in the work of economists Robert Ayers and Benjamin Warr, who have investigated the time series econometrics of growth models with some maverick results. In *Accounting for Growth,* they analyze economic growth since 1900, treating physical work as a factor of production and finding that it explains historical growth with high accuracy until the mid-1970s. They state, "In effect, the Solow residual (a number describing productivity growth) is explained as increasing energy-conversion (to work) efficiency."

A major contribution to growth is conventionally assigned to technological progress, something that, by its nature, is challenging to measure. Ayers and Warr propose resource inputs as factors of production, whereas conventional economics tends to treat resource consumption as a consequence of growth rather than as a factor of production. Whatever you may think of Ayers's and Warr's argument about energy as a factor of production, there is little doubt that our modern technological era has leveraged cheap energy for growth.

In this respect, Professor Gordon seems to have missed a crucial insight underscored by energy analyst Gregor Mac-Donald. He puts together the loose pieces of innovation in the modern centuries into a coherent big picture in his article "Paper vs. Real: Exit from Normal, Ecological Economics, and Probabilistic Regimes in One Chart." MacDonald states that even though human innovation and technology will continue, it will be limited to "small, incremental terms" based on the energy available. He goes on to say: "The advances made possible once humans started extracting fossil fuels, while likely to be repeated in humanistic terms, will not be repeated in industrial terms. Fossil fuels are not creatable. Their unique density made possible a whole range of laborious, constructive activities at a speed and scale that is not replicable."[22]

The Fantasy of Dematerializing the Economy

Advocates of energy efficiency, ever eager to confuse the public about dematerializing the economy, or decoupling economic growth from the growth of energy inputs (and thus the dreaded carbon emissions) extol the supposed benefits of declining energy intensity in the United States. They miss the fact that, as energy use per capita has declined, so have real wages, along with the genuine prosperity of the American middle class. These are symptoms of the declining state. In fact, one of the simpler explanations for the deindustrialization of the United States is that manufacturing was priced out of access to energy, leading energy intensive industries to move overseas. The push for energy efficiency was a major factor in the outsourcing of manufacturing.

Energy Shortfall Coincides with Signal Crisis: Productivity Plunge and Income Decline for Bottom 90 Percent

Bear in mind that the timeline that marks 1973 as the end of the rapid phase of energy input growth, associated with the postwar Great Prosperity, ties in with issues we explore in other chapters. For one thing, as indicated above, productivity growth sank after 1973. Robert Wiedemer put it this way: "Even the spurts of productivity growth in the 2000s don't change the overall pattern of much slower growth after 1973."[23] Not coincidentally, 1973, when the postwar surge of energy inputs in the US economy petered out, was the year when the share of Americans living in poverty bottomed. Then the next year, 1974, saw the first general decline in wages in a quarter of a century. As documented in chapter 5, wages fell by 2.1 percent, while median household income shrank by $1,500.

It is also notable that this proved to be the peak in the income share of the bottom 90 percent of earners. Soon thereafter the income share of the top 1 percent of earners bottomed out at about 9 percent and then began to soar. By 2012, it had more than doubled to 22.5 percent. These details underscore some of the dimensions of distress to which investors responded in triggering the signal crisis of US hegemony at that time: productivity growth collapsed, real income peaked, and broad-based prosperity began to recede. Richard Nixon had defaulted on the Bretton Woods commitments, and investors in droves turned away from business investments to place their free cash flow in financial assets.

The increasing cost of energy was a factor pushing the United States toward full-fledged financialization in which every effort was made to maximize profits through financial[24] manipulation (which, as you know, entails low energy inputs). This is why financial sector debt exploded and financial market capitalization as a percentage of the S&P 500 shot up from around 7 percent as recently as 1990 to more than 22 percent in 2007 on the eve of 2008's great recession.

It has been more than forty years since the rapid increase in the consumption of hydrocarbon fuel in the United States was checked by our encounter with what Jevons described in *The Coal Question* as not "a fixed and impassable limit, but as it were an elastic obstacle, which we may ever push against a little further, but with ever increasing difficulty."[25]

And so it has been. Since then, we have seen evidence of a "declining state" along many dimensions.

US Economic Growth Tracks World Energy Output per Capita

To summarize, the meanderings of US economic growth closely track world energy production per capita. From 1945 through 1973, world energy production per capita grew at a rate of 3.24 percent per year. During the same period, from 1945 through 1973, US real GDP grew accordingly, at exactly the same average rate of 3.24 percent. That is only a correlation, but it is about as close a correlation as you are likely to find in a confused world.

Notwithstanding the tripling of the price of oil in 1973 and a further jump after the Iranian Revolution, the growth of energy production per capita from 1973 to 1979 dwindled to an annual average rate of 0.64 percent. Between 1979 and 2000, energy production per capita declined at an average rate of 0.33 percent per year, also closely matching the decline in real GDP minus the federal deficit.

The soaring price of oil has not reversed the decline in energy production per capita as EROEI has plunged, strongly hinting that the barriers to enhanced production are biophysical, associated with the exhaustion of supplies of the most readily extracted, cheapest oil. In my view, the effect of declining energy intensity on the vitality of the energy-hungry US economy has been evident in the declining growth rate, as real GDP minus the federal deficit since 1980 has fallen at about the same rate as per capita energy production: 0.3 percent.

Gordon's thesis that "economic growth may not be a continuous long-run process that lasts forever" is well-placed heresy. Specifically, Gordon argues that high rates of growth previously experienced in the United States and other developed economies are "one-off" effects that cannot be compounded going forward. He predicts an "epochal decline in growth from the US record of the last 150 years." I think he may be right, but if I am correct about the cause of this decline in growth—in large part from biophysical causes—it makes little sense to suggest, as the International Monetary Fund (IMF) does, that countering it "depends on whether European and US policymakers deal proactively with their major short-term economic challenges." The epochal decline in growth cannot be countered by any feasible policy invention.

To the contrary, if I am correct, the causes of the slowdown Gordon identifies are baked in the cake. These are what I have called megapolitical rather than political. They will happen no matter who is president of the United States because they are informed by factors that lie outside the reach of short-term policy choices. Note that in "a provocative exercise in subtraction," Gordon suggests that "future growth in consumption per capita for the bottom 99 percent of the income distribution could fall below 0.5 percent per year for an extended period of decades."[26]

At that rate, it would take 139 years for income to double— about twice as long as the pace of income growth from December 2007 through Q1 2015. But, per Soddy, there is good reason to doubt that this truly medieval rate of growth could compound long enough to actually realize the doubling. Remember, prior to the Industrial Revolution, sporadic growth of the organic economy tended to either get absorbed by population increases or get cancelled by subsequent economic decline—usually associated with bouts of bad weather— tribulations that were clearly not caused by trace amounts of carbon dioxide in the atmosphere.[27]

The Zero-Sum Character of the Stationary State: Zero-Sum Gains and Crony Capitalism

Part of what you should understand in looking ahead to a long-term secular stagnation or stationary state is a point Kenneth Boulding made in "The Shadow of the Stationary State": a drawback of the stationary state, much less a declining one, is that income gains would be of a zero-sum character. In order for one firm or investor to gain income or market share in an economy without growth, other investors or businesses must lose an equivalent amount.[28]

As Boulding observed from a late-twentieth-century perspective, the logic of the zero-sum character of income gains in a no-growth society gives a powerful impetus to crony capitalism, encouraging privileged groups to seek profits by changing the rules in an antimarket direction. He wrote: "Unfortunately this increases the rate of successful exploitation—that is, the use of organized threat in order to redistribute income. In progressive societies; exploitation pays badly; for almost everybody, increasing their productivity pays better than trying to force redistributions in their direction. One can get $10 out of nature for every dollar one can squeeze out of a fellow man. In the stationary state, unfortunately, investment in exploitation may pay better than in progress. Stationary states, therefore, are frequently mafia-type societies in which government is primarily an institution for redistributing income toward the powerful and away from the weak."[29]

Boulding's logic is sound, but it is unclear in what context he concludes that "stationary states are frequently mafia-type societies." He must have been referring to stationary or quasi-stationary preindustrial societies, or what were known in the early '70s as "underdeveloped economies." Obviously, in a game of musical chairs, where the whole world competes for a dwindling number of good perches, the ablest and most nimble, along with those who are already successful, have a leg up.

Such is the world you live in, where crony capitalists buy laws to secure a larger piece of a declining pie at your expense. (Recall the details reported earlier of the vast costs calculated by Dawson and Seater at $37 billion in annual lost GDP as of 2011.)

Cheap Energy Helped Counter the Drag on Growth from Crony Capitalism

Another way of looking at the problem is that rapid growth in cheap energy in previous decades provided the propulsive force to overcome the drag on growth imposed by rapidly accumulating corporatist regulation. The economy needed a boost to overcome the inefficient antimarket impediments to growth.

Think of a heavily laden truck with flat tires that requires more fuel to move forward. Without such a boost from growing hydrocarbon inputs, economic growth becomes stagnation.

Certainly, a big part of the problem, as indicated above and in previous chapters, is the maneuvering of the great predators, as Braudel called them, to secure a larger piece of a declining pie at your expense. Not incidentally, their resort to antimarket legislation and regulations, as we have seen, has deleterious effects on growth, compounding the effects of the energy input slowdown in curtailing prosperity.

Constrained Economy Erupts in Crisis

Dramatic manifestations of the energy constraints on growth became apparent by 2008. The fatal flaw of fiat money, sporadically evidenced during cyclical downturns and now chronically in view with the plunge in EROEI, is that in the absence of growth, the requirement to pay interest on money borrowed into existence obliges debtors to curtail outlays, with the threat of deflationary contraction lying in the shadows of widespread debt default (hence, the subprime crisis and the collapse of Lehman Brothers).

When the financial crisis almost collapsed the world economy, we were missing a quantity of oil production equal to the annual output of Saudi Arabia. Clearly, this mattered. It is symptomatic of the chronic confusion that shrouds understanding of the energy intensity of economic growth that the Obama administration, along with green energy shills, applauds the recent decline in the number of BTUs per dollar of GDP. They miss the point that little of this decline in energy intensity reflects improved efficiency (higher returns from the energy we use).

Rather, close analysis shows that declining energy use in the United States mostly reflects structural shifts, such as offshoring of energy-intense manufacturing; a greater proportion of government spending in the GDP accounts, which mostly involves the electronic transmission of cash, requiring minimal energy requirements; and, yes, the minor efficiencies realized from shifts to higher quality fuels and more onsite generation. Add to that the declining returns associated with the massive inefficiency of the corporatist sector (i.e., education, health care, and the military), and declining energy intensity is nothing to celebrate.

This growth slowdown magnifies the unsustainable disconnect between primary energy consumption and the growth of debt. As Tim Morgan reminds us, the inevitable result to be expected from a widening gap between financial claims and the real energy economy of the future is that financial claims, meaning both debt and money, are destined to be destroyed on a truly enormous scale. In other words, we're headed for a version of the no-growth stationary state, culminating in the Breaking Point collapse.

The Debt Supercycle Endgame

The shortfall in energy inputs manifested itself in stagnant, or falling, income for most people, debt strains, defaults, and financial crisis. Taken together, these strains amount to an affordability crisis that almost collapsed the world financial system in 2008 and likely will do so during the coming Breaking Point. It is important to understand that there is little prospect that the terminal crisis can be avoided, as it would require astonishing breakthroughs in oil prospecting. Equally notable, it would require an unlikely abandonment of the corporatist establishment's ecofascist campaign to demonize carbon dioxide. Consequently, as Gail Tverberg points out, "adding one percentage point of growth in energy usage tends to add less and less GDP growth over time."[30]

Another factor that amplified the returns from the early integration of hydrocarbon energy into the economy was the high, early EROEI. When the EROEI was one hundred to one, as it was as recently as 1930, more energy surplus was available to grow the economy because less energy was required simply to extract the energy itself.

Unfortunately, the US government has painted itself, and the entire world economy, into a corner. Its attempt to preserve the untenable status quo—leveraged by quantitative easing into between $500 trillion and $700 trillion in derivative bets against higher interest rates—is running out of time. Derivatives—or as Warren Buffet memorably described them, "financial weapons of mass destruction"—are now worth as much as ten times more than the entire world economy. The fragility this entails makes a voluntary abandonment of further credit (or debt) expansion all but mathematically impossible. Since 1980, the shadow economy of monetary and debt claims on future energy have multiplied 400 percent faster than the underlying real economy.

And that does not account for the shadow claims on future production, embodied in unfunded liabilities for government entitlements that multiply by the trillions every year. According to an estimate by Professor Kotlikoff, the unfunded "fiscal gap" of the US government amounted to about $205 trillion as of 2013.

The Concertina of Debt Collapse

This is what is coming your way: either a global crack-up boom—an inflationary culmination of the terminal crisis of US hegemony in a final and total catastrophe of the currency system—or more probably, the terminal crisis will play out in a deflationary collapse. As Soddy explained, the money supply becomes a "concertina," expanding during the boom phase and contracting when debt is repaid or extinguished through default. I suspect this crack-up boom will also be the terminal crisis for the entire modern economic history dominated by nation-states at ever-greater scale. This won't merely be a crisis for the US imperium; it will be a global crisis of fiat money. As Darryl Schoon has pointed out, even "China's rapid growth was fueled by the unprecedented expansion of the US money supply—an expansion directly responsible for America's exploding appetite for consumer goods from China and the US dot-com stock market bubble in the 1990s."[31]

As I detail in chapter 20, China accounted for as much as 45 percent of the increase in world oil demand after 2004. Much of that demand proved to be artificial, leveraged from the Chinese credit bubble. The subsequent collapse in oil prices in 2014, along with the waterfall declines in other commodities, reflected the waning of the exaggerated credit-fueled demand as the Chinese bubble began to deflate.

To the extent that demand for oil occasioned solely by Bubblenomics is not duplicated by a subsequent credit-ramped artificial boom somewhere in the world, the collapse of economic growth, occasioned by the depletion of cheap hydrocarbon energy, may be delayed a few more years into this century of crisis. The twilight of fossil fuels heralds the end of fiat currency, as well as the eclipse of the consumer economy regulated by the all-powerful nation-state. Whatever else you do, however, be sure you put aside some gold and silver to prepare for the collapse of the shadow economy of money and debt.

A reputable source for acquiring and storing precious metals is Matterhorn Asset Management of Switzerland. They can secure you precious metals inside a mountain redoubt formerly used by the Swiss Army. For more details, contact Johny Beck, partner, Matterhorn Asset Management AG at jb@goldswitzerland.com. Their websites are www.goldswitzerland.com and www.matterhorngold.com.

Although the Great Depression looms as a period of mythic economic woe in the popular imagination, it involved only a temporary interruption in the rapid compounding of real GDP per head. While it does not seem serious as measured by the dubious national income accounting, the growth slowdown of the twenty-first century poses a much worse threat to future growth than did the Great Depression.

At the time of the Great Depression, the economy suffered from disruptions associated with the terminal crisis of British hegemony. As a consequence, the world monetary system was deranged, with capital flows from London to the periphery interrupted. True, energy was involved—remember British coal production peaked in 1913—but oil was plentiful and growth was not constrained by the dwindling availability of energy. Also, EROEI was still highly favorable in the 1930s.

The record confirms the inference that vibrant growth would rapidly restored. Lord Keynes wrote in "Economic Possibilities for Our Grandchildren" (1930) that he expected the real economy to have grown between four and eight times within one hundred years. He underestimated. Using the US economy as a yardstick, it had expanded by eightfold by 1985. In that same essay, Keynes declares himself on the opposite end to Soddy on the question of compound interest. "Perhaps it is not an accident that the race which did most to bring the promise of immortality into the heart and essence of our religions has also done most for the principle of compound interest and particularly loves this most purposive of human institutions."[32]

With high EROEI in 1930, there was plenty of scope for rapid growth in the post-Depression economy, which duly did grow in what F. A. Hayek called "The Great Prosperity."

To a large extent, the quarter of a century of Hayek's "Great Prosperity" really made for mass prosperity. Productivity rose by 97 percent, and median wages rose by 95 percent. The incomes of the poorest fifth jumped by 42 percent, while incomes of the wealthiest 20 percent climbed by 8 percent. Then Nixon repudiated the gold reserve standard, facilitating the shift to financialization.

Today, the prospects for renewed growth seem dim, with EROEI on new projects crashing toward single digits.[33] You can look forward to a future of dematerialized growth, involving leisure, presumably to play chess, learn to paint, read the classics by daylight, and otherwise enjoy life amplified by little or no exogenous energy. As Roger K. Brown suggests, however, there is more than a tinge of nonsense invested in inflated hopes for dematerialized growth as, no matter what, it could not continue forever. Brown notes:

> That dematerialized growth cannot continue forever is, I think, fairly obvious. Consider the logical end point of such activity; You give me a better back rub and I sing you a better song. Note the emphasis on increasing quality exemplified by the use of the word "better". I cannot consume exponentially increasing amounts of back rubs (or of any other dematerialized service) and you cannot listen to exponentially increasing amounts of my singing. The idea that generation after generation of venture capitalists can pay for their mansions by financing such dematerialized services is nonsense.[34]

And so "we stumble downward into a spiral of retrenchment, drift and collapse."[35]

Notes

1   Smith, Adam, *The Wealth of Nations* (Chicago: University of Chicago Press, 1976), book 1, ch. 8.

2   Boulding, Kenneth E., "The Shadow of the Stationary State," in *The No-Growth Society*, ed. Mancur Olson and Hans H. Landsberg (New York: W. W. Norton, 1973), 95.

3   Smith, *The Wealth of Nations*, 90–91.

4   Ibid., 179.

5   Ibid., 184.

6   Ibid., 185.

7   Wrigley, E. A., *Energy and the English Industrial Revolution* (Cambridge: Cambridge University Press, 2010), 239.

8   Jevons, *The Coal Question*, 205.

9   Ibid.

10 Ibid., 173–74.

11 Ibid., 178.

12 Mill, John Stuart, *Principles of Political Economy 1848*, repr. (Amherst, NY: Prometheus, 2004), 688.

13 Denhart, Chris, "How The $1.2 Trillion College Debt Crisis Is Crippling Students, Parents and the Economy," *Forbes*, August 7, 2013.

14 Gould, Elise, "Even the Most Educated Workers Have Declining Wages," Economic Policy Institute, February 20, 2015.

15 Jevons, *The Coal Question*, 173–74.

16 http://www.safehaven.com/article/20785/ben-bernankes-press-conference-we-dont-control-emerging-markets.

17 Sprott Money, "U.S. Retail Sales Fall, Again—the Next Crash Is Near," *Zero Hedge*, July 21, 2015.

18 Summers, "U.S. Economic Prospects: Secular Stagnation, Hysteresis, and the Zero Lower Bound," *Business Economics*, http://econpapers.repec.org/article/palbuseco/v_3a49_3ay_3a2014_3ai_3a2_3ap_3a65-73.htm.

19 Morgan, Tim, "Perfect Storm: Energy, Finance and the End of Growth," *Strategy Insights* 9 (London: Tullett Prebon), http://ftalphaville.ft.com/files/2013/01/Perfect-Storm-LR.pdf.

20 Summers, op. cit.

21 Gordon, Robert, "Is U.S. Economic Growth Over? Faltering Innovation Confronts the Six Headwinds" (NBER working paper no. 18315, August 2012). JEL No. D24,E2,E66,J11,-J15,O3,O31,O4,Q43.

22 MacDonald, Gregor, "Paper vs. Real: Exit from Normal, Ecological Economics, and Probabilistic Regimes in One Chart," *Gregor. US: Energy and Economics.*

23 Wiedemer, Robert, *Aftershock Investor Report* 3, no. 7 (July 2015), 2.

24 Ibid.

25 Jevons, *The Coal Question*, 174.

26 Gordon, "Is U.S. Economic Growth Over?"

27 O Grada, Cormac, "Ready for Revolution? The English Economy before 1800," September 24, 2014, http://www.lse.ac.uk/economicHistory/seminars/EconomicHistory/Papers14-15/READY-FOR-REVOLUTION.pdf.

28 Boulding, "The Shadow of the Stationary State," 95.

29 Ibid.

30 http://ourfiniteworld.com/2015/05/06/why-we-have-an-oversupply-of-almost-everything-oil-labor-capital-etc/.

31 Schoon, Darryl, "China, 2012 and Von Mises' Crack Up Boom," January 4, 2012, http://www.financialsense.com/contributors/darryl-schoon/2012/01/04/china-2012-and-von-mises-crack-up-boom.

32 Keynes, John Maynard, "Economic Possibilities for Our Grandchildren," in *Essays in Persuasion,* by John Maynard Keynes (New York: W. W. Norton, 1963), 358–73.

33 Ibid.

34 http://theworldisfinite.com.

35 Balakrishnan, Gopal, "Speculation on the Stationary State," *Occasion: Interdisciplinary Studies in the Humanities* 3 (March 15, 2012).

Chapter Eighteen

The Declining State

From a Downward Spiral of Retrenchment to Mad Max

*In their own ways, both bureaucratic socialism and its vastly
more affluent neoliberal conqueror concealed their failures
with increasingly arbitrary* tableaux economique. *By the
'80s the GDR's (German Democratic Republic's) report
of national income was revealed to be a statistical artifact
that grossly inflated its cramped standards of living . . .
The coming depression may reveal that the national income
statistics of the period of bubble economics were fictions, not
wholly unlike those operative in the old Soviet system.*
—Gopal Balakrishnan, "Speculations on the Stationary State"

There is No Tomorrow–Morrowland.
—Mad Max, *Mad Max Beyond Thunderdome*

Has Growth in the Real Economy Ceased?

In this chapter, we consider Dr. Tim Morgan's apparently wild-
eyed conjecture, prominently quoted in the epigraph in chapter
16, that "growth in the real economy ceased quite some years ago"
as the energy intensity of the economy declined. Dr. Morgan is
hardly as wild-eyed as Mad Max, the fictional hero of four movies whose adventures in the postgrowth world have been played
out before audiences of millions over the past thirty-six years.

Mad Max appeals because he is a survivor in a world that mainstream economists can't even imagine. His is the world of multidimensional collapse, where financial collapse has been compounded by industrial collapse and commercial collapse (the breakdown of supply chains), followed by political collapse, and ultimately culminating in social collapse. We first meet Max Rockatansky as a police officer in the Main Force Patrol of a future and rapidly collapsing version of Australia.

Science fiction is an attempt to imagine the future, just as history is the attempt to reimagine the past. Much that was seen in the past and then forgotten can be recognized in the present. Both history and science fiction may help us better understand our current dilemmas. As you will have recognized, the argument of this book draws mainly on history. But I am always open, as I hope you are, to whatever science fiction can tell us.

"It's the Oil, Stupid"

The *Mad Max* movies provide a good vantage for a thought exercise—to learn what you can from the imaginative people who make films. They have a way of reflecting and clarifying themes that are too serious to be tackled by the editorial board of the *New York Times*.

Meanwhile let's take a closer look at Tim Morgan's contrarian claim that growth in the real economy "ceased quite some years ago." This, of course, betrays skepticism on Morgan's part about the validity and usefulness of official measurements of "growth in the real economy." If you believe what you read in the newspapers, this may disqualify Morgan from further consideration.

Rather than dismiss his thesis out of hand, let's drill in to see what he is talking about and whether it could possibly be true. Of course, you have had a warm-up in previous chapters for the idea that declining energy inputs could inform a slowdown and even a decline in the economy.

A Measurement Adventure

It is important to recognize that measuring economic growth is more of an adventure than measuring your pants size. For one thing, in almost every circumstance you can imagine, the person with the tape measure has lively incentives to say that you are bigger than you really are. And further to that, there are nontrivial questions about what should be counted and what excluded.

The anonymous blogger FSK, who specializes in posts debunking supposed GDP growth (not the Fork Spoon Knife FSK of the cooking blog that famously featured a recipe for "Gluten Free Blueberry Pound Cake")—questions a feature of GDP accounting. In a July 2010 post, he gave the example of a toy imported from China for sale in the United States. When the toy arrives in the United States, it may have a value of three dollars, but after retailing for twenty dollars, the difference of seventeen dollars goes toward US GDP. FSK argues that even though the US company selling the product imported, marketed, transported, and sold the toy, it didn't add any tangible value.[1]

Another way of looking at it is to see the offshoring of manufactured production to China as a way of circumventing US environmental regulations that have sharply raised the cost of otherwise relatively low-cost energy from coal. For example, US utilities have to install flue gas desulfurization equipment, or "scrubbers," which cost hundreds of millions of dollars each. China's coal consumption has grown by leaps and bounds, while US plants are closing. In 2012, 10.2 gigawatts of coal-fired capacity was retired in the United States, while the World Resources Institute reported that China's government was planning to build 363 coal-fired power plants across China, with a combined generating capacity of more than 557 gigawatts.[2] China now consumes about as much coal as the rest of the world combined. Because American companies could not access energy from coal directly in the United States, they were content to do so indirectly in China.

If 100 percent of products sold in the United States were made in China, with profit margins like those on the toy example discussed, 83 percent of the sales would count as domestic product. If seen by a casual viewer with an unmindful squint, domestic production, as measured in national income accounts, would appear to be robust. As it happens, national income accounting is such that it accommodates the disintermediation of costly US regulations quite smoothly. The profits of US companies renting access to Chinese energy, and environmental regulations, count in US GDP.

The profits from subprime auto loans issued to finance used car sales may count in GDP tallies—fee-based net income from financial services is included as value-added and thus boosts GDP—but whatever fraction of the 15.6 million used cars sold for cash in 2014 otherwise did not show up in GDP accounts. However, some surprising things did.

Such as promises.

No. I am not joking. Currently, the government counts in GDP totals, under "wages paid," corporate promises to someday, maybe fund pension obligations.

As reported by the *Zero Hedge* blog, Elliott Management's Paul Singer explains that the BEA's GDP calculation includes the amount of money companies promise to pay into pension plans in the future, even though these promises are not fully funded.

> We have commented in the past on government statistical fakery and fudges, in the inflation numbers, in employment and long-term budgeting. But recent changes to the national GDP accounts by the Bureau of Economic Analysis may "take the cake." As part of the revisions, they change the way pension payments are counting in GDP. Previous to the change, when a company paid money into a pension plan, the money was counted as wages in the

GDP calculation. After the change, **what companies have promised to pay in the future, not what they are actually paying, will be added to GDP.** This is fantastic. <u>**The bigger the unpayable promise made to unsuspecting retirees (promises that are not fully funded), the more GDP supposedly goes up!**</u>[3]

Amazing intellectual dishonesty. It is pertinent that a standout expert among those who have studied national income accounting most closely, John Williams of *Shadow Government Statistics,* accords little credibility to the official narrative loudly proclaimed by Obama in his State of the Union speech: "We've seen the fastest economic growth." To the contrary, Williams says we are in the midst of "an unfolding, multiple dip economic collapse."[4] I agree.

In addition to methodological shenanigans, it is well known that politicians go to great lengths to distort the headline numbers. Dr. Carsten Holz, a visiting scholar in the Department of Economics at Harvard, points to both former president Lyndon Johnson and former president George H. W. Bush as guilty of this practice. If Johnson didn't like the GNP reports, he was known to send the estimates back to the Commerce Department until they came up with a number that he considered "correct." During Bush's administration, a senior member of the executive branch requested that a computer company exaggerate its sales in its report to the BEA: "Thanks to the heavy leverage of computer deflation, reported GDP growth enjoyed an artificial spike."[5]

Note another facet of the deception: today, you are told that GDP is the proper measure of prosperity. But as Dr. Holz reminds us, when Lyndon Johnson was forcing bureaucrats in the Commerce Department to fiddle the numbers, he wanted them to exaggerate Gross National Product (GNP). In the years since Johnson left the White House, GNP has been more or less forgotten while GDP has taken center stage.

Why?

It is simple.

Notwithstanding all that Johnson did to put the United States on the road to bankruptcy, with the Vietnam War and his Great Society programs, the United States was still a creditor nation in those days. Because GNP includes the total of incomes earned by residents of a country, regardless of where they earn it, the GNP of a creditor country is always higher than its GDP, which includes the total of all economic activity in the country, regardless of who owns the productive assets, and without deducting for interest and dividends paid abroad.

The United States now owes at least $6.2 trillion to other countries, and unlike the 1960s, a significant portion of US production is owned by companies domiciled abroad. For example, as of 2006, 36.4 percent of US automobile production came from foreign-owned plants.[6] If the United States were still using GNP as the yardstick of economic growth, whatever number the bean counters conjured up would be smaller than an equivalent GDP number.

According to John Williams, even though GDP is the most widely followed business indicator reported by the US government, it has become nearly worthless as an actual indicator of economic activity due to upward growth biases built into GDP modeling since the '80s.[7] Today, GDP reporting has become a political propaganda tool. The most fevered huckster of used cars is a personification of credibility compared to the bureaucrats who assemble and report data on the economy. The GDP measurement standards are so squirrely that Morgan's thesis that growth in the real economy ceased some years ago is by no means incredible.

A Morsel of Nonsense

The point that should stand out in this quick tutorial on national income accounting is that GDP is an intellectually dishonest propaganda construct. It has become one of those morsels of nonsense, like celebrity gossip disguised as news, that diverts infatuated people from thinking about what is really going on. In my view, the official propaganda about GDP has about as much substance as the latest twaddle about the Kardashians.

Look to the Footnotes, Not the Headlines

Look around: What do you see unfolding on a daily basis but the aftermath of the end of growth? Is it not a symptom of economic decline when the labor force participation rate of college graduates recedes to an all-time low and Ivy League schools have a higher acceptance rate than McDonald's?

Look to the footnotes for your bearings, not the headlines. They are less likely to be fiddled. The fact that the Social Security's Disability Insurance Trust Fund has gone bust after more Americans secured permanent disability status than found full-time work during the Obama presidency says that you are living in a declining retrograde economy.

But that is only one dismaying footnote. If you look closely, you can see that from 2007 through 2014, during the period of the imaginary recovery, workers in all education categories showed flat or declining real average hourly wages. During that time, the number of Americans living in poverty increased by 9.4 million, from 37,276,000 to 46,657,000.

That helps explain why the prospect of retirement is rapidly fading away. Witness the ordeals of legions of superannuated "workcampers,"[8] senior migrants who put in twelve-hour shifts in Amazon warehouses or hold down other menial jobs. As *Harper's* reports in "The End of Retirement," "Each successive generation is now doing worse than previous generations in terms of their ability to retire."

A similar hint of downward mobility: the officially reported Q2 2015 worker pay increase was the smallest on record, decidedly lower at 0.20 percent, than even at the depths of the Great Recession. This negative turn helps explain why labor force participation rates since 2000 have plunged for all age cohorts under the age of fifty-five, with the steepest drop, of about 17 percent, for workers aged sixteen to twenty-four. This also says that the world we knew of rapid economic growth is gone.

To be clear, Morgan's case is not merely a premonition that someday, in the by-and-by, growth may come to a halt if we don't balance the budget and eat our vegetables—his stark message is that the economy stopped growing years ago. Your challenge is to recognize what is really happening, think as clearly as possible about how to survive, and position yourself to succeed in a bankrupt world.

Another hint that we are caught in a downward spiral of retrenchment: companies aren't investing in the physical expansion of their businesses or in their employees because they don't believe the recovery is real. They see a consumer economy locked in a downward spiral where the average American is stretched too thin, saddled with too much debt, and has too little income to recover.

America's economy is teetering on an edge. The consumer is largely absent, and companies aren't investing either, except in share buybacks and financialization. You will wait in vain for official channels to concede that the status quo is shot. No established political system ever concedes that it is in the process of being superseded.

Look at more of the footnotes that attest to the long-term economic collapse happening all around you.

Recession or Worse?

I have no doubt that the economy is in decline. But it is not at all evident that the decline so vividly expressing itself is likely to be of "temporary" duration. For perspective, consider the etymology of "recession." The word made its first appearance in 1929, as "a noun of action" derived from "recess," meaning a temporary retreat or decline in economic activity. In that sense, a downturn that is not temporary is something other than a recession.

Consider the compelling evidence that median income is not merely in a temporary dip but in a long-term secular downtrend that shows no sign of reversing. *Shadow Government Statistics* has deflated the average weekly earnings of production and nonsupervisory employees from 1965 until today. Using the Shadow Stats CPI-W deflator, current real average weekly earnings are just half of what they were fifty years ago. And even the government's own fishy data (deflated by the official CPI-W) show the real average weekly earnings are lower than in 1965. This is not merely a recession. It is economic regression, a prelude to collapse.

A 2016 study by the Pew Charitable Trusts ("Household Expenditures and Income") shows the weakness in consumer spending power is even greater than a comparison of inflation-adjusted median income suggests. Why? My guess is that the ZIRP policies of the Federal Reserve have been too successful in raising inflation, while emptying the savings accounts of poorer Americans who no longer earn enough from interest income to offset the cost of bank fees. And don't forget the impact of political schemes like Obamacare that have emptied the already thin wallets of lower-income Americans, vastly increasing the cost of health care.

According to Pew, the typical household among the lower third (counting pretax, posttransfer income) suffered a decline in its annual balance of income over spending of $3,800 in the decade after 2004. By comparison, the typical household in the middle third of earners saw its surplus of income over expenditure drop from $17,000 in 2004 to $6,000 in 2014. (Of course, this was calculated before taxes so families had even less slack than the numbers suggest.)

The stated intention of the thoroughly detailed Pew study of household financial security was to more closely examine whether income is "sufficient to cover expenses." Overall, they concluded that "overall median household expenditures grew by about 25% between 1996 and 2014," while "income continued to contract" after the Great Recession. "By 2014 median income had fallen by 13% from 2004 levels, while expenditures had increased by nearly 14%."

Part of the story was that low income families had to spend a much greater share of their incomes than in the past on core needs, such as housing, transportation, health care, and food. In 2004, typical households in the bottom third of the income distribution had "$1,500 of income left over after expenses. But by 2014, 'the household surplus' had decreased by $3,800, putting them $2,300 in the red."

This raises an obvious question—where did the lowest income households find the $2,300 cash needed to fund the gap between their spending and their income? Remember, the Pew study already takes transfers into account. I doubt they all became Uber drivers. Presumably, they must have borrowed from relatives or depleted whatever meager savings they possessed. But with outlays exceeding income by $2,300 in 2014, it would seem impossible for the lower third of households to have continued spending at 2014 levels for any protracted length of time. Thus the insufficiency of income among the lower third of households to cover even core needs, such as housing, transportation, health care, and food, implies that time was running out on the economy in 2014.

The surge in the expenditure to income ratio could be interpreted in many ways. Part of it is undoubtedly due to Obamacare. Before 2010, families in the lower third of the income distribution not covered by employer health insurance could choose to go without it. If they got sick, they had to pay out of pocket or depend on charity and declare bankruptcy if the bill became unpayable. By 2014, the average cost after assistance subsidies for the 87 percent of those who qualified for cost assistance was about $69 a month for the second-lowest-cost Silver plan. So in other words, $828, or about 22 percent of the household deficit among the bottom third of households, could be attributable to Obamacare.

And announcements by insurance companies show that the predatory Obamacare squeeze on lower-income consumers was destined to skyrocket in 2017. Average premium increases proposed by insurers for individual Obamacare policy holders are topped by a 65.2 percent hike proposed by Humana in Georgia, a 38.4 percent hike proposed by Highland in Pennsylvania, a 31.6 percent hike proposed by New Mexico Health, and a 29.6 percent hike proposed by Provident Health Plan in Oregon. Ouch. If consumers were not already insolvent, another year or two in the tender embrace of Obamacare should complete the job.

Some of the surge in the spending by lower-income consumers may also reflect an adverse change in relative market prices that loomed larger for the lower third of the income distribution. Remember, while housing costs have been soaring for decades, during the height of the subprime boom, families in the lower third of the income distribution temporarily seemed to be benefiting. But that changed abruptly with the 2008 subprime financial crisis.

By 2014, households at the bottom spent more on gasoline than their counterparts spent on all transportation in 1996. Perhaps housing inflation required the poorer segment of the population to reside farther away from their jobs and thus commute farther, raising their required spending on gas disproportionately? Remember, housing costs have escalated sharply in recent decades. In most major cities, housing prices are up by 400–500 percent since 1980, with some like Boston (716.3 percent) and San Francisco (729.8 percent) up even more. If you are not rich or you didn't buy years ago, you would be hard-pressed to find shelter in those cities.

Another interpretation is that the ominous surge in the expenditure to income ratio confirms the *Shadow Government Statistics* conclusion that the CPI-W (the monthly Consumer Price Index for Urban Wage Earners and Clerical Workers) significantly understates the decline in consumer purchasing power. In this respect, it is noteworthy that the CPI-W was explicitly chosen as the index for the annual adjustment of benefits paid to Social Security beneficiaries and

Supplemental Security Income recipients. The idea was that a low-ball inflation adjustment would save trillions as compared to a more accurate index. Social Security outlays would be approximately double their current level if inflation had been accurately measured.

The *Shadow Stats Alternate CPI-W* (with 1990 as a base) is calculated, as John Williams of *Shadow Government Statistics* puts it, by excluding "gimmicked changes to reporting methodologies of the last several decades, which have tended to understate actual inflation and to overstate actual economic activity." The implication is not only that real (or inflation-adjusted GDP) is much lower than official data portray, but all other economic series deflated by official measures are overstated due to gimmicked reporting methodologies that undermeasure official inflation. The muddling of that statistical series with reports of fake prosperity merely pollutes the data, making it harder to tease out valid information you need to plan your investments and your life.

You often have to await the calculation of benchmark revisions to get a more realistic feel for how the economy has performed. Of course, this entails difficulties. For one thing, you may have to wait a long time for the government bean counters to grudgingly amend their lies. For another, you have to go clawing through the footnotes to find benchmark revisions because the mass media only report the headline confections, not the subsequent revisions that at least partially amend the record. News reports of benchmark revisions, if any, are confined to small articles in the business section.

For instance, if you were here across the table and prepared to make a friendly wager, even though I am not a gambling man, I would be willing to bet that you could easily have missed the May 18, 2016, benchmark revision to "Manufacturers' Shipments, Inventories and Orders." (Again, think durable goods.) The benchmark revisions show that 12 percent of the pickup in manufacturers' shipments since the officially declared end of the recession in 2009 actually never happened.

Not only did billions in imaginary manufactured shipments vanish in a twinkle, but $12.66 billion of business inventories, along with $57 billion of unfilled orders vanished as well. In other words, the recovery has not been nearly as strong as Obama and his minions pretended.

A hint of the magnitude of the coming economic adjustment can be gleaned from the fact that wholesale sales peaked in July 2014. This means that as of June 2016, the supply chain contraction in the US economy had already lasted more than twice as long as the nine-month supply chain adjustment in the Great Recession following the Lehman bankruptcy. Total business sales have been declining for years—as suggested by the Pew audit of consumer finances—and were running about 15 percent lower in 2016 than in late 2014.

Of course, the fact that $12.66 billion of business inventories don't actually exist makes the task of rectifying the supply chain somewhat less daunting. No store will have to stage bankruptcy sales to liquidate the billions of dollars of inventories that were never more than statistical fictions in the first place.

"Only 'Dummies' Believe the Unemployment Figure"—Donald Trump

Speaking of fake prosperity, I return to a sensitive topic— the chronic and remorseless lies fabricated by the Obama administration to portray the US job market as more vibrant than it is.

Not incidentally, a reason I respect Donald Trump is that he has tried to advance the national conversation by underscoring a point that should be evident to any thinking person— namely, that the "recovery" the establishment is so keen to have you embrace is a fraud. If elected president, Trump promises to draw back the veil of statistical flummery that disguises reality for credulous people. Trump is the first candidate in my memory to say he "will investigate the veracity of U.S. economic statistics produced by Washington—including 'the way they are reported.'" No wonder the establishment hates him. As George Orwell, the author of *Nineteen Eighty-Four,* put it, "The further a society drifts from truth the more it will hate those that speak it."

Let's look more closely to see why my comments and those of Donald Trump on the employment situation are not merely impudent name-calling but sober conclusions informed by the facts.

Start with the issue of business dynamism that lies at the heart of a lot of statistical mischief in government pronouncements on the job market. "Business dynamism is the process by which firms continually are born, fail, expand, and contract, as some jobs are created, others are destroyed, and others still are turned over. As indicated above, research has firmly established that this dynamic process is vital to productivity and sustained economic growth. Entrepreneurs play a critical role in this process, and in net job creation."

As economists Ian Hathaway and Robert E. Litan pointed out in research conducted for the Brookings Institution, "Historically one new business is born about every minute, while another one fails every eighty seconds." That was then. Since the Great Recession, not so much. Now there are more failures than start-ups.[9]

Business dynamism in the United States has been in long-term decline, so not all of the recent problems of entrepreneurial stagnation could be fairly attributed to Barack Obama. Nonetheless, extensive research shows that the old ratio of business births to deaths no longer obtains. Quite the contrary.

The rate of business dynamism collapsed when the subprime bubble popped. Obama's presidency is the first to see more firms go out of business than be created. As you will readily understand, it makes a difference in a supposed "economic recovery" if business deaths run considerably ahead of new firm formation.

One of the areas where it makes a big difference is in job creation. Historically, dynamic new firms have been a large source of new jobs. But that is no longer the case when old firms are going bust faster than new firms are being created. Obviously, if the Brookings Institution can figure out that more firms are going out of business than are being created, that insight should not elude the Bureau of Labor Statistics (BLS). But it has, primarily because it gives the lie to the fake job strength the BLS ballyhoos every month.

In fact, Obama's bean counters add about 200,000 imaginary jobs each month through the "Birth/Death" model that continues to suppose—contrary to the evidence—that more jobs were created in new firms (births) than lost in firms going out of business (deaths). These fake jobs account for a big percentage of the growth in employment announced by the BLS. The bottom line is that at least four and a half million jobs announced during the Obama presidency never existed. They were statistical adjustments inserted in the data reflecting outdated historical ratios that no longer hold true.

But this is only part of the story. The Brookings data, along with surveys conducted by Gallup, show that far from adding 200,000 jobs through the "Birth/Death" model, a more accurate report would have subtracted 70,000 jobs a month to account for the jobs that disappeared when firms died.

That would be another 840,000 annual jobs (or two and a half million jobs subtracted since 2014). All told, 6,950,000 (or 75 percent) of the officially announced 9,150,000 jobs supposedly created through the first quarter of 2016 were fake. I should point out that that might actually be a low estimate, as the BLS inflates jobs estimates with seasonal adjustment shenanigans that result in double counting of the same fake jobs and other frauds that are too complicated to get into here.

Fake Employees Are Not Paid

You don't need to be a Nobel Prize–winning economist to realize that fake employees cannot form the basis of a strong economy. Suffice it to say that employers are not writing checks to employees that don't exist outside of statistical models. The income those imaginary employees would be earning if they were real is not being spent at the businesses that are going out of business by the hundreds of thousands each year.

And inevitably, if business deaths continue to outstrip business formations in an environment of slack consumer demand, the result to be expected is economic collapse. The slow-motion insolvency of American consumers as the economy regresses implies a coming surge of economic distress. This will inevitably be construed as a "recession," although as explained above what is afoot is probably better understood as another installment of economic regression along the road to collapse.

Slow-Motion Musical Chairs
A good simile for the US economy is that it has performed like a cruelly disguised game of musical chairs. Each time the music stops, an ever-larger contingent find that their chairs have been taken away, and they are out of the game. And they had no clue by what rules they were playing.

If you think about the implications of the decline in median income over half a century a lot of other dimensions of economic weakness come into focus. For one thing, the supposedly strong US employment picture is not at all what Obama pretends it is. Actual US job growth is concentrated almost entirely in low-wage service work. Among the jobs the US economy supposedly added during 2015, 360,000 were waiters, bartenders, and baristas, while 12,000 were allegedly hired for manufacturing jobs.

Fake Jobs in Perspective
Why so many baristas?

Partly, that may reflect the fact that it is easier to fake the hiring of a 100,000 bartenders than it would be to fake 100,000 manufacturing jobs. A boom in manufacturing sufficient to account for a surge in manufacturing job growth would show up anomalies in many other statistical series. You can't pretend with a straight face that employment in manufacturing is booming when manufacturers' shipments are down in eight months out of nine.

Declining Productivity Exposes Fake Jobs

Yet another telltale statistical hint of the large number of fake jobs is the declining productivity that seems to puzzle so many mainstream economists. Duh. Of course productivity is disappointing. The millions of fake employees aren't actually doing much heavy lifting, are they? The fake jobs obviously skew the denominator for calculating productivity growth. All the actual work is done by real employees who show up, not by statistical hypotheses.

Fake Prosperity Winds Down

The long-term decline in median income, amplified in 2016 by the biggest drop in weekly earnings in history, puts the lie to the pretense of self-sustaining recovery. Average people don't have enough discretionary income to sustain expanded economic activity. And this shows up in lots of ways—if you care to look. In 2008, when the mortgage bubble burst, 18 percent of American children were officially living in poverty. By July 2015, after six years of supposed recovery, the Casey Foundation's 2015 Kids Count Data Book reported that the number of kids in poverty soared by three million, with the total having risen to 22 percent.[10]

Another detail that reflects the deterioration of living standards in the declining economy is the fact that federal outlays for the food stamp program have doubled since the last recession. They totaled $37 billion in 2008—by 2015 that number was $74 billion. Recall this telling detail that I have highlighted previously: the total number of business closures exceeded the total number of new businesses created during every year of Obama's presidency. When business failures exceed the number of successful start-ups, you are no longer living in a growing economy, but a declining one headed for collapse. It is new work that stimulates an intensification of the division of labor. When new firms that embody new work are failing, the average age of firms in the economy goes up, and new jobs reflecting new occupations disappear. This is the essence of a declining economy.

Worse than the Great Depression?

Another confirming datum—So far in this century, US manufacturing has suffered its worst performance ever. Americans lost 5.7 million manufacturing jobs, and the decline as a share of total jobs (33 percent) exceeded the rate of loss in the Great Depression.[11]

Dr. Robert Atkinson, the economist, elaborates:

> U.S. government statistics significantly overstate the change in U.S. manufacturing output, and by definition productivity, in part because of massive overestimation of output growth in the computer and electronics sector and because of problems with how manufacturing imports are measured.
>
> Measurement of the computers and electronics industry (NAICS 334) is a particular problem. Because of Moore's law computers get more powerful every year. But when a company makes a computer that is twice as fast than the one it did two years, ago, the government counts it as if they produced two computers. This is why according the government statistics, from 2000 to 2010, the computer and electronics sector increased its real U.S. output over 5.17 times. Compare this with electrical equipment, which saw a decline of 12 percent.
>
> It is hard to believe that the U.S. computer and electronics sector is producing 5.17 times more in the United States than it was a decade ago, given

the fact that its employment declined by 43 percent and according the U.S. Census Bureau's the number of units of consumer electronic products shipped from U.S. factories actually fell by 70 percent.[12]

Less to Growth than Meets the Eye

In short, even without a supercomputer and an advanced degree in economics, if you look carefully at the US GDP data, you can see that there is less to reported economic growth than meets the eye. To itemize the squirrely truth about US GDP accounting:

- There are nontrivial questions about what should be included and left out. In general, the government answers those questions in ways that inflate growth.
- Totals are distorted by "hedonic" adjustment of output, particularly of computers. (Today's computer with twice the processing power of an older model is counted as two computers in national income accounts.)
- GDP is distorted by nonsense like tallying mere promises to pay pensions in the future as current wages.
- There is evidence of intentional distortion and dishonesty in reporting economic growth, famously characterized by Lyndon Johnson's instructions to the Commerce Department to "correct" growth estimates.

This brings us to another crucial methodological issue. A large and growing percentage of the GDP growth recorded in the official accounts is bogus in another sense: it is based entirely on government spending out of an empty pocket.

The Evanescence of Decay

A case could be made that even if increased government spending were financed entirely by drawing down a reserve fund (of which none exists), such spending of past surpluses should not be misconstrued as growth. This would be double counting of past income, as would be obvious if you put it in terms of an individual's income statement. Say you made $500,000 in one year and saved $100,000. Then, a year later, you earned nothing but spent the $100,000 that you had saved. It would be misleading to say that your total income over the two years was $600,000.

Equally, if you merely secured a loan for $100,000 in the second year, that would not make your income $600,000. Borrowing money and treating that as growth mistakes the nature of growth and overstates the actual vitality of the economy.

Houston commodity trader Randy Degner, no econometrician himself, has had some fun analyzing US GDP data. Degner strongly disputes the standard practice for Washington to spend borrowed money and treat that as growth. If you follow Degner's lead and subtract the annual government deficit from GDP data, you see that much apparent growth is only the statistical trail of revenue shortfalls, borrowing, in Morgan's terms, against the "energy economy of the future."

I took Degner's suggestion and ran through the numbers. I used third quarter nominal GDP for each year in this century—to avoid getting entangled in the government's fishy deflator calculations—and subtracted the year-over-year growth of the national debt.

As fiscal years end with the third quarter and the national debt is measured nominally, all the data were comparable. Degner seems to have made his calculations current through fiscal year 2010. Degner concludes in a 2011 article, "U.S. Economic Growth: GDP Minus the Federal Deficit—Doug Short," that since 1980, there have been fifteen years with negative GDP growth, and the average GDP growth has been -0.3 percent. His data show that, without deficit spending, the GDP has actually been negative since the Reagan administration.[13]

The politicians want to downplay the deficit, so they have perfected a bag of tricks to make a bad situation look better than it is. As I tallied the nominal GDP growth for fiscal year 2009 minus the year-over-year growth of the national debt, it was -15.79 percent (Degner reckoned it to be -12 percent). Fiscal years 2011, 2012, and 2014 were also all negative.

The only year of the Obama presidency to show even a smidgen of growth in this light is 2013, in which GDP was up by the invisibly meager rate of 0.07 percent. Ironically, that meager measure of growth was attributable to extraordinarily cold weather that spiked industrial production as demand for power soared during the early months of the year. Utility demand is counted as industrial production. More to Morgan's point, growth so far in the twenty-first century has been decidedly negative, as you would expect from the fact that the national debt has doubled since 2008.

Economy Contracted in Every Year of Obama's Rule?

Another strong exhibit hinting that the US economy has been declining is the Chapwood Index, a twice-annual private survey of the actual prices of 500 broadly consumed products that middle-class people buy. Calculations are compiled under the sponsorship of Chapwood Investments, LLC in the fifty largest US cities.[14] For 2014, inflation according to the Chapwood Index was 9.7 percent. As measured by the Ministry of Truth, inflation was only 0.8 percent, implying that the real economy contracted by 4.1 percent. When real GDP growth is calculated and the Chapwood Index is used to adjust for inflation, the economy has been contracting during every year of Obama's presidency. Revised real GDP is down by 21.4 percent since 2011.

Of course, one could question the validity of tracking an unchanging, non–seasonally adjusted basket of consumer purchases. Eventually, purchasing patterns do change with the array of options in the market. So the academic rationalizations for the various gimmicks the government employs to understate the decline in living standards are not wholly ridiculous. Equally, there are clearly items whose prices have cascaded far beyond recorded CPI increases. Here I think of health care costs, but especially tuitions.

Declining Energy Intensity Means Declining Economy

This also points to a correlation to which mainstream economists seem chronically oblivious: how tightly the growth of America's economy, if any, has been correlated with the use of energy and, therefore, what the pronounced falloff in energy conversion means to you.

The end of growth in energy inputs entails a declining surplus from which to support the overhead costs of complexity. As we have explored in depth, economic growth in the United States, as in all advanced economies, has dramatically decelerated since the 1970s. In his 2014 article, "The Beginning of the End of the Fossil Fuel Revolution (From Golden Goose to Cooked Goose)," Jeremy Grantham illustrated this as a function of decline in the value of the useful energy surplus available for exploitation. The quintupling in oil prices after 1999 drove a fifty-dollar-per-barrel swath of lower-value uses of oil out of business. This $50 per barrel loss amounts to about $1,000 per person, per year in the United States.[15] It's easy to believe that Americans have experienced at least that much economic loss.

Recent growth rates are far too low to permit government debt, pensions, and welfare commitments to be met. Equally alarming, Morgan suggests we are closer than most people care to admit to a *Mad Max* moment when the structure of law, bureaucracy, and antimarket subsidies—those that have proliferated on the back of hydrocarbon energy over the past century and three quarters—collapses.

In 1840, the Federal Budget Was $29 Million

When you look back to the early 1840s, when hydrocarbon energy inputs were minimal, you see that government spending was unbelievably tiny by today's standards. In those long forgotten days, the anthracite coal industry was just beginning in Eastern Pennsylvania. Total production in 1840 was just 2.5 million tons. Coal was mostly used by blacksmiths, brewers, and bakers. A few isolated households used coal for heating when they happened to live near surface outcroppings. The first railroad in the United States, the Baltimore and Ohio, began operation in 1830. But coal-powered locomotives only took hold in 1870. In earlier decades, coal played a bigger role in the production of iron for building locomotives and rails. By 1840, eleven small iron furnaces had begun using "rock coal" as anthracite was originally known to smelt iron. It was all rather basic. In 1840, there was no vast energy surplus for politicians to commandeer in order to buy votes.

In that year, the federal government spent only $29 million. Think about that. Of course, those "dollars" were worth a big multiple of the dollars in your wallet today. A credible estimate is that each 1840 dollar was worth $3,333 current dollars. On that basis, the federal spending of 1840 would have been worth $96.660 billion today—a small fraction (about 2.46 percent) of today's federal spending of over $3.9 trillion.

Of course, in 1840 there were no entitlements. No Social Security. No Medicare Part B. No food stamps. And US military spending was not greater than that of all other countries combined.

Also note that the federal government in 1840 operated with a 17 percent surplus of revenues over spending—with $5 million going toward retiring the national debt. This year's cash deficit is projected at $564 billion, "only" 16.8 percent of revenues and 14.5 percent of spending. Obviously, there was a vast change in government spending after hydrocarbon inputs in the economy began to surge.

Why Government Grew

Do you suppose that the vast difference between the tiny solvent government in 1840 and the gigantic bankrupt government of today can be explained by the emergence of better, more coherent arguments for big government in the decades after 1840? If so, what were those arguments that never occurred to the Founding Fathers? You could parse the history books in vain looking for them. It was much simpler than that. Hydrocarbon energy had more of a say than you did. It made work so much more productive that the Treasury filled up with money the politicians quickly squandered to buy votes.

Another metric for measuring the relative size of government in 1840 is the percentage of GDP it comprised. Of course, there was no BEA afoot in 1840 to establish an official, if "nearly worthless," calculation of GDP. Nonetheless, economic historians (with no incentive to "spin" the data) credibly estimate US GDP in 1840 at $1.574 billion. That would have put federal spending in 1840 at just 1.8 percent of GDP.

This glance in the rearview mirror highlights a problem looming in the future. I cannot imagine any deliberate orderly process by which big government could be shrunk to even 18 percent of GDP—ten times its percentage of 1840—no matter how drastically energy inputs recede. There is a "ratchet effect" as government grows that disables the economy from shifting successfully into reverse. A requirement for more than marginal retrenchment implies such high social stress that it would collapse the system.

Before hydrocarbon energy inputs surged, the United States was too poor to support a massive government. Spending by any measure you care to make was a bare chemical trace of today's budget.

A crucial aspect of the story is that the growth in real per capita income surged alongside energy inputs, and came to a halt when the increase in per capita energy consumption stalled at about 70 million BTUs per head. It has been fluctuating around that plateau since 1972–73 (and has lately slipped even lower). Perhaps not by coincidence, productivity growth has plunged since the early '70s when the real income of production workers stalled out. Note that energy inputs and consumption per dollar of GDP have been sliding dramatically and are now less than half what they were in the early '70s.

As we have explored, economic growth in the United States as in all advanced economies, has dramatically decelerated since the 1970s. As reported by the IMF, the rolling five-year average of economic growth of the OECD countries plunged from 4 percent as recently as 1988 to peter out in just a 1 percent stall after 2009. And as we've seen, even that is exaggerated.

Telltale Arithmetic

While there's a danger of approaching too close for comfort to the telltale arithmetic that exposes the nonviability of the system, consider that recent growth rates are far too low to permit government debt, pensions, and welfare commitments to be met. Historically, oil demand has grown at 75 percent of the trend rate of GDP growth. Extrapolating from past GDP trends implies a 23 percent increase in oil consumption from 2004 through 2013.

It didn't happen.

The long-established "normal" growth trend was independent of price. When oil prices rose sharply, with US oil consumption rising at 1.8 percent per year, the US oil consumption trend flipped. From July 2004 through July 2013, it turned negative to -1.5 percent per annum.

Hydrocarbon inputs in the US economy plunged after July 2004. Thereafter, oil supplies failed to go up in response to massive increases in CapEx outlays by oil companies. By the end of 2005, symptoms of the downward spiral of retrenchment had begun to show themselves. As energy inputs receded, so did economic activity.

By 2008, we were missing a quantity of oil production equal to the annual output of Saudi Arabia. The economy was oil-supply constrained.

"This Sucker Could Go Down"
Of course, you remember what happened in 2008. The bankruptcy of Lehman Brothers triggered a financial crisis that brought the whole world economy to the threshold of collapse. It was then, with his $800 billion bailout package facing resistance in Congress that then president George W. Bush made this telling declaration: "If money isn't loosened up, this sucker could go down." In the event, he got the bailout. Then, according to official sources, a recovery began in 2009 and everything has been getting better ever since.

Or has it?

"A Reality-Gap of 13 Million Jobs"
While Barack Obama was crowing about "10 million new jobs," the government's own data showed that over the six-and-a-half-year period after 2008, the number of employed Americans had fallen by more than three million, in spite of population growth.

But it gets worse. In 2015, Jeff Nielson of *Sprott Money* reported that the "10 million new jobs" lie, and the fact that 3 million jobs were lost, results in "a reality-gap of 13 million jobs, or exactly 2 million jobs per year." Nielson stated that the US economy has been losing roughly half a million jobs every year of the "fantasy-recovery."

The American economy, as conventionally mismeasured, was growing by around 3.8 percent in 2004 and total US energy use was about 100 quadrillion (quads) BTU. It has since fallen below ninety-five quads without recovering, while GDP growth, even as reported in the official propaganda, crawled along. Even if real GDP growth in 2004 was grossly overstated in official headline reports, real economic activity seems to have receded from that level.

Economic growth since the Industrial Revolution has been powered by fossil fuels. Lower energy consumption means a lower level of productivity and a shrinking economy.

Growing economies use more energy. Declining economies use less energy.

The Link between Oil Consumption and Income

US oil consumption per employed person has been decreasing at about 0.5 percent per year, along with the percentage of the population with jobs. Diminishing returns in energy production are equivalent to a fall in productivity. This cuts income for nonelite workers, leaving them with insufficient capacity to buy many end products the economy produces.

The result is a slowdown in growth that can be only temporarily masked by expanding debt. The conventional view attributes the decline in oil consumption per person employed to greater energy efficiency. Yes, we now have more fuel-efficient cars. Between 1973 and 2010, there was a 47 percent increase in auto mileage per gallon. But a closer look shows that is hardly the whole story of the plunge in gasoline consumption and declining mobility in the United States.

A Three-Decade Low in Fuel Use

According to the University of Michigan Transportation Research Institute (UMTRI), average fuel consumption by US drivers in 2013 dropped to the lowest level since UMTRI began measuring it in 1984. According to UMTRI researcher Michael Sivak, "Fuel consumption is lower than a generation ago and is some 14 to 19 percent less than peak levels in 2003–2004." As reported by Bill Visnic in a March 2015 *Forbes* article, despite an 8 percent growth in population, the absolute amount of fuel consumed by light-duty vehicles decreased by 11 percent between 2004 through 2013.[16]

This is an unvarnished hint of economic decline. Only a small portion, less than 20 percent, of the huge drop in gasoline consumption since 2004 is due to improved mileage efficiency within that time frame. The biggest reason for the plunge in driving is not a cultural shift, but a lack of income to support the cost of operating an automobile. Only about 18 percent of people without a car in the United States have full-time jobs. As the UMTRI reported in Visnic's article,

"The number of vehicles owned per person and household are at the lowest points since the 1990s. Same goes for miles driven per person, driver, household and vehicle."

When you think about it, it is clear why suddenly cheaper gasoline could not abruptly reverse the trend and reliquefy a busted middle class. For one thing, people without cars don't save money on lower gas prices.

Dramatically Diminishing Returns

For more perspective on the sharp deterioration in EROEI, consider the astonishing fact that CapEx productivity in oil production has fallen by a factor of five since 2000. And the fall is even more dramatic if you compare the rising cost of oil exploration and production (E&P CapEx) since 1999. E&P CapEx costs between 1985 and 1999 rose at an annual rate of 0.9 percent. Since 1999, however, E&P CapEx costs have been escalating a magnitude faster at 10.9 percent per annum.

The EROEI, as measured by barrels of conventional oil production, have fallen sharply. Between 1998 and 2005, total CapEx spending of $1.5 trillion added 8.6 million barrels per day of crude production. Since 2005, $4 trillion bought a one million barrel *decline* in conventional oil production.

Going Deep for Lower EROEI

For a clear look at consequences of rapidly deteriorating EROEI, consider this comparison between the number of wells and their depth between the United States, Russia, and Saudi Arabia, each with similar daily production:

- USA = 11.7 million barrels of oil per day, 35,669 wells, 297 million feet
- Russia = 10.9 million barrels of oil per day, 8,688 wells, 83 million feet
- Saudi Arabia = 11.4 million barrels of oil per day, 399 wells, 3 million feet

In other words, we have had to drill eighty-nine times more wells, covering ninety-nine times more feet of pipe, to produce about the same amount of oil as Saudi Arabia. That is evidence of diminishing returns, with a vengeance. It also vividly underscores what I have been telling you: we face ever-tightening biophysical constraints on growth. The slowdown in energy conversion in the economy can be expected to accelerate decline as the accumulated wealth of the past two centuries is dissipated.

Return to the Organic Economy?

You see what this means. The economy in this century of crisis is being forced back into the straightjacket of Soddy's solar energy income, mostly the energy we can scavenge from photosynthesis in plants and animals that ate plants. Of course, this will be augmented in some locales by hydropower and various photovoltaic technologies for converting sunlight directly into electricity. But before alternative energy can amount to much, there will be a transition period of generations during which the industrial base upon which the transition depends will undoubtedly collapse. There will be no seamless reset of the system based on new energy systems.

This also underscores the pernicious implications of the trumped up anathema on carbon dioxide. If the UN carbon budget is enforced through mandatory limits, it could result in up to 85 percent of known reserves of fossil fuels being barred from use. To the extent that the modern economy is a surplus energy equation, as I argue it is, the result of the war on fossil fuels is likely to be an economic collapse.

The Breaking Point will tell across the whole spectrum of the modern economy as Jevons and Soddy hinted and Morgan proclaims. Already, the consequences for growth have been devastating. As David Stockman explained in a June 2015 *Contra Corner* article, since the conventionally measured pre-crash peak in December 2007, there has been a sharp deceleration in private sector wages and salary growth. According to Stockman, the United States now has a 1 percent growth economy (one-third its historic trend).[17] Meanwhile, the debt incurred to finance federal spending, which does not pay its way, has grown at a 10.24 percent compound rate since 2007. It doesn't take a divine genius to realize the situation is unsustainable when the shadow economy of debt is multiplying more than ten times faster than the real economy grows.

Indeed, by the time an economy growing at 1 percent, if that, could double, debt ballooning at a 10.24 percent annual rate would have expanded eight times over, without even counting the effect of compounding interest. This would bring the US government's debt to GDP ratio to a crushing 812 percent—far beyond the threshold of bankruptcy. Even if average interest rates paid on the debt remained frozen at today's minimal rate of about 2.5 percent, that would imply annual interest payments of $3.6 trillion.

Such is the doom-laden arithmetic of government finances. The debt that I imagine compounding at a 10.24 percent rate would undoubtedly compound at an accelerating rate going forward as the real economy weakens and the authorities try more desperately to stimulate the dying industrial world back to life. Unfortunately, it can't be done. The notional wealth that can be created by the promiscuous creation of fiduciary credit, or "fictitious capital," tends to rapidly vanish as capital markets react to and devalue malinvestment.

Little Remaining Margin of Income to Plunder
With US government spending having recently soared above 70 percent of wages and proprietors income 30 percent higher than in World War II, there is little scope to curtail debt by raising taxes.

The reserve capacity of the system is spent.

Losing the "Red Queen's Race"
With debt and entitlements growing by leaps and bounds, you can readily see why economies lack a reverse gear. They cannot

decline as smoothly as they advance, because the status quo has been built to assume exponentially increasing obligations from year to year. We require ever-greater sums to meet servicing obligations on a soaring debt and rapidly expanding welfare payments (because real incomes are falling for nonelite workers).

Recall Alice's discovery, courtesy of the Red Queen, in *Through the Looking Glass*, that the system must go faster and faster to stay in the same place. ("Now here, you see, it takes all the running you can do, to keep in the same place. If you want to get somewhere else, you must run at least twice as fast as that!")[18] In an economy plagued with diminishing returns, the de facto requirement to go faster and faster to avoid losing the "Red Queen's Race" underscores the high probability of collapse. With the disappearance of cheap to extract energy resources, we are headed for the Breaking Point.

Energy Shortfall Takes Marginal Players Out of the Game

Again, the primary manifestation of "peak oil" is not in soaring prices for the oil itself but in the flat-lining of economic growth among the advanced economies whose average consumers have been unable to grow their incomes in the absence of a continuing surge of affordable oil supplies. After Richard Nixon imposed pure fiat money on the world, launching history's great borrowing binge, GDP growth slowed, and income for average men in the United States began to decline. Those millions of average men could stay in the game only by sending their wives to work and then by borrowing. Because polygamy was out of the question, when their credit ran out, as it did for millions in the first decade of this century, the game stopped in a crisis of defaulted subprime mortgages that almost collapsed the world economy.

That is what happened in the run-up to the 2007–8 crisis, and something analogous has been happening more recently in Greece. As of May 2015, some sixty Greek businesses were closed and 613 jobs were lost for each business day of the year. According to data from the Hellenic Confederation of Commerce and Entrepreneurship, Greek retail sales had fallen by 70 percent.[19]

The "repossession" of the middle class lifestyle from marginal players in "advanced countries" as well as marginal countries has just begun. In that respect, the fall in oil prices that began in 2014 has ominous implications.

The Downward Ratchet

You can see the dynamic by which "lack of demand creates over time lack of supply" in the business headlines. The lead story in the July 27, 2015, issue of *The Financial Times* said it all: "Energy groups postpone $200 BN in projects as oil price slumps again: Wider commodities route hits spending plans; BP, Shell and Chevron among those cutting costs."[20] The story goes on to detail how the "plunge in crude prices since last summer has resulted in the deferral of 46 big oil and gas projects with 20 bn barrels of oil equivalent in reserves— more than Mexico's entire proven holdings—according to consultancy Wood Mackinsey . . . The upstream industry is winding back its investment in big pre-final investment decision developments as fast as it can." It added that the number of large upstream projects to be fully approved during 2015 could probably be "counted on one hand."

This plunge in exploration and production CapEx clarifies how the store of resources to meet future hydrocarbon demand was being curtailed by insufficient demand at high prices in 2014–15—a development that amplifies a dynamic that has been building ever since the post war surge of energy inputs stalled with the tripling of the oil price in 1973. The "downward ratchet" effect curtailing growth has intensified over time as EROEI fell, resulting in the Great Slowdown of the twenty-first century.

"US Wages Have Fallen EVERY Quarter of the 'Recovery'"

Part of the reason it has intensified, I believe, is that the declining energy intensity of measured GDP growth involves a growing percentage of statistical "fluff" that exaggerates growth in national income accounting. To put it another way, the growing financialization of the economy may add to GDP as currently measured, but it does not propel the same increase in demand associated with GDP growth as previously constituted. Most of the gains from financialization, as amplified by the creation of trillions in "fictitious capital" out of thin air through quantitative easing, accrued to the already wealthy. So while those on the upper rungs of the income distribution have gained trillions, **median household income in the United States fell by 4.6 percent from 2008 to 2014.** This contributed to the downward ratchet effect as declining demand increased the constraints on future growth by curtailing capital outlays for developing oil and gas prospects. Sprott Money, one of Canada's leading investment analyst and precious metals dealers, claims that "US wages have fallen EVERY quarter of the 'recovery.'"[21]

This is common to all "advanced" economies that are being pinched by a decline in cheap-to-extract hydrocarbon energy. Italy has experienced a 36 percent decline in oil consumption over the past decades. Courtesy of Mariana Mazzucato, we learn that "Mario Pianta has shown in his recent book *Nove su Dieci* (Nine Out of Ten: Why We Are Almost All Worse Off Than 10 Years Ago) the average salary of Italian workers has fallen by .1% every year for two decades." That type of accounting exercise would show similar declines in almost every "advanced" economy.

Given the downward ratchet effect on oil exploration and production (E&P) capital outlays, therefore, you can expect a further slowdown in world energy production per capita, which as we have seen, has been closely correlated to real US GDP growth.

Looming Ahead: Deflationary Collapse

Oil is merely the most prominent of many crucial commodities whose prices have plunged because they are too expensive to produce and because the Chinese credit bubble stimulated artificial demand on a massive scale—which provoked growth of expensive supply—and then fell away again.

For example, iron ore plunged from a 2011 peak of $190 per ton to a 2015 low of $44.59. And copper has plunged to multiyear lows. The same is true of aluminum, lead, nickel, and zinc. Prices of all the industrial metals were plunging in the summer of 2015, providing another strong hint that we are not witnessing an accelerating recovery. If the price of oil and other commodities fall far enough, of course, they will again become temporarily affordable. But when the current deflationary spiral began, they were not.

The process of ricocheting between deflationary slumps in commodity prices and episodes of partial recovery in which tepid economic activity resumes, supported by unprecedented amounts of fictitious capital conjured out of thin air, will probably cycle at greater amplitude as the system evolves toward collapse. Contrary to headline economic reports, the end of economic growth is happening now.

The Cycle of Retrenchment

Think about it. The S&L collapse of the early '90s opened the door for the Bill Clinton presidency late in the term of George H. W. Bush. Then eight years later, after the dot-com bubble burst, George W. Bush spent two terms in the White House, culminating in the mortgage collapse that paved the way for Obama. I rather expect a deep downturn to trigger the Breaking Point in the wake of the Obama presidency.

To date, the only apparent expedient for recovery from bubbles caused by runaway credit expansion is yet another round of credit expansion that involves shoveling gargantuan quantities of fictitious capital to the already wealthy. Not surprisingly, this has yet to work.

Now you face the end of another bubble. The signs are there if your eyes are open. Subprime debt has collapsed, as I forecast in 2014. Commodity prices are plunging. Notwithstanding government statistical fiddles to turn GDP positive, the broader, but long neglected, GNP contracted in Q1 2015 by 0.15 percent. The market has been choppy. No matter what the government does, it is not pushing stocks up. It's only a matter of time until the big fall. Unfortunately, contemporary economists have little to tell us about the declining state beyond what Adam Smith said. If we want to know more about the declining state, other than that it is "melancholy," we have to think it through ourselves.

Your homework assignment, if you care to do it, is to map out your personal survival kit. Put on your thinking cap and try to imagine how the declining economy will affect your well-being: your investments, your livelihood, and your family. I trust that this book has given you a good head start on that exercise. You certainly will not get much help from conventional information sources.

Most of the great and good economists whose names you know from the news are totally in thrall to the status quo. That is why they all failed to anticipate the mortgage crisis, or almost any other development that mattered over the past half century. They are particularly bound in fealty to the notion that creating fiduciary credit, or fiat money conjured out of thin air, is the culmination of human economic ingenuity. The only job of the establishment economists is to rationalize the status quo and help politicians confuse and mollify you.

Whatever you do, don't confuse yourself by imagining that you have nothing to worry about because the retrograde economy is not officially acknowledged. Only mavericks are telling you that the boilers are cold and the ship of state is drifting toward the shoals of collapse.

But the fact that the established economists have shied away from thinking, much less writing, about the retrograde economy does not mean you have nothing to worry about. They did not forewarn you about the mortgage collapse, either. The fact that they were silent offered no protection against the trillions of dollars in losses suffered in 2008 and since.

It's about Energy

The living mainstream economists have been mum about the importance of the collapse of EROEI on prosperity, but not everyone shares their reticence. There may have been nothing in the *Journal of Applied Econometrics* to help you understand why prosperity was falling away, but[22] Mel Gibson was willing to shout it out in a 1995 interview with *Playboy*: "It's about energy. It didn't spare anyone."[23]

Gibson earned his education in economics as a twenty-one-year-old Sydney drama student cast to play the lead role in *Mad Max*, a low-budget 1979 dystopian film about life after growth in the Australian outback. *Mad Max* was the brainchild of Sydney physician and movie producer George Miller, abetted by economist and film buff James McCausland.

McCausland was an early convert to the peak oil hypothesis of M. King Hubbert. In 1956, Hubbert predicted that US conventional oil production would peak in about fifteen years. In 1971, his prediction came true. He further predicted that world oil output would peak early in the twenty-first century, sometime around now.

Both Miller and McCausland were impressed by the disruptions and strains arising from the 1973 oil crisis. When the price of oil jumped from three dollars per barrel to almost twelve dollars, Australia's car-centric culture went into shock. The *Mad Max* creators drew on that experience to imagine how a long-term and deeper depletion of energy might be felt. Instead of an abstract treatise, they produced a high-voltage action film. They used their cinematic imaginations to help people understand the potential impact of the loss of energy inputs on an apparently fragile civilization. They certainly made more money and had more fun that they would have enjoyed preparing an academic study for the *Journal of Applied Econometrics*.

Mad Max cost just $350,000 to make, and it grossed $100 million worldwide. (It was for some time considered the most profitable movie ever made.) It was then followed by two somewhat higher-budget sequels: *Mad Max II: The Road Warrior* and *Mad Max Beyond Thunderdome*. A much higher-budget sequel, *Mad Max: Fury Road*, was released in 2015.

Imagine yourself as a bit player in the collapse to come in a variation on a *Mad Max* movie. Imagine yourself in any formerly rich, collapsing economy with critical resource shortages. If you have been a tourist in this postapocalyptic landscape, courtesy of your local cinema or via DVD, you will recall how the desperados and marauders manage to secure enough gasoline to indulge their high-octane hobby of road racing. In fact, they use gasoline as money.

Of course, this is fiction. But there is realism in the presumption that even when critical resource shortages pinch growth enough to throw the economy into a downward spiral of retrenchment—and even after total financial, industrial, commercial, political, and social collapse—there will still be residual supplies to be had from reworking abandoned refineries in Gas Town, enough to keep some people's V-8 engines revved up for generations of sequels after the Breaking Point. Hence the notion right out of *Mad Max* that gasoline distribution is likely to evolve into the hands of outlaw motorcycle gangs: in the future, instead of going to Shell or ExxonMobil, you may have to turn to Hell's Angels for the fuel to operate your car.

And we learn from *Mad Max Beyond Thunderdome* that even when the marauders destroy the last oil refinery in the outback, there will still be enough methane gas in Bartertown to power chainsaws for gladiatorial combat. Some tough cookie like Tina Turner's character, Aunty Entity, will make alternative fuel using slave labor in her Underground pig farm. But unlike the pious hopes of alternative energy shills, brewing methane gas in the Underground won't necessarily make the world a peaceful place, much less prosperous. Once prosperity collapses due to an unavailability of sufficiently cheap net energy, there is no easy path back.

The mainstream economists will tell you nothing about the declining/retrograde economy. But George Miller is in a higher pay grade than any mainstream economist. As of this writing, *Mad Max Fury Road*, in which the depletion theme in a parched world has been widened to include the lack of fresh water, has grossed $373 million worldwide, a sum that will loom even larger after the coming deflationary collapse.

Miller knows a good story when he sees one about strong, silent men (and women) obliged to battle leather-clad gangs for gasoline (and fresh water) in a postapocalyptic wasteland. All of which leads to a question: Will the coming deflationary collapse be as grim as that depicted in the *Mad Max* films?

I doubt it. For one thing, the liquidity deficit won't be felt only in an uninhabitable desert. Another reason is that part of the premise of the *Mad Max* series is that the collapse of urban civilization has been accelerated by nuclear war.

Peter J. Taylor has identified the Thirty Years' War as an important milestone of transitions of power in the world system. He writes: "As well as being on the winning side, the hegemon has a 'good war' economically. This is the case with the Dutch during the Thirty Years War, and it also fits the British during the Napoleonic war and the Americans during World Wars I and II."[24] Obviously, the patterns of the past are based on conventional conflict.

Notwithstanding the fact that war has been a common feature of the terminal crises of hegemony, it is possible to imagine collapse without a nuclear war. Indeed, given the easily imagined prospect of annihilation, one has to hope that collapse could proceed in a more ordered and less devastating way that does not entail humanity being all but extinguished by the widespread detonation of nuclear weapons.

Yes, I agree, hope is a flimsy strategy for avoiding a destructive war.

Yet the postcollapse world of Mad Max—where Sydney, as seen in *Beyond Thunderdome*, is a ghostly carcass of ruined skyscrapers—is not the only outcome you could expect from even a full-fledged collapse sequence. With better weather, and a splash of rain, your options in the declining state would not necessarily come down to a choice between joining Hell's Angels and morphing into a fifteenth-century peasant.

There will certainly be a crisis surrounding Tim Morgan's undeniably logical conclusion about the fate of a huge excess of claims that cannot be met by the real economy. As he states, "The only solution to this mismatch is the destruction of the value of money and debt on an unprecedentedly vast scale." Put simply: a collapse.

Notes

1 http://fskrealityguide.blogspot.com/2010/07/real-gdp-is-crashing-2000-2009.html.

2 http://www.wri.org/blog/2013/08/majority-china%E2%80%99s-proposed-coal-fired-power-plants-located-water-stressed-regions.

3 Durden, Tyler, "The Latest Contribution to US GDP: Promises . . . No Really," *Zero Hedge*, May 6, 2013.

4 Williams, John, *Shadow Government Statistics*, commentary number 740.

5 Holz, Carsten, "Here Be Dragons? China's Economic Data May Not Be All Bad," http://theconversation.com/here-be-dragons-chinas

-economic-data-may-not-be-all-bad-23047.

6 "Foreign-Based Companies Investing in the U.S. Auto Industry," Office of Aerospace and Automotive Industries International Trade Administration U.S. Department of Commerce, August 2007.

7 Williams, John, "Government Economic Reports: Things You've Suspected but Were Afraid to Ask!," *Shadow Government Statistics*, October 6, 2004.

8 Bruder, Jessica, "The End of Retirement: When You Can't Afford to Stop Working," *Harper's,* August 2014, 29.

9 https://www.scribd.com/document/222414663/Declining-Business-Dynamism-Hathaway-Litan.

10 http://www.aecf.org/blog/17-million-more-children-live-in-low-income-working-families-today-than-in/.

11 http://www.industryweek.com/global-economy/why-2000s-were-lost-decade-american-manufacturing.

12 http://www.huffingtonpost.com/robert-d-atkinson-phd/worse-than-the-great-depr_b_1368219.html.

13 Degner, Randy, "U.S. Economic Growth: GDP Minus the Federal Deficit Doug Short," http://www.advisorperspectives.com/commentaries/dshort_42811.php.

14 http://www.chapwoodindex.com.

15 Grantham, Jeremy, "The Beginning of the End of the Fossil Fuel Revolution (From Golden Goose to Cooked Goose)," *GMO Quarterly Letter,* Third Quarter 2014, 14.

16 Visnic, Bill, "Worrying Sign for Automakers: Americans Burning Least Amount of Gasoline a Generation," *Forbes*, March 25, 2015.

17 Ibid.

18 Carroll, Lewis, *Through the Looking-Glass and What Alice Found There*, chapter 2, https://www.gutenberg.org/files/12/12-h/12-h.htm.

19 http://www.ekathimerini.com/199997/article/ekathimerini/business/retailers-see-turnover-fall-by-up-to-70-pct.

20 http://www.ft.com/cms/s/d6877d5e-31ee-11e5-91ac-a5e17d9b4cff.

21 https://www.sprottmoney.com/blog/us-wages-have-fallen-every-quarter-of-the-recovery-jeff-nielson.html.

22 Tilly, Charles, "War Making and State Making as Organized Crime," in *Bringing the State Back In*, ed. Peter B. Evans et al. (Cambridge: Cambridge University Press, 1985), 169.

23 *Playboy* 42, no. 7 (July 1995), 51.

24 Taylor, Peter J., *The Way the Modern World Works: World Hegemony to World Impasse* (Chichester: John Wiley & Sons, 1996), 4.

Chapter Nineteen

Black Swans on the Horizon

The Accelerating Collapse of the Status Quo

Globalization creates interlocking fragility, while reducing volatility and giving the appearance of stability. In other words it creates devastating Black Swans. We have never lived before under the threat of a global collapse.

—Nassim Nicholas Taleb, *The Black Swan: The Impact of the Highly Improbable*

"Peasants Vote to Leave the Feudal Manor"

Unless you have been doing a Rip Van Winkle somewhere, you know by now that voters in the United Kingdom decided by a margin of about 52 percent to 48 percent to secede from the European Union on June 23, 2016. John Bolton, a former George W. Bush aide, quipped that the "peasants had voted to leave the manor." This act of insubordination hit world markets like an earthquake. Aftershocks rattled the foundations of the status quo. According to Bloomberg, $4 trillion in paper wealth vaporized on world stocks in the two trading days immediately following the vote. Most of those dramatic stock market losses were subsequently retraced, in the wake of central bank intervention and jawboning that helped spike an epic short squeeze, the biggest since the 2008 financial crisis.

On the other hand, the impact of the British vote, known under the shorthand of "Brexit," looks to have been more enduring effects in the bond and currency markets—enough to qualify Brexit as a world-changing Black Swan event as defined by Nassim Nicholas Taleb.

Currencies seem to have experienced a dramatic realignment, particularly the British pound. This, in turn, had carry-on consequences. For one thing, tourism to the United Kingdom surged as the weaker pound made travel in Britain more affordable. For another, Eleanor of Acquitaine's dowry fattened the coffers of Bordeaux wine-makers. As you may know if you are a wine snob or a medieval history buff, the Bordeaux region became a personal fiefdom of the English king, Henry II, when he married Eleanor of Aquitaine in 1152. From that point forward, England became a major market for Bordeaux wines. Many Bordeaux brands have traditionally been marketed from bonded warehouses in the United Kingdom and priced in pounds sterling. The plunge in the pound after Brexit stimulated a surge in orders with London wine merchants. BI, one of the foremost wine merchants in the world (sponsors of BI LiveTrade, the "only 2-way market-making screen for buying and selling top Bordeaux"), reported, "We literally had to close our screens at the moment of Brexit."[1] In an environment where many central banks have been angling to reduce the exchange value of their currency, Brexit produced an immediate eighteen-standard-deviation devaluation of the pound sterling. I joked that the Japanese should announce their intention to withdraw from the European Union.

Of course, that was a joke. But it appears likely that the Chinese could take advantage of the tumult associated with Brexit to permit a larger devaluation of the yuan. This could confound the efforts of the central banks of "advanced economies" to notch inflation higher and devalue their own currencies. A lower yuan would help China export its deflation to the West, as it faces what hedge fund superstar Kyle Bass calls "the largest macro imbalance in history"—an epic asset/liability mismatch (bad debt) equivalent to 10 percent of GDP.[2]

Compare this with gap of 2.5 percent in the United States during the 2008 financial crisis. As the Chinese authorities seek to fend off a 1929-style depression by caulking the cracks in China's $22 trillion edifice of "social financing" with still more credit, their effort to "buy time" is likely to translate into lower imported inflation in the West, as well as a stronger US dollar, implying a still more deflationary environment.

The blowback from Brexit in the bond markets testified to significant cross asset stress. The ten-year German bonds gapped higher in a larger move than that experienced on any day in 2008. Global bonds rose in price, as yields on sovereign debt traded to all-time lows, with $11.7 trillion in sovereign issues sporting negative yields. Swiss yields turned negative fifty years out, trading as low as -2.7 basis points.

Ever-lower interest rates imply ever-wider financial fallout.

For example, over $500 trillion in global derivatives trade based on bond yields. This may be one reason that the stocks of big banks and other financial firms with large derivative books did not participate as much as other sectors in the central bank-engineered stock rally that followed two days of waterfall selling in the wake of Brexit.

The fine print on the stock pages in the wake of Brexit offers another important "tell" on the world after Brexit. As noted by Gillian Tett in the *Financial Times*, a surprise among the worst performing stocks in the first trading days after Brexit was MetLife (MET NYSE), down 14 percent.[3] MetLife plunged not because it expected a drop in policy business in the United Kingdom. It has none. MetLife plunged because, as an insurance company already suffering from "Financial Repression" (or martial law for money), it was faced with a higher prospect of suffocation as Brexit deepened deflation expectations. With $11.7 trillion in sovereign issues sporting negative yields, the prospect of still lower long-term bond yields promises nothing but woe for insurance companies that have come to rely on income from long-term bonds for funding their policy liabilities. This challenge has gotten serious, according to *Bloomberg*, as North American insurance companies have experienced a plunge in their bond investment income back to 2011 levels. Insurers such as Prudential Financial and MetLife find themselves holding $132 billion of bonds either in or close to default. Most of these now distressed bonds, by the way, were "investment-grade bonds from energy drillers and retailers that ended up heading south."[4]

Note that in the ex-growth world of the twenty-first century, there will be a strong tendency for any Black Swan event to have deflationary repercussions. Why? Because governments have chosen to disguise the failure of growth with credit spun out of thin air. Almost any disruption will tend to jeopardize the ever-more fragile architecture of unpayable debt upon which the status quo depends. The logical consequence of an ex-growth economy is difficulty in meeting interest payments on outstanding debt. This was underscored in the wake of Brexit by the collapsing prices of European bank stock. Monte dei Paschi, the world's oldest bank, grabbed the headlines when it was warned by the European Central Bank that it needs to shed another €10 billion in nonperforming loans.

The Black Swan

More on the deflationary risk below, but shifting focus slightly, you might like to better understand why an innocent water bird, the *Cygnus atratus* is being widely associated with economic collapse. Here is the backstory.

Consider that the black swan has been emblematic of something improbable or vanishingly rare since the first century when the Roman poet Juvenal wrote about "a rare bird in the land, like a black swan." At the time, and for another fifteen centuries, it was taken for granted that the black swan did not exist.

That changed in 1697, when Dutch explorer Willem Hesselzoon de Vlamingh van Oost Vlieland (otherwise falsely credited for naming "Rats Nest Island") sailed into what is now the Swan River in Western Australia (then known as "New Holland") and found a number of large black swans, three of which he captured and carried away with him.

The Black Swan Asymmetry: Verifiability and Falsifiability

Black swans came to illustrate a shortcoming of inductive reasoning—namely, that even with a very large sample size, you cannot leap from particular observations to reach a valid conclusion (consequent) that generalizes from those observations (antecedents). The white swan/black swan example perfectly illustrates that.

Before the seventeenth century, when all swans were thought to be white, you could have seen every swan there was to see for a millennium and a half and apparently concluded without mistake that all swans were white. But this would still have been an abuse of logic, as a tally of white swans can never mount so high as to disprove the existence of black swans. But once a single black swan was discovered, the idea that all swans are white was forever falsified.

The philosopher of science, Karl Popper, analyzed this asymmetry that plagues exercises in probabilistic statistics. He made that a crucial factor in his doctrine of falsifiability in *The Logic of Scientific Discovery*: "My proposal is based upon an asymmetry between verifiability and falsifiability; an asymmetry which results from the logical form of universal statements. For these are never derivable from singular statements, but can be contradicted by singular statements"[5]

Hence the black swan is the exception that disproves the rule. That is why the Black Swan (in caps) has become an important metaphor for the risks inherent in trying to infer universal conclusions from particular data.

The Black Swan has been immortalized as the poster child for the "highly improbable events" that mathematician and hedge fund philosopher, Nassim Nicholas Taleb, has identified as likely to dominate history. Recall how this expressed itself in the innumerable "white swan sightings" that preceded the subprime mortgage crisis that brought the world economy to the brink of collapse in 2008.

At that time, the record of recent history offered no examples of large clusters of Americans defaulting on their mortgages. Equally, experts testified that housing prices always went up. And for those silly enough to appraise risk in the mortgage market without taking Taleb's care in considering the role of Black Swans, the data must have seemed convincing. From Alan Greenspan's swearing in as chairman of the Federal Reserve Board in August 1987, through the peak of the housing bubble in 2007, residential real estate in the United States soared from a value of $5.5 trillion to $22.5 trillion—a fourfold appreciation.

The white swans in view were all beautiful. No one among the bankers worried about the Black Swans that they couldn't yet see—until those Black Swans landed on Wall Street. But Taleb was attuned to the danger. He famously proclaimed, "I know that history is going to be dominated by an improbable event, I just don't know what that event will be."[6]

The Improbable Happens

In Brexit, you have witnessed another "improbable event" with the potential to dominate history. In a development that heralds the unraveling of the status quo globally, the United Kingdom voted on June 23, 2016, in a referendum to leave the European Union. As Taleb suggests in the comment quoted at the top of this chapter, "Globalization creates interlocking fragility, while reducing volatility and giving the appearance of stability. In other words it creates devastating Black Swans. We have never lived before under the threat of a global collapse."

You do now. A strong hint of the "interlocking fragility" that characterizes global finance was provided by the *Bloomberg* screens blinking red as the realization that "Brexit" would win dawned on previously complacent investors around the world. An abridged summary of the financial pandemonium occurring forty-eight hours after the vote:

- British pound falls as much as 11 percent to $1.3229—a three decade low and its greatest one-day loss in history—off an incredible eighteen standard deviations. Earlier that day (Thursday, June 23) the pound sterling traded at just under $1.49.
- Implied volatility on the pound/dollar trade reaches twice that seen in the Lehman collapse.
- Japan's Topix index leads Asian stock losses, down more than 7 percent, as the Japanese yen soars to a multiyear high.
- The Australian dollar loses 3 per cent to 73.8 US cents, as Australian stocks shed $50 billion.
- FTSE 100 Index futures tumble 9 percent; contracts on Euro Stoxx 50 slide 11 percent.
- Italian stocks (FTSE MIB) fall by 12.5 percent.
- Spanish stocks (IBEX 35) plunge 12.3 percent.
- S&P 500 Index futures are limit-down overnight; the DOW falls 900 points post-Brexit.
- Brazil's Bovespa stock index falls 2.8 percent.
- Yield on ten-year US Treasuries drops 29 basis points to 1.46 percent, the biggest daily decline since 2009.
- Big banks trading in Asia post double-digit losses overnight.
- The euro's fall overnight is its worst ever.
- Commodities (apart from precious metals) plunge as the US dollar soars.
- New York crude oil retreats 5.1 percent to $47.56 a barrel, poised for biggest loss since February 2016.

- Gold rallies as much as 8.1 percent to $1,358.54 an ounce, highest since March 2014.
- Poland's zloty drops by the most since 1993.
- The South African rand tumbles as much as 8 percent to the dollar, joining the sharp sell-off on world market.
- China devalues the yuan the most since the August crash, as Premier Li Keqiang warns "a disillusioned British butterfly flapped its wings and the entire global financial system could collapse."[7]

Tallying the Losses

I confess that I lack the patience to undertake the long-running exercise in forensic accounting needed to comprehensively quantify the losses in paper wealth occasioned by Brexit. But I am happy to credit *Bloomberg*'s handy estimate that some $4 trillion in shareholder wealth vanished in the first two trading days after Brexit. Here are some other approximations to help you put the pandemonium in perspective.

Bloomberg calculated that the overnight market movements after Brexit cost the world's 400 richest people $127 billion. And I did some admittedly back-of-the-envelope exercises to tally other aspects of the market backwash from Brexit. Take the 11 percent drop in the value of the pound. It implied a loss of £172,004 million based on the reported size of the British M2 Money Supply. In other words, £172 billion vaporized in one night—about a quarter of a trillion dollars measured against of the Thursday, June 23, high price for the pound sterling.

Of course, these calculations call out for multiple updates, as initial price movements stand to be reversed (or amplified) by subsequent market movements. For example, the first day of Brexit wiped £200 billion (about $273 billion) off the value of British stocks. Bank stocks were particularly hard hit (Barclay's down 20.5 percent, with Royal Bank of Scotland plunging 27.5 percent), and they continued to weaken in subsequent trading sessions.

Shortly before the vote, one of the United Kingdom's wealthiest billionaires, Peter Hargreaves expressed confidence that leaving the EU would be good for British business in the long run. He said it would get British "butts in gear." In an interview with *Bloomberg*, Hargreaves observed, "I have more money in the stock market than any other person in the UK. I have £2 billion in the UK stock market. No one has anything like that. Do you think I would be intent on leaving if I thought that was going to endanger my wealth?"

Evidently, Hargreaves was not day-trading his £2 billion portfolio, but hoping to optimize its value over the long run. After the relief rally in stocks, Hargreaves big bet must look better than it did after the Brexit votes were tallied.

Why Global Pandemonium?

You might well ask yourself why a decision by British voters to back out of the European Union triggered trillions in losses in apparently unrelated markets. Why do stocks in Shanghai, Tokyo, and Sao Paulo plunge when the United Kingdom exits the European Union? Why should the UK vote pull billions from the pockets of holders of the South African rand? And why should the Chinese yuan plunge with the pound and the euro? Why indeed?

The Gag Is Up

The simplest answer is that Brexit hints that "the gag is up." It says that the well-worn tricks of the establishment—bribes, propaganda, fear, and, yes, false flag dirty tricks—are no longer dependable recipes for bending the public to the will of the crony capitalist oligarchs. This has obvious consequences. It means that the status quo is shot. Kaput. Now it is only a matter of time—probably not long—until the crony capitalists lose control and the central bankers are sent packing.

In other words, Brexit implies the end of the global system in which "fictitious capital" is promiscuously created by central banks to inflate the value of investment assets like stocks and real estate for the benefit of speculators—while the majority suffers with a real economy that is starved for capital. It means that the prospects for stock markets around the world will no longer be levitated far above the prospects of companies in the real economy by quantitative easing. More on that below.

Jo Cox and the Tragedy of Brexit

Before I delve further into the dark magic of monetary policy, I need to say that for me the real tragedy of Brexit was not the trillions of fiat dollars in market losses but the assassination of Helen Joanne "Jo" Cox, (Labour) Member of Parliament for Batley and Spen, who was brutally murdered on June 16, 2016, at the age of forty-one as she campaigned for the "Remain in the EU" referendum.

Mrs. Cox, unlike so many of her fellow politicians, seen from a distance, seemed to be an admirable character. She was good looking and exceedingly intelligent (she made it through Cambridge as the equivalent of a scholarship student—the first member of her family to earn a college degree—while working odd jobs in a toothpaste factory). She was the mother of two young children, ages three and five, and she was a former leader of the international humanitarian charity Oxfam. Both inside and outside of Parliament, Jo Cox campaigned tirelessly for refugees and the downtrodden victims of the world. You would have been hard-pressed to identify another member of Parliament who would have been such a sympathetic figure to assassinate.

And that's where the tragedy lies. While I can't prove it, I can't shake the feeling that Jo Cox was sacrificed for nothing in an unsuccessful ploy by manipulators to change the public mood a week before the vote when polls showed Brexit gaining support.

In the days immediately following her death, I suspected that this despicable act might actually have worked to push the Remain vote to victory. Even Nigel Farage, head of the UK Independence Party, lamented, "We had momentum until this terrible tragedy."[8] Still, after a brief deflection of the momentum in favor of Brexit, the Leave campaign refound its footing, and even Cox's own constituency voted 55 percent to 45 percent to quit the EU. The manipulators did not realize how weak their position had become. Had they understood the unpopularity of the status quo, they might not have shot Jo Cox, because sadly, she died for nothing.

Martin Armstrong, the renowned economist, drew the connection that must have occurred to many when news of Jo Cox's murder crossed the wires: "There is disturbing opinion circulating that Jo Cox may have been assassinated to prevent a BREXIT vote. Many are starting to believe there is a conspiracy plot connecting the dots to ensure a sympathy vote to remain within the EU. People are pointing to the familiar tool of assassination often used to achieve political agendas." Armstrong summarized that for the powers-that-be, "there's too much at stake to allow Brexit."[9]

Whether the powers-that-be murdered her or not is unlikely ever to be known or publically acknowledged. All that can be confidently established is that she was assassinated at a time when the powers-that-be apparently had the maximum incentive to orchestrate a false flag dirty trick.

In case you don't know Armstrong, he is known for his theory that boom-bust cycles recur once every 3,141 days, or 8.6 years. (That is the number pi—approximately 3.14159 times 1,000.) Armstrong is also heralded for having become a self-made millionaire at the age of fifteen.

When Greed Turns Deadly

Armstrong's cynical view of the establishment was no doubt burnished by the many years he spent in prison for contempt of court on what he considered to be trumped up charges. If you are a well-bred person of good will, you may recoil from the notion that the usual suspects among the powers-that-be could be implicated in murder to influence an election result. That is totally contrary to the underlying assumptions of civilized, democratic society. A depressing thought, to be sure, but it should hardly be a shock. The establishment has often revealed itself to be without scruples.

I say that without pretending to understand the full ugliness of the covert chain of command by which the decision to kill Jo Cox could have been put into action. I have no idea how they can come up with the warped killer Thomas Mair, who has been charged with assassinating Cox. But I am equally sure that the inquest into her death will not come close to illuminating any "trade secrets" of covert action that could pin the blame on Mair's handlers, much less on the evil calculus that set the crime in motion. They won't investigate themselves.

The story, for now, is that Mair was a mentally ill British nationalist with ties to pro-Apartheid and neo-Nazi groups. Witnesses who saw the murder say they heard Mair scream something to the effect of "put Britain first" before he stabbed her.

He also had two letters printed in the South African magazine *Patriot-in-Exile*. He was quoted as saying, "I still have faith that the White Race will prevail, both in Britain and in South Africa, but I fear that it's going to be a very long and very bloody struggle."

In a decision I'm sure someone is regretting, on the night before the attack, Mair visited an alternative therapy center in Birstall seeking treatment for depression and was told to come back the next day.

So did Mair kill Jo Cox because he was a "Leave" sympathizer suffering a deep bout of depression? Or did the establishment use him, and his troubled story, to try to create a scenario in which Britain would stay in the EU?

We may never know.

If you think about it further, don't forget murder for financial gain is so common it is a cliché. CNBC has aired a long-running documentary series called *American Greed*. A number of its programs have detailed instances of murder for money. Among the episodes I was able to review, the average sum that seemed to inspire the featured homicides was $4,954,500. Some involved amounts as low as $174,000.

If prominent people will resort to homicide over about $5 million, much less $174,000, is it really far-fetched to suppose that powerful interests would be equally unscrupulous when trillions of dollars hang in the balance? I don't think so. Indeed, I am sure that whole countries could be wiped out for less.

Brexit Is "the Tip of the Iceberg"—Greenspan

Alan Greenspan was famous for making unintelligible pronouncements about the economy back when he was chairman of the Federal Reserve Board (1987–2006). In those days, the media hung on his every word. Parsing his famously garbled sentences became a high art. He must miss his lost status as a "Master of the Universe" because he has resorted to the ultimate "sneaky trick" to see himself more widely quoted. He actually flirted with talking sense. His sentences still don't exactly parse. But if you listen closely, you can tell what he is talking about. And some of it is even true.

When it came to Brexit, Greenspan told CNBC that it was the worst crisis he could recall. "There's nothing like it. Brexit is only the tip of the iceberg." He sees much more economic and market disruption to come. In my view, Greenspan correctly identified one of the crucial issues underlying the British decision to secede from the European Union. According to Greenspan, "It is caused essentially by output per hour in virtually every country slowing to a halt. The result of this is that real income is not going anywhere. This is causing a severe political problem."[10] He added, "We are in very early days of a crisis which has got a way to go."

Perhaps without intending, Greenspan pointed to an important aspect of the ongoing challenge you face. Collapse is a long-term process, not merely an episodic tribulation.

"A Terrible Mistake"?

Lest you forget that Greenspan was a high priest of the establishment, he went on to lament the fact the British people were given a voice to determine whether they wished to remain within the EU. He called the election a "terrible mistake." Greenspan opined, "It didn't have to happen."

Or did it?

The Megapolitics of Devolution

For many years, I have pointed out that big governments, much less a European super state, are anachronisms. This has been true for decades. The boundary forces that determine the scale at which violence can be successfully organized have decisively altered the logic of power. Since about 1950, the smaller party in asymmetric conflict has defeated the larger, ostensibly stronger power in wars the majority of the time.

This is exactly what you should expect if you have your eyes open. Think about it. US military outlays (including military spending disguised in the budgets of other departments than Defense) exceed those of all other countries combined. Even so, the United States failed to defeat a peasant army in Vietnam. And more recently the United States proved woefully unsuccessful in combatting ragtag bands of squalid terrorists in Iraq and Afghanistan.

Notwithstanding these spectacular failures, few have paused to consider what this implies for the architecture of government. We have had lots of navel gazing about "foreign-policy overreach," and the limitations of "nation-building."

And the operatives of the Deep State have outdone themselves in dreaming up far-fetched rationalizations for multi-billion-dollar weapons systems like the Littoral Combat Ship, ostensibly meant to improve the dwindling effectiveness of combatting asymmetric threats (or weaker foes). But few have dared to wonder what the faltering projection of power tells us about the viability of legacy institutions of big government.

You only need to look back a couple of hundred years into history to see that big government as it evolved in the twentieth century came along as a side effect of industrialism. There were no governments before the Industrial Revolution that spent even 10 percent of what current governments spend in real terms. They couldn't. It was impossible.

The feasibility of any government is inevitably tied to the underlying physical basis of the economy. No government can spend resources that do not exist. Big government only became feasible when factories powered by hydrocarbon energy permitted a vast increase in the value of the economy and thus the scale of warfare. Armies were outfitted with mass-produced weapons that could only be afforded by taxing away a big share of a rapidly growing economy. Competition in warfare at an industrial scale, as exemplified by World Wars I and II, required the capacity to mobilize vast resources that were beyond the reach of all but a big government.

But that time is passed now. Current events clearly show that it is no longer necessary to maintain a vast industrial base to achieve military effectiveness. Governments in the Middle East struggle to keep the upper hand over small, highly motivated groups of fanatics like ISIS.

Advantages to scale in the organization of violence have plunged, as they have in economic organization. The result has been a widening megapolitical disconnect between legacy institutions and the underlying physical and technological foundations of the economy. This is reflected in a chronic slowdown in economic growth, sky-rocketing government budget deficits, and the accumulation of unpayable debt.

This is part of the reason for the triumph of crony capitalism. As the late Kenneth Boulding suggested, an all-but-inevitable consequence of the growth stall is a relentless effort by special interests to make government an institution for redistributing income away from the weak and toward the powerful. The advantages enjoyed by larger enterprises in lobbying and the protections they enjoy from the rigors of the market by their success in purchasing regulatory favors entail artificial returns to scale.

The various expedients for disguising collapse—budget deficits, conjuring money out of thin air to finance malinvestment booms, crony capitalist rip-offs (antimarket regulations)—have the perverse effect of weakening the economy and making the ultimate collapse worse.

Contrary to Alan Greenspan, it was hardly a "terrible mistake" that "didn't have to happen" for the UK to withdraw from the EU. It was only a matter of time until some concatenation of events occasioned a crisis to bring the institutions of the status quo into better alignment with megapolitical conditions.

The decentralization of production as digital information has come to play a larger role in the production process implies that ever-smaller units of government could be effective in providing the conditions for free market prosperity. Equally, this implies that diseconomies plague big governments.

Free Trade Alliance or Big Government Cartel?

That, in turn, helps explain why the European Union was created in the first place. Not simply as a free trade alliance as it is often described, but as a cartel to help shore up big governments by protecting them from competition. The late free market economist Murray Rothbard saw the EU as "part of a very long campaign to integrate and cartelize government in order to entrench the interventionist mixed economy. In Europe, the campaign culminated in the Maastricht Treaty, the attempt to impose a single currency and central bank on Europe and force its relatively free economies to rachet up their regulatory and welfare states." Rothbard elaborated, "Brussels has forced low-tax European countries to raise their taxes to the Euro-average or to expand their welfare state in the name of 'fairness,' a 'level playing field,' and 'upward harmonization.'"[11]

In short, quoting Rothbard's EU critique, "the socialistic Eurocrats have tried to get Europeans to surrender to the super-statism of the European Community."

The leaders of this enterprise were in no mood to see it derailed by popular revolt. Martin Schulz, president of the European Parliament, expressed a brazen contempt for the views of the "little people." Said Schulz, "The British have violated the rules. It is not the EU philosophy that the crowd can decide its fate."

Unless you are a tycoon in the upper fractions of the 1 percent, he is talking about you. Charming, isn't it?

"Bravo for Brexit"—David Stockman

David Stockman took the opposite attitude to that of Alan Greenspan and Martin Schulz. Stockman weighed in with a "Bravo for Brexit," pointing out:

> At long last the tyranny of the global financial elite has been slammed good and hard. You can count on them to attempt another central bank based shock and awe campaign to halt and reverse the current sell-off, but it won't be credible, sustainable or maybe even possible.
>
> The central bankers and their compatriots at the EU, IMF, White House/Treasury, OECD, G-7 and the rest of the Bubble Finance

apparatus have well and truly over-played their hand. They have created a tissue of financial lies; an affront to the very laws of markets, sound money and capitalist prosperity.[12]

My old friend Marc Faber, speaking to CNBC, saw that "Brexit is a victory of ordinary people, common sense and people who are prepared to take responsibility for the sake of freedom against a political and financial elite that only cares if stocks go up or down and does not care about the interests of the average British citizen."[13]

Note the contrast between Greenspan's view—that even permitting the British public the opportunity to decide on continued EU membership was a "terrible mistake"—and Stockman's view—that it was a good thing to slam "the tyranny of the global financial elite." Stockman goes on to declare, "The days of the Financial Elite's rule are numbered."

I believe he is right. The days of the status quo are numbered. Even before Brexit, it was ripe for a fall. The United States, along with most of the world, is already in recession, and the central bankers, along with the other mandarins of statism, haven't a clue what to do about it. Incomes for non-elite workers have been falling for about half a century. And even in a quasi "sort-of" democratic system that was eventually bound to have consequences. As Faber underscored in a CNBC interview, the revolt against the establishment "is already well underway. Brexit is a huge boon for Trump and a wake-up call to Hillary that ordinary people are sick and tired of being lied to and cheated by the crony capitalistic system."[14]

Or "Time for the Elites to Rise Up against the Ignorant Masses"?

Battle lines are drawn. *Foreign Policy* magazine has published an article by James Traube proclaiming, "It's time for the elites to rise up against the ignorant masses." According to Traube, "It's not about the left vs. the right; it's about the sane vs. the mindlessly angry."[15] He seems to think it is entirely appropriate for bankers and the high nabobs of crony capitalism to use the powers of government to empty the pockets of the "ignorant masses." But woe to those ignorant masses who dare to repudiate "the bankers and economists and Western heads of state" who instruct them on the boundaries of permissible anger. Perhaps one of the reasons for the virulent reaction against the "ignorant masses" is the instinctive understanding by Traube and other defenders of the status quo that anything that encourages people to think more deeply is subversive.

Why Uncertainty Is a Solvent Dissolving the Status Quo

The status quo is an engineering marvel, a convection erected on the flimsy footing of fake statistics, unfunded liabilities, preposterous growth forecasts, and funny money accounting. Upon inspection, it is evident that national debts (sovereign paper), far from being high-quality "riskless assets," are predestined to become little more than souvenirs of lost causes like Confederate money.

All the advanced economies are Looney Tunes productions at risk of a Wile E. Coyote moment. They are all suspended in thin air, resting on nothing but an ill-placed confidence that could be wiped away as investors contemplate this or the next Black Swan.

The status quo has been collapsing for decades. Evidence of this is apparent in decelerating economic growth and the fact the governments of all advanced industrial economies are unable to pay their way. You need only consider the astonishing, previously reported fact that $11.7 trillion in government debt is trading with negative interest rates.

Thanks to the growth stall, insolvent governments cannot afford to pay honest interest rates on their rapidly metastasizing debt. In other words, conditions are so weak and the options for deploying large sums in investment seem so uncertain that people are prepared to pay governments for the privilege of lending them money. According to Fitch's, the credit rating agency, the total value of bonds trading with negative yields has soared by $1.3 trillion in June 2016 alone.[16]

This tells you that the deflationary dynamic characterized by Exter's Pyramid is already at work in a big way. It calls into question all the derivative illiquid investment categories at the top layers of that unstable, inverted structure, including ultimately the purportedly safe government bonds themselves.

That is why I think anyone with the capacity to do so would be well-advised to prepare for the worst and put a few hundred thousand dollars aside in actual gold bullion in a repository outside the banking system. I believe we are headed for deflationary collapse. But it is also possible that elites desperate to teach "the ignorant masses" a lesson could also engineer hyperinflation as the whole economy collapses.

Either way, the real price of gold is destined to go higher. This is obvious for hyperinflation. But gold should gain relative value in a deflationary environment precisely because the deflationary liquidity pressures may force the sellers of paper gold claims to buy large quantities for delivery. Or default. Be that as it may, it underscores the drawbacks of relying on the leverage in futures trading to profit from "paper gold."

I doubt that you would go wrong in a worst case circumstance if you purchase actual gold and warehouse it in safe vaults outside the banking system in Switzerland. For more information, contact Johny Beck, partner, Matterhorn Asset Management AG at jb@goldswitzerland.com. Their websites are www.goldswitzerland.com and www.matterhorngold.com.

Meanwhile, keep your eyes open for other precious metals investment opportunities for a world in crisis. As legendary trader Jim Rogers says, "This is going to be worse than any bear market that you've seen in your lifetime."

Rogers forecasts, "The EU as we know it will not exist, the Euro as we know it will not exist . . . I'll tell you what I'm doing, people have to make their own decisions, going into this I'm long the U.S. Dollar, I'm short U.S. stocks, I own some Chinese shares, I own agriculture around the world. These are things that might do well no matter what happens . . . these are going to be perilous times, I hope I get it right."

You should be entertaining similar thoughts.

For better or worse, anything that cannot go on forever will inevitably come to an end. The Black Swans fluttering overhead are omens of deep tectonic disturbance. For decades, pressures have been building along the fault lines of our civilization. One fine morning, something will give way and the rickety edifice could tumble down.

Notes

1   Greenhalgh, Hugo, "Bordeau Vintners Raise a Glass to Brexit Effect as Wine Sales Reach Five-Year High," *Financial Times*, August 13/14, 2016, 1.

2   https://goldsilver.com/blog/china-the-next-crisis-kyle-bass/.

3   Tett, Gillian, "Now Watch the Shift in Interest Rates," *Financial Times*, July 1, 2016.

4   Durden, Tyler, "North American Life Insurers 'Accidentally' Pile Up Massive Distressed Debt Holdings," *Zero Hedge*, August 12, 2016.

5   Popper, Karl, *The Logic of Scientific Discovery* (London: Routledge, 2002), 19.

6   Taleb, Nassim Nicholas, *The Black Swan: The Impact of the Highly Improbable* (New York: Random House, 2007).

7   https://peoplestrusttoronto.wordpress.com/2016/06/26/china-devalues-yuan-most-in-10-months-as-premier-li-warns-of-brexit-butterfly-effect-on-financial-markets-economy/.

8   http://www.zerohedge.com/news/2016-06-19/nigel-farage-brexit-we-had

-momentum-until-terrible -tragedy-here-are-latest-odds ?page=1.

9   http://sgtreport.com/ 2016/06/assassination-the -conspiracy-theory-to -prevent-brexit-vote/.

10 http://www.usatoday.com/ story/money/business/2016/ 06/24/greenspan-brexit-euro -eu-greece-oecd-economy/ 86336802/. Note: *USA Today* editors chose to narrow the allocation of Greenspan's com- ments in a way that they do not apply to the United States. Read them without those brackets. They do.

11 https://mises.org/library/nafta -myth#.UppdJ83nE1A.reddit.

12 http://davidstockmans contracorner.com/bravo -brexit/.

13 http://www.zerohedge .com/?page=2&feed_me= Conventionally.

14 http://www.zerohedge.com/ print/564731.

15 http://foreignpolicy.com/ 2016/06/28/its-time-for-the -elites-to-rise-up-against -ignorant-masses-trump -2016-brexit/.

16 http://finance.yahoo.com/ news/fitch-brexit-vote-pushes -negative-150600583.html.

Chapter Twenty

The Idiot Principle of Deflation, and Why I Am One of the Idiots Who Sees It Happening

It should be patently obvious to anyone with two synapses to rub together that the Idiot Principle of Deflation is utter gibberish, and cannot possibly add up, when one simply views the economic dynamics (and definitions) in their proper context . . . Sadly, this infantile error in logic/arithmetic of which all the Deflationists are guilty cannot be attributed to mere ignorance. It is (has been) nothing less than abject stupidity.
—Jeff Nielson, "Hyperinflation Cannot Be Prevented by Debt/Deflation," *Sprott Money*

The last time it seemed so certain that my IQ had receded into double digits was after I forecast the collapse of the Soviet Union. That made me really stupid for a while. The few authorities who admitted giving any heed to my unconventional prophecy were absolutely convinced it was, as *Newsweek* put it, "an unthinking attack on reason."

That experience should have warmed me up for the rant from Jeff Nielson of *Sprott Money*, who has been unleashing double-barreled insults against anyone with the temerity to suggest that the bankrupt status quo could collapse in debt deflation. I suppose it would be churlish to point out that "idiot" is a noun, not an adjective. But equally, we are entitled to wonder what it means that ungrammatical insults carry a greater punch of authenticity at this stage in the credit cycle. Perhaps it is a quasi-indicator of things coming unhinged, like the "hemline theory" that supposes the length of women's skirts are strong tip-offs to prosperity, or the lack thereof, with shorter hemlines being more bullish.

Dark Nail Polish and the Future of the Economy

Then you have the closely observed alternative theory posited by *Forbes* contributor Lee Shepard. She argues in "Fashion's True Leading Economic Indicator" that dark nail polish colors foretell a dark economic future.[1] She says, "Dark nail polish would qualify as a leading indicator—telling people things were headed into the porcelain plumbing before it was otherwise evident." She also notes that "ballet-slippers pink" was in style in the boom years of the 1980s, and it remains popular with denizens of the upper East Side because "economic life is always good for them." Unfortunately, Ms. Sheppard doesn't give us any hints about whether fingertips adorned with Chanel's reddish-black Vamp are pointing toward hyperinflation or deflationary debt collapse—or perhaps both. To understand that, we have to put the ungrammatical insults aside and figure it out for ourselves.

Nielson's argument in "Hyperinflation Cannot Be Prevented By Debt/Deflation" turns on some definitional slight-of-hand, as it defies an incontrovertible principle of alternative medicine. There is no telling how many cancer deaths have been prevented by heart attacks. It is possible that deflationary collapse will quench the country's thirst for artificial monetary stimulus and thus forestall the launch of helicopter money that otherwise seems likely to hover like a dark cloud on the horizon.

Nielson is eager to tell you that every unit of currency came into existence through "our bankrupt governments literally borrowed every unit of currency into existence." This means that these units of currency are/were literally the IOUs of our governments—our bankrupt governments. He asks, "What is the value of an IOU issued by a bankrupt Deadbeat?" His response: "Zero."

A nice, tight little syllogism.

But not so fast. I agree that the government is bankrupt, especially when viewed in terms of GAAP accounting. As you may recall, two leading congressional budget experts, former congressmen Chris Cox, one-time chairman of the Task Force on Budget Process Reform, and Bill Archer, a past chairman of the House Ways and Means Committee, admitted in a *Wall Street Journal* editorial, titled "Why $16 Trillion Only Hints at the True US Debt," that the government would have to raise revenue by $8 trillion a year to achieve solvency. Not an easy task. That targeted tax raise was greater than every penny of adjusted gross personal income for persons earning $66,193 per year, $5.1 trillion, as well as all reported corporate profits, $1.6 trillion, for a total of $6.7 trillion in 2006, when corporate income peaked before the recession.[2]

A path to solvency that requires taxing away more income than people earn is a dead end. So I agree wholeheartedly that the government is hopelessly bankrupt. Where I beg to differ is with Nielson's heavy-handed conclusion that there can never be a deflationary collapse. Mr. Nielson has led himself, and others, astray by missing the fact that values in the market are set by the price mechanism, not by arbitrary definitions. You can't resolve the question of whether the Breaking Point is more likely to take the form of a deflationary collapse or a hyperinflationary one by enlisting a better lexicographer. It isn't a matter of definitions; it is a matter of market dynamics.

Investment Syllogisms Run Amuck

For my part, I see lots of drawbacks in an investment strategy formulated on the basis of tautological definitions and syllogisms. I can easily postulate a similarly misleading construct that could inform a highly unprofitable investment.

Take this example. Say that the major premise of your syllogism is that the shares of bankrupt companies are worthless. Then say that the minor premise of your syllogism is that you believe that the Framus Corporation is bankrupt. Therefore, you could leap to the conclusion that if you sell short shares of the Framus Corporation at $43.44, their price must immediately fall to zero and you will make a lot of money.

Sounds pretty simple and quite logical. It is a proposition exactly like that of Jeff Nielson's assertion that the value of an IOU issued by a bankrupt deadbeat government is zero. But one little hitch should be obvious to anyone who thinks for a moment about Nielson's deduction that money is worth "zero" because "these units of currency are/were literally the IOUs of our governments—our bankrupt governments." The hitch is that the deduction that money is worthless is remote from the facts.

Market Realism over Rhetoric

Money is not worthless. And I very much doubt that Mr. Nielson would take his own conclusion so seriously as to convert his monthly paycheck into cash and scatter the supposedly worthless currency along Bay Street, Queen Street, or any other street, for that matter.

If he did, the resulting commotion as passersby scrambled to collect the currency would prove to anyone who can't fathom it otherwise that currency is not worthless. Far from it. Yes, the government may well be bankrupt according to rigorous standards of accounting. Indeed, I would say that the US government, with a fiscal gap of $205 trillion according to Professor Laurence Kotlikoff, is arguably the most hopelessly bankrupt government in history.[3] But the value of currency is not established by definition. Lexicographers have no influence in determining the value of money. None. Value is determined by the market.

The market tells us that $100 bills are emphatically worth picking up off the street and, indeed, even working hard to earn, the aggravated Mr. Nielson notwithstanding. More to the point, there is ample evidence as I write that the value of the dollar has been appreciating.

The Supposedly Worthless Dollar Soars

If you followed the currency markets in 2015, you would have seen that the trade-weighted value of the dollar had been soaring for two years at the time. *Bloomberg* reported that the dollar was in the middle of its strongest rally since 1984, when it surged 32 percent in two years, and there was likely little anyone could do to stop it. It surged 20 percent against the yen and 17 percent against the euro. The Fed's dollar index climbed more than 18 percent between the end of 2013 and 2015, approaching the record high of February 2002.[4]

Such developments, while not dignified by Nielson's syllogisms, reflect market dynamics. They certainly run counter to the notion that the dollar is a worthless IOU of a bankrupt government. In fact, it is an increasingly valuable IOU of a bankrupt government.

Why? What accounts for the dollar's strength? How could the IOUs of a bankrupt government be soaring? To better understand what is afoot, let's go back to my alternative syllogism where I warned that you could not necessarily expect to profit by selling short the shares of the Framus Corporation, even if you were convinced that Framus was actually bankrupt. Although it may not be obvious, there is a close link between the market dynamics that sometimes raise stock prices of bankrupt companies and the dynamics that underlie the rally in the US dollar, an intrinsically worthless fiat currency.

As another step toward realism, let's change the name of the bankrupt company in our example from the fictitious Framus Corporation to Enron. As you recall, Enron was a real company that filed for bankruptcy on December 2, 2001, in what was then the largest corporate bankruptcy in US history. The Enron story was not just the account of a business failure; Enron's collapse involved a major scandal.

The essence of the Enron scandal was that company executives, particularly CEO Jeffrey Skilling and CFO Andrew Fastow, used inaccurate financial reporting, accounting loopholes, and special-purpose, off-balance-sheet entities to disguise billions of dollars of debt in failed deals and projects.

You could see this as similar to the way Congress hides unfunded liabilities and complicates understanding of the federal budget. Indeed, this is why Professor Kotlikoff has solicited the endorsement of fifteen Nobel Prize winners in economics for his The Inform Act. Dr. Kotlikoff and his fellow economists contend, "The country needs to do honest accounting." The professor charges, quite rightly, that the government is "disguising the true problem."[5]

Shades of Enron. The authors of one best-selling book, *Enron: The Smartest Guys in the Room: The Amazing Rise and Scandalous Fall of Enron*, put it this way, Enron executives "created off-balance sheet vehicles, complex financing structures, and deals so bewildering that few people could understand them."[6]

Unfortunately, it is not far-fetched to draw an analogy between Enron's finances and those of the federal government. One eluded the understanding of investors—the other eludes the understanding of citizens. In both cases, the books were kept in a fishy way. In both cases, the public was misled with a constant stream of data detailing fake successes. In Enron's case, fake profits piled up. For the US government, the malpractice of measurement involves overstating employment and economic growth. Those of us who look more closely at the numbers know that they depict a fake prosperity animated by an unsustainable growth of debt.

A Short Seller Explains

One person who did make a point of trying to understand Enron's books was James Chanos, the famous New York short seller. Chanos provided his view of Enron in testimony to the Securities and Exchange Commission in 2003, essentially explaining that he believed Enron had been bankrupt for years:

> The first Enron document my firm analyzed was its 1999 form 10-K filing, which it had filed with the SEC. What immediately struck us was that despite using the "gain-on-sale" model, Enron's return on capital, a widely used measure of profitability, was a paltry 7% before taxes. That is for every dollar in outside capital Enron employed, it earned about seven cents. This is important for two reasons; first, we viewed Enron as a trading company that was akin to an "energy hedge fund." For this type of firm, a 7% return seemed abysmally low, particularly given its market dominance and accounting methods. Second, it was our view that Enron's cost of capital was likely in excess of 7% and probably closer to 9%, which meant from an economic point of view, that Enron wasn't really earning any money at all, despite reporting "profits" to its shareholders. This mismatch of Enron's cost of capital and its returns on investment became the cornerstone for our bearish view on Enron and we began shorting Enron, common stock.[7]

His view was amply ratified by evidence that came to the surface after Enron collapsed. The pertinent point here is that proof exists to demonstrate that Enron had, in fact, been bankrupt for many years. Yet Enron's stock price shot straight up during 2000, rising from $43.44 on January 3, 2000, to as high as $89.63 on September 18, 2000.

Of course, no one understood what Enron was up to. Its accounts were intentionally complicated to disguise the fact it was losing money. These shenanigans went almost

426 | The Breaking Point

unnoticed because Arthur Anderson, one of the world's foremost auditing firms until that time, had given Enron a stamp of validity. And don't forget as well, Enron was always announcing impressive, though fictitious, earnings. This whole fake picture was further disguised in a gilded frame when Enron was repeatedly hailed as perhaps the leading company of its time. *Fortune* magazine named Enron the "Most Innovative Company in America" for six years in a row, from 1996 to 2001—the very year that Enron filed for bankruptcy protection.

This relates directly to the "idiot principle of deflation." (I am not correcting Nielson's grammar; if he wants to put it that way, let him.) Just as Enron's share price could skyrocket notwithstanding the fact that it was actually bankrupt, so the IOUs of the bankrupt government can go up in value, as they have been.

The $9 Trillion Deflationary Short Squeeze

Nielson unknowingly highlighted a crucial element in this dynamic in his rant in "Hyperinflation Cannot Be Prevented By Debt/Deflation." His exact words were, "Our bankrupt governments literally borrowed every unit of currency into existence." Yes, it is a characteristic of our fiat money that it is mostly borrowed into existence. This is precisely what makes deflation more likely.

Every dollar that is borrowed into existence is a de facto "short" position. Like a short stock position, the borrowed dollars must be repaid. When selling short stocks, you must be alert to the danger of a "short squeeze" that could oblige you to buy back the shares you have sold at a loss. While professional investors have different standards for judging the risk, they generally agree that the higher the open short interest rises, as percentage of the total float, the more likely it is that a short squeeze will develop, driving the price of the underlying instrument higher. Of course, where the dollar is concerned, the short interest is at least 90 percent of the float—far higher than is ever seen in even the dodgiest stock.

As of August 13, 2015, there was $1.38 trillion cash in circulation. The other nine-tenths of the money supply was borrowed into existence.

The Fed Darkens the Shadows in the Shadow Banking System

Part of the black magic of QE was the fact that dollars created in the United States were multiplied as dollar-borrowers morphed into so-called nonbank banks and created cascading layers of dollar debt. This has occurred on a truly massive scale, much of it in emerging markets (EMs), particularly in China.

As it happened, there was a special attraction in exporting the easy money conjured up by QE to countries where local interest rates were higher than the invisibly low rates or zero interest rate policy (ZIRP) dictated by the Fed. In effect, by creating the formula for a profitable carry trade, in which borrowers could use dollar funding to invest at home and profit from the spread between dollar and local interest rates, the Fed gigantically multiplied the world's shadow banking system.

As the *Economist* reported in March 2015, stock of dollar debts owed by nonfinancial borrowers outside the United States had grown by 50 percent since the financial crisis of 2008, reaching $9 trillion—EMs accounted for half of that amount. Dollar-denominated loans in China went from $200 billion in 2008 to more than $1 trillion in 2015.[8]

In effect, the Fed helped finance the huge credit bubble that artificially inflated Chinese economic growth in recent years. Since 2008, private debt in China has grown by at least 80 percent of stated GDP. Data on China's shadow banking system leaves much to be desired; it involves obscure interlinkages with the official banks and a bunch of trusts, wealth management products, money market funds, and loan-guarantee companies, along with entities of various description deploying foreign-currency borrowings. The *Economist* puts Yangzijiang Shipbuilding "at the forefront" of shadow banking.[9]

In 2010 alone, private debt in China soared by 35 percent of reported GDP, as the Chinese credit bubble became the biggest in history. According to McKinsey, China's debt nearly quadrupled from 2007 to mid-2014, rising from about $7 trillion to almost $28 trillion.[10] Since 2008, Chinese banks loans have expanded by 50 percent more than the combined total of money created by the Federal Reserve, the European Central Bank, the Bank of England, and the Bank of Japan.[11]

The unprecedented magnitude of China's credit bubble supported a fixed investment orgy that could not have been better designed to set the deflationary trap that has now begun to spring shut on the global economy. About half of Chinese loans are directly or indirectly tied to China's vastly overbuilt and overheated real estate market.

I could deploy a number of charts to underscore the point that China's credit bubble blown up much more than earlier bubbles in either the United States or Japan, much less the South Sea bubble or the Tulip Mania. But one astonishing and revealing statistic makes that point all by itself.

China Used More Cement from 2011 to 2013 than the United States Used in the Entire Twentieth Century

You have heard of the ghost cities in China, built out in every respect except without people. And you have no doubt seen TV reports recorded in vast, new Chinese shopping malls complete with top-brand anchor tenants but no customers. A marker of this fantastic overbuilding is the Chinese consumption of cement. They used 6.6 gigatons—a gigaton is one billion tons—in the three-year period between 2011 and 2013, almost 50 percent more than the 4.5 gigatons of cement the

United States used to build its modern cities and infrastructure during the whole of the twentieth century.[12]

That is a lot of cement.

This credit-fueled building binge not only dwarfs the subprime bubble build-out of McMansions in the United States; it also helps underscore the deflationary dynamic that became so evident in world commodity markets after 2014.

Build It, and They Will Come . . . or Will They?

You see, it isn't just cement that has been used to excess in China's credit-ramped building binge. When the Chinese government decided to keep the measures of GDP soaring after 2008, they launched a massive, one-off infrastructure build, financed by an increase in debt that ranged somewhere between $21 trillion and $25 trillion.[13] Money on that scale bought more than just cement. Lots of other raw materials were sucked into China's historic building spree—the equivalent of erecting one thousand World Trade Centers each year. Among other things, this also sucked up a lot of steel and copper, and China accounted for 45 percent of the increase in world oil demand.

While some of the empty towers and shopping centers were flipped to investors as the bubble expanded, the trusting Chinese investors who bought must have been bummed: empty apartments, offices, and shopping blocks could not possibly pay their way. As David Stockman put it, this was "the most massive malinvestment of real economic resources" in history. The losses it engendered are radiating around the globe. An astonishing seventy million new luxury apartments stand empty in China.[14] For perspective, note that there are 2,581,170 apartment units in New York. China's empty apartments could house New York City twenty-seven times over.

The Greatest Margin Call in History

Of course, as the orgy of malinvestment inevitably slowed, demand for commodities receded from exaggerated levels.

Consequently, prices of many key industrial commodities, including oil, have plunged, triggering margin calls, devaluing currencies, and spelling bankruptcy for many commodity suppliers and whole countries.

Most of China's construction has been for high-rise apartment complexes and office towers. In 2010 alone, total residential construction in China was an astonishing 25.8 billion square feet, while office construction totaled another 19.4 billion square feet. That equates to more than ten square feet of office space for every man, woman, and child in China in 2010, according to the *Economist Intelligence Unit.*

Think about it. The call on commodity markets for such tremendous quantities of resources did not just constitute a passing bid-on-the-spot market. It gave rise to a whole additional layer of demand for the raw materials needed to build the mining machinery, earthmovers, drill rigs, refineries, power plants, steel furnaces, and mills, as well as the ships and tankers that were part of the logistics tail required to fill the demand for commodities at the gargantuan scale drawn forth in China's credit bubble.

The additional stimulus to malinvestment was all the greater in the case of a key commodity, copper. Why? Because geological limitations as evidenced by continuing declines in copper grades at Chilean mines (38 percent of world supply) made it difficult to even maintain, much less increase, production without massive capital expenditures. The Chilean copper company Codelco announced in 2010 that its production of copper would fall by 50 percent within a decade without an intensive CapEx program. This culminated in massive new investments to deepen mines and improve recoveries of metals, such as copper, that were in high demand in China's building binge. Such programs became part of a worldwide capital-spending spree that has expanded capacity for many commodities far beyond what can economically service China's now slumping demand, especially with new production coming on line from years of vast malinvestment in new capacity globally.

Chinese Steel Capacity Now Twelve to Fifteen Times US Annual Consumption

Consider the steel industry. Chinese capacity of about 100 million tons annually in 1995 soared to upwards of 1.2 billion tons today. Capacity has multiplied by twelve times over in just two decades—growth equivalent to twice the total world capacity in 1995. Compare this with estimates of current sell-through demand for steel in auto and appliance production, as well as replacement cycles for apartment blocks, office towers, ships, shopping malls, and rail lines in China. Not more than 500 million tons of steel would be required, and that is a huge amount. For reference, in 2013, the United States consumed 95.6 million tons of steel; China consumed 700.2 million tons.[15]

A well-built skyscraper doesn't need replacement on a short-term basis. In fact, engineers estimate that even without maintenance, a skyscraper should be good for half a century before it has to be abandoned or replaced.[16]

Given the scale of recent Chinese fixed asset investment, there was no way it could continue unabated. Much of China's recent gluttonous consumption of commodities involved one-off demand from the infrastructure boom, spurred by one of history's more extreme credit expansions. It is unlikely to be repeated any time soon, if ever.

China Meltdown Ahead

At the very least, the wind down from this credit bubble will entail a significant depreciation of capital stock put in place to service the boom. But something much worse is in the cards. The research arm of Daiwa, Japan's second biggest investment bank, put the prospect for a China meltdown in perspective. As reported by *Zero Hedge* in 2015, if China's economy were to experience a meltdown, the world's economy would more than likely be sent into a tailspin, creating an impact that could be the worst the world has ever witnessed.[17]

In a 2015 *Zero Hedge* article, David Stockman pointed to the August 3, 2015, bankruptcy filing of Alpha Natural Resources as a "metaphor for the central-bank enabled crack-up boom now underway on a global basis."[18] Alpha Natural Resources is a US public company that produces coking, or metallurgical (met), coal. *Forbes* reported that the company "was overwhelmed by big debts it had accumulated to finance the purchase of coal mining assets." Alpha achieved a market cap of $11 billion in 2011 when it acquired Massey Energy for $7 billion. That seemed like a bargain at a time when prices of met coal inflated by the Chinese infrastructure bubble reached $340 a ton. As I write, the price of met coal has plunged by 87.5 percent to $42.50 per ton, and ANRZ is worth zero.

The collapse in met coal prices bagged another corporate victim when state-owned Longmay Group, one of China's biggest met coal miners, announced that it would cut 100,000 jobs—40 percent of its 240,000 person labor force. Excess capacity drives down prices. Today's met coal price is only one-eighth of the price at the 2011 commodity peak. As commodity prices fall, it becomes ever more of an adventure for the leveraged borrowers to repay their debts. Like Alpha Natural Resources, many of them won't.

Debt contracted to discount cash flow from the sale of met coal at $340 per ton became unpayable when increased production and weakened demand drove the price of a ton of met coal down by 87 percent. No wonder Alpha Natural Resources went broke and Longmay is firing 100,000 workers. It is the fate that awaits much of the world as the unsustainable credit-based spending winds down.

The *Titanic* Sinks Again?

Meanwhile, the collapse of Alpha Natural Resources could have a parallel on a larger scale in Glencore, PLC, the UK-listed trading company. Glencore plays a pivotal role in trillions of derivatives as what may be the biggest commodity trading counterparty. With $30 to $35 billion in debt and scant possibility of paying at current commodity prices, Glencore's credit default swaps have blown out to a record 757 basis points as I write, hinting at junk status to come.

The company's half-year 2015 results showed $6.5 billion in earnings before interest, taxes, depreciation, and amortization (EBITDA). Note, however, that according to the company itself, EBITDA drops by $1.2 billion for every 10 percent drop in copper prices. Also note that Glencore's outstanding bonds have slumped to record lows. For example, the GLEN €1.25 billion notes due March 2012 sunk to €0.78. With Glencore bonds following the copper price down the chute, a credit downgrade would hardly be a shock. It could entail significant follow-on consequences for the fragile financial system.

Glencore's trading business requires large tranches of short-term credit to finance commodity deals. It could ill afford to lose its investment grade status, as this could trigger demands by its counterparties to deposit higher collateral—a requirement that the cash-strapped company would be hard-pressed to meet.

As Glencore demonstrates, the linkages between commodity prices and the tottering edifice of global debt are many and complex. Hence you have the current deflationary market dynamic. The credit bubble, augmented by the $9 trillion global carry trade stimulated by QE, has induced a wide spectrum of malinvestment in commodity production as well as the infrastructure of commodity export, including ships and ports. As increases in commodity supply—in the wake of massive CapEx stimulated by artificial Chinese demand in recent years—collide with weak demand, prices for many crucial commodities have plunged, drastically undermining the value of commodity assets. Note that $9 trillion is greater than the economies of Germany and Japan combined. No small sum.

To further illustrate the capitalization effects of plunging commodity prices, consider Glencore's experience with the Cosmos nickel mine in Australia. As Glencore scrambled to clean up its balance sheet in June 2015, it sold Cosmos for $19 million. Glencore's Xstrada subsidiary purchased that mine for $2.6 billion in 2007, when nickel was trading for $32,000 a metric ton on the London Metal Exchange. As I write, the price of nickel has slumped to $9,835 per ton. The 70 percent fall in nickel prices brought on a 99.3 percent fall in the value of the mine.

The Era of Bubblenomics Draws to a Close

History's greatest debt supercycle is coming to an end. That is what the noise and grumbling in today's news disguises. You can expect a deflationary collapse proportionate to the excesses that preceded it. The $9 trillion global short position, contracted on the collateral of a commodities supercycle that peaked years ago, will continue to unwind. That means you can expect most natural resource prices to continue going south. They will plunge until they are lower than production costs for the marginal producer. Then they will overshoot further on the downside until they fall below the cost of production of the low cost producer. Then, when almost everyone is bankrupt, the bottom will be in.

Many, like Jeff Nielson, will tell you that the result to expect is hyperinflation. They point to the great German hyperinflation of the Weimar era. They point to Zimbabwe, always an entertaining spectacle. (I carry a 100 billion Zimbabwean dollar bill in my wallet.) But while a currency note for $100 billion Zimbabwe dollars is an interesting curiosity, on a par with a two-headed frog, much would have to change before you would see hyperinflation in the United States.

I don't deny that desperate central bankers may, indeed, long to gas up the helicopters in a last-ditch attempt to save the tottering edifice of debt by showering big crowds with bucketloads of freshly printed notes.

But they run into a problem in trying to distribute digital money from a helicopter. I suppose they could scatter iPhones preloaded with digital money programmed to disappear if you don't spend it within thirty days. Such devices certainly could not be dropped from a great height, for the obvious reasons.

And I doubt it will ever happen. To the best of my knowledge, there has never been an episode of hyperinflation that began in an economy where the majority of the money supply was borrowed into existence.

Will They Abolish Cash or Print More of It?

Before hyperinflation could overtake the United States, there would have to be a transition period while ever-greater amounts of currency were dumped into circulation. This would represent a major about-face as the high priests of the status quo are now talking about increasing the already predominant role of the banking system in creating money.

In my view, the utter fragility of the system makes it unlikely that the authorities would risk the transition period that would be required to move from 90 percent credit-based money to a system incorporating a greater circulation of currency. The problem is that the largely insolvent system would implode if a lot of digital money were converted into physical cash. And here we are not talking about the commonplace observation that illiquid banks cannot honor the simultaneous withdrawal of deposits if many wish to withdraw at once.

This is a much more acute problem, illustrated by run-on money market funds. When $500 billion, about a quarter of money market investments, were withdrawn in just four weeks in 2008, the market seized up, threatening the liquidity of commercial paper. Of course, a major part of the problem was that the pioneering money market mutual fund, the Reserve Fund, broke the buck when it had to write off short-term paper issued by Lehman Brothers after the firm declared bankruptcy.

The result was a run on the shadow banking system. This undercut the market for commercial paper—money market mutual funds were afraid to compound the maturity mismatch between their obligation to redeem shares immediately on demand and commercial paper with maturities of up to thirteen months. As liquidity in the market evaporated, the money market funds backed away from buying commercial paper.

The resulting drop in demand for commercial paper prevented companies from rolling over their short-term debt, raising the specter of an acute liquidity crisis. The prospect of companies being unable to issue new debt to repay maturing debt implied that many would default on their obligations and perhaps even have to file for bankruptcy protection. That was in 2008. But the Fed and other central banks still fret that the demand for cash by investors seeking to protect themselves could compound debt deflation, as many investors catch up with John Exter's insight that as more and more debt is compounded, digital money becomes less safe.

That explains why Andy Haldane, chief economist of the Bank of England, has been beating the drums for a cashless society. He wants to eliminate cash as a way of circumventing the "zero bound" so central banks could lower interest rates substantially below zero. Haldane also argues that abolishing cash would make it easier for central banks to raise the general level of inflation to 4 percent, which he favors as a cushion against deflation in the future. As Allister Heath put it in the *Telegraph* of London, Haldane's concerns about a possible massive shock to global demand led to his desire to reduce the risk of "prices plunging too far into deflation."[19] In other words, the attack on cash is a crucial feature of financial repression. With no cash in circulation, you could not escape the penalty of negative interest rates by hiding your money under the mattress.[20]

And without cash, I would argue, you could not get hyperinflation. If 100 percent of money were borrowed into existence, the open short interest in the dollar would be 100 percent, and a deflationary short squeeze would be inevitable.

Doubling down on credit expansion means digging ourselves deeper into a deflationary hole. It never made good sense to multiply debt at twice the rate of income growth. And it makes even less sense to increase the multiple of debt growth, as income growth stalls, which is happening in many economies. The McKinsey Global Institute reported this tidy detail: total world debt has grown by $57 trillion since 2008.[21] That is a compound annual growth rate of 7.3 percent. Meanwhile, world GDP, as calculated by official sources, grew by no more than about $15 trillion at a compound growth rate of 3.2 percent. Debt grew more than twice as fast as income.

And of course, another fatal flaw in the plan for infinite credit expansion is the patently evident fact that there is not an infinite stock of good collateral (too many Cosmos mines), and there are not infinitely liquid markets in which to hypothecate, rehypothecate, and redeem highly leveraged collateral. That's why Glencore debt prices were plunging as I wrote, along with the high-yield debt of the world. Long before the Fed starts monetizing dirty underwear, the whole system will have succumbed to deflationary collapse.

Meanwhile, the longer the Ponzi credit expansion continues, the more it turns out that principally the same collateral is overmortgaged by being pledged in multiple transactions. When the system devolves into crisis once more, as it did in 2008, it will soon become evident again that the derivative linkages calmly enshrined in instruments such as credit default swaps are fragile and subject to rapid devaluation, as the $85 billion bailout of AIG demonstrated.

Hyperinflation arises only with the wholesale printing of currency. As indicated above, currency currently accounts for a small fraction, about 10 percent, of the US money supply. Most of our money has been spun out of bank credit. Hyperinflation is exceedingly unlikely, as a high rate of monetary depreciation limits the incentive of banks to undertake further lending. If money is rapidly losing value, the payoff from the banker's "extravagant privilege" of creating money through the fractional reserve system falls. That is why you don't see hyperinflation engineered solely through bank credit.

Hyperinflation erupts with the direct creation of currency on a massive scale. For example, the 1923 hyperinflation in Germany was the result of runaway deficit spending funded by ever-increasing print runs of banknotes. By mid-1923, Germany had more than 30 paper factories, almost 1,800 banknote printing presses, and 133 companies with government contracts to print and issue banknotes. Printing currency was notoriously one of the few profitable industries in Germany in that troubled time. The money printers lived up to their contracts. By November 1923, a loaf of bread cost 200 billion marks.

You'll know you need to start worrying about hyperinflation when the government buys more high-speed presses to crank out paper money on a vast scale. That may happen. But if it ever does, you will see it beginning long before it advances as far as global deflationary meltdown has already advanced. If hyperinflation is a problem, it is a problem for the future. The more immediate problem you face is the tidal wave of global deflation that could sweep you away.

How do you protect yourself? As is so often the case, simpleminded clichés are likely to lead you astray. You are told that gold is a hedge against inflation but not deflation. I agree with the late John Exter that gold is the ultimate hedge against deflation.[22] Exter warned that the more debt money that was created, the more quantitative easing, the bigger the drag on economic activity, and thus the more severe the ultimate deflation would be. Exter believed the deflationary crash ahead will make the 1930s look like a boom. Referring to gold, he suggested, "Buy it now while it's still cheap," as it will be the best investment to own when the crash occurs.

Exter was preternaturally alert to the implications of continued credit expansion in magnifying deflationary forces in the economy. He foresaw that, as the terminal crisis of the credit supercycle took shape, the excess proliferation of derivative claims would set in motion a powerful deflationary adjustment.

Exter's Precarious Inverted Pyramid

He saw that investors, slowly at first, then in greater numbers, would desert the more derivative and illiquid expressions of wealth in favor of more basic and liquid assets.

Yes, gold and silver are natural resources that are produced in costly and elaborate processes like other commodities. But as monetary metals they are in a different category than met coal, iron, copper, aluminum, nickel, and zinc. When you mine for gold, you are mining for liquidity.

Exter did not believe that the decision of how the overburden of debt would be liquidated was ultimately a political choice: he thought it would be resolved by the market. He is best known today for "Exter's Inverse (or Inverted) Pyramid," or simply "Exter's Pyramid," by which he sought to harness intuition about how deflation would unfold.

Exter's Pyramid has the appearance of an Egyptian pyramid standing precariously upside down on its apex. Its layers are organized in an inverse relation to safety. The sketchiest and least safe assets are at the top, with safety increasing as you move down the pyramid. The widest layer represents the hundreds of trillions, if not a quadrillion, of dollars' worth of derivatives, like credit default swaps, currency swaps, collateralized debt obligations, and mortgage-backed securities. According to the Bank for International Settlements, 55 percent of collateralized debt obligations (CDOs) now being issued are based on leveraged loans.

Exter's Inverted Pyramid is top-heavy, with the upper levels comprising precarious derivatives—financial claims that are furthest removed from the physical world and the least liquid. Think also of unfunded government liabilities (the soon-to-be-worthless promises of politicians), small business assets, real estate, collectibles, OTC stocks, commodities, municipal (muni) bonds, corporate bonds, listed stocks, government bonds, treasury bills, and physical currency notes. Ultimately, at the inverted apex of the pyramid sits gold, the asset of preference in a deflationary collapse.

Gold is an asset that is not someone else's liability. Presumably, silver fits somewhere near the inverted apex of the pyramid in a thin layer somewhere above gold. Exter did not mention silver, but the logic of his argument is quite clear.

It is also worth noting that derivative items at the top of the inverted pyramid have highly inflated values that, in aggregate, greatly exceed the value of all privately owned tangible assets on Earth. The notional value of paper markets vastly exceeds the underlying physical assets from which they are derived. Further to this, the leveraged derivatives entail liabilities that dwarf the equity of the banks and other entities that issue them, so that for all intents and purposes their recovery value could approach zero.

252 Ounces of Gold Purchased on the Comex for Every Deliverable Ounce of Gold

Consider the example of "paper gold." It has been alleged for many years that physical gold borrowed from the vaults of central banks has been sold over and over again like producer shares in *Springtime for Hitler*, as imagined by Mel Brooks. But "paper gold" has another meaning as well. *Zero Hedge* reported on September 16, 2015, that "the number of paper claims through open futures interest for every ounce of deliverable gold" on the Comex had soared to 252. In other words, there was only one ounce of deliverable gold to satisfy every 252 paper claims through open futures interest. (You can see why Exter recommended acquiring physical gold to protect yourself in a bankrupt world.)

The deflationary collapse is working its way from the periphery to the center. Most people in the United States are still in denial. They imagine that the wizards at the Federal Reserve will concoct some new expedient for juicing credit when the music stops. Don't hold your breath. With a new record high of 252 ounces of gold claims on the COMEX (Commodity Exchange, Inc.), a division of the New York Mercantile Exchange (NYMEX) for each ounce of deliverable gold, even before the crisis hits the headlines, it is clear that you may be unable to count on delivery of futures purchases of gold.

Or to put it another way, the real price of gold is destined to go higher in a deflationary environment precisely because the deflationary liquidity pressures may force the sellers of paper gold claims to buy large quantities for delivery. Or default. Be that as it may, it underscores the drawbacks of relying on the leverage in futures trading to profit from "paper gold." That is why I recommend that you purchase actual gold and warehouse it in safe vaults outside the banking system in Switzerland. For more information, contact Johny Beck, partner, Matterhorn Asset Management AG at jb@goldswitzerland.com. Their websites are www.goldswitzerland.com and www.matterhorngold.com.

Remembering the Great Depression

It is little remembered today that the depression that began after 1929 in the United States began much earlier for commodity-producing countries at the periphery. Commodity prices peaked between 1927 and 1928. Most of the commodity-producing countries entered the Great Depression before the US stock market crashed. Argentina and Australia, for example, peaked in 1927 and were already in depression in 1928. The same goes for Brazil, Mexico, Uruguay, and Chile. In addition, a number of European countries were in depression in 1928, including Germany, along with some peripheral European countries like Bulgaria and Finland.

Apparently, some investors have done their homework. Others must have intuited that they could gain greater safety by shifting investments into dollars—the reserve currency of the fading hegemonic power. Though it may be bankrupt, it is still the closest approximation of safety among fiat currencies in a bankrupt world.

The Can Has Run Out of Road

The artificial economy, leveraged on fictitious capital spun out of thin air, has been stimulated to little better than sporadic episodes of pseudogrowth. Recurring bubbles have been successively inflated to gain another short lease on life, while the powers that be struggle to invent some expedient to expand credit even further in a world already saturated in debt.

I foresee limited prospects for kicking the can much farther down the road. So there you have my confession about why I am one of the "idiots" who expects the collapse of the insanely inflated global credit boom in the vortex of deflation.

Those glossy Vamp fingernails you see everywhere are pointing to deflationary debt collapse. They may yet point up to the emergency Federal Reserve helicopters hovering overhead. But if so, that is a story for another day.

Look out below.

Notes

1 http://www.forbes.com/sites/leesheppard/2013/10/06/fashions-leading-economic-indicator/#787caf804448.

2 Cox, Chris, and Bill Archer, "Why $16 Trillion Only Hints at the True U.S. Debt," *Wall Street Journal*, November 28, 2012, http://www.wsj.com/articles/SB10001424127887323353204578127374039087636.

3 http://usawatchdog.com/america-in-worse-fiscal-shape-than-detroit-professor-laurence-kotlikoff/.

4 http://www.bloomberg.com/news/articles/2015-09-15/dollar-gaining-like-1980s-evokes-plaza-accord-angst-before-fed.

5 http://www.sermonaudio.com/new_details.asp?ID=38473.

6   McLean, Bethany, and Peter Elkind, *Enron: The Smartest Guys in the Room: The Amazing Rise and Scandalous Fall of Enron* (New York: Penguin, 2003), 132–33.

7   Chanos, James, "Hedge Fund Strategies and Market Participation" (Prepared Statement to US Securities and Exchange Commission: Roundtable on Hedge Funds panel discussion, Thursday, May 15, 2003).

8   "The Mismatch Point: The Rise of the Dollar Will Punish Borrowers in Emerging Markets," *The Economist*, March 21, 2015.

9   "Shadow Banking in China: Battling the Darkness," *The Economist*, May 10, 2014.

10   Dobbs, Richard, Susan Lund, et al., "Debt and (Not Much) Deleveraging," http://www.mckinsey.com/insights/economic_studies/debt_and_not_much_deleveraging.

11   http://www.zerohedge.com/news/2015-09-23/welcome-newer-normal-your-complete-guide-world-which-fed-no-longer-control.

12   http://www.washingtonpost.com/news/wonkblog/wp/2015/03/24/how-china-used-more-cement-in-3-years-than-the-u-s-did-in-the-entire-20th-century/.

13   http://davidstockmanscontracorner.com/chinas-25-trillion-debt-bubble-fracturing-bad-loans-mount-at-big-four-banks/. Note that the $21 trillion estimate is at the low side of the McKinsey calculation discussed above.

14   http://davidstockmanscontracorner.com/chinas-monumental-ponzi-heres-how-it-unravels/.

15   "World Steel in Figures 2014," World Steel Association, Evere, Belgium, https://www.worldsteel.org/dms/internetDocumentList/bookshop/World-Steel-in-Figures-2014/document/World%20Steel%20in%20Figures%202014%20Final.pdf.

16   https://www.reddit.com/r/AskEngineers/comments/1z02k9/what_is_the_life_expectancy_of_a_skyscraper/.

17   Durden, Tyler, "A Major Bank Just Made Global Financial 'Meltdown' Its Base Case: The Worst the World Has Ever Seen," *Zero Hedge*, September 9, 2015, http://

www.zerohedge.com/news/
2015-09-12/major-bank
-just-made-global-financial
-meltdown-its-base-case
-worst-world-has-ever-se.

18 Stockman, David, "The
Worldwide Credit Boom Is
Over, Now Comes the Tidal
Wave of Global Deflation,"
Zero Hedge, August 3, 2015.

19 http://www.telegraph.co.uk/
finance/economics/11875529/
We-musnt-ban-cash-or
-inflate-the-pound.html.

20 http://www.telegraph.co.uk/
finance/economics/11875529/
We-musnt-ban-cash-or
-inflate-the-pound.html.

21 http://www.mckinsey
.com/insights/economic
_studies/debt_and_not_much
_deleveraging.

22 http://www.kitco.com/ind/
Taylor/2014-07-21-Monetary
-Velocity-John-Exter-s
-Inverse-Pyramid.html.

Chapter Twenty-One

The Next Stage of Capitalist Development

In antiquity the freedom of the cities was swept away by a bureaucratically organized world empire within which there was no longer a place for political capitalism . . . [In] contrast with antiquity [in the modern era the cities] came under the guise of competing national states in a condition of perpetual struggle for power in peace or war. The competitive struggle created the largest opportunities for modern Western capitalism. The separate states had to compete for mobile capital, which dictated to them the conditions under which it would assist them to power . . . Hence it is the closed national state which afforded to capitalism its chance for development—and as long as the national state does not give place to a world empire capitalism will also endure.

—Max Weber, *General Economic History*

If your eyes are open, and you don't spend all your time in a tattoo parlor, by now you have experienced many premonitions of the Breaking Point. If you read the fine print, four-inch articles in the financial press, you may know that even the former chief economist of the Bank for International Settlements, William White, has warned, "This looks like to me like 2007 all over again, but even worse." As reported in 2013 by *Zero Hedge*, White stated that all the previous imbalances still existed, while total public and private debt levels were 30 percent higher, as a share of GDP in the advanced economies, than they were in '07. He also pointed out an entirely new problem: the emerging market bubbles ending in a bust-boom cycle.[1]

The repeated failure of monetary methods to generate more than an illusion of growth reflects the faltering efficacy of the nation-state. Big government is ill suited for today's megapolitical realities. The fact that inadequate remedies to previous crises have set the stage for even greater crisis to come underscores the thesis of John Micklethwait and Adrian Wooldridge in *The Fourth Revolution: The Global Race to Reinvent the State*. They argue that pervasive malfunction calls for nothing less than deep restructuring of the state system.[2]

You don't need to become a connoisseur of quantitative easing, or translate the European Central Bank's lies about the quality of Italian government collateral, to know that a crisis awaits. The history of the past 500 years says so. So do the last few decades, as well as the most perceptive literature on the dynamics of collapse. Joseph Tainter tells us in *The Collapse of Complex Societies* that "once a complex society enters the stage of declining marginal returns, collapse becomes a mathematical likelihood, requiring little more than sufficient passage of time to make probable an insurmountable calamity."[3] In a previous chapter, I sketched out a rough outline of the cycles of hegemony over the past five centuries. With evidence now pointing to a terminal crisis that will bring the US imperium to a close, an important question for investors arises: What comes next?

A first step toward answering that question is a step back. In order to see what may come next, you have to realize that much of your current view of the world is imagined, if not imaginary.

What do I mean? A vivid example was provided by the Apollo astronauts, one of whom, looking back to earth, was amazed by the fact that he couldn't see any boundaries between countries.[4] What the astronauts saw was not a mosaic of nation-states of varying colors spanning the globe but a striking blue marble in the black void of space.

This view was famously captured in NASA photo 22727 taken by the Apollo 17 crew traveling toward the moon on December 7, 1972, directly conflicted with the "taken for granted state-centric Ptolemaic model or image of world space most modern people carry around in their heads."[5]

Straddling the Boundary between Myth and Reality

The astonishment of an astronaut that he could not discern national borders from space shows how deeply imprinted the notion of the nation-state has become in the metageography of the modern world.

As geographer Peter J. Taylor explains, "*Metageography* is the collective geographical imagination of a society, the spatial framework through which people order their knowledge of the world. It provides the geographical structures that constitute unexamined discourses pervading all social interpretation."

According to Taylor, metageography "straddles the boundary between myth and reality providing a grounding for both the necessary information and the necessary belief within a society." Taylor makes the crucial point that metageography carries over from the territorial realm and informs the way we think about society. He argues that the so-called social sciences—economics, sociology, and political science—were invented in the nineteenth century as part of the effort to organize understanding in nationalist terms within the boundaries of nation-states. Just as the idea of nationalist citizenship was invented to help mobilize large armies as the scale of power and warfare rose, so economics, sociology, and political science all united around a collection of statistics, which Taylor better describes as "state-tistics," to focus attention on developments as defined within the territories of national governments.

An accompanying metageographic anachronism is the mapping of political, economic, and sociological attitudes along a "left" and "right" axis based on imagined affinities for control of the state. This is a labeling hocus-pocus that confuses the crucial issue of where your own interests lie.

You see the implication: if your income is defined within territorial boundaries as a derivative of national GDP per capita, then your success is implicitly a function of national economic policy. It is bound up with that of everyone else within the national boundaries—or with the state itself. Equally, if low-skill jobs migrate offshore to Third World countries—another metageographical conceit as there is, of course, only one world—the greater income gap between persons in First World and Third World populations becomes a "foreign aid" or "foreign policy" problem. But if income differentials increase between high-skilled and low-skilled persons within the same territory, this expression of territorial, ethical myopia becomes a "political" issue that implies the need for predatory taxes on the successful to combat income inequality.

To put it another way, the anachronistic metageography that defines well-being in statist terms distracts attention from the fact that the nation-state charges magnitudes more for its "protection services" than they are worth—magnitudes more than the cost of providing such services and far more than approximations of such services could be secured through alternative sources. You are required through predatory taxation to buy a bundle of protection services that comes tied to monetary confusions and inflationary boom-bust disruptions arising from enshrinement of fiat money through legal tender laws. Then add to those the host of corporatist impositions, FDA regulations, entitlement programs, and other politically inspired antimarket distortions that do not pay their way. What you get in exchange for the taxes you pay is no bargain.

From Territories to "Spaces of Flows"

This is why there is scope for entrepreneurs to gain adherents by shaping the provision of protection services more attractively in the Information Age. As the territorial component of the economy recedes, and Manuel Castells's "spaces of flows" (i.e., networks and cyberspace) become more important, this implies a potentially major shift in the work of the "guardians" who control government.[6] As noted by Jane Jacobs in *Systems of Survival*, their main focus had heretofore been "protecting, acquiring, exploiting, administrating or controlling territories."[7] As more and more of the material supply chain is replaced with digital information, the relative importance of protecting large territories recedes. This opens the possibility for greater entrepreneurial input in structuring the policy mixes of government without creating monstrous hybrids— those that arise when justice is commercialized and sold to the highest bidder, or when commerce is politicized, as it was in the late Soviet Union.

Lee Kwan Yew: Going beyond Redistributive Mass Democracy

Here I think of a signal example of a deft political entrepreneur that I mentioned earlier: the late Lee Kwan Yew. He shaped Singapore from a colonial backwater into one of the world's leading economies, richer on a per capita basis than the United States. Lee made Singapore a city-state and attracted investment at a large scale by making it one of the world's most attractive places for doing business.[8]

The unbundling of Singapore's attractions as a domicile for doing business from the crushing costs of maintaining a nation-state was an informing example of institutional entrepreneurship by Lee Kwan Yew. Notwithstanding a reputation as a left-wing lawyer with early backing from the Communist Party of Malaya, Lee did not take Singapore on the well-worn path to redistributive mass democracy.[9] In fact, Lee Kwan Yew's Singapore is probably better understood as a proprietary city-state than a democratic one. His aim was to make

Singapore a "first-world oasis in a third-world region"—not to make it a welfare state.

In this respect, Lee also distinguished himself from most past examples of proprietary governments. As Frederic Lane suggests, more commonly, the "proprietor's" overriding objective is to enrich himself rather than enhance the well-being of the community. Lee departed from both the examples of "a prince or emperor so absolute that he could be considered the owner of the protection-producing enterprise"[10] and the more conventional model of mass redistributive democracy.

A prime example of Lee's departure from welfare state orthodoxy is Singapore's Medisave program. Its key principle is that no health treatments are provided free of charge. Within Medisave, each citizen accumulates funds that are individually tracked to his or her account under a compulsory savings scheme. The vast majority of Singapore citizens have substantial savings in this scheme (more than $50,000). These funds can be pooled within and across an entire extended family. Citizens have the right to choose one of three levels of care. Lee told me, with considerable pride (in a private meeting in his office in 1995), that if citizens wished to avoid depleting their accounts, he had arranged that they could opt for cheaper hospital rooms without air conditioning. If they preferred a higher-class ward or a private hospital, they paid extra for it.

9.1 Percent Compound per Capita GNP Growth

Lee was able to design a successful political program under which GNP per capita rose at a compound annual rate of 9.1 percent during his thirty-one years as prime minister. One reason was that Singapore is a city-state of just 277.3 square miles. He was close to voters and could reach them on a retail basis without resorting to redistribution on the nation-state scale. Unlike in a large nation-state where one of the surest ways to compose a consensus is by promising to redistribute income to a hefty fraction of the voters, Lee could leverage his success in facilitating a rapid rise in real income. It increased

200 times over from the time he assumed power in 1958. Per capita income was about $400 a year then; in 2014, based on World Bank calculations, Singapore was the world's fourth richest jurisdiction, with GDP at per capita purchasing power parity in international dollars of $82,024. That was 150 percent of the US value for the same year ($54,629).

Note also that unlike the United States, where malpractice of economic measurement routes GDP calculations through the Ministry of Truth, Singapore's robust growth is confirmed by energy proxies. Bruce Podobnik, author of *Global Energy Shifts*, reports that data covering coal, oil, and natural gas, along with nuclear, hydro, geothermal, and other alternative energy, show that per capita energy consumption, expressed in kilograms of oil equivalent, rose in Singapore from one-tenth the US level in 1958 to 110 percent of the US level in 1998.[11]

Successful Depoliticization of the Economy

As a quasi-proprietary city-state, Lee's Singapore was in many ways a unique jurisdiction in that it actually seemed to cater to its customers rather than try to maximize tribute. Singapore's success arose from policy aimed at facilitating well-functioning markets rather than subordinating them to democratic control. Singapore achieved real growth without relying on the monetary methods of simulating illusions of prosperity through inflation, public debt, and private debt, as practiced in the United States and other "advanced" economies. Lee provided a high-caliber jurisdiction that appealed to international investors by securing the rule of law and rooting out corruption. Singapore is ranked each year among the world's least corrupt jurisdictions.

With more corruption-free, proprietary city-states, some would no doubt offer first class infrastructure, while adopting a more tolerant attitude toward chewing gum. (As you may know, Lee Kwan Yew famously outlawed chewing gum in Singapore.) It will be interesting to see what policy configurations are offered as the scale of governance falls and policy entrepreneurs begin to supplant electorates in determining the economic offerings available for protection and other government services.

The Spatiotemporal Fix

David Harvey offers an interesting twist on James Scott's observation that movement is the enemy of the state. In *Seeing like a State*, Scott sets out to understand why states tend to treat "people who move around" so badly.[12] Among those he cites who "have always been a thorn in the side of states" are nomads, hunter-gatherers, gypsies, pastoralists, slash-and-burn farmers, vagrants, homeless people, itinerants, and others whose preferred lifestyles tend to involve what Castells called "spaces of flows," more than "spaces of places."

Movement undermines the exercise of power. For a state to exercise power over a large population, it seeks to make life "legible," simplifying and standardizing local practices so the people are more readily controllable by political power. This becomes more challenging, even impossible, where caravans of gypsies are crisscrossing the country and hunter-gatherer bands roam the woods. The same would also have held true for "donkey caravaneers" like the Hebrew Patriarchs to whom God promised land and progeny.[13]

This brings me to David Harvey's fascinating analysis of what we might call "territorial inertia." Harvey speaks of a "spatio-temporal fix" in which capital is increasingly imprisoned within immobile physical and social infrastructures that support specific types of production (e.g., labor processes). With an increase in quantities of fixed capital, territorial alliances become more powerful in an effort to maintain current privileges and investments, while protecting them from competition over space. This means no new spatial configurations can be created, leading to an "uneven geographical development of capitalism." This form of capitalism is "highly inconsistent with sustained accumulation either within the region or on a global scale."[14]

The nation-state is the superglue that holds the spatiotemporal fix in place. It represents territorial inertia that fosters immobility and is obviously at cross-purposes with the development of a network economy composed of "spaces of flows." The full economic potential of cyberspace is unlikely to be realized so long as capital remains "imprisoned within immobile physical and social infrastructures" fastened in place by the legacy institutions of the nation-state.[15]

The whole suite of economic policies, programs, and initiatives undertaken by nation-states, supposedly in pursuit of prosperity, is the legacy of past hegemonies. The fact that every First World nation-state is now incurring massive budget deficits, and resorting to financial repression, says much about the fragility of the status quo. The anachronistic nation-state cannot afford to pay market interest rates on its metastasizing debt. Nor can it confront astronomical unfunded liabilities for social welfare programs that no longer pay their way.

This confirms that the Breaking Point looms ahead.

Bismarck's Bribe

You live in a world dominated by anachronistic institutions. Governments grew during the nineteenth century as the scale of warfare and the scale of enterprise rose. The first German Chancellor, Otto von Bismarck, invented the welfare state, by his own confession, as a way of "bribing" ordinary people into believing that the state existed for their benefit. He wrote: "My idea was to bribe the working classes, or shall I say, to win them over, to regard the state as a social institution existing for their sake and interested in their welfare."[16]

Bismarck's bribe paid off handsomely when great numbers of the German working class volunteered to fight in World War I. Bismarck's bribe continues to work (after a fashion) in high-income economies today. Some 75 million Americans who either are retired or soon will retire as recipients of a "pay-as-you-go" pension system have a vested interest in the survival of these entitlements.

Thinking "Outside the Box"

You have heard the expression "thinking outside the box." You may have wondered what the "box" was. Here is the answer. The mental box that you are well advised to think "outside of" is the prevailing *metageography*—the legacy of old hegemonies. As suggested earlier, it colors the way you see the world in more ways than one.

This is obvious when you encounter antique *metageographies* on display in old maps embodying imaginations informed by cultures different than our own. Modern "mosaic" maps are presented from a fixed viewpoint, but this, too, is a *metageographic* convention. The "Cempoala map," a rare indigenous map from sixteenth-century Mexico, by contrast, has no fixed orientation. It looks at East, West, North, and South at the same time. Viewing it requires constant reorientation, as features that cannot be taken in from the same viewpoint are scattered around the map.

One of the unexamined conventions of the mosaic, nation-state metageography is the fixed orientation of the map with the north at the top. This is mostly an artifact of the invention of the magnetic compass that points to the north of the Earth's magnetosphere. Consequently, most maps in use by European sea captains were oriented to the North to comport with the compass. (Early Chinese compasses were designed to point South—merely a matter of looking down the other end of the needle.)

In pure logic, compasses aside, other map orientations are possible. At various times, maps oriented in all directions have been used to depict our world. But prior to the Age of Exploration, most maps were oriented with the East at the top because the sun rises in the east.

Consider the so-called T and O flat earth map as drawn by the Christian cartographers of the Middle Ages. This was the standard European map of the world until the sixteenth century. The representation it embodies is clearly a schematic social abstraction, rather than a report of geographic reality measured "to scale."

In the "T and O" map, there is seldom anything you would recognize as geographic detail, only lines in a stylized T-form, symbolic of the cross, meant to signify water bodies separating the continents, with Asia (the East) on the top, Africa (the South) on the bottom right, and Europe (the North) on the bottom left. No territorial jurisdictions are indicated. At the point where the crossbar of the "T" intersects its leg, at the very center of the map, is Jerusalem. In reality, a landlocked city, Jerusalem's placement at the intersection of three bodies of water is not a realistic geographic detail but a symbolic representation of the city as the spiritual focus of Christendom. Surrounding the map is a large circle (thus the "O"), representing the circumfluent ocean that was thought to surround the flat Earth.

Antique Sino-centric maps feature China as the "Middle Kingdom" in representations that could be mistaken for schematic depictions of magnified amoebas. Europe is condensed in foreshortened form in the upper northwest margin. Many of the Chinese maps also show the typical flat Earth representation of territories surrounded by an ocean crowding the borders of the map.

Metageographic conventions other than our own are almost invariably obscure and difficult to interpret. For example, ancient Roman maps of Italy, as preserved in medieval copies, contain geographic representations but are practically unintelligible to a modern eye, as they are oriented with the East at the top. Old Islamic maps divide the world is in a counterintuitive way into two spheres—*dar al-Islam* (House of Islam) and *dar al-harb* (House of War). Many early Arab cartographers oriented their maps with the South at the top.

Time and the Imagination

Measurement of time is another variable of the collective imagination. Although time is not experienced as a physical dimension (notwithstanding Einstein's theory of relativity, in which time is an aspect of the universe whose measurement depends on the observer), our sense of time, too, is parsed according to a conventional framework for thinking about the world.

It seems second nature to think of an hour divided into equal minutes that are in turn composed of sixty equal seconds, with twenty-four hours in the day and seven days in a week. However, measuring time that way is an arbitrary and relatively recent convention. Standardized hours were an essential innovation to make way for the time clock and the factory system. As G. J. Whitrow documents in *Time in History: Views of Time from Prehistory to the Present Day*, the concept of the hour as a unit of standard duration (initially called the "equinox hour") was introduced in the late Middle Ages. Before the invention of the mechanical clock to mark off seconds and minutes, hours were of unequal length—a practice that dated to the ancient Egyptians.

Other societies, and even Western societies in the past, have had completely different conventions of time.[17] The Chinese divided the whole day into twelve parts rather than twenty-four.[18] "The modern practice of numbering the days of the month consecutively from the first to the last," as Whitrow reports, "came to the West from Syria and Egypt in the second half of the sixth century."[19]

The Mayans, who had an elaborate calendar but no clocks, measured the passing of time with a system of numeration based on months with twenty days, each of which had a distinct name. They counted both a 13-month, 260-day cycle (Sacred Year) and a solar year of 365 days "composed of 18 months of 20 days each and five intercalary days."

The combination of the sacred year and the solar year was a larger cycle of 18,980 days—"the least common multiple of

260 and 365." Mayans also parsed time into another division—the *katun*, comprising twenty years of 360 days. The Mayans believed that the world had been created and destroyed repeatedly. They kept a "Long Count" calendar of the days from the most recent starting point of the creation of the world, corresponding to August 10, 3113 BC, on our calendar.[20] This gained a lot of attention in 2012 when the Long Count calendar supposedly expired, suggesting to some excitable people that the world would come to an end. It didn't.

We measure the start of a new day at midnight. But for much of history, the day began at dawn. Or at noon, which was the easiest time to measure before clocks. The medieval Islamic day began at sunset.

The Hopi Indians have "often been cited," according to Whitrow, as a people "whose language contains no words, grammatical forms, constructions, or expression that referred to time or any of its aspects."[21] Interestingly, Old English, as spoken before the Norman Conquest, "contained no distinct words for the future tense."[22]

The conversion of sun time into standardized time zones has become part of the modern metageographic (or if you prefer, "metatemporal") framework. As difficult as it now is to imagine, as late as the fifteenth century, it wasn't just the hours that were not standardized; there was no general agreement within nearby areas on what year it was. You could travel fifty miles and find yourself in another year. R. L. Poole illustrates: "If we suppose a traveler set out from Venice on March 1, 1245, the first day of the Venetian year, he would find himself in 1244 when he reached Florence; and if after a short stay he went on to Pisa, the year 1246 would already have begun there. Continuing his journey westward he would find himself again in 1245 when he entered Provence and on arriving in France before Easter (April 16) he would be once more in 1244."[23] It takes an act of imagination to conceive of time and space as they were ordered in the metageographies of the past. You probably could not keep time if someone handed you an

Islamic astrolabe from the Middle Ages, any more than you could find your way to Jerusalem using a medieval, flat earth "T and O" map.

Seeing maps informed by anachronistic metageographies underscores the fact that there have been many transitions when an existing metageography gave way to a new framework that better reflected the facts and values associated with a new imagination of the world. Now that we are traveling the well-worn path that leads to the breakdown and renewal of civilization, we can expect an upheaval in *metageography* to accompany the coming upheaval in the world system. Peter Taylor argues that the predominant mosaic nation state *metageography* has already been undermined: "the fundamental spatial framework of our thinking is being dismantled. In other words, the demise of embedded statism has arrived."[24]

As suggested above, Taylor says that the starting point for the erosion of the mosaic *metageography* of states was "the impact of the photographs of the Earth from space where, as one of the astronauts exclaimed, a world without boundaries is on display."[25] Taylor concludes, however, that while it is "relatively easy to discern the demise of the old *metageography*, . . . Identifying the new replacement is a very different type of argument."[26]

The Non-Euclidian Geometry of Economic Space in the Twenty-First Century

Not the least reason that the next metageography is difficult to imagine is that the economy has outgrown three dimensional Cartesian mapping. The incorporation of increasing amounts of digital information in the production process raises the map of economic space beyond three dimensions. As we try to describe this new world in mathematical terms, we will see that it is often a high-dimensional chaos. To live successfully in the new economy of the twenty-first century, we need to learn to better understand and predict its high-dimensional chaotic dynamics.

When novelist William Gibson coined "cyberspace" in his 1984 book, *Neuromancer*, he set the stage for understanding that information technology created "a world within a world." Here is the initial passage that famously christened "cyberspace": "A consensual hallucination experienced daily by billions of legitimate operators, in every nation, by children being taught mathematical concepts . . . A graphic representation of data abstracted from banks of every computer in the human system. Unthinkable complexity. Lines of light ranged in the nonspace of the mind, clusters and constellations of data. Like city lights, receding."[27] Gibson's coining of the term "cyberspace" reflected "a critical foresight," claimed analyst Alex Monroe Ingersoll, "in relation to the melding of virtual and physical spaces that are programmed to map data circulation and information flows."[28]

Hence the puzzle inherent in the reimagining of the world. The "spaces of flows" as importantly represented in cyberspace do not obey the laws of Euclidean geometry. This presents a mathematical challenge to the imagination. As mathematicians Edward J. Wegman and Jeffrey L. Sofka put it, "The analysis of high-dimensional data offers a great challenge to the analyst because the human intuition about the geometry of high dimensions fails."[29]

Still to come is the metageographical mapping of the "spaces of flows," the "consensual hallucinations" that compose cyberspace. Indeed, disentangling the many strands of influence that will shape the institutional reset post–Breaking Point, takes us beyond the reach of simple inference. It is easy enough to see, in a general sense, that big government is dysfunctional, lumbered with debts, and seemingly incapable of adjusting to new megapolitical realities. This disconnect implies that change is coming. But exactly when the Breaking Point will come and what will follow are less evident.

The Decline of the West?

Oswald Spengler foresaw a century ago "the going down of the West," "another decline entirely comparable to it (the decline of Classical civilization) in course and duration, which will occupy the first centuries of the coming millennium but is heralded already and sensible in and around us today—the decline of the West."[30] You don't have time to read both volumes of *The Decline of the West* by German historian Oswald Spengler. But sometimes—like now—it is good to know a little history.

That is why I have excerpted a crucial passage below. Read it carefully and you'll see that the *Citizens United* Supreme Court decision that struck down limits on corporate campaign contributions may have changed little after all:

> One can make use of the constitutional rights only when one has money. That a franchise should work even approximately as the idealist supposes it to work presumes the absence of any organized leadership operating on the electors (in its interest) to the extent that its available money permits. As soon as such leadership does appear, the vote ceases to possess anything more than the significance of a censure applied by the multitude to the individual organizations, over whose structure it possesses in the end not the slightest positive influence. So also with the ideal thesis of Western constitutions, the fundamental right of the mass to choose its own representatives—it remains pure theory, for in actuality every developed organization recruits itself. Finally, the feeling emerges that the universal franchise contains no effective rights at all, not even that of choosing between parties. For the powerful figures that have grown up on their soil control, through money, all the

> intellectual machinery of speech and script, and
> are able, on the one hand, to guide the individual's
> opinions as they please above the parties, and, on
> the other, through their patronage, influence, and
> legislation, to create a firm body of whole-hearted
> supporters (the "Caucus") which excludes the rest
> and induces in it a vote-apathy which at the last it
> cannot shake off even for the great crises.[31]

Almost a century ago, Spengler had a premonition of a situation where 10 percent of the Democratic Party's Super Delegates—the unelected "dignitaries" who help chose the party's presidential nominee—are registered lobbyists.

Spengler's insights also help anticipate the heartaches Donald Trump has caused the grandees of the Republican Party—by threatening to nullify the power of money exercised by special interests. Trump's campaign sought to bypass the "organized leadership operating on the electors (in its interest)" that has managed to keep politics in the United States well-bounded by the permissible consensus of the establishment since World War II.

You have to judge for yourself to what extent Spengler's foreboding bears on the terminal crisis of US hegemony. I certainly agree that the twenty-first century is a century of crisis. But I don't fully share Spengler's doom-laden perspective.

As illustrated through numerous examples in the discussion above, a major part of the social construct involves the imagination, the metageography of your worldview. I firmly believe that it is possible to combine insight with optimism about the future.

Change is inevitable, whether we embrace it or not. The tendency to shelter incumbent businesses and legacy institutions is a natural human inclination—a reflection of the spatiotemporal fix that informs the nesting instinct at a group level. Cleaving too tightly to the old may leave economies particularly vulnerable to disruptive change. I see the coming transition, creative destruction writ large, not as the end of civilization, but a transition leading to another, and perhaps freer and better, phase of postmodern capitalist civilization. Human ingenuity will always find a way through, whatever the circumstances.

Alternative Futures

So what comes next? I continue to believe that the future evolution of society will be informed by the characteristics of technology that establish the scale of production, as well as determine the balance of advantage between projecting and resisting power.

What should you expect as the next stage of capitalist development? Various connoisseurs of hegemony in the world system foresee several quite distinct potential outcomes from the collapse of US hegemony. The late Giovanni Arrighi outlined three of what might be termed "conventional" extrapolations from the patterns of the past:

1. Perhaps the most conventional forecast is for the return of Chinese hegemony, after a lapse of 600 years, organized according to Chinese values with a noncapitalist market economy.[32]

2. "As a reaction to increasing systemic chaos, it is possible," in Arrighi's words, "that over the next half-century or so such a world empire will actually be realized."[33] There is also the potential for the creation of a full-fledged world government. Arrighi guessed that the "substantive nature of this world empire" could be "saving the planet from ecological self-destruction." (A special case of a full-fledged world government is an ecofascist world system, in which a type of "global apartheid," as described by Peter Taylor, replaces capitalism.) Certainly, the celebration of the UN's global goals initiative shows that, if nothing else, crony

capitalists think big. The UN's creepy and expensive "new universal agenda" for humanity amounts to a blueprint for a global Big Brother data surveillance state.

3. Another possibility would be, as Arrighi put it, "endless, worldwide chaos."[34]

4. "Eco-Fascist World System." This is a special case of full-fledged world government, which fulfills Arrighi's hunch about the substantive nature of the projected "world empire." Peter Taylor elaborates in projecting that an "impasse" following the collapse of America hegemony could result in what he describes as "Eco-Fascism." Taylor writes:

> With no capital accumulation or inter-state system, this is the end of capitalism replaced by a postmodern global apartheid which we can call an eco-Fascist world system. . . . Delineating possible worlds from a disintegration transition is more difficult than for the outcome of a controlled transition. With less continuity a greater leap of imagination is required. Hence, with eco-Fascism the politics of limits can be reduced to a simple strategy of "maintain what you can and ditch the rest". The usual modernist alternatives to fascism have no simple projection to a postmodern world. As . . . redistribution of resources creates a future of shared poverty.[35]

I can't say that that sounds promising.

5. The most appealing alternative, at least in my view, is that information technology has created a cyber realm that transcends territoriality. As outlined by Nuno Pessoa Barradas in *Empire without Emperor*, no single state could reach hegemony in this cyber realm. This means no given state would be able to lead in the emerging cycle of capital accumulation. The new hegemony will be, in a word, "hegemonless."

Furthermore, in cyberspace, even the construction of walls on national borders cannot conclusively halt the spread of information.

Barradas draws on *The End of the Nation-State* by Jean-Marie Guéhenno to propose that in the new world of information technology "no single state can attain hegemony, and hence the emerging systemic cycle of accumulation of capital will not be led by any given state. The new hegemony, which we will call 'Empire without Emperor,' is hegemonless . . . We thus arrive at the concept of the non-geographic core-periphery structure, that is superimposed to the traditional geographic one."[36] He concludes, "National borders have no influence in the spread of information" in cyberspace.

The United States Joins the "Third World"

An implication of the nonterritorial character of information technology is that it will assign a considerable fraction of the populations of the formerly core countries to peripheral roles. Instead of sorting prosperity by jurisdiction, the emerging system incorporates the new Third World periphery within the territory of the old core states. In that sense, it is not slander to consider the United States an increasingly Third World country. That is just what should be expected. It is a consequence of changing megapolitical conditions. At the same time, it underscores the anachronistic character of nation-states that foster a political imperative to redistribute income at a magnitude that no longer pays its way.

The basic assumption of common interests and social affinities between hundreds of millions of people who happen to live within the confines of a continental economy like the United States is, at best, an exaggeration—as is so clearly illustrated by the recurring fiscal impasses in Washington.

As the terminal crisis of US hegemony unfolds, it will become increasingly evident that efforts by the US security state to eavesdrop on every conversation and monitor every email on Earth represent not only a departure from the rule of law but a vast overreach that is destined to fail. To the extent that US leaders persist in attacking every manifestation of global privacy, it will make it an unalloyed disadvantage to be domiciled in the current version of the United States (as IBM and Oracle found in Q3 2012 when their sales in the BRIC countries plunged).

I can only cross my fingers and pray that the collapse of US hegemony, unlike the three immediately preceding cases, will not entail an additional "thirty years' war." Peter J. Taylor has identified the "thirty years' war" as an important milestone of transitions of power in the world system. He writes: "As well as being on the winning side, the hegemon has a 'good war' economically. This is the case with the Dutch during the Thirty Years War, and it also fits the British during the Napoleonic war and the Americans during World Wars I and II."[37] I would hope that the passing of the United States as the world's hegemon does not entail another thirty years' war on the scale of those in the past. For one thing, such an all-out conflict in the age of nuclear weapons would cause incredible destruction and loss of life.

Of course, one could argue that the "thirty years' war" of American decline is actually the half century of war that began in 1965 with the deployment of American ground troops in Vietnam and has continued more or less ever since, particularly in Iraq and Afghanistan, where the United States has squandered trillions chasing, according to the head of the CIA, one hundred or fewer al-Qaeda operatives.

A seemingly conservative and measured calculation in the *Kabul Press* by Matthew J. Nasuti suggests that it has cost American taxpayers $50 million for each Taliban fighter killed in the war.[38] A close read of his calculations, however, shows this to be woefully underestimated. For one thing, Nasuti's estimates of the costs of the war could be on the low side by a magnitude. He includes only the Pentagon's published costs. The highest credible estimates I have seen (from Nobel Prize–winner Joseph Stiglitz and Linda Bilmes of Harvard) put the current out-of-pocket and already incurred future costs of the Afghan and Iraq wars around at least $6 trillion.[39] According to a report in *Defense One*, a military newsletter, covered by RT, after holding at about $1.3 million, "The cost of keeping each American soldier in Afghanistan" nearly doubled to $2.1 million.[40] Furthermore, Nasuti's estimate of Taliban killed annually could be exaggerated by as much as three times over. When the costs of pensions for war widows and caring for hundreds of thousands of wounded and injured troops are compiled, along with compound interest on amounts borrowed to pay these bills, the all-in cost to kill each Taliban fighter could easily be $500 million.

Such incredibly expensive and inconclusive wars have emphatically demonstrated the inability of the US Armed Forces to project power against small groups of squalid terrorists. There could scarcely be a more emphatic demonstration that American hegemony is in its twilight. So a question to be answered in projecting the next phase of capitalism is, "Will there be a next phase of capitalism?" Or will a bureaucratically organized world empire crush economic freedom?

There have been alarms aplenty about black helicopters and dangers posed by the threat of one world government. While the fact that the leading governments have been losing control over crucial aspects of the world economy for decades may help explain the longing for world government on the part of some control freaks (i.e., the big crony capitalists), it also underscores why the US government is unlikely to be able to convert its disintegrating hegemony into a world empire. Megapolitical conditions—as reflected in the ghastly expenses incurred by the United States in its ongoing war on terror, conducted not against any state but against ragtag nonterritorial groups—testify to the collapsing scale at which violence can be effectively organized.

A report from Brown University concluded that the total US costs for wars in Iraq, Afghanistan, and Pakistan over the past decade (the Afghan conflict has continued for thirteen years—longer than the Civil War, World War I, and World War II combined) is at least $3.2 to $3.4 trillion.[41] While this is 50 percent lower than the Joseph Stiglitz and Linda Bilmes estimate, it is ruinously high.

It is pertinent here to consider the grotesque incompetence evidenced in the prosecution of US intervention in the Middle East. When I say "grotesque incompetence," consider the Obama administration's "Train and Equip" program announced in May 2015. It was to train and equip an army of 5,400 moderate Syrian fighters by the end of 2015—at an expense of $500 million. But by the autumn, General Lloyd Austin of the US Central Command told Congress that the total number of Train and Equip troops actually fighting was "four or five." Not four thousand or five thousand; four or five. But the grotesque incompetence may have been marginally less astounding than it at first seems. You see, it did not cost $100 million each to outfit and deploy as many as five moderate Syrian rebels. The cost could have been no greater than $77 million per fighter, because only $383 million of the earmarked $500 million was actually spent.

Perhaps more important than the skyrocketing costs for projecting power (plunging returns to violence) is the fact that technological developments have dramatically reduced the scale at which enterprise must be organized. Technological innovations have created a new nonterritorial realm where money can be made: the virtual reality of cyberspace.

It might be good to recall that for 99 percent of human existence, when megapolitical conditions offered no leverage for predatory violence, government did not exist. Some experts believe that, anatomically, modern humans have inhabited the earth for as long as one million years. During 990,000 of those years we lived in relative peace, if not abundance, as hunters and gatherers in the "Garden of Eden." (Or was that the "City Garden of Eden"?)

The Football Fan's View of History

If the saga of human existence on Earth were mapped on an American football field, the introduction of farming about ten thousand years ago was an event happening on the one-yard line. The height of the Roman Empire at AD 117 would have occurred on the seven-inch line. The advent of the Industrial Revolution would have taken place one inch from the goal line—the equivalent of the width of a golf ball resting on a football field. Perhaps the next stage of capitalism will be played out in the end zone?

After long centuries in which power was organized in hegemonies of ever-greater scale organized by nation-states, megapolitical conditions now point to the devolution of power to a smaller scale. The Information Age implies a radical devolution of power. It will expose diseconomies of scale embodied in anachronistic forms of big business capitalism. And it will even more emphatically undermine the returns to complexity embodied in the anachronistic nation-state. It is beyond the scope of this analysis to detail a full litany of the implications of this revolution in human affairs. But broadly and simply, as epitomized by 3-D printing, information technology will ensure that economic and political power devolve back toward the individual. Market forces will replace politics and crony capitalism in determining the distribution of income.

Res Publica Romana

It is all very well to recognize that the arc of history has turned and that the big government nation-state has outlived the megapolitical factors that gave it existence. But that doesn't tell you when the other shoe will drop.

In the mid-1980s, when I mustered the nerve to begin forecasting the collapse of the Soviet Union, it was a prelude to something amazing. On December 25, 1991, Mikhail Gorbachev resigned as the last president of the Soviet Union and declared his office extinct. At 7:32 p.m. that evening, the

Soviet hammer and sickle flag was lowered from the Kremlin for the last time. The Soviet Union ceased to exist.

I later regretted that I had not gone to Ladbroke's or another legal betting agency to wager a million-dollar bet that the Soviet Union would collapse. A few years earlier, I probably could have gotten great odds. And with the evidence of December 25, 1991, I would have collected. There could have been no argument about whether I was right.

It might have been a different story, however, if you were a rogue Roman who had bet a million denarii in 42 BC, after the Battle of Phillippi, that the Roman Republic would cease to exist within fifteen years. I think it highly unlikely that your counterparty would have paid when the Senate granted Octavius extraordinary powers in 27 BC and he assumed the title "Augustus." That could have postponed settlement of your winnings for as long as 1488 years.

Notwithstanding the fact that Wikipedia tells us that the Roman Republic ended in 27 BC with the establishment of the Roman Empire, it is merely reporting the current consensus among historians of the de facto end of the Roman Republic. Professor Anthony Kaldellis tells us in his provocative new history, *The Byzantine Republic: People and Power in New Rome*, that Byzantium, as the Eastern incarnation of the Roman Republic has been known since the sixteenth century, was indeed "a Roman republic."[42] (The term "Byzantine Empire," unknown to the supposed Byzantines themselves, was invented in 1557, about a century after the fall of Constantinople by German historian Hieronymus Wolf, in his work *Corpus Historiae Byzantinae*). The use of "Byzantine" to describe the Eastern remnants of Rome was further popularized by the eighteenth-century French political philosopher, the Baron de Montesquieu.

The Byzantines thought themselves the surviving expression of the Roman Republic.[43] In a de jure sense, the Roman Republic soldiered on for another millennium and a half until July 1461, when the last garrison of the Roman army defending the Castle of Salmeniko, in the *Peloponnese region of Southern Greece,* capitulated to the forces of the Ottoman Turks. As Gibbon confirms, in their minds, the people we now call "Byzantines," thought of themselves as Romans. "They alleged a lineal and unbroken succession from Augustus and Constantine; and, in the lowest period of degeneracy and decay, the name of **ROMANS** adhered to the last fragments of the empire of Constantinople."[44]

Without venturing further into the lowercase *b* byzantine complexity evidenced in the evolution of the institutional character of the Roman Republic over the 1488 years between its de facto end in 27 BC and its final de jure extinction in July 1461, you will recognize the highlighted difference between the de facto and the de jure.

Bearing this in mind may help to better understand the many potential permutations of the wind down of the nation-state. Ponder, if you will, the vast difference between the rapid and permanent de jure collapse of the Soviet Union and the protracted de jure afterlife of the Roman Republic.

A review of the history of republican Rome shows that the system underwent many radical changes, with the commoners, or plebians, gradually achieving some protections from the law. For example, after several gestures of secession, in which plebeians walked out of Rome, the principle was established that debtors could no longer be executed for failure to pay. Anyone confirmed by the courts as owing a debt would be given thirty days to pay—only after this could he be sold into slavery by his creditors.

The specifics of Rome's republican political contentions are less important than the fact that Rome had already thrived for twice as long as the United States has existed when the Senate granted Octavian the title Augustus. *Res Publica Romana* had a good reputation, so it made sense for Octavian and other autocrats who followed to conserve that good name. So they did.

Also note that, almost from the beginning of the Roman Republic, there had been intervals of authoritarian rule. The first dictator was appointed in 501 BC, less than a decade after the founding of the republic. Equally, it is notable that Marcus Furius Camillus, who was the five-times-appointed dictator of Rome, was also celebrated as "the second founder of Rome." With this background, it was less contradictory to republican tradition than it may seem to a modern observer to have Octavian appointed as essentially "dictator for life."

While Rome enjoyed a good reputation that may have seemed worth preserving, the Soviet Union did not. Its reputation was bad and getting worse with its population, and because the Soviet republics were organized along ethnic lines, a Soviet breakup predictably opened the door to more power for many of their leaders. Consequently, men like Boris Yeltsin and Nursultan Nazarbayev, leaders of the two largest Soviet Republics, were only too glad to explore de jure as well as de facto change. Today, it seems likely that the distinction between de jure and de facto transformation could play a role in this century of crisis.

The Devolution of Nation-States

As the breakdown of nation-states works its way like a contagion from the periphery to the core, we can already see overt campaigns for devolution to split the sovereignty of even advanced nation-states. There was a closely divided referendum for Scotland to withdraw from the United Kingdom. The "no" side carried the day by 55 percent to 45 percent.

An apparently popular campaign for Catalan independence from Spain works its way into the headlines sporadically. Indeed, there is such a headline as I write on September 27, 2015: Catalan independence claimed a decisive victory in regional parliamentary elections. According to Reuters, secessionist parties secured 72 of 135 seats in the region,[45] which consists of 7.5 million people and includes Barcelona.

In Canada, the elected government in Quebec has several times sought to split the country with the Bloc Québécois favoring independence for Quebec. That outcome was only narrowly defeated in 1995.

And the United States?

By contrast, there have been fewer contemporary efforts to dissolve the United States. A Reuters/Ipsos poll in 2014 showed that local sentiment for withdrawing from the United States was strongest in Texas, Oklahoma, New Mexico, and Arizona, where one in three favored the move.[46] In a report on that poll, under the headline "A Third of Texans Support Seceding from the Union?!," the *Dallas Morning News* reported that the national average in support of dissolving the United States is 24 percent, as compared to one-third of Texans.[47]

Unlike the situation in most states, there is already a movement for Texas independence that has gathered signatures for a nonbinding 2016 ballot initiative endorsing independence. In 2012, a petition to the White House asking for Texas independence sported 125,746 signatures. James Gaines, Reuters global editor-at-large, analyzed follow-up phone calls with a small random sample of prosecession respondents to the Reuters national poll. He reported that the people he spoke with did not fall along simple red or blue lines: their signatures were a form of protest against a lack of jobs postrecovery, low-paying jobs, mistreatment of veterans, war, political corruption, assault on marriage, assault on same-sex marriage, the government in general, the president, both political parties, and more.[48]

Gaines stated, "By the evidence of the poll data as well as these anecdotal conversations, the sense of aggrievement is comprehensive, bipartisan, somewhat incoherent, but deeply felt . . . this should be more than disconcerting; it's a situation that could get dangerous." The status quo is on a slippery slope when it is held in pervasive contempt for a multitude of often contradictory reasons. About which, here are a couple of observations:

1. The polychromatic complaints of the proponents of secession, apart from gripes about a recovery that has not yet produced jobs and against jobs that don't pay, underscore the growing challenge of trying to run a one-size-fits-all continental economy. Smaller polities could better appeal to people on the basis of otherwise divisive policies. For example, those opposed to same-sex marriage could enjoy living with others sharing their views while leaving those who don't to prosper with alternative arrangements in other venues.

2. Presumably, the fact that the United States has enjoyed one of the world's highest standards of living and nonetheless manifests extraordinary levels of discontent suggests that support for the status quo will be less than stalwart in the aftermath of the coming terminal crisis of US hegemony.

I admit that I am surprised that support for the status quo seems so shallow, with up to 34 percent of respondents in a reputable poll opting in favor of decisive institutional change even before terminal crisis strikes home. The level of disaffection is greatest among young men. Whether it is pervasive enough to lead to Soviet-style de jure collapse, rather than a de facto reorganization a la the Roman Republic, will be a matter of great interest in the years to come.

Madison and Jefferson Ride Again?

While the macro logic makes a powerful case for the greater efficacy of smaller jurisdictions in the Information Age, the prospects of de jure devolution seem problematic. Not the least reason is because there is no particular tribal or ethnic leverage to accelerate independence projects in the United States as there was in the former Soviet Union and there is in Scotland, Quebec, Catalonia, and to a lesser extent, the North of Italy.

Consequently, I rather expect the devolution to a smaller scale of governance in the current United States to involve mutations of the current system. De facto devolution may come into play in the spirit that Madison expressed in the Virginia Resolution of 1798 in which he decried the federal government's enlargement of its powers and resulting destruction of the meaning and effect of the Constitution.[49] Madison saw the federal government consolidating the states into one sovereignty and feared the consequences: a transformation of the US republican system into an absolute or mixed monarchy system. Jefferson went further in the Kentucky Resolution and explicitly advocated nullification by the states of federal actions deemed beyond proper bounds.[50]

No doubt, you could find some chatty law professor who would tell you that the "doctrine of nullification," along with its sister ship, "the doctrine of interdiction," was sunk in the Civil War, never to float again. Of course, the law professor would be wrong in the sense that counts. Centralization and decentralization perpetually swing on a pendulum. No legalistic prohibitions can check the swings subject to the powerful megapolitical gravity. Devolve they will: one way or another, layered sovereignty will be realized at the local level.

As a thought exercise, I can see at least two obvious channels through which that might be achieved:

1. Through nullification or interdiction of federal laws. Notwithstanding the chatty law professor's assurance to the contrary, "Nullification is a growing practice." For example, there are more than two hundred sanctuary cities in thirty-two states where federal immigration law is not enforced. Also, since 1996, twenty-three states plus the District of Columbia have legalized marijuana for medical and/or recreational use. In the wake of the Breaking Point, it is reasonable to suppose that the US government will

command much diminished resources (for reasons explored throughout this book).

In particular, fiat money is likely to be discredited. Localities may take the lead in reconstituting money on a more sound footing. Texas has already moved in that direction with legislation proposed by State Representative Giovanni Capriglione to create a Texas Bullion Depository where Texas could store its gold. They have some. The University of Texas Investment Management Co. (UTIMCO) heeded the pithy advice of Kyle Bass, a member of UTIMCO's board. Bass said, "Buying gold is just buying a put against the idiocy of the political cycle." According to reports in 2011, UTIMCO bought $1 billion in gold bullion.

One can imagine nullification or interdiction extending to tax laws and other areas allowing states and even metropolitan areas to achieve de facto independence. After all, the United States began as a federation. It could potentially evolve into something akin to a latter-day Hanseatic League, a commercial and defensive confederation of de facto city-states.

2. Another crevice in the edifice of sovereignty that might be pried open to provide de jure cover for the devolution of power to the local level involves the quasi-independence of American Indian bands from US law. Ironically, perhaps some of those bands would be deft enough to leverage their status for more productive uses than casino gambling. For example, the Muwekma Ohlone Tribe formerly lived around San Francisco Bay, and the Miccosukee Tribe of Indians of Florida have been trying for decades to assert control over land near Miami.

This is a thought exercise, not a prediction. It seems far from likely that a South Florida version of Singapore will evolve under the leadership of the Miccosukee Tribe of Indians. But considering this unlikely prospect is a useful exercise going into the Breaking Point—something that seems unlikely now will happen. You need to be ready for almost anything.

For too long, our thinking has been trapped in antique intellectual constructs. It is time we ploughed new furrows. When you view the economy exclusively in terms of twentieth-century business cycles, or even long waves (also a twentieth-century construct), you adopt an unexamined discourse that may lead you astray. It is too easy to assume that slowdowns and downturns automatically lead to upturns and booms as matters of clockwork. They need not. The green shoots are turning brown.

I suspect that the resurgent phase of capitalist growth requires creative destruction at a scale that can shatter the spatiotemporal fix that imprisons capital within deeply entrenched, immobile infrastructures subject to sharply falling marginal returns. Simply by eliminating the counterproductive anti-market contrivances that are held in place by big government, the world could realize significant efficiency gains that could yield twentieth-century-style growth surges to economies now in the thrall of the twenty-first-century secular stagnation.

I have already shared with you the astonishing 2013 study from the *Journal of Economic Growth* that concluded that increased regulation since 1949 had cost the US economy $37 billion in lost annual GDP, as of 2011, implying that the average American would enjoy an additional $125,000 in annual income if not for all the crony capitalist rip-offs. Presumably, eliminating this regulation could lead, after a transition, to something better.

The potential for realizing a huge one-off surge in income from a shift to efficiency was illustrated in the wake of the collapse of the Soviet Union. Based on World Bank figures, GDP in Russia, and the other former Soviet Republics, took a steep dive after the 1991 collapse of the Soviet Union. Yet also based on World Bank figures, probably subject to large measurement errors, one could nonetheless argue that current per capita GDP in Russia is as much as fourteen times higher than it was on average from 1991 through 2000. And GDP in Kazakhstan is now twenty-three times higher than its 1991–2000 average. Estonia, which had the highest per capita GDP in the former Soviet Union according to the World Development Indicators of the World Bank, has managed a bit less than a tenfold increase in per capita GDP in this century.

The pertinent point is that after a maximum decline estimated at 39 percent from 1991 levels in 1998, Russia's GDP per capita subsequently grew by twenty-three times to $25,248 by 2013 according to the World Bank. Equally, Kazakhstan suffered a maximum decline of 28 percent, bottoming in 1995. From that point, GDP per head in Kazakhstan seems to have multiplied thirty-twofold, based on World Bank figures, to $23,214.

Much like the former Soviet Union, Western economies, lumbered with innumerable counterproductive regulations and crony capitalist big government, have the potential to enjoy a considerable boost to growth by ditching antimarket distortions. The big government nation-state has outlived the megapolitical foundations that gave it existence. Big government was built on high and rising returns to scale in the organization of violence and in the production process.

There was a time, as Napoleon assured us, when "God was on the side of the big battalions." No longer. In the majority of asymmetrical conflicts since 1950, the smaller, ostensibly weaker combatant has won. This negates the most pressing reason for big government.

Another major issue tangled up with the dysfunction of big government is the apparent conflict between democracy and capitalism. Prior to the Industrial Revolution, as evidenced in the United States during the late eighteenth century, there were substantial property restrictions on the vote. In urban areas, only about 40 percent of white males had the franchise, while up to 70 percent voted in rural areas. (Six states also permitted free black males who met property requirements to vote.) Perhaps because there were megapolitical advantages to be realized from government at a larger scale, the franchise was expanded almost everywhere, granting propertyless males and females the vote. This inevitably led to greater income redistribution.

Indeed, today one of the major functions of big government is income redistribution. It is an obvious route for gaining the affiliation of support populations that otherwise may have little in common. Composing a single policy that commands majority support among persons of wildly different skills, values, incomes, and education levels has proven challenging across the globe.

If big governments reigning over the advanced economies do collapse in the long run, as seems likely, I would expect the scale of governance to shrink dramatically. Probably the most viable form of government going forward would be the metropolitan city-state, in which dynamic cities and their hinterlands would achieve independence.

As Philip Stephens suggested in a bold article in the *Financial Times*, "London should break free from Little England," devolution to a smaller scale would remind Britain that "power is best exercised close to the people." Even better, Europhobes would no longer have an influence on the city, thus ensuring it would stay "open to Polish doctors, Italian designers and French mathematicians." Stephens laments that conservatives are refusing immigration, as he sees immigrants as the city's "lifeblood." He imagines a new London city-state that would attract the best and brightest from around the world, leaving "anti-immigration pressure groups . . . to their anguished debates about identity."[51]

The divergence of interests that divides residents of the home counties in England from their wealthier cousins in London has parallels in the United States. These were highlighted in a 2014 demographic analysis in the *Washington Post*. It showed that in 210 counties of the United States, income peaked more than forty-five years ago. In another 572 counties, income peaked thirty-five years ago. In only 380 counties, many of them sites of active oil exploration and production, did income peak in the decade of the 2010s.

I referred earlier to the plans of my friend Peter Thiel, and other high-tech billionaires, to create a workspace for incubating high-tech companies beyond the laws of the United States. As you may recall, their project, Blueseed, will be an artificial island hosting a startup community for entrepreneurs. It will be launched on a cruise ship anchored in international waters, twelve nautical miles from the coast of San Francisco.

This will allow startup entrepreneurs from anywhere on the globe to launch or grow companies near Silicon Valley without the need for a US work visa. The ship will be converted into a coworking and coliving space, with high-speed Internet access and daily transport to the mainland via ferryboat. To date, over 1,500 entrepreneurs from 500 startups in more than 70 countries have expressed interest in living on Blueseed. This seems a much inferior solution to what could be achieved when San Francisco becomes a city-state.

Also, in a world in which exogenous energy is destined to be at a premium, cities offer the obvious advantage of hosting and facilitating the greatest density of logistical interlinks and transactions at the lowest cost in energy inputs.

Still another hint that the age of the microstate draws near is provided by a glance at the CIA's *World Factbook* table that ranks the sovereignties of the world on the basis of per capita GDP. Among a dozen or so that rank higher than the United States, every one, except oil-rich Norway (population 5.14 million), is either a city-state or a ministate: Monaco, Macau, Liechtenstein, Qatar, Luxembourg, Hong Kong, Singapore, Jersey, Bermuda, Brunei, Falkland Islands, and Isle of Mann. And if you think about it, Norway's population is roughly similar to that of Singapore, and Hong Kong's population is 2.1 million greater than that of Norway.

It should not be a surprise that the jurisdictions with the highest per capita incomes in the world are city-states and minisovereignties. Governance is more effective at a smaller scale in which many of the policy impasses that stump nation-states can be ignored altogether because it is not necessary to insist upon a one-size-fits-all solution to stretch over a continental economy.

Microsovereignties are capable of providing a setting for free-market prosperity in the future. After five centuries during which the scale of governance, the scale of warfare, and the organization of business inexorably rose, that long historical trend has been short-circuited by the invention of microprocessing and the advent of the information economy, as reflected in the paradigm example of 3-D printing.

Just as mass production gave rise to big government, I believe that microproduction will give rise to microsovereignties. Remember, there were 300 city-states in Italy alone in 1250. Their time will come again. The new sovereignties that will emerge from the coming transition crisis will be microsovereignties: small states on the scale of cities and provinces rather than continental economies.

Philip Stephens has taken a step forward in thinking about what comes next in proposing that London should become a city-state. He did not write overtly about reinventing government in response to crisis, but crisis itself will take care of that in the long run.

As little as we may wish to confront the long run, someday it will confront us. The arc of history has turned. The status quo has exhausted it potential. Whatever comes next will inevitably confront us as an adventure. As Helen Keller suggested in a wise rumination about the long run, "Security is mostly a superstition. It does not exist in nature, nor do the children of men as a whole experience it. Avoiding danger is no safer in the long run than outright exposure. Life is either a daring adventure, or nothing."

Notes

1   http://www.zerohedge.com/print/478912.

2   Micklethwait, John, and Adrian Wooldridge, *The Fourth Revolution: The Global Race to Reinvent the State* (New York: Penguin, 2014).

3   Tainter, Joseph A., *The Collapse of Complex Societies* (Cambridge: Cambridge University Press, 1990).

4   Beaverbrook, Jonathan V., Roland G. Smith, and Peter J. Taylor, "World City Networks: A New Metageography," *Annals of the Association of American Geographers* 90, no. 1: 123.

5   Ibid.

6   See Castells, Manuel, *The Rise of Network Society* (Oxford: Blackwell, 1996).

7   Jacobs, Jane, *Systems of Survival: A Dialogue on the Moral Foundations of Commerce and Politics* (New York: Vintage Books, 1994), 29.

8   Taylor, Peter J., "World Cities and Territorial States: The Rise and Fall of Their Mutuality," in *World Cities in a World System*, ed. Paul L. Knox and Peter J. Taylor (Cambridge: Cambridge University Press, 1995), 59.

9   Turnbull, C. M., *A History of Modern Singapore: 1819–2005* (Singapore: NUS Press, 2009), 252.

10 See Frederic C. Lane, "Economic Consequences of Organized Violence," in *Profits from Power: Readings in Protection Rent and Violence—Controlling Enterprises* (Albany: State University of New York Press, 1973), 54.

11 Podobnik, Bruce, "Global Energy Inequalities," in *Global Social Change: Historical and Comparative Perspectives*, ed. Christopher Chase-Dunn and Savatore J. Babones (Baltimore: Johns Hopkins University Press, 2006), table 7.1.

12 Scott, James, *Seeing like a State: How Certain Schemes to Improve the Human Condition Have Failed* (New Haven, CT: Yale University Press, 1998), 1.

13 Albright, William F., Introduction to Herman Gunkel, *The Legends of Genesis: The Biblical Saga & History* (New York: Schocken Books, 1964), x.

14 Harvey, David, *The Limits to Capital* (Chicago: University of Chicago Press, 1982), 428–29.

15 Ibid.

16 See http://www.fee.org/the
    _freeman/detail/marching
    -to-bismarcks-drummer
    -the-origins-of-the-modern
    -welfare-state#ixzz2k5u8pwmj.

17 Whitrow, G. J., *Time in History:
    Views of Time from Prehistory to
    the Present Day* (Oxford: Ox-
    ford University Press, 1988).

18 Ibid.

19 Ibid., 84–85.

20 See Ibid., 92–93.

21 Ibid., 8.

22 Ibid., 15.

23 Quoted in ibid., 84.

24 Taylor, P. J., "A Metageograph-
    ical Argument on Modernities
    and Social Science," *GaWC
    Research Bulletin* 29 (Septem-
    ber 4, 2000).

25 Ibid.

26 Ibid.

27 Gibson, William, *Neuromancer*
    (New York: Berkley Publish-
    ing Group, 1984), 51.

28 Ingersoll, Alex Monroe,
    *Place in Flows: A Contin-
    uum of Virtual Transduction
    and the Work of Locating the
    Mobile Mob* (University of
    Colorado, 2008), 74, https://
    books.google.com/books
    ?id=ErpgxxsUCmYC&pg
    =PA74&lpg=PA74&dq=
    graphic+representations+of
    +spaces+of+flows&source

    =bl&ots=GtXQSj1iYs
    &sig=KKKAtifhLhUccFEie
    krQibj8pwo&hl=en&sa=X
    &ved=0ahUKEwjB3ozznJb
    KAhUGXB4KHZLZCwEQ
    6AEIVzAJ#v=onepage&q=
    graphic%20representations
    %20of%20spaces%20of%20
    flows&f=false.

29 Wegman, Edward J., and Jeffrey
    L. Sofka, "On Some Mathe-
    matics for Visualizing High
    Dimensional Data," http://binf
    .gmu.edu/jsolka/PAPERS/
    MathVisRevision.pdf.

30 Spengler, Oswald, *The De-
    cline of the West*, trans. Charles
    Francis Atkinson (New York:
    Modern Library, 1962), 74.

31 Ibid., vol. 2, 456.

32 Arrighi, *The Long Twentieth
    Century*, new ed. (New York:
    Verso, 2010), 380.

33 Ibid., 381.

34 Ibid.

35 Taylor, Peter J., *The Way the
    Modern World Works: World
    Hegemony to World Impasse*
    (Chichester: John Wiley &
    Sons, 1996), 218–19.

36 Barradas, Nuno Pessoa, *Em-
    pire without Emperor*, 13.

37 Taylor, *Way the Modern World
    Works*, 4.

38 Nasuti, Matthew J., "Killing
    Each Taliban Soldier Costs

$50 Million," September 30, 2010, http://kabulpress.org/my/spip.php?article32304.

39 See http://www.thedailybell.com/editorials/34748/Paul-Craig-Roberts-What-Is-The-Real-Agenda-Of-The-American-Police-State/#sthash.umPApiTG.dpuf.

40 See "Collateral Damage: Cost of Each US Soldier in Afghanistan Soars to $2.1 Million," October 25, 2013, http://rt.com/usa/us-afghanistan-pentagon-troops-budget-721/.

41 Crawford, Neta, and Catherine Lutz, "Economic and Budgetary Costs of the Wars in Afghanistan, Iraq and Pakistan to the United States: A Summary," *Costs of War*, Brown University.

42 Kaldellis, Anthony, *The Byzantine Republic: People and Power in New Rome* (Cambridge, MA: Harvard University Press), 2015.

43 Ibid., 28.

44 Gibbon, Edward, *The Decline and Fall of the Roman Empire* (New York: Modern Library, 1995), 3:298–99.

45 Toyer, Julien, "Victorious Catalan Separatists Claim Mandate to Break with Spain," http://www.reuters.com/article/2015/09/28/us-spain-catalonia-idUSKCN0RQ0RN20150928.

46 http://www.dallasnews.com/news/politics/headlines/20150906-texan-declares-own-brand-of-secession.ece.

47 Stockdale, Nicole, "A Third of Texans Support Seceding from the Union?!," *Dallas Morning News*, September 23, 2014, http://dallasmorningviewsblog.dallasnews.com/2014/09/a-third-of-texans-support-seceding-from-the-union.html/.

48 http://blogs.reuters.com/jamesrgaines/2014/09/19/one-in-four-americans-want-their-state-to-secede-from-the-u-s-but-why/.

49 From the Virginia Resolution, http://avalon.law.yale.edu/.

50 From the Kentucky Resolution, http://avalon.law.yale.edu/.

51 Stephens, Philip, "London Should Break Free from Little England," *Financial Times*, December 11, 2014.

Chapter Twenty-Two

Pirenne's Pendulum and the Return of the Organic Economy

Thus we are looking at a few more years of steady decline before the lights start going out. This, then, is the key distinction: the USSR collapsed promptly because it was already skin and bones, whereas the US and the EU have plenty of subcutaneous fat to burn through. But they are, in fact, burning through it. And so, the conclusion is, the collapse will come, but here it will take a little longer.

—Dmitry Orlov, "How to Time Collapses," *ClubOrlov*

In reviewing my analysis of the declining state retrograde economy in previous chapters, I suspect that I may have dwelled too much on the potential for total financial, industrial, political, and social collapse. Yes, it could happen. You could end up as an unpaid extra in a *Mad Max* sequel. It is probably more likely than we care to imagine.

Yet you could also end up like St. Godric of Finchale, who was born the better part of one thousand years ago in the eleventh century. What little we know of him after his birth in 1065 to poor peasants in Wallpole, Norfolk, is that he was "from infancy . . . forced to use his ingenuity to find the means of livelihood." He seems to have gotten his start as an entrepreneur with a lucky find of wreckage cast up by the sea. From there he became a wandering peddler, from which he earned a sufficient sum to join a "troop of town merchants" and from there, he chartered a boat for coastal trading "along the shores of England, Scotland, Denmark and Flanders. His company is highly successful. Godric is now a man of wealth." Then, suddenly overtaken with religious enthusiasm (or merely hard-pressed to invent a better way to retire), Godric "renounces his fortune, gives his goods to the poor and becomes a monk."[1]

You would risk overlooking or misreading Godric's genius if you interpreted his sudden religious conversion solely in mod-ern terms. Remember when he reached the age of forty-five in the year 1110, there was nothing remotely like an old age pension. There was no Social Security. There was no wealth management industry designing strategies for a secure re-tirement. Godric had to invent his own path. Because of the prohibition against usury, re-enforced by the "Capitularies of Charlemagne" (issued 803 AD) banning transactions "where more is asked than is given," the form of financial instruments was limited by opposition from the church. For example, there were no circulating bonds from which to build a retirement portfolio. There were no modern investment instruments. No stocks. (The first joint stock company, Le Bazacle, was to be launched in France in the late fourteenth century—far too late to have been of any use to Godric in planning his retirement.) And even had the Bazacle "eschaus" (shares) been issued ear-lier, it would have been highly unlikely that an Englishman like Godric could have secured an allocation to buy any. Re-cords indicate that the initial issue of history's first stock was snapped up by councilors of the Parlement of Toulouse and "other local notables."[2] There were no stock investments avail-able in Godric's time, and even when they came along cen-turies later, it is unlikely that an outsider would have been able to buy shares. The London Stock Exchange traces its history to 1698, so Godric would have had a long wait to find a blue chip stock investment to fund his retirement. There were no insurance companies in 1110 offering annuities to would be retirees.

The closest approximation to a medieval annuity was the "census" contract—an instrument of credit that obliged the seller, usually a large landholder, a religious order, a local monopolist, or a taxing body, "to pay an annual return from fruitful property."[3] So Godric conceivably could have acquired or employed census contracts. Perhaps he did. A hint that he may have orchestrated a financial foundation for his retirement comes with the surviving details of his religious conversion. Godric was visiting the English tidal island of Lindisfarne possibly searching for a hiding place for his mercantile treasure, when he reported an encounter with St. Cuthbert. This was considered more credible in the Middle Ages than it would be today, as Cuthbert had been dead since March 20, 687. Be that as it may, Godric was supposedly inspired by the vision of Cuthbert to renounce his fortune and retire to a life of devotion. After several pilgrimages to Jerusalem and a couple of years living with an elderly hermit, Godric approached Ranulf Flambard, the Bishop of Durham, whom he persuaded to give him a grant of land on the River Wear on which to establish a hermitage.

Note the coincidence that Godric's conversion was inspired by a vision of St. Cuthbert rather than the Virgin Mary, John the Baptist, or the Apostle Paul. It so happened that Bishop Ranulf was engaged in a project to cultivate the cult of St. Cuthbert that included a multidecade project to build Durham Cathedral with a design that included a shrine in which Cuthbert was re-entombed. Also note that Bishop Ranulf earned a reputation as a creative financier who pioneered new ways of raising money as a minister in the courts of King William the Conqueror and his son, King William Rufus. If any leading church authority would have been receptive to a creative proposal from Godric to facilitate his retirement, it was Bishop Ranulf Flambard. Anselm, the Archbishop of Canterbury, arranged for Bishop Ranulf's trial in a papal court for simony. If you are not up-to-date on medieval ecclesiastical crimes, "simony" involves "the buying or selling of a church office or ecclesiastical preferment."[4]

Godric was a successful capitalist, an entrepreneur in a society that condemned entrepreneurs. But his story is still legible to us, almost a millennium later, because Godric decided to become a hermit monk in a long, sixty-year retirement (he lived to age 105), and thus his story was entrusted to the church—the literate substratum of early medieval society.

Another monk, Reginald of Durham wrote Godric's biography. Among other accomplishments, Godric took several pilgrimages to Jerusalem and gained a reputation as a wise and holy man, honored for his intelligence. His reputation spread far enough that Pope Alexander III sought his advice. Godric also wrote four hymns that are still performed. They are among the first identified works by an English songwriter.

The great historian Henri Pirenne, recounts the adventures of St. Godric of Finchale, as they embody Pirenne's thesis in *Stages in the Social History of Capitalism*. Pirenne argued that capitalism began long before Marx imagined. Pirenne finds evidence as far back as records are kept. And he tells us that the group of capitalists of a given epoch "does not spring from the capitalist group of the proceeding epoch. At every change in economic organization we find a breach of continuity. It is as if the capitalists who have up to that time been active, recognize that they are incapable of adopting themselves to conditions which are evoked by needs hitherto unknown and which call for methods hitherto unemployed. They withdraw from the struggle and become an aristocracy."[5]

Pirenne continues: "In their place arise new men, courageous and enterprising, who boldly permit themselves to be driven by the wind actually blowing and who know how to trim their sails to take advantage of it."[6]

St. Godric was such a man.

So was Romano Mairano (1152–1201). Mairano was a Venetian entrepreneur of humble beginnings who made several fortunes in the twelfth century trading in Constantinople and the Levant. But the primary reason that his story is known is that his son and business partner, Giovanni, seems to have encountered fatal misfortune and died sometime before November 1201, when Romano Mairano was last known to be alive. Upon his death, his sole heir was his daughter, a nun. She inherited his business papers. Or rather, her convent did. Thus the details of Romano Mairano's business transactions were preserved to the delight of modern historians. If her brother Giovanni Mairano had outlived his father, the business papers undoubtedly would have been left to him and seven pages of the *Cambridge Economic History of Europe* could not have been devoted to telling the story of Romano Mairano's exploits as an entrepreneur.

The point, which is really Pirenne's point, is that in any environment, particularly where some change in economic organization has made itself felt, some people will be able to succeed and attain great wealth. (The tales of St. Godric of Finchale and Romano Mairano stand out because, uncharacteristically, the church preserved them.) Pirenne tells us that there were many others like them, including their occasional partners whose details have been ill-preserved over the centuries.

The encouraging point from your perspective is that even in the slow-growth organic economy of the early medieval period, when wealth was engrossed by landed aristocrats, or war lords, intrepid men could invent their own unsanctioned versions of capitalism and even design a version of retirement through which he survived to the age of 105. While the medieval aristocracy generally showed no interest in profiting from commerce, it was nonetheless possible for enterprising men to start from nothing and accumulate a fortune.

There will be new opportunities to achieve independence and wealth in a decelerating world. Even if you have not been hugely successful in navigating the crony capitalist status quo, the coming terminal crisis of US hegemony may create an opening in which you can succeed beyond your wildest dreams. In Pirenne's words, those who succeed are often "parvenus brought into action by the transformation of society, embarrassed neither by custom nor by routine, having nothing to lose and therefore the bolder in their race toward profit."[7]

While it is all but impossible to project precisely how the chief crisis in this century of crisis will unfold, you can look to a crucial regularity that was identified by the great historian Henri Pirenne almost a century ago.

That is the tendency, known as Pirenne's Pendulum, for succeeding eras of capitalist development to swing back and forth between periods of heavy regulation and economic freedom. In his *Stages in the Social History of Capitalism*, Pirenne describes the regularity of the phases of economic freedom and of regulation to succeed each other. He clearly saw that "our own epoch of social legislation" involved a decided swing away from economic freedom. That implies that Pirenne's Pendulum is primed to swing your way.

Worse than the Great Depression?

It would be tempting to suppose that the post-Lehman woes of the economy are merely a long-wave cyclical depression and not evidence of the "Secular Cycle" of collapse. More tempting still is the conventional notion that the Great Recession was just the twelfth garden-variety post–World War II downturn that has been left in the dust of a conventional recovery. That was the view that the guardians of the status quo pressed on you. Don't buy it.

In fact, I suspect that even the interpretation of the Great Recession as a later day version of the Great Depression of the 1930s represents too sanguine a view of what is actually afoot. All signs point to a secular growth slowdown, at least a partial return to preindustrial conditions due to a slowdown in the growth of energy inputs that remained robust even during even the darkest days of Depression after 1929. While the economy shrank then, it later rebounded so vigorously that the average growth rate over the first half of the century did not trail off.

As explored in previous chapters, the growth of energy inputs has stalled today with consequences that weigh against the conventional view that the status quo is sustainable. It is hardly necessary to rehearse all the points introduced earlier in a summary analysis to show that we approach the Breaking Point.

The paltry growth rate of the net private economy in the United States in the twenty-first century is within the range reached in the "organic" economies that prevailed before the Industrial Revolution. Ominously, nominal economic growth is too slow to keep pace with the compounding cost for serving debt amounting to 300 percent of GDP, even at the lowest interest rates in 5,000 years. The result to be expected is a financial crisis culminating in the Breaking Point.

As false forward assumptions about growth are disappointed, the ability of the economy to generate new credit will decline. This places the continued debt-financed surge in government spending in doubt. It also undercuts the illusion that debt spiked growth can continue forever.

The national debt soared from $5.800 trillion in 2001 to $13.561 trillion in 2010—a jump of 133 percent. You don't have to be a mathematical genius to recognize that the system is flirting with collapse when the burden of the national debt compounds 3,000 percent faster than the productive economy grows. And this is without consideration of the multi-trillion-dollar annual increase in unfunded liabilities for future spending on programs such as Social Security and Medicare.

Looking back over the sixty years from 1949 to 2009, annual average GDP growth in the United States was 3.3 percent. The thirty-year growth rate slid to 2.7 percent. Over twenty years, the average growth rate notched down to 2.5 percent. The ten-year rate (from 1999 through 2009) was 1.9 percent, with the five-year average annual growth rate declining to 0.9 percent. Shades of *Mad Max*, the modern progressive economy has been coasting to a stop like an automobile that has run out of gas. Each period of decline in growth was marked by ever-greater amounts of government, business, and consumer borrowing.

While the Ministry of Truth tells you there has been a recovery since 2009, it is a statistical mirage. But even taking it at face value, it came at the cost of $7.703 trillion added to the national debt during this short time. As gaudy as that number is, it understates the unsustainability of the federal budget situation. The US government GAAP-based budget deficit hit a record of $6.6 trillion for 2012 alone. GAAP is shorthand for "generally accepted accounting principles"—the same accounting rules to which every legitimate business and public company must adhere. If those rules were applied to the federal government—the annual federal deficit would be almost ten times larger than the publicly announced number.

Not only were the true operating costs of government vastly greater than the authorities in Washington like to pretend, but between three quarters and 100 percent of the "official" cash operating deficit will have been monetized by the Federal Reserve in the course of its exercises in "quantitative easing." Borrowers have not been willing to buy US securities at the artificially low rates at which the government wants to sell, so they have had to resort to digitally creating money at the Federal Reserve to pay the US Treasury for the debt notes.

Never in history has any nation been so deeply indebted. Never has an economy suffered with so many distortions and efficiency losses due to domination by crony capitalists who use political power to fashion a self-serving antimarket economy to reward themselves at your expense.

All the predatory antimarket sectors, exemplified by education, health care, and the military, are characterized by dramatically falling returns. Perhaps fifty years ago one might have argued that for every dollar taxpayers invested in education, they received a return of three dollars or more, as an educated populace joined the workforce and created wealth.

If that were ever true, it no longer is. As standout investor Peter Thiel explained, higher education has become a bubble.

"If a college degree always means higher wages, then everyone should get a college degree. But how can everyone win a zero-sum tournament? No single path can work for everyone, and the promise of such an easy path is a sign of a bubble."[8]

The marginal returns to education have declined dramatically. In some cases, increased spending may have had a negative effect. Numerous studies show despite massive spending boosts and educational "reforms," test results have actually declined. The cost of a college education for a bachelor's degree has quadrupled during my lifetime, while the median income of those gaining bachelor's degrees has plunged from $53,320 in 2000 to $46,900 in 2012 (expressed in constant 2012 dollars)—a drop of 12 percent in the first twelve years of this century.

Equally, as Charles Hugh-Smith points out, the US military adopts weapon systems "that cost four times as much as the system they replace while being less effective and more costly to maintain/repair."[9] Nothing so vividly illustrates Hugh-Smith's point as the F-35 attack fighter. The F-35 program has squandered $400 billion on an aircraft that can't even fly in the rain.[10]

Sick care in the United States provides perhaps a competitively egregious example of declining returns. The United States spends $3.8 trillion a year on medical care—more per capita and a higher percentage of GDP (22 percent) than any other country. Yet according to the World Health Organization, US life expectancy (78.4 years at birth) ranks fiftieth among 221 nations and near the bottom at twenty-seventh out of the thirty-four industrialized OECD countries.

"When It Gets Serious, You Have to Lie"

If real median income were adjusted for inflation by the same methodologies used to calculate it by the US government through the Carter administration, median income would be lower today than it was when Eisenhower was in the White House. This tells you something. There is a meta-message on the transparent inadequacy of official inflation adjustments. They may not measure how far the value of the dollar has fallen, but they do hint at how far along the downward grade the government has gone in terms of honesty in the past six decades. As Gopal Balakrishnan shrewdly observed in his *Occasion* essay, "Speculations on the Stationary State," the current US depression "may reveal that the national economic statistics of the period of bubble economics were fictions, not wholly unlike those operative in the old Soviet system."[11] The twenty-first-century growth stall of the US economy has proven too serious to be treated truthfully in the sense that European Commission president Jean Claude Juncker highlighted in his famous comment: "When it gets serious you have to lie."[12]

The growth stall hints at an unspeakable truth, much as it was out of the question that the Soviet Central Statistical Directorate (TsSU) would publish accurate figures detailing the negligible rates of growth that characterized the last decades of the Soviet Union.

By 1987, whistleblowers Grigory Khannin and Vasily Selyunin had already spilled the beans on the TsSU. They reported that official statistics had overstated the Soviet national income in 1985, compared to the base level of 1928, by a factor of almost thirteen times. Peter J. Boettke summed up the "malpractice of economics measurement" nicely in *Why Perestroika Failed*. Referring to the overstated economic growth, he wrote, "In fact, the whole peculiar art of Soviet economic management amounted to the production, and distribution of this illusion."[13]

US growth rates have now dwindled to the range actually experienced in the Soviet economy in its final years. But the production and distribution of the illusion that the United States is continuing to recover toward a long-term average of 3.27 percent GDP growth is a major preoccupation of the political establishment.

If you have a family to support and look forward to some comfort in retirement, you are one of the principal targets of the elaborate pretense that the US economy is growing as before. The wizards in Washington want you to run out to the mall to buy lots of junk you don't need. The last thing they want is for you to save your money, much less buy gold, as you might be well advised to do if you realize how close this exhausted system is to collapse.

Better late than never, you should prepare for the Breaking Point. The American easy chair today is floating on the biggest ocean of red ink in the history of the earth, with total credit market debt of $59.4 trillion, as of March 31, 2014. The middle class is being reduced to poverty.

The causes and consequences of the slow-motion secular growth stall that began in the 1970s have grown clearer over the decades. The futility of attempting to base prosperity upon bubbles stimulated by the inflation of fiat money by the Federal Reserve was underscored when the US economy almost collapsed along with Lehman Brothers in 2008. Trillions of dollars of inflated wealth were wiped away and trillions more were funneled into bailouts of big banks, Wall Street investment houses, and two-thirds of the auto industry.

What happens if, as now appears likely, the postmodern economy is destined to revert more emphatically to a declining state because of radically falling returns on the energy investments required to obtain new hydrocarbon fuels? What would this mean? Here are some possible implications:

1. A continued plunge of EROEI from one hundred to one in 1930, to thirty-seven to one in 1990, to fifteen to one in 2010, and just ten to one by 2020 implies that middle-class living standards and debt levels in advanced economies like the United States are unsustainable.
2. This suggests that collapse will prove to be a long-term process, not merely an episodic tribulation.

3. You can expect "the world of day-to-day realities and that of make-believe well-being" to increasingly part ways—to steal Mikhail Gorbachev's characterization of the last days of the Soviet Union. Every effort will be made to infatuate you with bogus statistics supposedly indicative of robust economic growth.

4. As Kenneth Boulding suggested, an all-but-inevitable consequence of the growth stall is an increasing, relentless effort by special interests to make government an institution for redistributing income away from the weak and toward the powerful.[14]

5. Upward mobility will decline as government legislates greater prosperity for the powerful. Incumbent firms will tend to enjoy greater artificial economies-to-scale so over time they will tend to capture greater market share so long as they enjoy political protection from startups.

6. Continued production from legacy fields opened during periods of greater EROEI suggests a gradual falloff of hydrocarbon energy inputs. But the overlay of cyclical movements over a secular decline imply the reverse of the picture of economic growth described by Henri Pirenne. Rather than "an inclined plane," it would resemble "a staircase"—every step of which is liable to fall abruptly rather than rise "above that which precedes it." Recoveries from cyclical downturns will continue to disappoint expectations informed by the modern experience of rapid 3.25 percent growth in advanced economies.

7. Dimitri Orlov suggests that the timing of collapse can be estimated by determining when a significant drop in energy consumption took place. He says you can then calculate how long the "collapse clock" is yet to tick by dividing the total wealth of a country's people by the economic shortfall of the economy. The gag will continue until the government "has

managed to strip citizens completely of everything they have."[15]

8. Eventually, there will be a Breaking Point, the inevitable crisis foreseen by F. A. Hayek—a collapse or "rapid decline in social-political complexity," as described by Joseph A. Tainter. Tainter points out in *The Collapse of Complex Societies* that what "may be a catastrophe to administrators" need not be to others. People who have the opportunity or ability to produce their own food resources may avoid this catastrophe.[16] In 1980's "The Role of Climate in Affecting Energy Demand/Supply," MacKay and Allsopp point out that Europe and North America then used about 17 percent of their total energy for food production (while developing countries currently use 30 percent to 60 percent of their energy in food systems).[17] A collapse in net energy availability would therefore presumably be a disaster for hundreds of millions or billions of people with uncertain access to food.

9. Institutional transformation at, or subsequent to, the Breaking Point is likely to be a tangled process, shrouded in make-believe continuity, confusion, and lies.

10. After the Breaking Point, depending on how far energy inputs fall, there could be a dramatic drop in the carrying capacity of the temperate economies. As Tim Morgan points out in *Life after Growth*, most work in today's economy is powered by exogenous sources. Morgan writes, "Of the energy—a term coterminous with 'work'—consumed in Western developed societies, well over 99% comes from exogenous sources, and probably less than 0.7% from human labor." He concludes, "A sharp decline in EROEI could bomb societies back into the preindustrial age. . . . The reality is that energy is completely central to all forms of activity, so the threat

posed by a sharp decline in net energy availability extends into every aspect of the economy, and will affect supplies of food and water, access to other resources, and structures of government and law."[18]

11. I would expect governments to become less democratic in form as well as substance. Remember, industrial democracy emerged after the Industrial Revolution to complement the organization of power at a large scale. As government institutions devolve, the poor, being a much larger percentage of the whole, will be reimagined with much less income redistribution.

12. State-sponsored old age pension systems are likely to collapse post–Breaking Point.

13. Fiat currencies will likely be replaced with money based on gold and/or silver, perhaps in competition or in conjunction with some crypto-currencies like Bitcoin.

14. The heavily regulated corporatist economy is likely to give way to a more free entrepreneurial economy, post–Breaking Point, as governments will lack the resources to bribe electorates and reward crony capitalists.

15. I expect a proliferation of sovereignties with governments organized on a smaller scale. This will permit a more entrepreneurial stance by the leaders of city-states and microsovereignties, much as the late Lee Kwan Yew devised new options in governance that made Singapore one of the richer jurisdictions in the world, without becoming what Jane Jacobs construed as a "monstrous hybrid."

16. As net energy availability from hydrocarbons declines, the importance of solar energy conversion, by plant photosynthesis and direct radiation, will grow. Under those conditions, one would expect higher living standards in upland regions of the tropics where the impact of the climate requires less energy-intensive remediation. According to MacKay and Allsopp,

more than one-third of all energy consumed in industrialized North America and about one-half of the energy consumed in Europe is used to heat homes and commercial buildings in winter and, to a lesser extent, cool them in the summer.[19]

17. An interesting question is how enormous amounts of computing power now available will shape the evolution of the stationary, declining state in the future. With luck, perhaps it can help expand the percentage of the population who can live well to as much as a talented tenth.

These are some of the issues that are better thought through now than later when it may be too late. And you may need to keep your eyes open for a Mad Max look-alike in your neighborhood.

Notes

1 Pirenne, "Stages in the Social History of Capitalism," in *Class, Status and Power*, ed. Richard Bendix and Seymour Martin Lipset (Glencoe: Free Press, 1953), 507–8.

2 See Hellier, Henry, *Labour, Science and Technology in France, 1500–1620* (Cambridge: Cambridge University Press, 1996), 14.

3 Homer, Sidney, and Richard Sylia, *A History of Interest Rates*, 4th ed. (Hoboken, NJ: 2005), 73.

4 http://www.merriam-webster.com/dictionary/simony.

5 Pirenne, "Stages in the Social History of Capitalism," 501–2.

6 Ibid., 502.

7 Ibid., 516.

8 https://www.washingtonpost.com/opinions/peter-thiel-thinking-too-highly-of-higher-ed/2014/11/21/f6758fba-70d4-11e4-893f-86bd390a3340_story.html?utm_term=.4c3a37f87a5e.

9 Hugh-Smith, Charles, "How Economies Collapse: Systemic Friction and Debt Are Self-Liquidating," *Zero Hedge*, August 5, 2014.

10 http://www.alternet.org/fail -400-billion-military-jet-cant -fly-cloudy-weather.

11 Balakrishnan, Gopal, "Speculations on the Stationary State," http://arcade.stanford .edu/occasion/speculations -stationary-state.

12 http://www.pressreader .com/ireland/irish -independent/20150630/ 282699045781010/TextView.

13 Boettke, Peter, *Why Perestroika Failed: The Politics and Economics of Socialist Transformation* (London: Routledge, 1993), 4.

14 Boulding, Kenneth, "The Shadow of the Stationary State," in *The No-Growth Society*, ed. Mancur Olson and Hans Landsberg (New York: W. W. Norton, 1973), 92, 95.

15 Orlov, Dmitry, "How to Time Collapses," *ClubOrlov*, February 4, 2014, http:// cluborlov.blogspot.com/2014/ 02/how-to-time-collapses .html.

16 Tainter, Joseph A., *The Collapse of Complex Societies* (Cambridge: Cambridge University Press, 1990), 198.

17 McKay, G. A., and T. Allsopp, "The Role of Climate in Affecting Energy Demand/Supply," in *Interactions of Energy and Climate*, ed. W. Bach, J. Pankrath, and J. Williams (Dordrecht, Holland: D. Reidel, 1980), 53–72.

18 Morgan, *Life after Growth*, 68–69.

19 Jager, Jill, "Scope 27 Climate Impact Assessment," http:// www.scopenvironment.org/ downloadpubs/scope27/ chapter09.html.

Acknowledgments

If you studied the history of the thank-you note in publishing, you would be disappointed. There is not much to go on. If you are enough of a bibliophile to own first editions published in centuries before the industrial period—or even early in it—you will find few (or no) acknowledgments. The earliest I can find record of is Li Qingzhao's (1084–1155) "Thanking note to revered Chong Li," appended to her volume of Song dynasty poems. I don't know whether this hints that the Chinese were more polite than Western cultures and thus felt an earlier need to acknowledge intellectual debts. Or perhaps it is merely an artifact of my somewhat erratic research methods. I tried to outsmart the search algorithms on Google and DuckDuckGo well enough to get a hint of "what is what" about book acknowledgments. That brought me to Li Qingzhao.

I do know that Adam Smith did not append acknowledgments to *An Inquiry into the Nature and the Causes of the Wealth of Nations* (1776). He launched right in with "Introduction and Plan of the Work." This made him the object of criticism in the last century. The late free-market theorist Murray Rothbard saw Smith's lack of acknowledgments as indicative of plagiarism:

> Even in an age that had fewer citations or footnotes than our own, Adam Smith was a shameless plagiarist, acknowledging little or nothing and stealing large chunks, for example, from Cantillon. Far worse was Smith's complete failure to cite or acknowledge his beloved mentor Francis Hutcheson, from whom he derived most of his ideas as well as the organization of his

economic and moral philosophy lectures. Smith indeed wrote in a private letter to the University of Glasgow of the "never-to-be-forgotten Dr. Hutcheson," but apparently amnesia conveniently struck Adam Smith when it came time to writing the *Wealth of Nations* for the general public.[1]

As unlikely as it may seem that future generations of intellectual historians will toil over *The Breaking Point,* seeking to deconstruct the numerous influences that informed my thinking, I have hoped to make that unnecessary by footnoting the text and, further, with the more general acknowledgments I spell out here. Firstly, I want to thank Bill Bonner, who graciously penned a foreword to this book, for a lifetime of stimulating conversation. We witnessed the gaudy decline of the American political economy from the privileged perspective of Baby Boomers. And through the subversive device of inventing our own work, we found ourselves in positions to think independently about what has gone amiss. *The Breaking Point* gives my take on it.

I was encouraged in that direction by a stint as graduate student at the Institute for Renaissance Studies, where one fine afternoon, a guest lecturer holding forth on *synderesis* made the telling point that one could no more understand the Renaissance knowing no theology than he or she could understand the modern world knowing no economics. My determination to understand was doubled at that moment. Bill Bonner and I shared decades of conversation in the struggle to decipher the determining factors that seem to have deflected the future from the positive trajectory we expected a lifetime ago.

I also want to thank Peter Thiel for generously sharing ideas in numerous brainstorming sessions over the past five and a half years. I have been stimulated by our discussions, and perhaps unrealistically, I had hoped that he might fill the void left by the death of Lord Rees-Mogg. I distinctly miss being able explore and share ideas with a sympathetic and well-informed freethinker. William was a polymath who knew a lot about a lot of things. Peter is too. But he is a busy billionaire with too many calls on his attention to spontaneously take calls from me whenever some idea strikes my fancy. Still, he has been very generous with his time, for which I thank him. In particular, Peter drew my attention back to the haunting forward vision in *Atlas Shrugged*.

"You may know society is doomed when you see that in order to produce, you need to obtain permission from men who produce nothing; when you see that money is flowing to those who deal, not in goods, but in favors; when you see that men get richer by graft and by pull than by work, and your laws don't protect you against them, but protect them against you; [and] when you see corruption being rewarded and honesty becoming a self-sacrifice." Ayn Rand wrote that without seeing a single redacted email about Uranium One and the Clinton Foundation.

I owe a debt of thanks for many creative suggestions to Charles Delvalle, Aaron De Hoog, Heath King, and my colleague and partner in Newsmax, Chris Ruddy. Chris has given me more than one forum to develop my ideas. I appreciate his friendship. I also owe thanks to Mary Glenn and her whole editorial team for laboring over the various drafts of the text.

Several innocent parties, who had no idea they were contributing to *The Breaking Point*, nevertheless did. Simon Mitton at the Cambridge University Press contributed his wisdom in the form of Mitton's Law—the caution that for every equation in a book, its readership will be halved. You can add your thanks to mine for the fact that there are no equations in *The Breaking Point*. The not-so-dumb blonde Morgan Fairchild helped introduce me to the corrupt culture of Florida's sugar barons—a tutorial that came in handy in drafting chapter 14. Jim Rodgers also confirmed and amplified my alarm about the unsustainable nature of the financialized debt economy.

I particularly want to thank Dr. Habibullo Abdussamatov, head of the Space Research Laboratory at the Pulkovo
Observatory of the Russian Academy of Sciences for his
encouragement. Courtesy of Peter Thiel, Dr. Abdussamatov visited the United States, and we were able to spend
five stimulating hours discussing the fraud that alleges the
earth is threatened by human-caused global warming. John
Casey, author of *Dark Winter: How the Sun Is Causing a 30-
Year Cold Spell*, graciously read chapters 10 through 12. I
thank him. Of course neither Dr. Abdussamatov nor John
Casey bear responsibility for any mischaracterizations of
solar physics or the geoid that may remain in the text. I also
thank Dr. Al Sears for helping educate me on the shortcomings of mainstream sick care. Thinking independently is a
gamey proposition. It is exciting to talk to others who are
not in thrall to various rackets that inform public opinion in
the twenty-first century.

As Nelson Demille noted in his acknowledgments to *Wild
Fire*, "There is a new trend among authors to thank very famous people for inspiration, non-existent assistance, and/or
some casual reference to the author's work. Authors do this
to pump themselves up." His clever note notwithstanding, I
am resisting the temptation to thank the Queen of England
for the ceremony and grace that helped punctuate my time at
Oxford. I do thank Donald Trump for his ever-stimulating
contribution to public dialogue. Before he became a presidential candidate, he was a gracious host in Palm Beach, where
he frequently encouraged me and others to think about why
"America doesn't win anymore."

And finally, I want to thank my beautiful wife, Sabine,
who fell in love with me and proved it by leaving her life in
Europe to start anew with me in sunny Florida. She soon
caught on precociously to remarkably many of the ills that
beset us. She is smart and insightful and had the encouraging hugs—the vitamin S—I needed from time to time to
function at full strength. My mother told me that "unless

you love someone, nothing else makes sense." Sabine is the proof of that. I thank her humbly and lovingly for putting up with me while I puzzled out which of the many drawbacks of the Fed's zero interest rate policy (ZIRP) would prove more fatal to prosperity.

And though almost every fiber of the Kardashian/Caitlyn Jenner culture inspires us to blame others for our shortcomings, I don't. I accept full responsibility for errors and shortcomings of this book.

Note

1   See Rothbard, Murray, *An Austrian Perspective on the History of Economic Thought* (Northampton, MA: Edward Elgar, 1995), ch. 16.

Index

population
  decline, 82
  growth, 3, 93, 176
Population Reference Bureau, 151
Porsche, Ferdinand, 37
pound, British, 403–4
poverty, 372
Poverty of Philosophy, The (Marx), 54
power
  centralization of, 33–34
  cost of projecting, 467
  devolution to small scale, 468
  territorial and personal, 31–32
  See also violence
predatory rule, 126
preindustrial societies, 347
Principia (Newton), 197, 208
privacy, 129, 465
privileged groups, 241–42
Procter & Gamble, 284
production, misdirection of,
  89–90
productivity, 314, 372
productivity growth, 73–74
profits, manufacturing, 102
programmers, 72–73
progressive state, 327–35
propaganda, science research, 199
property rights, 69–70, 78, 125
"Property Rights and Time
  Preference" (Mulligan), 69
proprietary governments, 450
prosperity, 352
  fabricated, 9–10
protection services, 448
public opinion, 282

purchasing patterns, 376
Pursuit of the Millennium
  (Cohn), 79
Putilnik, Lev A., 219
Putin, Vladimir, 249–50

Q

quantitative easing (QE), 6–7,
  48–50, 69, 161–69, 250–54,
  427, 491
Quebec independence, 471–72
Quincey, Saire de, 124–28, 133–34
quota systems, 270

R

Rae, Douglas W., 317
Ramsey, Drew, 276
Rand, Ayn, 96–97
RAND Corporation, 10
Rankka, Maria, 250
ransoms, 82
real estate investors, 166
reality gap, 381
recession, 363
recovery, 368–70
redistribution of hunt, 76–77
redistribution of income, 51, 478
Red Queen's Race, 386
redress of grievances, 159
Rees-Mogg, William, 2–3, 7, 16,
  22, 27, 34
reference ellipsoids, 208–9
regime changes, 14
Reginald of Durham, 487
regulation, 17, 47, 88–89, 130–31,
  157–58, 476

GET OUR EXPERTS' SECRETS TO WEALTH TODAY!

The **Financial Intelligence Report** is a monthly newsletter bringing together some of the sharpest minds from the worlds of finance, investing, and economics.

Containing insights and opinions not found anywhere else, the **Financial Intelligence Report** gives readers an unprecedented look at how events are likely to unfold in the United States and across the globe over the coming weeks, months, and years, as seen by our panel of experts.

This distinguished group comprises individuals from numerous countries with a broad range of backgrounds and fields of expertise, including **James Dale Davidson**, investment guru **Jim Rogers** and renowned financial publisher **Steve Forbes**.

The consortium has put together a track record that is impressive not only for its success, but also for its ability to accurately predict many of the events that have impacted the global economy over the last few years.

To immediately gain access to this valuable information, you can join the **Financial Intelligence Report** today by going to the website listed below.

Go To: Newsmax.com/Breaking